Practicing Texas Politics

A BRIEF SURVEY

D0073737

Practicing Texas Politics

A BRIEF SURVEY
Eighth Edition

Lyle C. Brown
Baylor University

Joyce A. Langenegger
San Jacinto College

Sonia R. García
St. Mary's University

Ted Lewis
Cy-Fair College

HOUGHTON MIFFLIN COMPANY   BOSTON   NEW YORK

Publisher: Charles Hartford
Sponsoring Editor: Katherine Meisenheimer
Development Manager: Beth Kramer
Senior Project Editor: Carol Newman
Editorial Assistant: Robert Woo
Manufacturing Coordinator: Renee Ostrowski
Executive Marketing Manager: Nicola Poser

Printed in the U.S.A.
Library of Congress Control Number: 2003110154
ISBN: 0-618-43743-6

1 2 3 4 5 6 7 8 9—QUF—09 08 07 06 05

Contents

3 *Local Governments* 76

4 *The Politics of Elections and Parties* 112

Preface

This Eighth Edition of *Practicing Texas Politics: A Brief Survey* describes and analyzes state and local politics as practiced within the Lone Star State. Published for college and university students early in the twenty-first century, our textbook gives readers a realistic and up-to-date picture of how the state and its cities, counties, and special districts are governed. Approximately nine-tenths of *Practicing Texas Politics: A Brief Survey* consists of text material written jointly by co-authors who critically examine public policy-making within Texas. Each chapter features a selected reading.

The Co-authors

Ted Lewis, the latest addition to our team of co-authors, draws on his personal experience in Texas politics to explain the organization and functions of political parties and the actions of politicians. Sonia García provides valuable insights based on her teaching and research, as well as her involvement with women's organizations and San Antonio's Latino community. Joyce Langenegger is a law school graduate. She practiced law for several years before obtaining a graduate degree in political science and becoming a college instructor and administrator. Her background and experience have strengthened our coverage of the Texas judicial system and public finance. Lyle Brown has studied and taught in Mexico, has published articles on Mexican politics and U.S.-Mexican relations, and has been a co-author of *Practicing Texas Politics: A Brief Survey* since the first edition in 1984.

Important Features of This Edition

The Eighth Edition of *Practicing Texas Politics: A Brief Survey* gives special attention to political developments since 2000. To include descriptions and analyses of recent political events and governmental changes, the narrative has been significantly rewritten. Topics given special attention include

population changes documented by the 2000 census, recent state constitutional amendments, proposals for constitutional revision, attempts to generate revenue for economic development at the local level and to address
the problems of *colonias* in counties along and near the Rio Grande, party
primaries and the general election of 2004, the roles of interest groups and
political action committees (PACs) in recent elections, the importance
of interest group lobbying and the results of Republican majorities in
both chambers of the 78th Texas Legislature, actions by Governor Rick
Perry and other executive officials in 2003 and 2004, changes in the
state's administrative agencies, the politics of taxing and spending in the
Perry era of "no new taxes," and issues facing Texas's courts and penal
institutions.

A summary is provided at the end of the text for each chapter. It is followed
by a list of the key terms that are printed in boldface type where first presented in the text and defined in the glossary, a list of discussion questions,
and a list of Internet resources featuring URLs for agencies and organizations
relevant to the chapter. Endnotes document information provided in the text
and suggest additional reading for further study. To provide fresh views on
current issues, we have included a reading at the end of each chapter. Every
reading has a brief introduction to prepare readers for what follows.

At the end of the book, students may consult a glossary featuring definitions of the key terms. In addition, graphic illustrations and useful data are
presented in maps, diagrams, photographs, cartoons, and tables throughout
the book. Each chapter includes "How Do We Compare" data for the four
most populous U.S. states (California, Florida, New York, and Texas) and the
four U.S. states bordering Texas (Arkansas, Louisiana, New Mexico, and
Oklahoma). For some subjects, data are provided for the four Mexican states
bordering Texas (Chihauhua, Coahuila, Nuevo León, and Tamaulipas). All
chapters of this Eighth Edition feature "Points to Ponder" information relevant to the text and "Point/Counterpoint" arguments on a current issue. An
extensive and periodically updated bibliography of books and articles for
each chapter of *Practicing Texas Politics: A Brief Survey* is available on the
Houghton Mifflin Political Science home page described in the next section.

The Complete Teaching and Learning Package

A companion web site for students is available on the Houghton Mifflin Political Science home page, accessible through *politicalscience.college.hmco.com.*
The site includes chapter outlines, links to Texas government and politics
sites, ACE practice tests featuring multiple-choice and true-or-false questions, and an updated bibliography of books and articles for further reading
and research. Also, updates will be posted when major events affect the content of the text.

The instructor web site, which is password protected, contains the online *Instructor's Resource Manual* (IRM), prepared by Robert K. Peters of Tyler Junior College. The IRM offers a complete lecture outline for each chapter in *Practicing Texas Politics,* multiple-choice questions, essay exercises, suggested class activities, and a listing of numerous audiovisual and Web resources. Also available is a computerized ClassPrep CD-ROM containing the test questions from the IRM and Powerpoints.

Acknowledgments

We are indebted to many political scientists as well as scholars in other disciplines. They have shared generously the results of their research and have stimulated our effort to produce a better textbook for classroom use. In particular, we thank Dr. John Glassford, Angelo State University; Dr. Tony Payan, University of Texas at El Paso; and Kyle W. Smith, Assistant Professor of Government at Western Texas College; who served as reviewers for this edition of our textbook. They read the manuscript and provided many useful comments and suggestions for which we are grateful.

We are also indebted to many personal friends, government officials and their staff, political activists, lawyers, and journalists who have stimulated our thinking. Likewise, we owe much to librarians and archivists who located hard-to-obtain facts, photos, and new readings. We also appreciate the professional assistance rendered by the editorial staff of Houghton Mifflin Company and the freelancers who worked on the book. Without the benefit of their publishing experience, this textbook and its ancillaries would be of much less value to students and instructors.

Of course, expressions of appreciation are due to secretaries and others who helped to produce this new edition of our book and to spouses and other family members who have learned to cope with the irregular working hours of authors struggling to meet deadlines. Last and most important, we dedicate this book to Texas students and political science instructors who, we hope, will continue to be the chief beneficiaries of our efforts to describe and analyze the practice of Texas politics.

Lyle C. Brown
Joyce A. Langenegger
Sonia R. García
Ted Lewis

Practicing Texas Politics

A BRIEF SURVEY

Chapter 1

★

THE ENVIRONMENT OF TEXAS POLITICS

Gary Brookins, *Richmond Times-Dispatch*

You ask me what I like about Texas
I tell you it's the wide open spaces!
It's everything between the Sabine and the Rio Grande. It's the Llano Estacado,
It's the Brazos and the Colorado;
It's the spirit of the people who share this land![1]*

---

*I*n 2000, as depicted in the preceding cartoon, census takers counted a rapidly growing U.S. population. Texas ranked second among the 50 states with almost 21 million, up from nearly 17 million in 1990. California ranked first with close to 34 million; New York was third with less than 19 million. The new total for the Lone Star State included about 15 million men and women of voting age (18 years or older). Of course, some of them could not legally cast ballots because they lacked qualifications concerning residence, voter registration, or U.S. citizenship. Nevertheless, most Texans are involved in political activities, even if their actions are limited simply to talking about politics or merely listening while others talk, and everyone is affected by the words and deeds of politicians, government officials, and public employees.

Legislative actions, executive decisions, and court proceedings, as well as popular elections and lobbying activities, are parts of the political struggle that determine, in the words of political scientist Harold Lasswell, "who gets what, when, and how."[2] **Politics** involves conflict between political parties and other groups that seek to elect government officials or to influence those officials when they make public policy, such as enacting and interpreting Texas laws.

Political Behavior Patterns

This book focuses on politics as practiced in Texas and on the diverse and rich cultural heritage of the Lone Star State. Our analysis of the politics of Texas's state and local governments today is intended to help readers understand political action and prepare them for informed participation in the political affairs of the state and its counties, cities, and special districts. In addition, we introduce readers to important political actors, most of them high-ranking party activists or government officials who have been elected or appointed to public office. In politics, as in athletics, people need to identify the players before they can understand the game.

Government, Politics, and Public Policy

Government may be defined as a public institution with the authority to allocate values in a society. In practice, values are allocated when a state or local government formulates, adopts, and implements a public policy, such as raising taxes to pay for more police protection or better streets and high-

---

*Source: "What I Like About Texas," lyrics by Gary P. Nunn. Copyright © Nunn Publishing Co. Reprinted by permission.

The south side of the Texas State Capitol in Austin (Courtesy of the Texas Department of Transportation)

ways. At the state level, each **public policy** is a product of political activity that may involve both conflict and cooperation among legislators, between legislators and the governor, within the courts, and among various governmental agencies, citizens, and **aliens**. (Aliens are persons in the United States who do not have U.S. citizenship, including those holding a valid visa as well as undocumented people who have entered without a visa or have entered legally but have stayed after their authorized visa has expired.)

Policymaking involves political action intended to meet particular needs or achieve specific objectives. For example, a state policy to promote public health by reducing or eliminating the use of certain pesticides alleged to cause cancer might be proposed to a legislator by the governor or by another government official, by a nongovernmental organization such as the environmentalist Sierra Club, or by any interested person. Next, the proposal would be incorporated into a bill and submitted to the Texas Legislature by a state senator or representative who favors the new policy. Then, in committee hearings and on the floor of the Senate and the House of Representatives, the bill would be discussed and debated in the presence of lobbyists representing interest groups, journalists reporting the news, and concerned citizens. When the bill is passed by the legislature and signed by the governor, the pesticide proposal becomes law. Next, the new public policy must be implemented, or put into operation. That responsibility might be assigned by law to the Texas Department of Agriculture or to some other governmental agency. But the policy measure could also be challenged in court. Judges might uphold all or part of the legislation, or nullify it entirely if it violates some provision of the Texas Constitution or the U.S. Constitution. In sum, politics is the moving force that produces public policy, which in turn determines what government does and who is affected.

Political Culture

Politics is influenced by **political culture**, which consists of the values, attitudes, traditions, habits, and general behavior patterns that develop over time and shape the politics of a particular region. Political culture is the result of both remote and recent political experiences. According to political scientist Daniel Elazar, "culture patterns give each state its particular character and help determine the tone of its fundamental relationship, as a state, to the nation."[3]

Texas Political Culture

The foundations of Texas's political culture were laid and developed under the flags of six national governments: Spain, France, Mexico, the Republic of Texas, the Confederate States of America, and the United States. Unlike most of the other 49 states, Texas was not a U.S. territory prior to statehood. As an independent republic (1836–1845), Texas received diplomatic recognition from the governments of the United States, England, France, Holland, and Belgium. With a popularly elected president and congress, the republic maintained its own army and navy, operated a postal system, printed paper money, administered justice through its courts, and provided other governmental services.

Texas Individualism Elazar asserts that the political culture of Texas is strongly individualistic, in that government is supposed to maintain a stable society but intervene as little as possible in the lives of the people. He identifies the state's politics with economic and social conservatism, strong support of personal politics, distrust of political parties, and minimization of the latter's importance.

An important source of Texas's conservatism is the nineteenth-century **frontier experience**. In the early nineteenth century, Anglo settlers (non-Hispanic whites, mostly from the United States) moved to Texas individually or with leaders such as Stephen F. Austin who received land grants from Spain. Many of these settlers had been unsuccessful in business or wished to escape their pasts, and Texas provided them with new opportunities. After the Anglo settlers and some Tejanos (Mexicans residing in Texas) rebelled and won independence from Mexico in 1836, the Republic of Texas developed its own economy, military force, and education system. The Texas republic's main success was its endurance. Relying largely on their own resources, Texans displaced Native Americans, created farms and ranches, built homes, organized communities, and overcame economic challenges.[4] They were survivors in a harsh and dangerous environment, but their deeds have been enlarged over time by historians and fiction writ-ers emphasizing the violent aspects of Texans' struggle for independence from Mexico and their clashes with Native Americans who unsuccessfully resisted the westward movement of Anglo settlers. Thousands of Native Americans and settlers—men, women, and children—were slain on the Texas frontier from the 1820s to the mid-1870s. Frontier warfare lasted longer in Texas than in other states.

After the Texas frontier was secured, there remained the task of bringing law and order to the land. In some areas, range wars, cattle rustling, and other forms of lawlessness and violence continued to menace law-abiding citizens into the twentieth century. As a result of these experiences, many Texans grew accustomed to using force in settling disputes and struggling for survival. In 1995, when the legislature legalized the carrying of concealed handguns by licensed owners, some people interpreted the measure as another influence of frontier days, when many Texans carried concealed weapons or bore pistols openly in holsters. Today, shootings and other violence may be as common in Texas's inner cities and elsewhere as they were on the state's frontier in the nineteenth century.

Elements of the individualistic culture persist in other areas as well. Compared with other, more densely populated states, Texas has a limited government with restricted powers. This government has a legislature that meets biennially, with salaries that can be increased only after approval by Texas voters; a governor who has limited budgetary, appointment, and removal powers; and an elected judiciary with multiple levels of courts. Many Texas politicians boast that their state has a climate very favorable to business. It remains one of the few states without a personal or corporate income tax. Government spending for social services on a per capita basis is consistently among the lowest in the nation. Participation in politics and voter turnout continues to remain low. Public perception of government and elected officials is very negative.

Texas Traditionalism   The traditionalistic culture of Texas can also be traced to the early nineteenth century. The plantation system thrived in the rich, fertile soil of East Texas, and cotton was by far the state's largest money crop. Prior to Texas's entry into the Confederacy, much of its wealth was concentrated in a few families. Although slave owners controlled 60 to 70 percent of the wealth and dominated state politics, approximately 75 percent of the state's population and 67 percent of the farmers did not own slaves.[5] After the Civil War (1861–1865), **Jim Crow** laws limited African Americans' access to legal protection and public services. In the late nineteenth and early twentieth centuries, literacy tests, grandfather clauses, poll taxes, and all-white primaries further restricted the voting rights of black citizens.

Today, many Texans are descendants of migrants from traditionalistic states of the Old South, where conservatism, elitism (upper-class rule), and one-party (Democratic party) politics were long entrenched. Although urbanization and industrialization, together with an influx of people from other states and countries, are changing the cultural patterns of Texas's population, Elazar insists that the traditionalist influence of the Old South still lingers. He notes that many Texans have inherited southern racist attitudes, which for decades were reflected in state laws that discriminated against African Americans and other minority groups. In 2000, however, two Civil War plaques were removed from the Texas Supreme Court building as demanded by the National Association for the Advancement of Colored People. One plaque bore a likeness of the Confederate battle flag, and the other displayed the official Confederate seal. Similar symbols of Texas's role in the Confederacy remain in public places throughout the state and are a source of continuing controversy.

The traditionalistic influence of Mexico is discernible among some Mexican American Texans who are affected by a political culture featuring the elitist *patrón* (protecting political boss) **system** that still dominates certain areas of South Texas. In the last four decades, however, the old political order of that region has been challenged—and, in many instances, defeated—by a new generation of Mexican Americans.[6] Compared with other areas of the state, however, voter turnout still remains much lower in counties along the Mexican border.

The traditionalistic culture can be seen in the social and economic conservatism of the state. Religious groups have influenced government policies on matters such as abortion, casino gambling, sale of alcoholic beverages, pari-mutuel betting, and the state lottery. City councils have drawn public criticism for publicly financing corporate ventures or providing certain businesses with property tax abatements. Powerful families continue to play an important role in state politics and influence public policies.

A Changing Culture?   Beginning in the mid-1970s, Texas has experienced a large population influx from other areas of the nation. With regard to Elazar's appraisal of Texas's conservative political culture, important questions arise: How long will particular sociocultural influences last? Aren't cultural influences of the past being replaced by new ones? Will Texas's cultural identities, inherited largely from the nineteenth century, survive indefinitely in the face of widespread urbanization, industrialization, education, communication, and population change? Will a **moralistic culture** ever take root and flourish in the Lone Star State?

Elazar explains that the moralistic culture originated in New England with Puritanism. In this culture, the people view government as a public service. They expect government to provide goods and services to advance the public good. They also see it as their duty to become active in governmental decision making through participation in town councils and other representative bodies or by close monitoring of their leaders. The people generally have high expectations of their government because they hold it accountable. Today, this culture has spread across the northern states to the Pacific Northwest.

The Land

Like people everywhere, Texans are influenced by their geography as well as by their history. Texas's mountains, plains, seacoasts, climate, mineral deposits, and other geographic features affect the state's economy, its political culture, and the part the Lone Star State plays in national and international affairs. By the twenty-first century, Texans had cleared the land to establish and operate thousands of farms and ranches, built hundreds of towns and cities, organized many banks and businesses, and produced much of the nation's oil and natural gas, cotton and mohair, fish and meat, wheat and sorghum, fruits and vegetables, computers and computer chips.

The Politics of Geography

From the start, Texas politics and public policy have been molded in part by the state's size. Its very large area and diverse physical geography create strong regional interests. Some of these interests are shared with the four neighboring U.S. states (Arkansas, Louisiana, New Mexico, and Oklahoma) and with the four bordering Mexican states (Chihuahua, Coahuila, Nuevo Léon, and Tamaulipas). Regardless of where they live, however, most citizens of the Lone Star State strongly identify with their state and are proud to be called Texans (see Figure 1.1).

Size   With over 267,000 square miles of territory, Texas is second only to Alaska in area. The Lone Star State is as large as the combined areas of New York, Pennsylvania, Ohio, Illinois, New Hampshire, Connecticut, Vermont, Rhode Island, Massachusetts, and Maine. As can be seen from data in "How Do We Compare . . . in Area?," Texas has a much larger area than any of its four neighboring U.S. states or the four bordering Mexican states.

Moving south in a straight line from the northwestern corner of the Texas Panhandle to the state's southern tip on the Rio Grande near Brownsville, one must travel 800 miles. Almost equally long is the distance from Newton County's Louisiana border (south of the Sabine River's Toledo Bend Reservoir) to the New Mexican border near El Paso. Such great size has necessitated the building of about 222,000 miles of roadways in the state, including more than 79,000 miles of major highways constructed and maintained under the supervision of the Texas Department of Transportation. No other state has so many miles of roadways.

| **Points to Ponder** | • The longest highway in Texas is US 83. It extends from the Oklahoma state line in the Panhandle to the Mexico border at Brownsville. It is 899 miles long. |
| | • The shortest highway in Texas is loop 168 in downtown Tenaha in Shelby County. This road is 0.074 mile long, or about 391 feet. |

Figure 1.1   Population Comparison: Texas vs. Other States

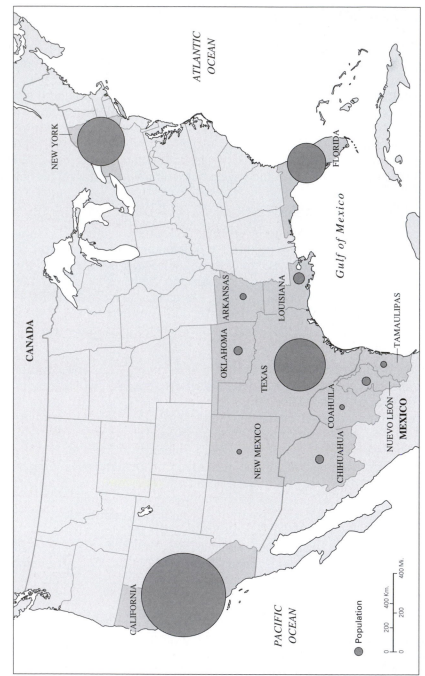

Source: Cy-Fair College GIS

☆ **How Do We Compare . . . in Area?**

Throughout the book, we use this feature to compare Texas with the other three most populous U.S. states, and with four neighboring U.S. states. Some How Do We Compare boxes also include information about the Mexican states bordering Texas: Chihuahua, Coahuila, Nuevo León, and Tamaulipas.

Land and Inland Water Area Combined

Most Populous U.S. States	Area (sq. miles)	U.S. States Bordering Texas	Area (sq. miles)	Mexican States Bordering Texas	Area (sq. miles)
California	163,707	Arkansas	53,182	Chihuahua	95,400
Florida	65,758	Louisiana	54,813	Coahuila	58,522
New York	54,475	New Mexico	121,593	Nuevo León	25,126
Texas	**267,339**	Oklahoma	69,903	Tamaulipas	30,734

Because of the state's vast size and geographic diversity, Texas developed a concept of five areas—North, South, East, West, and Central Texas—as five potentially separate states. In fact, the congressional resolution by which Texas was admitted to the Union in 1845 specifies that up to four states "in addition to said state of Texas" may be formed out of its territory and that each "shall be entitled to admission to the Union." Various plans for carving Texas into five states have been proposed to the Texas Legislature, none of which has been taken seriously by most legislators or other Texans.

Regions Geographically, Texas is at the confluence of several major phys- iographic regions of North America. The four principal **physical regions** of the state are the Gulf Coastal Plains, the Interior Lowlands, the Great Plains, and the Basin and Range Province. (For a map showing these regions, see Figure 1.2.)

The **Gulf Coastal Plains** region in East Texas is an extension of the Gulf Coastal Plains of the United States, a region that stretches westward from the Atlantic coast and then southward into northeastern Mexico. The inter- nal boundary of the Gulf Coastal Plains follows the Balcones Fault, so named by Spanish explorers because the westward-rising hills resemble a line of balconies. Immediately east of the fault line is the Blackland Belt. From 15 to 70 miles in width, this strip of black soil stretches southward from the Red River, which marks the eastern half of the Oklahoma border, to the Mexican border. The international boundary follows the Rio Grande in its southeastern course from El Paso to Brownsville and the Gulf of Mex- ico. (Mexicans call this international stream the Rio Bravo, which means "brave river" or "fierce river.") By early in 2001, however, the Rio Grande ceased its flow into the Gulf of Mexico because it ran dry downstream from Brownsville. Not until 2003 did a small volume of the river's water begin flowing again into the gulf.

Figure 1.2   Texas Geographic Regions

Source: "Texas Geographic Regions" from *2000–2001 Texas Almanac and State Industrial Guide.* Reprinted by permission of the *Texas Almanac,* published by the *Dallas Morning News.*

Within the Gulf Coastal Plains region lies the Coastal Prairies area. Bordering the Gulf of Mexico, between the Piney Woods of East Texas and the Rio Grande Plain of South Texas, this flat area has been the scene of Texas's greatest industrial growth since World War II, particularly in the section between Beaumont and Houston. Here are the state's chief petrochemical industries, which are based on oil and natural gas. In contrast to the arid plains of West Texas, this is the greenest region of the state, with certain areas receiving over 50 inches of rain annually.

The **Interior Lowlands** region encompasses the North Central Plains of Texas. This territory is bounded by the Blackland Belt to the east, the Cap Rock Escarpment to the west, the Red River to the north, and the Colorado River to the south. Farming and ranching are important activities within this largely prairie domain. The major cities in the region are Abilene, Dallas, Fort Worth, and Wichita Falls.

In 1999, after decades of controversy and negotiation stemming from the Adams-Onís Treaty between the United States and Spain (1819), the governments of Texas and Oklahoma entered into the Red River Boundary Compact. It established the south bank of the river where vegetation begins as the boundary between the two states.

Immediately west of the Interior Lowlands and rising to higher altitudes, the Texas **Great Plains** area is a southern extension of the Great High Plains of the United States. From Oklahoma at the northern boundary of the Panhandle, this area extends southward to the Rio Grande and into the Mexican state of Coahuila. The Panhandle–South Plains portion of the region is known principally for its large-scale production of cotton and grain sorghum. These irrigated crops draw their water from the Ogallala Aquifer, formed thousands of years ago by runoff from the Rocky Mountains. This underground, water-bearing rock formation extends northward from Texas to North Dakota, underlying parts of eight states. The chief cities of the Panhandle–South Plains are Lubbock and Amarillo.

Centered in Nevada, the **Basin and Range Province** region of the United States enters western Texas from southern New Mexico. The only part of the Lone Star State classified as mountainous, this rugged triangle provides Texans and many non-Texans with a popular vacation area that includes the Davis Mountains and Big Bend National Park. The state's highest mountains, Guadalupe Peak (8,749 feet) and El Capitan (8,085 feet), are located here. Among the few cities in this large area are the small city of Alpine (site of Sul Ross State University) and the big city of El Paso (on the north bank of the Rio Grande, just across the border from Mexico's more populous Ciudad Juárez in the state of Chihuahua).

Points to Ponder	• Brownsville is closer to Mexico City than to the Panhandle town of Texline. • El Paso is closer to Los Angeles on the Pacific Coast than to Port Arthur on the Gulf Coast of Texas. • Texarkana is closer to Chicago, Illinois, than to El Paso. • Port Arthur is closer to Jacksonville, Florida, on the Atlantic Coast than to El Paso.

Economic Geography

Although geographic factors do not directly determine political differences, geography greatly influences the economic pursuits of a region's inhabitants, which in turn shape political interests and attitudes. Geography has encouraged rapid population growth, urbanization, and industrialization in East Texas; in arid West Texas, geography has produced a sparsely populated rural and agricultural environment. In the course of its economic and political development, the Lone Star State has been influenced greatly by three land-based industries: cattle, cotton, and oil.

Cattle   The origin of Texas's cattle ranching may be traced to Portuguese and Spanish cattle primarily transported from the Madeira and Canary Islands in the Atlantic Ocean west of Spain to the West Indies and then to colonial Mexico. Descendants of such animals were later brought to Texas by Spanish explorers and settlers. Genetic testing indicates that these cattle provided the basic stock for development of the hardy Texas Longhorns that thrived on the open range.[7]

Plentiful land and the relative absence of government interference encouraged the establishment of huge cattle empires by determined entrepreneurs such as Richard King and Mifflin Kenedy. Today the famous King Ranch is composed of four separate units that total more than 825,000 acres or almost 1,300 square miles in Kleberg County (with the county seat at Kingsville, near the ranch headquarters) and five other South Texas counties.[8] Ownership of the Kenedy Ranch's 370,000 acres has been contested by the descendants of José Manuel Ballí, claiming that Kenedy acquired this land illegally. A state district judge in Corpus Christi ruled against the claims of the Ballí family, but the case has been appealed. Other highly publicized, legal actions were taken to obtain DNA testing of the remains of John G. Kenedy, who died in 1948, to determine if he could have fathered the daughter of his one-time housemaid. A charitable trust and a foundation controlling the Kenedy estate opposed these actions.

After the Civil War, an estimated 5 million cattle ranged over Texas's nearly 168 million acres of land. During the 25 years following that war, approximately 35,000 men drove about 10 million cattle and 1 million horses north along the Chisholm and Goodnight-Loving Trails to Kansas railheads. By the late 1880s, when the railroads were built closer to Texas ranches, the cattle drives ended, and large ranches developed. In time, the beef business as a political and economic force leveled off in the wake of newly emerging industries. Although Texas cattle production has declined in recent years, Texas still has more cattle than any other state: about 13.6 million, including more than 300,000 dairy cows. In fact, livestock and their products account for about two-thirds of the agricultural cash receipts in the state. Texas ranks first nationally in all cattle, beef cattle, and cattle feed production. It also leads the nation in the production of sheep, goats, wool, and mohair.

Cotton   Although popular culture romanticizes the cowboy and cattle drives of the nineteenth century, the backbone of the state's economy at that time was cotton. Before Spaniards brought cattle into Texas, cotton was already growing wild in the region. The rich, fertile soil led to its easy cultivation, begun by Spanish missionaries. In the 1820s, the first hybrid, or improved, cotton was introduced into Texas by Colonel Jared Groce, known as the founder of the Texas cotton industry. Groce and other Anglo Texans first cultivated cotton in East and Central Texas, where crop conditions most closely resembled those in the Old South. Prior to the Civil War, when slaves were available to perform much of the field labor, cotton production spread. During that war, revenue from the sale of Texas cotton to European buyers aided the

Confederacy. As more frontier land was settled, cotton production moved westward and increased in volume.

Currently, the High Plains region of West Texas accounts for about 60 percent of the state's annual cotton yield. With more than 6.4 million acres of Texas farmland devoted to cotton production (about 40 percent of the country's cotton acreage), the annual harvest usually exceeds 4.5 million bales of lint and 1.5 million tons of cottonseed. The annual value of this crop has ranged from $1.0 billion to $1.7 billion in recent years. Much of Texas cotton is exported.

Oil Long before Europeans arrived, Native Americans used oil seeping from the Texas soil for medicinal purposes. Early Spanish explorers in the sixteenth and seventeenth centuries used it to caulk their boats. By the late nineteenth century, thousands of barrels had been produced from crudely dug wells in different areas of the state. Before the twentieth century, however, Texas petroleum was a largely unknown quantity and had very limited commercial value. Not until 1901, when the **Spindletop Field** was developed near Beaumont, did petroleum usher in the industry that dominated the state's economy for nearly a century. After the Spindletop boom, other wells were drilled across Texas. Over the next 50 years, Texas evolved from a predominantly agricultural culture into an industrial society. Oil brought industrial employment on a grand scale to rural Texas. It offered an immediate and attractive alternative to life down on the farm or ranch for tens of thousands of Texans. Many oil companies, such as Gulf Oil Corporation, Humble (later Exxon-Mobil Corporation), Magnolia Petroleum Company, Sun Oil Company, and the Texas Company (later Texaco and more recently ChevronTexas), grew rapidly. In 1919, the legislature gave the **Texas Railroad Commission** limited regulatory jurisdiction over the state's oil and natural gas industry.[9]

At its peak in the early 1980s, the Texas petroleum industry employed half a million workers earning more than $11 billion annually, and it was estimated that oil and natural gas production accounted for almost one-third of the state's economy. By that time, the state's oil business had expanded into gasoline refineries, petrochemical plants, and factories for manufacturing a wide range of tools and equipment used in drilling, transporting, and refining operations. Meanwhile, an increasing number of banks willingly financed these costly enterprises. In 1982, an oil price slump began that produced a near panic in the industry, and the number of operating drilling rigs plunged from more than 1,000 to near zero by 1986. At that time, the price of oil dropped to less than $10 per barrel, its lowest level in more than a decade. As a result, many oil operators, businesspeople in related industries, and real estate developers were unable to meet their loan obligations. Consequently, hundreds of banks and savings and loan institutions became insolvent and were closed. From 1987 to 1989, more Texas financial institutions failed than at any other time since the Great Depression of the 1930s.[10] Many other banks and savings and loan institutions merged with healthier financial institutions that were often controlled by out-of-state interests.[11] At the same time, tens of thousands of laborers, technicians, engineers, managers, and others lost their jobs and joined the ranks of the unemployed, found employment in other industries, or left Texas to find jobs elsewhere.

In the century-long development of the Texas oil industry, its political impact has been inevitable. Because of the large amounts of oil money contributed to candidates for public office and collected as revenue from taxes and lease holdings by state and local governments, Texas politics could hardly escape the industry's influence. From the mid-1980s until 1999, however, cheap oil and falling production plagued Texas's petroleum industry. Among the consequences of hard times in the Texas oil patch were reduced revenues for state and local governments, and less election campaign money contributed by political action groups connected to the industry. Although petroleum prices have risen steadily since 1998, and soared during the United States occupation of Iraq (more than $50 per barrel in October 2004), oil is not expected to regain its former level of influence over the Lone Star State's economy and politics.

Today, the oil and gas industry accounts for less than 6 percent of the state's economy. But about 200,000 Texans work in this industry, and more than 200,000 others depend on energy-related industries for their employment. Most oil and gas jobs (including those in refineries and other petrochemical plants) pay relatively high wages and salaries. Meanwhile, there is a growing awareness that oil-based fuels burned in automobiles, trucks, buses, and airplanes are the world's principal source of air pollution. In addition, immeasurable harm to the world's oceans has resulted from oil spills in the Gulf of Mexico and other waters around the globe. Groups such as the Sustainable Energy and Economic Development (SEED) Coalition, the Lone Star Chapter of the Sierra Club, the Texas Campaign on the Environment, and the Texas Clean Air Working Group (a project of the Texas Conference of Urban Counties) have identified alternative fuel strategies for the Lone Star State.

The People

Texas has a large, ethnically diverse population that is about twice the size of the combined populations of the four neighboring U.S. states or the combined populations of the four bordering Mexican states. In every decade since 1850, Texas's population has grown more rapidly than the overall population of the United States. Like the population of the nation, Texas's population is aging as the post–World War II baby-boom generation (persons born between 1946 and 1964) has reached middle age. The U.S. Bureau of the Census estimates that the population of persons over the age of 64 will more than double by 2020. Since early 2005, it is estimated that about half of all Texans are either African Americans or Latinos (also called Hispanics).[12] The remainder are predominantly Anglos (non-Hispanic whites), with a small but rapidly growing number of Asian Americans and fewer than 70,000 Native Americans (also called American Indians).

Most Populous U.S. States	Population	U.S. States Bordering Texas	Population	Mexican States Bordering Texas	Population
California	33,871,648	Arkansas	2,673,400	Chihuahua	3,052,907
Florida	15,982,378	Louisiana	4,468,976	Coahuila	2,298,070
New York	18,976,457	New Mexico	1,819,046	Nuevo León	3,834,141
Texas	**20,851,820**	Oklahoma	3,450,654	Tamaulipas	2,753,222

Demographic Features

According to the federal census of 2000, Texas's population totaled 20,851,820—an increase of 23 percent from the 1990 total of 16,986,510. At the national level, the total population in 2000 was 281,421,906—an increase of 13 percent from the U.S. population of 248,709,873 in 1990. Texas also had three of the top ten fastest-growing metropolitan areas in the nation from 1990 to 2000. McAllen-Edinburg-Mission (fourth) grew at a rate of 49 percent, Austin-San Marcos (fifth) grew at a rate of 48 percent, and Laredo (ninth) grew at a rate of 45 percent. Although the U.S. Census Bureau estimated that about 3.3 million Americans (1.2 percent) were missed by census takers in 2000, the administration of President George W. Bush decided that raw totals would be used rather than figures based on statistical sampling. Latinos and African Americans, especially those in big cities, are most likely to be undercounted. Because creation of congressional and legislative districts, as well as allocation of federal grants and state tax money, are affected by census figures, those areas with large minority populations tend to receive less representation and lower funding.[13] Additionally, by relying on raw census totals, Texas stands to lose millions of dollars in federal programs and aid over the first decade of the twenty-first century.

Population Distribution Just as Texas's physical geography makes the state a land of great contrasts, so too does the distribution of its inhabitants. Densely populated humid eastern areas contrast with sparsely populated arid regions in the west. At one extreme is Harris County (containing Houston and most of its suburbs). Located in the southeastern part of the state, Harris has more than 3.5 million inhabitants. At the other extreme is Loving County, on the New Mexican border, where the 2000 census counted only 67 people. Today, Texas's four most populous counties (Harris, Dallas, Bexar, and Tarrant) have a combined population of over 9 million, more than 40 percent of all Texans. These four urban counties (along with Travis County, which has the state capital) are located within the Texas Triangle. This triangle is roughly outlined by segments of Interstate Highways 35, 45, and 10.

In the 1980s and 1990s, **population shifts** within Texas matched the national pattern: movement from rural to urban areas and from large cities to suburbs. Regions where the economy depended largely on oil and agriculture either decreased in total population or grew more slowly than the state as a whole.

Population Changes To provide today's public policymakers and business-people with demographic information that will allow them to plan for the future, state demographer Steven H. Murdock and his associates in the Population Estimates and Projections Program (now located in the Institute for Demographic and Socioeconomic Research at the University of Texas at San Antonio) have prepared alternative scenarios of population growth. According to Murdock, if the rates of net migration for 2000–2040 are half those for 1990–2000, the state's population will be 35 million by 2040; but if the rates continue to be the same as for 1990–2000, there will be about 50.6 million people in the state by 2040.[14]

Urbanization Migration of people from rural regions to cities results in **urbanization**. Urban areas are composed of one or more large cities and their surrounding suburban communities. A suburb is a relatively small town or city, usually outside the boundary limits of a central city. For a century after statehood, Texas remained primarily rural. Then came urbanization, which progressed at an accelerated rate. Whereas Texas was 80 percent rural at the beginning of the twentieth century, by 1970 it was 80 percent urban. Today, Texans living in metropolitan counties constitute about 85 percent of the state's population. Meanwhile, suburbs adjoining or near central cities continue to spread into rural areas and surrounding counties.

Metropolitanization **Suburbanization** on a large scale creates a metropolitan area, a core city surrounded by a sprawl of smaller cities and towns. Like most states, Texas is experiencing suburbanization on a very large scale. Between 1980 and 2000, Texas suburbs experienced explosive growth. **Metropolitanization** concentrates large numbers of people in urban centers, which become linked in a single geographic entity. Though socially and economically integrated, a metropolitan area is composed of separate units of local government, which include counties, cities, and special districts.

Since 1910, federal agencies have defined metropolitan areas (MAs) for census purposes. The general concept of an MA is that of a core area containing a large population nucleus, together with adjacent communities having a high degree of economic and social integration with that core.

In 1949, the then U.S. Bureau of the Budget (predecessor of the Office of Management and Budget) issued standard definitions of metropolitan areas. These definitions were changed over the following years, and in 2003, the Office of Management and Budget established the current designations and criteria:

- **Micropolitan statistical area**: at least one urban cluster with a population of at least 10,000, but less than 50,000
- **Metropolitan statistical area**: the basic unit, comprising a freestanding urbanized area with a total population of at least 50,000
- **Combined statistical area**: a geographic entity consisting of two or more adjacent core based (micropolitan or metropolitan) statistical areas (CBSAs)

▪ **Metropolitan division:** a county or group of counties within a CBSA that
   contains a core with a population of at least 2.5 million

By 2004, the United States (including Puerto Rico) had 565 micropolitan statistical areas (41 in Texas), 370 metropolitan statistical areas (27 in Texas),
116 combined statistical areas (7 in Texas), and 29 metropolitan divisions (2
in Texas: one consisting of Dallas–Plano–Irving, and the other consisting of
Fort Worth–Arlington).

Cities are eager to obtain the highest possible statistical designation
because many congressional appropriations are made accordingly. For
example, to qualify for mass transit funds, an area must be a metropolitan
statistical area (MSA). The business community also uses data on population concentrations for market analysis and advertising.

Texas's rate of population growth is consistently greater in the metropolitan stastical areas than throughout the state as a whole. Most of these population concentrations are in the eastern part of the state and the Rio
Grande Valley of South Texas. Texas's metropolitan statistical areas contain
more than 80 percent of the state's population but less than 20 percent of
the 254 counties. It is politically significant that these 48 counties potentially
account for about four out of every five votes cast in statewide elections.
Thus, governmental decision makers are answerable primarily to people living in one-fifth of the state's counties. The remaining four-fifths, constituting
the bulk of the state's area, have one-fifth of the people. Urban voters, however, are rarely of one mind at the polls; they do not tend to overwhelm rural
voters by taking opposing positions on all policy issues.

Racial/Ethnic Groups

When answering questions on ethnicity and race for the 2000 census, 32
percent of all respondents in Texas indicated that they were Hispanic or
Latino (without identifying race), 1.1 percent claimed a heritage of two or
more races, and 66.9 percent said they were neither Hispanic nor Latino and
were of one race. Categories within the group claiming to be neither Hispanic nor Latino were as follows:

White	52.4 percent
Black or African American	11.3 percent
Asian	2.7 percent
American Indian and Alaska Native	0.3 percent
Native Hawaiian and other Pacific Islander	0.1 percent
Some other race	0.1 percent

In 1980, two-thirds of all Texans were called Anglos (that is, white people
who were not identified as Hispanics or Latinos). By 2000, only slightly more
than half of the Texas population could be classified as Anglo. As of 2004,
about 60 percent of births in the state are minority births, with Latino births

accounting for half of all newborns. Murdock projected the following population percentages for the year 2010 if the rates of net migration from other countries and other states decrease to one-half of those for 1990–2000: Anglo, 47.6; Hispanic, 37.2; Black (African and African American), 11.3; and other (Asian and Native American), 3.9. In this scenario, Anglos would no longer constitute a majority; they would be outnumbered by the combined total of other groups. In a similar scenario, Murdock projected the following population percentages for the year 2040: Anglo, 32.5; Hispanic, 52.5; Black, 9.4; and other, 5.6. At this point, Hispanics would constitute a majority. In case the rates of net migration do not decrease but remain the same as for 1990–2000, Murdock's projections for 2010 are as follows: Anglo, 45.2; Hispanic, 39.2; Black, 11.1; and other, 4.5. Similarly, for this scenario, these are his projections for 2040: Anglo 24.2; Hispanic, 59.1; Black, 7.9; and other, 8.8.[15]

Anglos As commonly used in Texas, the term **Anglo** is not restricted to persons of Anglo-Saxon lineage. Traditionally, the term applies to all whites except Latinos. By 1800, Anglo settlements began to appear in East Texas. Prior to the Civil War, over half of the state's Anglo residents had migrated from Alabama, Arkansas, Georgia, Kentucky, Louisiana, Mississippi, Missouri, and Tennessee.[16] Most remained in the eastern half of the state as farmers. Although the first non-Spanish-speaking immigrants to Texas were largely of English ancestry, some were of Scottish, Irish, or Welsh ancestry. Additional European settlers included French, Scandinavian, and Eastern European peoples, together with a scattering of Italians, Greeks, and others.

A significant number of German immigrants established settlements in the Hill Country west and north of San Antonio before the Civil War. It has been estimated that as many as 24,000 German immigrants and descendants were settled in the Hill Country by 1860. Most opposed slavery on principle, whereas others simply had no need for slaves. As a result, fourteen counties in Central Texas voted 40 percent or higher against secession in 1861. The area was scarred by what a historian called "a civil war within a Civil War,"[17] as hundreds of Union and Confederate sympathizers were killed in armed confrontations. Although Anglo migration into the state declined during the Civil War and Reconstruction, it resumed by the 1870s. By the beginning of the twentieth century, the largest migration came from neighboring U.S. states (Arkansas, Louisiana, New Mexico, and Oklahoma), the Northeast, and the Midwest.

Latinos Until 1836, Texas history is part of the history of Spain and Mexico. From 1836, when Texas rebelled and won independence from Mexico, until 1900, immigration from Mexico all but ceased. **Latinos** remained concentrated in settlements such as Goliad, Laredo, and San Antonio, founded during the eighteenth century. However, most of the Latino population was located within the regions of Central and South Texas.

Early in the twentieth century, the rise of commercial agriculture created the need for seasonal laborers. Consequently, many Latinos picked cotton, fruits, and vegetables. Others found work as day laborers or used their skills

as ranch hands or shepherds. Although Texas became more urbanized following World War I, Latinos remained mostly an agrarian people. After
World War II, however, increased numbers of Latinos left agricultural work
and sought employment opportunities in the industrializing cities. Most of
them experienced improvements in wages and working conditions in
unskilled or semiskilled positions, although a growing number of Latinos
entered managerial, sales, and clerical professions.[18] In the second half of
the twentieth century, Texas's Latino population was enlarged by a relatively
high birth rate and a surge of both legal and illegal immigration from Mexico and other countries in the Western Hemisphere. In the 1980s, Texas's
Latino population became more diverse in terms of country of origin, following an increase in immigrants from Central America, South America,
and the islands of the Caribbean.

By 2000, Texas Latinos numbered about 6.7 million, or nearly one-third of
the state's population. More than 76 percent of Texas Latinos are of Mexican origin. Texas ranks second in the nation in the number of Latino residents; only California, with about 11 million in 2000, has more. In 24 Texas
counties, more than 61 percent of the population is Latino (see Figure 1.3).

Figure 1.3   Percent of Persons Who Are Hispanic or Latino (of Any Race), Texas by
County Census 2000

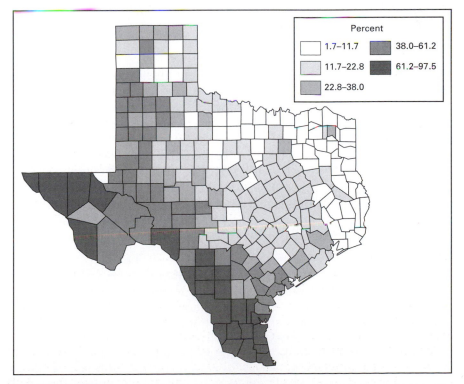

Source: U.S. Census Bureau

Both the economic and political strength of Texas's Spanish-surnamed citizens are on the increase. Latinos typically have larger families and are younger than the Anglo population. Immigration from Mexico and other Spanish-speaking countries is expected to continue throughout the twenty-first century.

African Americans   The first **African Americans** entered Texas as slaves of Spanish explorers in the sixteenth century. By 1792, it was reported that Spanish Texans included thirty-four blacks and 414 mulattos.[19] Some of them were free men and women. About the time slavery was abolished in Mexico, Anglo settlers brought larger numbers of black slaves from the United States to Texas. In addition, a few free African Americans came from northern states before the Civil War. By 1847, African Americans accounted for one-fourth of the state's population. During Reconstruction, there was a small wave of former black slaves who migrated into Texas. Many African Americans also moved from the state's rural areas to large cities. They often resided in freedmantowns that became the distinct black neighborhoods on the outskirts of these cities. A few of these freedmantowns have been preserved by various historical associations. Black labor also contributed substantially to the economic development of Texas cities and helped make the state's transition from its agrarian roots to an increasingly industrialized society. In 1880, the African American population in Texas numbered about 400,000.

In 2000, Texas had 2.4 million African Americans, more than 11 percent of the state's population. Although the number of African American Texans has continued to grow, it has increased at a slower rate than the rate of Latinos. Today, Texas has the third largest number of African Americans in the nation after New York and California. Most are located in southeast, north central, and northeast Texas, where they are concentrated in large cities. In recent years, a significant number of Africans have immigrated to the United States and settled in Texas. Their search for employment and their desire for a higher standard of living have prompted this immigration from Africa. Over half of the state's African Americans reside in and around Houston (approximately 630,000), Dallas (450,000), Fort Worth (185,000), San Antonio (100,000), and Beaumont (85,000) in Jefferson County. Although African Americans do not constitute a majority in any Texas county, according to 2000 census figures, Jefferson County has the largest percentage of African Americans (33.7 percent).

Asian Americans   Few Texans are aware that the Lone Star State is home to one of the largest **Asian American** populations in the nation. Most of Texas's Asian American families have immigrated to the United States from Southeast Asia (Cambodia, Laos, and Vietnam in particular), but a growing percentage of Texas Asians are American born. Compared with Latinos and African Americans, however, Asian Americans are newcomers to Texas.

Most Asian Americans settle in the state's largest urban centers, Houston and the Dallas–Fort Worth Metroplex. According to 2000 census data, Texas has two counties among the top fifty in the nation with the highest concentration of Asian Americans by percentage: Fort Bend, with 39,706 Asian Americans (11.2 percent of the population) ranks 22nd, and Collin, with 34,047 (6.9 percent) ranks 43rd. Although many are unskilled laborers, about half of Texas's Asian immigrants entered this country with college degrees or completed degrees later. The intensity with which the state's young Asian Americans focus on education is revealed by enrollment data for the University of Texas at Austin. Although Asian Americans account for only 2.7 percent of the total population of the state, they comprised approximately 13 percent of the enrollment at the University of Texas at Austin and 15 percent of the enrollment at the University of Texas at Dallas in the spring 2004 semester.

Native Americans   The Lone Star State owes part of its cultural heritage to **Native Americans**, who were called *indios* by Spanish explorers and American Indians by Anglo settlers. Today, relatively few Texans are identified as Native Americans; but some counties (Cherokee, Comanche, Nacogdoches, Panola, Wichita), cities and towns (Caddo Mills, Lipan, Nocona, Quanah, Watauga, Waxahachie), and other places have names reminding us that Native Americans were here first. In fact, the state's name comes from the word *tejas,* meaning "friendly," which was also the tribal name for a group of Indians within the Caddo Confederacy.

Estimates of the number of Native Americans in Texas when the first Spaniards arrived range from 30,000 to 150,000. Traveling in the Lone Star State in 1856, after three decades of Anglo-Indian warfare, one observer estimated the state's Native American population at about 12,000.[20] In 2000, Texas's Native Americans numbered less than 70,000. Most of them reside in towns and cities, where they work in a variety of jobs and professions.

Only a few Native Americans live on Texas reservations. About 1,000 remnants of the Alabama and Coushatta tribes are found on a 4,351-acre reservation in Polk County in the Big Thicket region of East Texas. Far across the state, near Eagle Pass on the United States–Mexican border, live a few hundred members of another Indian group, the Kickapoo tribe. The governments of Mexico and the United States allow them to move back and forth between Texas and the Mexican state of Coahuila. A third Native American group, the 1,400-member Tigua tribe, inhabits a 100-acre reservation near El Paso.

Searching for New Economic Directions

Once identified in the popular mind with cattle barons, cotton kings, and oil millionaires, the image of the Lone Star State is changing. Because the petroleum industry is not expected to regain its former leading role in Texas business, restructuring the state's economy has been vigorously pursued since the 1980s. In so doing, leaders in business and government have launched new industrial programs within the context of rapidly changing national and international circumstances. Today, Texas is part of middle-class America, with its share of professionals and businesspeople employed by varied enterprises: law firms; universities; federal, state, and local government bureaucracies; real estate and insurance companies; wholesale and retail sales firms; and manufacturing, communication, and transportation industries. However, a continuing struggle to provide jobs and market goods and services calls for effective public policies, an educated and productive labor force, an adequate supply of capital, and sound management practices.

For more than half a century, petroleum production and related enterprises led Texas's industrial development. Then, devastated by plunging oil prices in the mid-1980s, the entire Texas petroleum industry declined sharply. Even by the 1990s, with the price of oil on the rebound, Texans understood the danger of being overly reliant on one industry and recognized the need to develop an economically diverse economy. New industries have quickly spread across the state, making an impact on the Texas economy and now playing an important role in the national economy. In *Fortune*'s 2004 listing of the 500 largest private corporations in the United States, 44 were headquartered in Texas cities. Only two states had more than Texas: California with 53, and New York with 51. Among the 21 cities having 5 or more of the *Fortune* 500, New York City led with 41, and Houston was second with 19. Dallas was among five cities tied for sixth place, with seven of the *Fortune* 500 corporations.[21]

Energy

A natural offspring of the state's expansive oil and gas industries, the four largest private corporations in Texas, as identified in *Fortune*'s 2004 listing, were energy and energy-related. Two of these corporations, Exxon-Mobil (second) and Conocophilips (seventh) were among the seven largest corporations in the United States. Although oil and gas continue to be the major sources of energy in the Lone Star State, Texans are increasingly turning to alternative sources of energy such as wind. (For a detailed study of wind energy in Texas, see this chapter's selected reading, "Watts in the Wind.")

High Technology

The term **high technology** applies to research, development, manufacturing, and marketing of a seemingly endless line of electronic products. Among these are computers, calculators, digital watches, microwave ovens, telecommunications devices, automatic bank tellers, aerospace guidance systems, medical instruments, and assembly-line robots. Although high-technology businesses employ less than 6 percent of Texas's labor force, these enterprises contribute about 10 percent of all wages paid to private-sector employees. Most "high-tech" jobs are in manufacturing. Approximately 85 percent of all high-tech employment in Texas is centered in Austin, Dallas, El Paso, Fort Worth, Houston, and San Antonio. Major high-tech manufacturers include Motorola, Dell Computer, Compaq Computer (now a part of Hewlett-Packard), Texas Instruments, and Applied Materials (which produces machinery for manufacturing semiconductors).

The occupational structure of many high-tech companies differs from those of most other industrial firms. High-tech enterprises employ larger percentages of professional, technical, and managerial personnel. More than one-third of all high-tech jobs are in these categories, and wages and salaries are well above average. Recent reports of the American Electronic Association show that Texas has continued to rank second only to California in the size of its high-tech workforce. Early in 2001, more than 411,000 Texans held high-tech jobs paying nearly twice as much as the average for other private-sector positions. That same year, faced with weighty inventories and faltering personal computer sales worldwide, Austin-based Dell and Houston-based Compaq Computer were among several high-tech companies laying off or terminating large numbers of employees in highly publicized downsizing operations. In May 2002, Compaq announced its merger with Hewlett-Packard, laying off additional employees in Texas. Largely because of the weak personal computer market, the state's semiconductor and electronic component producers have also fared poorly. In mid-2002, Plano-based Electronic Data Systems announced that it was releasing more than 2,000 employees. Recently, Governor Rick Perry and other leaders in Texas government and business have called for greater efforts to expand the state's high-tech industry, encourage relocation of high-tech companies from other states (especially California), and challenge Texas's community colleges and universities to educate more students for high-tech careers.

A developing area in the field of technology is **nanotechnology** (a nanometer means one billionth of a meter). Texas is a leader in nanotechnology research and development. It's the only state with three Nobel laureates leading active research in nanotechnology. Additionally, most of the major universities in Texas have nanotechnology programs. In 1997, Richardson-based Zyvex Corporation, the first company in the world dedicated exclusively to molecular nanotechnology, was founded. Since then, 12 additional nanotech companies have settled in the Lone Star State. In 2002, Jim Von Ehr, the founder and CEO of Zyvex corporation, started the Texas Nanotechnology Initiative. It is a statewide consortium focused on bringing nanotechnology companies, researchers, and funding together. [22]

Biotechnology

The history of **biotechnology** dates back more than 6,000 years, when the Egyptians began using yeast to leaven bread, brew beer, produce wine, and make cheese. Today, biotechnology ("biotech") is exerting a growing influence on the state's economy. This multibillion-dollar industry produces many new medicines and vaccines, exotic chemicals, and other products designed to benefit medical science, human health, and agricultural production. In the last two decades, biotech-related jobs have increased four times faster than the overall increase in employment in Texas.

In 1999, a Summit on Biotechnology for Agriculture, Food, Fiber, and Health was convened in Austin to develop a strategic plan that would make Texas a national leader in agricultural biotechnology and allied technologies. Texas A&M University has become a recognized national leader in the biotechnology revolution in agriculture. Supported by Monsanto and other biotech companies, scientists at Texas A&M University have played an important role in research leading to production of genetically modified organism (GMO) crops, such as corn, soybeans, and cotton. However, Greenpeace and other environmental groups have opposed the marketing of gene-altered products without long-term safety tests and have called for labeling of all foods containing GMOs.[23]

Services

One of the fastest-growing economic sectors in Texas is the service industry. Employing one-fourth of all Texas workers, this sector continues to provide new jobs more rapidly than all other sectors. Service businesses include health care providers (hospitals and nursing homes); personal services (hotels, restaurants, and recreational enterprises such as bowling alleys and video arcades); and commercial services (printers, advertising agencies, data processing companies, equipment rental companies, and management consultants). Other service providers include investment brokers, insurance and real estate agencies, banks and credit unions, and a large variety of merchandising enterprises.

In 2001, the Texas service sector lost jobs for the first time in over 30 years. Many of these jobs were part-time positions in the areas of business services (personnel supply), the motion picture industry, and hotels. Terrorism concerns and economic weakness contributed to this loss. However, influenced by an aging population, the availability and use of new medical procedures, and the rapidly increasing cost of prescription drugs and other medical services, health services employment has steadily risen. The Texas comptroller of public accounts estimates that the Texas service sector will grow at a rate of 4 percent annually.

Most service jobs pay lower wages and salaries than employment in manufacturing firms that produce goods. A decade ago, journalist Molly Ivins warned, "the dream that we can transform ourselves into a service economy and let all the widget-makers go to hell or Taiwan is bullstuff. The service sector creates jobs all right, but they're the lowest paying jobs in the system. You can't afford a house frying burgers at McDonald's, even if you're a two-fryer family."[24] Her words still apply to service jobs in Texas.

Agriculture

Endowed with a wide range of climates, hundreds of thousands of acres of arable land, and adequate transportation and harbor facilities, Texas's farmers and ranchers are well positioned to produce and market huge amounts of food and fiber. Today, Texas ranks second in the nation in agricultural production. It leads the country in total acreage of agricultural land and numbers of farms and ranches, as well as in production of beef, grain sorghum, cotton, wool, and mohair (from Angora goats).

Gross income from the products of Texas agriculture amounts to about $14 billion annually, making agriculture the second-largest industry in Texas. The estimated value of agricultural assets in the state (such as land, buildings, livestock, and machinery) is more than $80 billion. The nation's second-largest exporter of agricultural products (behind California), the Lone Star State leads the country in exported cotton, much of which goes to Korea and Taiwan. Mexico is the largest buyer of Texas's farm and ranch products, and Japan is a major consumer of Texas-grown wheat and corn. Beef is the state's most important meat export.

Despite these impressive statistics, less than 2 percent of the state's jobs and total income are provided by farming and ranching. Furthermore, most agricultural commodities are shipped abroad or to other parts of the United States without being processed in Texas by Texans. Consequently, industrial development for processing food and fiber is needed if Texas is to derive maximum economic benefit from its agricultural production.

The number and size of Texas farms and ranches have changed greatly over the past century. These developments are due largely to the availability of laborsaving farm machinery and the use of chemicals to kill weeds, defoliate cotton before harvesting, and protect crops from insects and diseases. In the 1930s, there were more than 500,000 farms and ranches in Texas, with an average size of 300 acres. In 2004, the number of farms and ranches was about 230,000, and the average size was approximately 575 acres.[25]

Most small farms are operated by part-time farmers or by farmers who are able to farm only because a spouse has nonfarm employment. Although agri-business adds more than $80 billion to the Texas economy each year, the combined net annual income of all Texas farmers is under $3.1 billion. A large majority of them net less than $20,000 per year after production costs. When farm commodity prices are low (because of overproduction and weak market demand) or crops are poor (sometimes as a result of too much rain but usually because of drought), many farmers end the year deeply in debt. Some are forced to sell their land—usually to larger farm operators and sometimes to corporations. But some rich corporate executives, professional people, and politicians purchase agricultural property (especially ranchland) because such ownership is a status symbol they can afford—even though their land provides little or no income. Some use their agricultural property ownership to qualify for various exemptions and reductions for sales and property taxes at the state or local level and for federal income tax deductions. For economic reasons, much farmland and ranchland in the vicinity of expanding cities is being sacrificed to urban sprawl. According to the U.S. Department of Agriculture, every minute, half an acre of Texas farmland is converted into part of a road, shopping mall, or subdivision.

Trade

In 1993, the U.S. Congress approved the **North American Free Trade Agreement (NAFTA)**, to which the United States, Canada, and Mexico are parties. By reducing and then eliminating tariffs over a 15-year period, the agreement has stimulated U.S. trade with both Canada and Mexico. Because more than 60 percent of U.S. exports to Mexico are produced in Texas or transported through the Lone Star State from other states, an expanding foreign trade produces more jobs for Texans, more profits for the state's businesses, and more revenue for state and local governments.

Maquiladoras (assembly factories) on the Mexican side of the border typically use cheap labor to assemble imported parts for a wide range of consumer goods (for example, computers and TV sets) and then export these goods back to the United States. Only the value added in Mexico is subject to U.S. import taxes. Consequently, Texas border cities (especially Brownsville, McAllen, Laredo, and El Paso) have attracted many manufacturers who set up supply and distribution facilities in Texas that serve the maquiladoras in Mexico.[26] In late 2002, a report made by the director of the United Nations Development Fund for Women revealed that labor policies at maquiladora assembly plants, including late shifts and turning away employees for tardiness, endangered women in Ciudad Juárez, a Mexican city across the border from El Paso, where more than 75 women have been raped and murdered.[27] NAFTA is not without its critics. Texas's garment industry has been adversely affected, especially in border counties. Most clothing manufacturers have closed their plants and moved to Mexico, Central America, the Caribbean islands, or Asia. Likewise, some fruit and vegetable producers in Texas have been hurt by Mexican competition. A growing volume of trucking on highways between Mexico and Canada has contributed to the air pollution in Texas and causes serious traffic problems that endanger the lives of all motor vehicle drivers and passengers while slowing the transportation of goods.

Since 1995, a succession of political and economic crises in Mexico has raised serious questions concerning the future of NAFTA. In fact, the survival of Mexico's political system has been jeopardized by assassinations of public figures, kidnappings of wealthy businesspeople, drug-related corruption of government officials, attacks on tourists, widespread unemployment and hunger in both urban and rural areas, and acts of armed rebellion (especially in the southern states of Chiapas, Oaxaca, and Guerrero).[28] However, the election of President Vicente Fox in 2000 raised hopes for expanding political democracy, reducing poverty, and suppressing crime and corruption in Mexico.[29] After dominating Mexican politics for 71 years, the Institutional Revolutionary Party (PRI) lost the presidency to Fox and his National Action Party (PAN). Fox's victory demonstrated Mexico's capacity for peaceful political change, but his country has serious economic and social problems, and little has changed. A more prosperous and stable Mexico would help reduce the flow of jobless workers to Texas and other parts of the United States. At the same time, the volume of trade between the two countries could be expected to grow even faster. Recently, however, many Mexican *maquiladoras* have been shut down as multinational corporations have shifted production to plants in China and other parts of Asia where labor is even cheaper.[30]

Meeting New Challenges: Social and Economic Policy Issues

As we continue to move deeper into the twenty-first century, Texans are greatly affected by public policy decisions concerning the state's economy and its entire social order. The most important of these decisions relate to immigration and Texas's workforce, protection of the ecological system, job-creating economic development, technological changes in communications and industry, and restructuring and financing of public schools and institutions of higher education in the state.[31]

Social and economic influences on government, politics, and policymaking have been recognized since the days of ancient Greece. In recent years, Texas has experienced a wave of uncontrolled immigration and rapid economic change. Both of these developments pose problems for policymakers.

Immigration: Federal and State Problems

Since Texas became part of the Union, the Texas-Mexico boundary formed by the meandering Rio Grande has been the source of many controversies. Controlling the flow of aliens across the river, deciding how long they can remain within U.S. territory, determining what labor (if any) they may perform, and other immigration policy matters are issues that affect state, national, and international politics. Persons entering the United States in violation of federal immigration laws are called **undocumented aliens**. Although they supply Texas employers with cheap labor, some compete with U.S. citizens for jobs and require costly social services for themselves or for their children who come into this country or are born here. As with immigration issues involving other racial and ethnic groups today and in earlier periods of American history, passions and prejudices produce explosive politics.

In response to heavy political pressure and 14 years of debate and political maneuvering, the U.S. Congress enacted into law the Immigration Reform and Control Act of 1986. This federal statute was designed to restrain the flow of illegal immigrants into the United States by penalizing employers who knowingly hire undocumented aliens and by appropriating funds to provide more enforcement personnel for the U.S. Immigration and Naturalization Service (INS), especially border patrol officers, whom Latinos refer to as *la migra*. Despite this act, hundreds of thousands of undocumented aliens have continued to enter Texas each year since 1986. Many are arrested, detained, and subsequently expelled from the country. Others voluntarily return to Mexico and other countries after earning money to support their families. However, many thousands of undocumented aliens remain in Texas and often are able to arrange for family members to join them. Some undocumented aliens are shamelessly exploited by employers, merchants, and landlords. Others receive fair wages and humane treatment. All, however, live and work in fear of arrest and deportation.

In the 1990s, an anti-immigration groundswell developed throughout most parts of the United States. Central to the controversy is the issue of costs and benefits resulting from both legal and illegal immigration. In 1994, Texas joined other states in suing the federal government to recover various costs (for example, health, welfare, education, and law enforcement) incurred from illegal immigration. That same year, U.S. border patrol personnel intensified their efforts to halt the influx of undocumented aliens. In 1996, the U.S. Congress enacted the Immigration Control and Financial Responsibility Act, which was cosponsored by Representative Lamar Smith, a Republican from San Antonio. In addition to increasing the number of border patrol officers, the law increases penalties for immigrant smuggling and speeds up the deportation of illegal immigrants who use false documents or commit other crimes while in the United States.

In the wake of the terrorist attacks of September 11, 2001, the United States Congress passed the Enhanced Border Security and Visa Entry Reform Act of 2002, which President George W. Bush signed into law. The act concerns tracking international students accepted by educational institutions, issuing visas, and other matters involving foreign nationals. It authorizes an additional 200 inspectors and 200 investigators for the Immigration and Naturalization Service in each of the fiscal years 2003 through 2006. In addition, the act increases the pay and training of INS personnel, including border patrol agents. The act also provides an additional $150 million for improved border control technology, provides for creation of electronically maintained visa files that will be available to immigration inspectors, and requires the INS to integrate all of its data systems into one system. In 2003, INS was folded into the U.S. Department of Homeland Security's new Bureau of Immigration and Customs Enforcement and is now called the Citizenship and Immigration Service (CIS).

Despite legal obstacles to immigration, low wages and high levels of unemployment in Mexico motivate masses of Mexican workers to cross the border in search of jobs. At the same time, many businesspeople, farmers, and ranchers in Texas and elsewhere are willing to violate U.S. law (and run the small risk of incurring fines) by hiring undocumented aliens. They do so because other labor is unavailable or because illegal immigrants will work harder for lower wages.

Water

With the state's population expected to double by the middle of the twenty-first century, Texas faces a formidable challenge in meeting the water needs of its citizens. The state's current dependable water supply will meet only

POINT / COUNTERPOINT

Recognition of the *Matricula Consular* by the State of Texas[32]

THE ISSUE

The 11 Mexican consular offices in Texas issue the *matricula consular* (consular registration) to Mexican nationals—both undocumented and legal—living in the state. This photo identification card is accepted by many banks throughout the country for the purpose of opening an account, and at the beginning of 2004 it was recognized as valid identification by 13 state governments. Although the governments of 18 Texas cities and 6 counties recognize the *matricula consular*, in 2003 the 78th Legislature rejected proposals that would have required the Texas Department of Public Safety to accept it as proof of identity for a driver's license applicant.

Arguments For Recognition

1. *Identification.* The *matricula consular* would help state officials and agencies to determine the identity and residence of holders who are now unidentifiable.
2. *Public Safety.* Law enforcement officers could more easily identify card-carrying crime suspects, witnesses, and victims.
3. *Immigration.* Neither a *matricula consular* nor a driver's license, which is required for obtaining auto insurance, is proof of U.S. citizenship or legal residency; so undocumented aliens with these ID cards could still be arrested and deported.

Arguments Against Recognition

1. *Identification.* The *matricula consular* is too susceptible to fraud, and there is no central database for tracking recipients of these cards.
2. *Public Safety.* Homeland security would be compromised by ID cards that could be used by criminals and terrorists to move around the state and engage in financial transactions to support their activities.
3. *Immigration.* State recognition of the *matricula consular* would encourage illegal immigration and give cardholders a quasi-legal status that would hinder enforcement of U.S. immigration laws.

about 70 percent of projected demand by the year 2050. Complicating the water problem in Texas is the long-established rule or law of capture, allowing landowners to pump as much water from beneath their property as they wish, even if it affects their neighbor's wells. The Rule of Capture was upheld by the Texas Supreme Court in 1999. As the population continues to shift from rural to urban areas, and with the migration of people from other states to Texas cities, urban demands will increasingly compete with rural communities and agricultural interests for the same water. To meet this challenge and to provide necessary flows of water for maintaining the environment, Texas will need to rely on water conservation and alternative water management strategies.[33]

After a devastating drought in the 1950s, the Texas Legislature created the **Texas Water Development Board (TWDB)** in 1957 and mandated state-wide water planning. Since then, the TWDB and the Texas Board of Water Engineers have prepared and adopted seven state water plans, including *Water for Texas—2002*. This plan differs from previous plans in that it was developed as a result of public participation (nearly 900 public meetings were held across the state) at each step in the process, and local and regional input contributed to decisions to produce 16 regional water plans to form the basis of the State Water Plan. *Water for Texas—2002* makes several recommendations for development, management, and conservation of water resources and for preparation and response to drought conditions so that sufficient water may be available for the foreseeable future.[34]

Environmental Protection

Serious health problems are caused by the low quality of the air that many Texans breathe and the impurity of the water they drink and in which they wade and swim. (For more on environmental issues, see Chapter 8 on "Bureaucracy, Public Policies, and Finance.") Some effects of environmental pollution are revealed in observations concerning fish and wildlife populations. For example, Texas (along with California, Hawaii, and Florida) leads all other states in the number of endangered fish and wildlife species.

Bordered by Florida, Alabama, Mississippi, Louisiana, and Texas, the Gulf of Mexico covers nearly 700,000 square miles, or seven times as much area as the Great Lakes. Industries in each of these states and Mexico release toxic chemicals directly into the gulf or into rivers that flow into it. Also contributing greatly to environmental problems in the gulf is the continuing flow of nitrate-laden rivers that draw their water from the chemically fertilized farms of rural areas and the lawns and gardens of cities large and small. With declining catches of fish, shrimp, and oysters from gulf waters, Texans must do with less seafood or import it from abroad. Of course, an obvious solution to the problem would be environmental protection measures designed to clean up the Gulf of Mexico and restore its productivity.[35]

Points to Ponder

Texas ranks
- #1 in toxic and hazardous waste.
- #1 in "hazardous air pollutants" emissions.
- #1 in toxic manufacturing emissions.
- #1 in toxic water emissions.
- #1 in cancerous manufacturing emissions.
- #1 in toxic air emissions.
- #1 in cancerous air emissions.
- #1 in carbon dioxide emissions.

Yet only
- #18 in per capita spending on air quality.
- #49 in per capita spending on water
- #38 in water-quality planning.

Source: Texans for Public Justice

Education and Economic Development

Along with a poor record of environmental protection, Texas gets low marks in other critical areas that affect its residents' quality of life and economic welfare. More well-paying jobs, along with rising productivity, depend largely on a well-educated Texas workforce. Teachers are the key element in any educational system, but from year to year the Lone Star State is confronted with a shortage of certified personnel to instruct its 4 million elementary and secondary school students. Included within this total are more than half a million students with limited English proficiency.

Although estimates of the teacher shortage vary, the Texas Education Agency reports that about one-fifth of the state's 250,000 teachers quit teaching each year. Some retire, but most of them abandon their profession for reasons that include inadequate pay and benefits, low prestige, and time-consuming chores such as grading that often must be done at night and on weekends. Contributing to their decision to seek other careers is stress over student performance on standardized tests and classroom problems affected by the poverty and troubled home life of many students. In 2004, many public school teachers in Texas retired to take advantage of a provision that would allow them to collect spousal Social Security benefits. Most Texas teachers participate in the state's Teachers Retirement System rather than in Social Security. Congress changed this law early in 2004. However, teachers who retired prior to July 1, 2004 could still collect Social Security benefits provided that their last day was spent working in a job that was covered by the federally funded program, usually a janitorial or maintenance position within the school district. Although the public tends to overlook the needs of teachers, many Texans complain about students' high dropout rates, low levels of academic achievement, and inadequate preparation for work or college.

Success in dealing with educational needs will be especially important in determining Texas's ability to compete nationally and internationally in business as well as in science and technology. The urgency of this matter is suggested in studies that rank Texas near the bottom of the nation in the literacy of its residents. Of special concern to employers is the fact that one out of every three Texans cannot read and write well enough to fill out a simple job application. Moreover, the state loses many billions of dollars annually because most illiterate Texans, along with many who are poorly educated, are doomed to unemployment or low-paying jobs and thus generate little or no tax revenue.

Poverty and Social Problems

Although many of America's public figures stress the importance of family values, serious social and economic problems affect homes throughout the country. In the Lone Star State, there are alarming numbers of children living in poverty and in single-parent homes, births to unwed teenagers, juvenile arrests, and violent acts committed by teenagers and preadolescents.

More than one of every five Texas children lives in poverty, and many children at all levels of society suffer from abuse and neglect. Estimates of the number of homeless people (including many children) vary widely, but at least 100,000—and perhaps more than 200,000—Texans are unable to provide themselves with shelter in a house or apartment. In 2004, more than one-third of Texas workers were earning less than $18,850 a year, below the federal poverty level for food stamps for a family of four.

Texas's limited response to the social and economic needs of its people continues to be the subject of much debate. Some Texans argue that any public assistance for the poor is too much. They believe government help encourages dependence and discourages self-reliance, personal initiative, and desire to work. Other Texans advocate greatly increased government spending to help people who are unable to care for themselves and their families because of mental or physical health problems, lack of job opportunities, or age. Between these extremes are Texans who support a limited role for government in meeting human needs but call for churches and other nongovernmental organizations to play a more active role in dealing with social problems.[36] Texas voters, however, tend to support candidates for public office who promise lower taxes, tighter government budgets, fewer public employees, and reduction or elimination of social services. As a result, the Lone Star State ranks near the bottom of the 50 states in governmental responses to poverty and social problems.

Looking Ahead

As the process of economic development and diversification goes forward in Texas, some of the state's cherished values are being sorely tried. Many jobs are lost while others are being created, and old industries decline or die as new ones are established. Meanwhile, the lives of all Texans are affected— some for better and others for worse. Critical environmental problems— including air, water, and soil pollution—must be resolved at the same time that the state's water supply is declining.

Natural disasters such as hurricanes, tornadoes, floods, and droughts will continue to present problems for individuals, businesses, and governments at all levels. Further, as indicated by federal census statistics, together with economic and social data from other sources, Texas policymakers must deal with an expanded aging population and a high incidence of poverty. Above all, both ordinary citizens and public officials must realize that their ability to cope with public problems now and in the years ahead depends largely on how well homes, schools, colleges, and universities prepare young Texans to meet the crises and demands of an ever-changing state, nation, and world.

The following chapter, "Federalism and the Texas Constitution," examines the position of the states within the federal Union and looks at the constitutional development of the Lone Star State, especially its much-amended Constitution of 1876.

☆ Chapter Summary ☆

■ The political culture of Texas is both individualistic and traditionalistic. The individualist culture is rooted in the state's frontier experience and includes economic and social conservatism, strong support of personal politics, distrust of political parties, and minimization of parties' importance. The traditionalistic culture grew out of the Old South, where policies were designed to preserve the social order, a one-party system developed, and the poor and minorities were often disenfranchised. Today, these two cultures can still be found in the values, attitudes, traditions, habits, and general behavior patterns of Texans and in governmental policies of the Lone Star State.

■ With over 267,000 square miles of territory, Texas ranks second in size to Alaska among the 50 states. Cattle, cotton, and oil have at different times dominated the Texas economy and influenced the state's politics. Today, Texas is a highly industrialized state in which high-technology products are of increasing importance.

■ Texas has a rapidly growing population (about 21 million according to the 2000 census). More than 80 percent of all Texans live in the state's most highly urbanized counties. The three largest groups are Anglos, Latinos (mostly Mexican Americans), and African Americans. Texas has a small but growing population of Asian Americans, but fewer than 70,000 Native Americans.

■ Although the state's petroleum industry has declined in importance, Texas has become a leading manufacturer of computers and other high-tech products. Agriculture continues to be important in the state's economy but employs relatively few Texans. Service businesses provide many low-paying jobs.

■ Challenges facing Texas are the need for measures that will more effectively address immigration, protect the environment, develop educational programs to meet the demands of an industrial society, and formulate policies for combating poverty and social problems.

Key Terms and Concepts

politics	frontier experience
government	Jim Crow
public policy	*patrón* system
aliens	moralistic culture
political culture	physical regions

Gulf Coastal Plains
Interior Lowlands
Great Plains
Basin and Range Province
Spindletop Field
Texas Railroad Commission
population shifts
urbanization
suburbanization
metropolitanization
micropolitan statistical area
metropolitan statistical area
combined statistical area
metropolitan division

Anglo
Latino
African Americans
Asian American
Native Americans
high technology
nanotechnology
biotechnology
North American Free Trade
   Agreement (NAFTA)
maquiladoras
undocumented aliens
Texas Water Development
   Board (TWDB)

Discussion Questions

1. In what ways is Texas's political culture (individualism and traditionalism) reflected in politics, policies, and the people's attitudes about, and expectations of, government today?
2. What political advantages are there to Texas's being the second most populous state in the nation?
3. What challenges for government are presented by the growing urban population of the state in cities such as Houston, San Antonio, Dallas, and Fort Worth? How can government respond to these challenges?
4. What challenges for government are presented by the state's shrinking rural population? How can government respond to these challenges?
5. How have various ethnic and racial groups contributed to the state's culture and economic development?
6. What challenges for government are presented by the racial and ethnic diversity of Texas? How can government respond to these challenges?
7. What industries are essential to sustain and continue to develop the Texas economy in the twenty-first century?
8. What social services are essential to sustain and continue to develop the Texas economy in the twenty-first century?

Internet Resources

The Handbook of Texas Online: **www.tsha.utexas.edu/handbook/
   online**
Texas Department of Agriculture: **www.agr.state.tx.us**
Texas Railroad Commission: **www.rrc.state.tx.us**
Texas State Data Center: **www.txsdc.utsa.edu**

Texas State Library and Archives Commission: **www.tsl.state.tx.us**
United States Census Bureau: **www.census.gov**
Window on State Government: **www.window.state.tx.us**

Notes

1. Gary P. Nunn. "What I Like About Texas," from *What I Like About Texas* (Campfire Records, 1997).
2. Harold Lasswell, *Politics: Who Gets What, When, How* (New York: McGraw-Hill, 1936).
3. Daniel Elazar, *American Federalism: A View from the States,* 3d ed. (New York: Harper & Row, 1984), p. 134.
4. See "A Brief Sketch of Texas History," *Texas Almanac* 2004–2005 (Dallas: Dallas Morning News, 2004), p. 41.
5. Ibid., pp. 42-43.
6. For a case study of the *patrón* system, see J. Gilberto Quezada, *Border Boss: Manuel B. Bravo and Zapata County* (College Station: Texas A&M University Press, 1999).
7. For more on Texas Longhorns, see J. Frank Dobie, *The Longhorns* (Austin: University of Texas Press, 1980). Results of the most recent research on the origin of longhorn cattle are found in T. J. Barragy, *Gathering Texas Gold: J. Frank Dobie and the Men Who Saved the Longhorn* (Corpus Christi, Tex.: Cayo de Grullo Press, 2003). Barragy disputes assertions in Don Worcester's popular *The Texas Longhorn: Relic of the Past, Asset for the Future* (College Station: Texas A&M University Press, 1987) that English Bakewell Longhorns and other British breeds played a significant role in the genetic makeup of Texas Longhorns.
8. See Don Graham, *Kings of Texas: The 150-Year Saga of an American Empire* (Hoboken, N.J.: John Wiley & Sons, 2003); Jane Clements Monday and Betty Bailey Colley, *Voices from the Wild Horse Desert: The Vaquero Families of the King and Kenedy Ranches* (Austin: University of Texas Press, 1997); Armando C. Alonzo, *Tejano Legacy: Rancheros and Settlers in South Texas, 1734–1900* (Albuquerque: University of New Mexico Press, 1998); Andrés Tijerina, *Tejano Empire: Life on the South Texas Ranchos* (College Station: Texas A&M University Press, 1998); and Daniel D. Arreola, *Tejano South Texas: A Mexican American Cultural Province* (Austin: University of Texas Press, 2002).
9. For an account of the history of the early years of the oil industry in Texas, see Roger M. Olien and Diana Davids Olien, *Oil in Texas: The Gusher Age, 1895–1945* (Austin: University of Texas Press, 2002).
10. "Boom, Bust and Back Again: Bullock Tenure Covers Tumultuous Era," *Fiscal Notes* (December 1990), pp. 6-7.
11. For details concerning Texas's economy in the 1980s, see M. Ray Perryman, *Survive and Conquer: Texas in the '80s: Power, Money, Tragedy, Hope!* (Dallas: Taylor Publishing, 1990).

12. For a personal view of Hispanic (or Latino) culture, see Richard Rodriguez, "What Is a Hispanic?" *Texas Journal of Ideas, History and Culture* 22 (Summer 2000): 32–41.
13. See Daryl Janes, "Politics and Purse Strings: Why the Census Counts," *Fiscal Notes* (March 2000): 3–4.
14. *See* Steve H. Murdock et al., *The New Texas Challenge: Population Change and the Future of Texas* (College Station: Texas A&M University Press, 2003), p. 24.
15. Ibid.
16. Terry G. Jordan, "The Imprint of Upper and Lower South on Mid-Nineteenth-Century Texas," *Annals of American Association of Geographers* 57 (December 1967): 667–690.
17. Kent Biffle, "If At First You Don't Secede," *Dallas Morning News*, 3 November 2002.
18. Arnoldo De León, "Mexican Americans," in *The Handbook of Texas Online* (2002) <www.tsha.utexas.edu/handbook/online/articles/view/MM/pqmue.html>.
19. Alwyn Barr, *Black Texans: A History of African Americans in Texas, 1528–1995,* 2d ed. (Norman: University of Oklahoma Press, 1996), p. 3.
20. Frederick Law Olmsted, *A Journey Through Texas* (New York: Dix, Edwards, 1857; reprint, Burt Franklin, 1969), p. 296. For more information on Texas Indian tribes, see Richard L. Schott, "Contemporary Indian Reservations in Texas: Tribal Paths to the Present," *Public Affairs Comment* (Lyndon B. Johnson School of Public Affairs, University of Texas at Austin) 39:3 (1993): 1–9; and David La Vere, *The Texas Indians* (College Station: Texas A&M University Press, 2004).
21. *Fortune*, 14 April 2004, p. F-32.
22. "Sweating the Small Stuff: A Report on Texas' Bid to Become the Center of the Nanotechnology Industry—And the Ways That Industry, Academia, and the Legislature Can Support This Effort." Developed by the Texas Nanotechnology Initiative, February 2003.
23. For criticism and questions concerning genetic engineering for food production, see Nate Blakeslee, "Banking on Biotech: Is the Latest Food Science from Aggieland a Lemon?" *Texas Observer,* March 30, 2001, pp. 6–9, 14; Sandra Kill Leber, "Biotechnology: Curse or Cure?" *State Government News* (January 2000): 23–26; and Ronnie Cummins, "Exposing Biotech's Big Lies," *BioDemocracy News* 39 (May 2002) <http://www.organicconsumer.org/newsletter/blod39.cfm>. Concerning the use of GMOs to reduce risks of chronic diseases, see Edward A. Hiler, "Houston Has a Stake in High-Tech Agriculture, Too," *Houston Chronicle,* 18 June 2001.
24. Molly Ivins, "Top to Bottom Reform of Financial Structures Essential," *Dallas Times Herald,* 3 June 1990.
25. These statistics were provided by the Texas Agricultural Statistics Service, Texas Department of Agriculture.

26. For a case study of an assembly-line manufacturing job that passed (with big pay cuts) from Paterson, New Jersey, to Blytheville, Arkansas, to the Mexican border city of Matamoros (across the Rio Grande from Brownsville, Texas), see William M. Adler, *Mollie's Job: A Story of Life and Work on the Global Assembly Line* (New York: Scribner, 2000).

27. "UNIFEM Head Decries Feminization of Poverty," *UN Wire*, 3 December 2002 <http://www.unwire.org/UNWire/20021203/30674_story.asp>.

28. See Denise Dresser, "Mexico: Uneasy, Uncertain, Unpredictable," *Current History* 96 (February 1997): 51–54.

29. See Lucy Conger, "Mexico's Long March to Democracy," *Current History* 100 (February 2001): 58–64; Carlos E. Casasillas and Alejandro Mújica, "Mexico: New Democracy with Old Parties?" *Politics* 23 (September 2003): 172–180; and Julia Preston and Samuel Dillon, *Opening Mexico: The Making of a Democracy* (New York: Farrar, Straus and Giroux, 2004).

30. See Pamela K. Starr, "Fox's Mexico: Same As It Ever Was?" *Current History* 101 (February 2002): 58–65; Jorge G. Casteneda, "NAFTA at 10: A Plus or a Minus? *Current History* 103 (February 2004): 51-55; and Sidney Weintraub, "Scoring Free Trade: A Critique of the Critics," *Current History* 103 (February 2004): 56-60.

31. For 150 indicators assessing Texas's environment, education, economy, human services, public safety, and democracy, see Paul Robbins and Andrew Wheat, eds. *The State of the Lone Star State: How Life in Texas Measures Up* (Austin: Texans for Public Justice, 2000). For each indicator, Texas's ranking is compared with rankings of the five highest and five lowest states.

32. This Point/Counterpoint section is based on Kellie Dworaczyk, "Should Texas Recognize Mexican-Issued Identity Cards Held by Immigrants?" *Interim News* No. 78-20 (Austin: House Research Organization, Texas House of Representatives, 20 January 2004): 1-6.

33. For an excellent overview of the state's water problems, see Ann Walther, *Texas at a Watershed: Planning Now for Future Needs,* Focus Report No. 75-13 (Austin: House Research Organization, Texas House of Representatives, April 15, 1997); see also Hope E. Wells, *Managing Groundwater for Texas' Future Growth,* Focus Report No. 76-21 (Austin: House Research Organization, Texas House of Representatives, 23 March 2000).

34. Jan Gertson, Mark MacLeod, and C. Allan Jones, *Efficient Water Use for Texas: Policies, Tools, and Management Strategies,* report prepared for Environmental Defense by Texas Agricultural Experiment Station, Texas A&M University, College Station, Texas (September 2002).

35. For information on all aspects of Texas's environmental problems, see Mary Sanger and Cyrus Reed, comps., *Texas Environmental Almanac,* 2d ed. (Austin: University of Texas Press, 2000).

36. See Governor's Advisory Task Force on Faith-Based Community Service Groups, *Faith in Action: A New Vision for Church-State Cooperation in Texas,* full report (Austin, December 1996).

SELECTED READING

★ ——————————————————————————————

Watts in the Wind: Texas Wind Industry Rushes to Meet Growing Demand*

Clint Shields

This reading examines the wind industry as a source of alternative energy in Texas. Currently, more wind energy is generated than can be delivered to Texas consumers because existing transmission lines are inadequate.

Twenty years ago it was an oddity to spot a field of sleek windmills on a flat stretch of West Texas plain. Today, the "wind farms" of electricity-generating turbines are as common as cactus. Fossil fuels and nuclear power are still the mainstays of the Lone Star State—as much as 98 percent of Texas' electricity supply comes from those sources. But the availability and pollution-free performance of wind in Texas has made it the most in-demand form of renewable energy across the state, according to the Texas Comptroller's State Energy Conservation Office (SECO). Despite high demand for wind power, the existing transmission infrastructure can't handle the amount of power wind generates on any given day. The Texas Public Utility Commission (PUC) and the Electric Reliability Council of Texas (ERCOT) say they are working to bring delivery in line with production.

Blowin' Energy

Each year, Texas produces more wind energy than any state except California, according to the American Wind Energy Association (AWEA). "Texas is currently second behind California, where it all began in December of 1981," said Tom Gray, AWEA's director of communications. "California has about 1,832 megawatts (MW), Texas about 1,096 MW, but both are expected to climb a little at the end of this year." A megawatt, or one million watts, can provide electricity for about 300 homes over the course of a year.

AWEA, a trade association representing companies with interests in wind power ranging from turbine manufacturers to insurance companies, expects two new wind-energy projects to come online in Texas by the end of 2003: the 160 MW Brazos Wind Ranch south of Lubbock; and the 37.5 MW Sweetwater wind project. The addition of nearly 200 MW will bump the state's production by 20 percent, with plans for even more wattage.

*"Watts in the Wind" by Clint Shields. Reprinted by permission of Texas Comptroller of Public Accounts.

"About 2 percent of Austin's requirement in electricity is coming from wind, with 86 megawatts of wind under contract right now," said Mark Kapner of Austin Energy. "We also have a third wind contract with Cielo [Wind Power], which is yet to be built, and we're going to city council on October 2 to approve a fourth contract. Cielo will add 40 megawatts, and the fourth is to be 93. Those additional megawatts will make our energy total a little more than 4 percent from wind."

Kapner said renewable energy like wind power has become important to consumers because it is cleaner to produce than traditional, coal-fired electricity and, perhaps surprisingly, customers will pay extra for it.

"The customer is helping by causing the electrical provider to burn less [coal] to produce electricity," he said. "Why do people do it? They want to see us burn less and not put pollutants into the air or the environment and are willing to pay more up front to do it." Austin Energy purchases a little less than 10 percent of the state's wind power output, Kapner said.

Transfer Trouble

Texas has the available wind power and is working to harvest it. More new wind energy generation—951 MW—was installed in Texas in 2001 than in any state in U.S. history, according to AWEA. The Texas Panhandle, South Plains region and Davis Mountains area offer the best wind in the state, with consistent wind speeds of at least 15 miles per hour at 50 feet above the ground, a common height for wind turbines, according to SECO.

Kapner said the wind is in the west but the need is further east. "The market's not West Texas, it's North and Central Texas," he said. "Can the energy get to the market? That is the question." Robby Abarca of the PUC said the state's existing transmission lines are unable to accommodate the power generated by the turbines in West Texas.

"If all the turbines are running, it can create an overload," Abarca said. To protect the transmission lines, ERCOT can instruct the owners of the turbines to cease running them to guard against overloading the lines and to prevent large power outages, he said.

ERCOT's Ken Donohoo said each day ERCOT determines how much space is available on the state's power grid and works from there. "We know the [generating] capacity of each wind farm," he said. "We look every day at how much we can handle and then pass the word along as to how much the turbines can generate that day and they have to stay within that number."

Overpowered

Reaping energy from the wind is more complicated than just putting a few spinning blades in the sky. Repairing blown transmission lines is expensive and time-consuming, Kapner said. Turbines constantly produce energy that must be used or it will be lost. Production is a delicate balance. "There's more wind energy production than can move through the power lines when the wind is strong," he said. "Some turbines have to be curtailed in those times, and the owners of the wind farms suffer when they're offline."

Abarca said the transmission problems can be overcome but adds it will require some time and creative thinking. "Wind generators can be built relatively quickly," he said. "The transmission lines take much longer. Eventually, we'll catch up but it takes time to evaluate different transmission alternatives. What we do out in West Texas [will] affect the rest of the state in some way." He said one alternative is building wind farms in areas where there are existing transmission lines to handle the load of the generating facility, but the trick to that is finding lines and a location with wind suitable for electric generation.

Donohoo said ERCOT is quickly closing the gap between generation and transmission by improving existing lines and adding new ones, but he said the speed of wind power construction is hard to keep up with. "It's a clear fact that 1,000 megawatts of wind power is out there, and we're moving fairly quickly in getting transmission lines up," Donohoo said. "We're up to 400 megawatts now; by the end of next year we should be up to 650 and up to 1,000 by 2006. The amazing thing about wind is [wind farms] can go up in as little as six months, where it takes anywhere from two to three years to build a regular [coal or natural gas] generation facility."

The Sky's the Limit

Austin-based Cielo Wind Power has been in the business of wind farm maintenance and construction since 1994. The company started out repairing old wind turbines and later began designing wind farms. Walter Hornaday, Cielo's president, confirmed one problem is the time difference between developing a wind farm, which includes activities such as selecting sites and obtaining permits in addition to construction, and constructing the transmission lines to carry its load. "Basically it takes about 18 months to develop and build a wind project in Texas, but four to five years to build transmission lines," he said. "With wind projects, you have to build where the wind is right and getting electricity to major hubs like Dallas and Houston is difficult." While the electric route to metropolitan areas is a difficult one to map out, Hornaday said one advantage to wind farms in West Texas is the effect on the local economy. "Most of West Texas is windy," said Hornaday. "We see the biggest attraction [there] as arid and dry counties that can't get big, industrial facilities to locate there. "The great thing about wind power is [wind farms] can go in rural areas where there isn't water to cool generators [of coal-burning plants], and they can be a great economic development tool for areas like that."

Landowners benefit from a constant revenue source from royalty and lease payments, according to Hornaday, as well as benefits to schools, hospitals and county services from what Hornaday called "considerable property taxes" when installing a wind development. Hornaday said whenever someone chooses wind power as their energy source, the chances of a new turbine going up in Texas increases. As many as 200 employees are usually needed during construction of a typical, 80 MW installation, he said. Once it is running, it requires about 10 full-time employees for jobs that normally require at least a technical college associate degree and pay comparable to high-tech oil field and agriculture wages in Texas, Hornaday said.

Purchasing Power

Texas consumers have a choice when it comes to the electricity powering their homes. The 1999 Legislature passed S.B. 7, calling for, among other things, a capacity of 2,000 MW of renewable energy on the Texas electric grid by 2009. The creation of more renewable energy sources means more Texans can choose wind as their power source. Getting the word out is SECO's job.

"Wind is becoming very popular right now, so people want to know about what's popular," said SECO's Pam Groce. "The majority of my job is educating people about renewable energy and providing info on being an educated consumer." Groce conducts wind power demonstrations around the state aimed at large- and small-scale applications. "We do some small-scaled demonstrations because 'small wind' has been around for a very long time," she said. "In remote areas, wind [power] is still very popular as long as you're in a windy area." Small wind, according to the U.S. Department of Energy, is electrical power from a wind turbine rated at less than 100 kilowatts (KW). Small wind generally is used to provide power for single homes and small businesses.

Groce said SECO helped the Texas Department of Transportation (TxDOT) establish wind-powered rest areas in Pine Springs in East Texas and Alanreed in the Panhandle in 2003. TxDOT paid $115,000 for the two turbines, and SECO will handle the cost of maintenance on the turbines. SECO budgeted about $35,000 for maintenance. Groce said the hope is that the two rest areas, along with a 3 KW wind turbine SECO installed in Hale County, will help with future educational demonstrations by providing answers to questions about cost. "We're gathering [data on] how much power they generate so that it's not just a facility that generates electricity, but also gives us data that we can make available to the public," she said. "Questions like 'How often does it [break] down and why?' There are moving parts within wind turbines and they can break, but how often?"

Groce says that type of information is not available at the state level because the state hasn't actually owned wind farms in the past, and turbine owners who keep accurate maintenance records are not required to send that information to SECO.

"Utilities are investing in wind because it's economical," Groce said. "Consumers are the ones demanding that companies do more renewable generation."

Goin' Green

Consumers in Austin and San Antonio can opt to purchase wind power. Austin Energy's "Green Choice" program allows residents to purchase renewable energy, such as wind, solar and biomass, which is methane gas released from materials in landfills. Austin Energy's Mark Kapner said the wind projects Austin Energy is associated with make up the majority of the power supplied to GreenChoice customers. "The four wind projects [we use] make up about 85 percent of the energy provided in GreenChoice," he said. "Our renewable energy projects have all been developed in response to customer demand."

When customers opt for GreenChoice, Kapner said they pay a little more each month for electricity, but the price per kilowatt-hour will not go up when the price of fossil fuels—such as natural gas—rises. Recent price hikes for fossil fuels have driven traditional power costs closer to GreenChoice rates, Kapner said. It does not, however, mean a customer will be served solely by renewable energy; that's something Kapner said is just not possible. "In terms of energy flow, we're not pretending that [renewable] electricity is controlled to only GreenChoice customers," he said. "It just doesn't work that way. But the customer is helping by causing the electrical provider to burn less to produce electricity."

Kapner says about 7,000 residential customers and more than 300 businesses participate in the GreenChoice program. GreenChoice energy sales make up about 3 percent of Austin's total. Other electricity providers in Texas use wind power, but only Austin and San Antonio provide it as a consumer option.

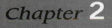
★

Chapter 2

FEDERALISM AND THE TEXAS CONSTITUTION

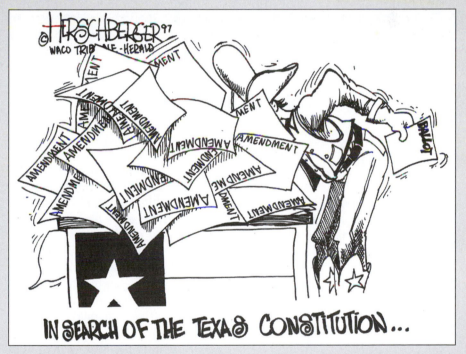

IN SEARCH OF THE TEXAS CONSTITUTION...

Waco/Tribune-Herald/Herschberger/Herschberger Cartoon Service

*T*he Texas Constitution, adopted in 1876, serves as the Lone Star State's fundamental law. This document outlines the structure of Texas's state government, authorizes the creation of counties and cities, and establishes basic rules for governing. It has been amended frequently over 13 decades (as illustrated by the cartoon at the beginning of the chapter). Lawyers, newspaper editors, political scientists, government officials, and others who consult the state constitution tend to criticize it for being too long and for lacking organization. Yet despite criticism, Texans have expressed strong opposition to or complete lack of interest in proposals for wholesale constitutional revision.

The Texas Constitution is the primary source of the state government's policymaking power. The other major source of its power is membership in the federal Union. Within the federal system, state constitutions are subject to the U.S. Constitution.

The American Federal Structure

Federalism can be defined as a structure of government characterized by the division of powers between a national government and associated regional governments. The heart of the American federal system lies in the relationship between the U.S. government (with the Capitol in Washington, D.C.) and the governments of the 50 states. Since 1789, the U.S. Constitution has prescribed a federal system of government for the nation, and since 1846 the state of Texas has been a part of that system.

Political scientist David Walker emphasizes the important role that states play in federalism: "The states' strategically crucial role in the administration, financing, and planning of intergovernmental programs and regulations—both federal and their own—and their perennial key position in practically all areas of local governance have made them the pivotal middlemen in the realm of functional federalism."[1]

Described by North Carolina's former governor Terry Sanford as "a system of states within a state," American federalism has survived two centuries of stresses and strains. Among the most serious threats were the Civil War from 1861 to 1865, which almost destroyed the Union, and a number of economic crises such as the Great Depression that followed the stock market crash of 1929.

Distribution of Powers

Division of powers and functions between the national government and the state governments was originally accomplished by listing the powers of the national government in the U.S. Constitution and by adding the **Tenth Amendment**. The latter asserts: "The powers not delegated to the United

States by the Constitution, nor prohibited by it to the States, are reserved to the States, respectively, or to the People." Although the Tenth Amendment may seem to endow the states with powers comparable to those delegated to the national government, Article VI of the U.S. Constitution contains the following clarification: "This Constitution, and the laws of the United States which shall be made in pursuance thereof; and all treaties made, or which shall be made, under the authority of the United States, shall be the supreme law of the land; and the judges in every State shall be bound thereby, anything in the Constitution or laws of any State to the contrary notwithstanding." Referred to as the **national supremacy clause**, it emphasizes that the U.S. Constitution and acts of Congress, as well as U.S. treaties, must prevail over state constitutions and laws enacted by state legislatures.

Delegated and Implied Powers   Article I, Section 8, of the U.S. Constitution lists powers specifically delegated to the national government. Included are powers to regulate interstate and foreign commerce, borrow and coin money, establish post offices and post roads, declare war, raise and support armies, provide and maintain a navy, levy and collect taxes, and establish uniform rules of naturalization. Added to these **delegated powers** is a clause that gives the national government the power "to make all laws which shall be necessary and proper for carrying into execution the foregoing powers, and all other powers vested by this Constitution in the government of the United States, or in any department or officer thereof." Since 1789, Congress and the federal courts have used this grant of **implied powers** to expand the authority of the national government. For instance, the U.S. Supreme Court, in a case originating in Texas, gave significant leeway to Congress to legislate in matters traditionally reserved to the states. In this case, the Court allowed Congress to set a minimum wage for employees of local governments.[2]

Limitations on the States   As members of the federal Union, Texas and other states are constrained by limitations imposed by Article I, Section 10, of the U.S. Constitution. For example, they may not enter into treaties, alliances, or confederations or, without the consent of Congress, make compacts or agreements with other state or foreign governments. Furthermore, they are forbidden to levy import duties on another state's products. From the outcome of the Civil War and the U.S. Supreme Court's landmark ruling in *Texas v. White* (1869), Texans learned that states cannot secede from the Union. In the *White* case, the Court ruled that the national Constitution "looks to an indestructible union, composed of indestructible states." More recently, in 1994, the states learned that a state legislature cannot limit the number of terms for members of the state's congressional delegation. The U.S. Supreme Court held that term limits for members of Congress could be constitutionally imposed only if authorized by an amendment to the U.S. Constitution.[3]

Other provisions in the U.S. Constitution prohibit states from denying any-one the right to vote because of race, gender, failure to pay a poll tax, or age (if the person is 18 years of age or older). The Fourteenth Amendment for-bids states from denying anyone the equal protection of the laws or the priv-ileges and immunities of citizens of the United States. Furthermore, no state may deprive persons of life, liberty, or property without due process of law.

Guarantees to the States   The U.S. Constitution provides all states with an imposing list of **constitutional guarantees**. For example, states may be nei-ther divided nor combined with another state without the consent of the state legislatures involved and Congress. Texas, however, did retain power to divide itself into as many as five states under the terms of its annexation to the United States.

Each state is guaranteed a republican form of government (that is, a rep-resentative government with elected lawmakers). To serve the ends of fed-eralism, the framers of the U.S. Constitution gave the states an important role in the affairs of the central government. Accordingly, each state is guar-anteed that it will have two senators in the U.S. Senate and at least one member in the U.S. House of Representatives. Because of population growth, as determined by the 2000 census, Texans now elect 32 representa-tives. As provided by the U.S. Constitution, Texas and the other states par-ticipate in presidential elections through the electoral college. A state has one electoral vote for each of its U.S. senators and each of its U.S. represen-tatives. All states participate equally in approving or rejecting proposed amendments to the U.S. Constitution. Approval requires ratification by either three-fourths of the state legislatures (used for all but the Twenty-First Amendment, which repealed Prohibition) or by conventions called in three-fourths of the states. In addition, each state is entitled to protection by the U.S. government against invasion and domestic violence, although Texas may also have its own militia (National Guard units). Finally, Texas is assured that trials by federal courts for crimes committed in Texas will be conducted in Texas.

Points to Ponder

The Twenty-Seventh Amendment to the U.S. Constitution became effec-tive in 1992 but was actually proposed in 1789. The congressional joint resolution proposing this amendment was discovered in 1982 by Gregory D. Watson, an undergraduate student at the University of Texas at Austin, while he was researching a paper on the Equal Rights Amendment. This forgotten proposal would prevent congressional pay raises until after an intervening congressional election had been conducted. At the time of Watson's discovery, only nine states had ratified the proposal. Since the joint resolution contained no time limit, completion of ratification by the required three-quarters of the state legislatures was still possible. Watson received a grade of C for his paper, but he was motivated to undertake a 10-year personal crusade that led to ratification by the necessary number of states (including Texas).

Interstate Relations and State Immunity

Article IV of the U.S. Constitution provides that "citizens of each state shall be entitled to all **privileges and immunities** of citizens in the several states." This means that residents of Texas who are visiting in another state are entitled to all the privileges and immunities of citizens of that state. It does not mean, however, that such visiting Texans are entitled to all the privileges and immunities to which they are entitled in their home state. In 1823, the U.S. Supreme Court defined "privileges and immunities" broadly as follows: protection by government, enjoyment of life and liberty, right to acquire and possess property, right to leave and enter, and right to the use of courts. Although corporations are legal persons, they are not protected under the privileges and immunities clause.

Article IV also states that "full faith and credit shall be given in each State to the public acts, records, and judicial proceedings of every other State." The **full faith and credit clause** means that any legislative enactment, state constitution, deed, will, marriage, divorce, or civil court judgment of one state must be officially recognized and honored in every other state. This clause does not apply to criminal cases. A person convicted in Texas for a crime committed in Texas is not punished in another state to which he or she has fled. Such cases are handled through extradition, whereby the fugitive would be returned to the Lone Star State at the request of the governor of Texas. Furthermore, for some felonies, the U.S. Congress has made it a federal offense to flee from one state to another for the purpose of avoiding arrest. One of the more recent controversies regarding the full faith and credit clause revolves around whether states must recognize same-sex marriages. In 2003, the Texas Legislature passed a law that prohibits the state or any agency or political subdivision (such as a county or city) from recognizing a same-sex marriage or civil union formed in Texas or elsewhere. The leadership of the state legislature, as well as Governor Rick Perry, expressed support for President Bush's call in February 2004 for a proposed U.S. constitutional amendment that would ban gay marriage.

The Eleventh Amendment states that "the Judicial power of the United States shall not be construed or extend to any suit in law or equity, commenced or prosecuted against one of the United States by citizens of another state." Recent U.S. Supreme Court rulings have ensured that a state may not be sued by its own citizens, or those of another state, without its consent, nor can state employees sue the state for violating federal law.[4] This assurance of sovereign immunity, however, is not absolute. When Texas was sued in federal courts on behalf of several families for the state's failure to provide federally required Medicaid programs, the lower federal courts ordered the state to correct the problem after the plaintiffs and state officials agreed to a consent decree. Texas appealed to the U.S. Supreme Court, arguing that "sovereign immunity" did not allow federal courts to enforce the consent decree. The Supreme Court, ultimately, held that this was not a sovereign immunity case because the suit was against state officials (not the state) acting in violation of federal law. The Eleventh Amendment did not bar enforcement of a consent degree; enforcement by the federal courts was permitted to ensure enforcement of federal law.[5]

State Powers

Nowhere in the U.S. Constitution is there a list of state powers. As mentioned, the Tenth Amendment simply states that all powers not specifically delegated to the national government, nor prohibited to the states, are reserved to the states or to the people. The **reserved powers** of the states are therefore undefined and often very difficult to specify, especially when the powers are concurrent with those of the national government, such as the taxing power. Political scientists, however, view reserved powers in broad categories:

- Police power (protection of the health, morals, safety, and convenience of citizens, and provision for the general welfare)
- Taxing power (raising revenue to pay salaries of state employees, meet other costs of government, and repay borrowed money)
- Proprietary power (public ownership of property such as airports, energy-producing utilities, and parks)
- Power of eminent domain (taking private property for highway construction or other public use at a fair price)

Needless to say, states today have broad powers, responsibilities, and duties. They are, for example, responsible for the nation's public elections—national, state, and local; there are no nationally operated election facilities. State courts conduct most trials (both criminal and civil). States operate public schools (elementary and secondary) and public institutions of higher education (colleges and universities), and they maintain most of the country's prisons.

Identifying a clear boundary line between state and national powers is still often complicated. For example, not until *United States* v. *Lopez* (1999), a case that originated in Texas, did the U.S. Supreme Court indicate that the U.S. Congress had exceeded its powers to regulate interstate commerce when it attempted to ban guns in the public schools. Operation of public schools has traditionally been considered a power of state and local governments.[6] Since the establishment of the American federal system, however, states have operated within a constitutional context that has been modified to meet changing conditions.

Federal-State Relations: An Evolving Process

The framers of the U.S. Constitution sought to provide a workable balance of power between national and state governments that would sustain the nation indefinitely. The fact that the American federal system has endured more than 200 years of stresses and strains attests to the foresight of its framers. The ultimate test of endurance occurred during the Civil War, which pitted North against South in a struggle to settle the issue of states' rights versus national supremacy regarding slavery. Despite the Union army's victory in 1865, federalism did not end. The policymaking authority of the national government after the Civil War was not necessarily broader than before, although for a period of time, Texas was subject to military rule. Each state's position within the nation was essentially left intact, but southern states could no longer legalize slavery.

Between 1865 and 1930, Congress acted vigorously to regulate railroads and interstate commerce; and through grants of money to the states, it influenced state policymaking. With the onset of the Great Depression of the 1930s, the federal government's role began to expand to other policy areas that were typically within the realm of state and local governments. Concurrently, the number and size of **federal grants-in-aid** grew as Congress gave more financial assistance to the states. As federally initiated programs multiplied, the national government's influence on state policymaking widened accordingly, with loss of state control over many areas. Beginning in the 1980s, and particularly in the 1990s and later, however, state and local governments have been given more freedom to spend federal funds as they choose. In some areas, however, such as public assistance programs, they have been granted less money to spend.

This latest development in federal-state relations has been termed **devolution**. The underlying concept in devolution is to bring about a reduction in the size and influence of the national government by reducing federal taxes and expenditures and by shifting many federal responsibilities to the states. Because one feature of devolution involves sharp reductions in federal aid, states are compelled to assume important new responsibilities with substantially less revenue to finance them. Consequently, Texas and other states have been forced to assume more responsibility in formulating and funding their own programs in education, highways, mental health, public assistance (welfare), and other areas. In some cases, federal programs are shared, whereby the states are required to match federal monies in order to benefit from a program, such as the CHIP (Children's Health Insurance Program).

Another important feature of devolution is use of **block grants** by Congress when distributing money to state and local governments. Block grants are fixed sums of money awarded according to an automatic formula determined by Congress. Thus, states receiving block grants have greater flexibility in spending. For example, welfare programs have been primarily the responsibility of the federal government, beginning with actions of the administration of President Franklin D. Roosevelt (1933–1945) in response to widespread unemployment and poverty of the Great Depression. The Clinton administration (1993–2001) and a Republican-controlled Congress forced states to assume more responsibility in administering welfare programs.[7] President George W. Bush continued these trends and added a new twist to devolution by giving federal financial assistance to faith-based organizations that provide social services to the poor. However, recently enacted federal laws, such as the No Child Left Behind Act of 2001, suggest that the Bush administration is aggressively pursuing policies that once again expand the role of the federal government. This law, which among other things requires federal testing in public schools, expands the national government's reach into a traditional area of state and local responsibility.[8]

The Texas Constitution: Politics of Policymaking

Political scientists and legal scholars generally believe that a constitution should not attempt to solve specific policy problems. Instead, it should indicate the process by which problems will be solved, both in the present and in the future. Presumably, if this principle is followed, later generations will not need to adopt numerous amendments. The Texas Constitution establishes the state's government, defines governing powers, and imposes limitations thereon; but in many areas it mandates specific policies in great detail.

The preamble to the Texas Constitution begins, "Humbly invoking the blessings of Almighty God, the people of the state of Texas do ordain and establish this Constitution." These words are the start of a 28,600-word document that became Texas's seventh constitution in 1876. By the end of 2004, it had been changed by no fewer than 432 amendments and had grown to more than 93,000 words.

The major flaws of the present Texas Constitution are its unwieldy length and a lack of coherent organization of provisions. It has grown by amendment chiefly because the framers spelled out policymaking powers and limitations in minute detail. This, in turn, made frequent amendments inevitable, as constitutional provisions had to be altered to fit changing times and conditions. For more than a century, the Texas Constitution has continued to grow through an accumulation of amendments, most of which are essentially statutory (resembling a law made by the legislature). The result is a document that more closely resembles a code of laws than a fundamental instrument of government. To fully understand the present-day Texas Constitution, we will examine the historical factors surrounding its adoption, as well as previous historical periods and constitutions.

Historical Developments

The Texas Constitution provides the legal basis on which the state functions as an integral part of the federal Union. But the document is also a product of history and an expression of the dominant political philosophy of Texans living at the time of its adoption.

Generally, constitution drafters have been pragmatic people performing an important task. Despite the idealistic sentiment commonly attached to constitutions in the United States, however, the art of drafting and amending constitutions is essentially political in nature. In other words, these documents reflect the views and political interests of the drafters, as well as the political

☆ How Do We Compare . . . in State Constitutions?

Comparison of Age and Length of State Constitution of Various U.S States

Most Populous U.S. States	Year of Adoption	Approximate No. of Words	Bordering Texas	Year of Adoption	Approximate No. of Words
California	1879	54,000	Arkansas	1874	59,500
Florida	1968	52,000	Louisiana	1974	54,100
New York	1894	51,700	New Mexico	1911	27,200
Texas	**1876**	**93,000**	Oklahoma	1907	79,100

Mexican States Bordering Texas	Year of Adoption	Approximate No. of Words
Chihuahua	1950	23,900
Coahuila	1918	29,400
Nuevo León	1917	20,700
Tamaulipas	1921	13,600

Sources: The Book of States, 2003 ed., vol. 35 (Lexington, Ky.: Council of State Governments, 2002), 14; Instituto de Investigaciones Jurídicas de la Universidad Nacional Autónoma de México, http://info4.juridicas.unam.mx.

environment of their time. With the passing of years, constitutions also reflect the political ideas of new generations of people who add amendments.

The **constitutional history** of Texas began nearly two centuries ago, when Texas was a part of Mexico. Each of its seven constitutions has reflected the political situation that existed when the document was drafted.[9] In this section, we see the political process at work as we examine the origins of these constitutions and note the efforts to revise and amend the current Texas Constitution.

The First Six Texas Constitutions   In 1824, three years after Mexico gained independence from Spain, Mexican liberals established a republic with a federal constitution. Within that federal system, the former Spanish provinces of Tejas and Coahuila became a single Mexican state that adopted its own constitution. Thus, the Constitution of Coahuila y Tejas, which was promulgated in 1827, marked Texas's first experience with a state constitution.

Political unrest among Anglo Texans, who had settled in Mexico's northeastern area, arose almost immediately, however. A number of factors led the Texans to declare independence from Mexico, such as their desire for unrestricted trade with the United States, Anglo attitudes of racial superiority, anger over Mexico's abolition of slavery, an increasing number of immigrant settlers, and insufficient Anglo representation in the 12-member Texas-Coahuila legislature.[10] On 2 March 1836, at Washington-on-the-Brazos (between present-day Brenham and Navasota), a delegate convention of 59 Texans issued a declaration of independence from Mexico. The delegates then drafted the Constitution of the Republic of Texas, modeled largely after the U.S. Constitution. During this same period, in an effort to retain Mexican sovereignty, General Antonio López de Santa Anna defeated the Texans in San Antonio in the siege of the Alamo that ended on 6 March 1836. Shortly afterward, Sam Houston's troops crushed the Mexican forces in the Battle of San Jacinto on 21 April 1836. Part of Texas's unique history is that it was as an independent nation for close to ten years.

After his victory over Santa Anna, Texas voters elected Sam Houston as president of their new republic; they also voted to seek admission to the Union. Not until 1845, however, was annexation authorized by a joint resolution of the U.S. Congress. Earlier attempts to become part of the United States by treaty had failed. Texas president Anson Jones called a constitutional convention, whose delegates drew up a new state constitution and agreed to accept the invitation to join the Union. In February 1845, after Texas voters ratified both actions of the constitutional convention, Texas obtained its third constitution and became the twenty-eighth state of the United States.

These events, however, set the stage for the war between Mexico and the United States (1846–1848). Historians argue that U.S. expansionist politicians and business interests actively sought this war. When the Treaty of Guadalupe Hidalgo between Mexico and the United States was signed in 1848, Mexico lost over half of its territory and recognized the Rio Grande as Texas's southern boundary.

The Constitution of 1845 lasted until the outbreak of the Civil War. When Texas seceded from the Union, the Secession Constitution was adopted in 1861, with the aim of making as few changes as possible in the structure and powers of the government. Only those changes necessary to equip the government for separation from the United States were included. Following the defeat of the Confederacy, however, the Reconstruction Constitution of 1866 was drafted amid a different set of conditions. Here, the framers sought to restore Texas to the Union with a minimum of changes in existing social, economic, and political institutions. Although the Constitution of 1866 was based on the Constitution of 1845, it nevertheless recognized the right of former slaves to sue in the state's courts, to enter into contracts, to obtain and transfer property, and to testify in court actions involving blacks (but not in court actions involving whites). The Constitution of 1866 protected the personal property of African American Texans, but it did not permit them to vote, hold public office, or serve as jurors.

The relatively uncomplicated reinstatement of Texas into the Union ended abruptly when the Radical Republicans gained control of the U.S. Congress following the election of November 1866. Refusing to seat Texas's two senators and three representatives, Congress set aside the state's reconstructed government, enfranchised former slaves, disenfranchised prominent whites, and imposed military rule across the state. Military officers replaced civil authorities. As in other southern states, Texas functioned under a military government.

Under these conditions, delegates to a constitutional convention met in intermittent sessions from June 1868 to February 1869 and drafted yet another state constitution. Among other things, the new constitution centralized more power in state government, provided compulsory school attendance, and guaranteed a full range of rights for former slaves. This document

E. J. Davis and some of the Constitutional Convention delegates of 1875 (left: Portrait by William Henry Huddle/Texas State Library and Archives Commission; right: Texas State Library and Archives Commission)

was ratified in 1869. Then, with elections supervised by federal soldiers, Radical Republicans gained control of the Texas Legislature. At the same time, Edmund Jackson Davis (commonly identified as E. J. Davis), a former Union army general, was elected as the first Republican governor of Texas.

Historians have described the Davis administration (January 1870 to January 1874) as one of the most corrupt in Texas history. The governor imposed martial law in some places and used police methods to enforce his decrees. His administration was characterized by extravagant public spending, property tax increases to the point of confiscation, gifts of public funds to private interests, intimidation of newspaper editors, and control of voter registration by the military. In addition, hundreds of appointments to various state and local offices were made. Although the Constitution of 1869 is associated with the Reconstruction era and the unpopular administration of Governor Davis, the machinery of government created by this document was quite modern. The new fundamental law called for annual sessions of the legislature, a four-year term for the governor and other executive officers, and gubernatorial appointment (rather than popular election) of judges. It abolished county courts and raised the salaries of government officials. These changes centralized more governmental power in Austin and weakened government at the local level.

Democrats gained control of the legislature in 1872. Then, in perhaps the most fraudulent election ever conducted in Texas, Governor Davis (with 42,633 votes) was badly defeated in December 1873 by Democrat Richard Coke (with 85,549 votes). When Davis refused to leave his office on the ground floor of the Capitol, Democratic lawmakers and Governor-elect Coke are reported to have climbed ladders to the Capitol's second story where the legislature convened. When President Grant refused to send troops to protect him, Davis left the Capitol under protest in January 1874. But he locked his office and kept the key. Governor Coke's supporters had to use an ax to open the office door. In that same year, Democrats were able to wrest control of the state courts from the Republicans. The next step was to rewrite the Texas Constitution.

Drafting the Constitution of 1876   In the summer of 1875, Texans elected 75 Democrats and 15 Republicans (6 of whom were African Americans) as delegates to a constitutional convention; however, only 83 attended the gathering in Austin. The majority of the delegates were not native Texans. More than 40 percent were members of the **Texas Grange** (the Patrons of Husbandry), a farmers' organization committed to strict economy in government (reduced spending) and limited governmental powers. Its slogan of "retrenchment and reform" became a major goal of the convention. So strong was the spirit of strict economy among delegates that they refused to hire a stenographer or to allow publication of the convention proceedings. As a result, no official record was ever made of the convention that gave Texas its most enduring constitution. (See this chapter's Selected Reading, "Of Rutabagas and Redeemers: Rethinking the Texas Constitution of 1876," for a new view of Grange influence during the convention.)

In their zeal to undo the policies of the Davis administration, the delegates overreacted on occasion. Striking at Reconstruction measures that had given Governor Davis control over voter registration, the overwrought delegates inserted a statement providing that "no law shall ever be enacted requiring a registration of voters of this state." Within two decades, however, the statement had been amended to permit voter registration laws.

As they continued to dismantle the machinery of the Davis administration, the delegates restricted the powers of state government for each of the three branches. They reduced the governor's salary, powers, and term (from four to two years); made all executive offices (except that of secretary of state) elective for two-year terms; and tied the hands of legislators with biennial (once every two years) sessions, low salaries, and limited legislative powers. All judges became popularly elected for relatively short terms of office. Justice of the peace courts, county courts, and district courts with popularly elected judges were established. In addition, public services were trimmed to the bone. Framers of the new constitution limited the public debt and severely curbed the taxing and spending powers of the legislature. They also inserted specific policy provisions. For example, they reinstated racially segregated public education and repealed the compulsory school attendance law, restored precinct elections, and allowed only taxpayers to vote on local bond issues.

Texas's most enduring constitution was put to a popular vote in 1876 and was approved by more than a two-to-one majority. Although Texans in the state's largest cities—Houston, Dallas, San Antonio, and Galveston—voted against it, the much larger rural population voted for approval.

Distrust of Government and Its Consequences   Sharing in the prevailing popular distrust of and hostility toward government, the framers of the **Texas Constitution of 1876** sought with a vengeance to limit and thus control policymaking by placing many restrictions in the state's fundamental law. The general consensus of the time held that a state government could exercise only those powers that were listed in the state constitution. Therefore, instead of being permitted to exercise powers not denied by the U.S. Constitution, Texas lawmakers are limited to those powers that are spelled out in the state's constitution.

Today: After More Than a Century of Usage

The structural disarray and confusion of the Constitution of 1876 compound the disadvantages of its excessive length and detail. Yet with all its shortcomings, the Constitution of 1876 has endured for more than 125 years.

It was inevitable that filling the Texas Constitution with many details and creating a state government with restricted powers would soon lead to constitutional amendments. In fact, many substantive changes in Texas government require an amendment. For example, an amendment is needed to change the way the state pays bills, to abolish an unneeded state or county office, or to authorize a bond issue pledging the revenues of the state. Urbanization, industrialization, the communication revolution, population explosion, education demands, and countless social service needs contribute to pressures for frequent constitutional change.

Texas Governor Rick Perry promotes Proposition 12 at a rally in a private hospital in Houston, Friday, September 12, 2003. Proposition 12, which would allow the state legislature to limit lawsuit damages, and twenty-one other constitutional amendments were approved by voters during Saturday's special election. (Michael Stravato/AP-Wide World Photos)

Most amendments apply to matters that should be resolved by statutes enacted by the Texas Legislature. Instead, an often uninformed and usually apathetic electorate must decide the fate of many frequently complex policy issues. In this context, special interests represented by well-financed lobbyists and the media often play an influential role in constitutional policy making.

In 2003, for instance, Proposition 12 resulted in an unprecedented level of lobbying activity and media coverage as public debate focused on setting limits for medical malpractice awards.[11] Although restricted to noneconomic damages, such as for pain and suffering, approval of the amendment would give lawmakers authority to set similar limits in other kinds of lawsuits. High malpractice insurance premiums for physicians and some large, well-publicized settlements prompted the amendment's proposal. Despite opposition by plaintiffs' lawyers and some public interest groups, 51 percent of the voters (751,896) supported the amendment while 49 percent (718,647) opposed it.

Along with Proposition 12, the 78th Legislature proposed 21 other amendments. Subjects included granting tax exemptions on property owned by religious groups for expansion, freezing elderly and disabled homeowners' property taxes, permitting wineries to sell wine for consumption both on and off premises, and allowing homeowners to establish home equity lines of credit. All 22 proposals were submitted to voters on 13 September 2003 rather than the traditional November election day. Voters approved all of these constitutional amendment proposals. Most were approved with comfortable majorities.[12]

Points to Ponder

Among the joint resolutions proposing constitutional amendments that were considered but rejected in the 78th Legislature's regular session were ones reforming the judicial selection process, regulating campaign contributions, lowering the voting age, placing a moratorium on executing persons convicted of capital offenses, giving Texans a right to privacy, and even one authorizing a casino in Harris county to fund public education.

In addition to constitutional amendments that apply to all parts of Texas, some examples of policymaking by constitutional amendment affect categories of counties or single counties. For instance, in 2001, voters approved a tax exemption for green coffee and raw cocoa inventories held in Harris county.

To modernize the Texas Constitution, one amendment adopted in 1999 authorized elimination of certain "duplicative, executed, obsolete, archaic and ineffective provisions of the Texas Constitution." Among resulting deletions were references to the abolished poll tax and the governor's authority "to protect the frontier from hostile incursions by Indians." A similar amendment to eliminate several obsolete or duplicative provisions was approved by the voters in 2001. Despite these measures to improve the Texas Constitution, problems still exist.

Constitutional Amendments and Revision

Each of the 50 American state constitutions provides the means for changing the powers and functions of government. Without a provision for change, most constitutions could not survive very long. Revisions may produce a totally new constitution to replace an old one. Courts may alter constitutions by interpreting the wording of these documents in new and different ways. Finally, constitutions may be changed by formal amendment, the chief method by which the Texas Constitution has been altered.

Because Texas's registered voters have an opportunity to vote on one or more proposed amendments nearly every year—and sometimes twice in a single year—an understanding of the steps in the **constitutional amendment process** is important. Article XVII, Section 1, provides a relatively simple procedure for amending the Texas Constitution. The basic steps in that process are as follows:

- A joint resolution proposing an amendment is introduced in the House or in the Senate during a regular session or during a special session called by the governor.
- Two-thirds of the members in each chamber must adopt the resolution.
- The secretary of state prepares an explanatory statement that briefly describes the proposed amendment, and the attorney general approves this statement.
- The explanatory statement is published twice in Texas newspapers that print official state notices.
- A copy of the proposed amendment is posted in each county courthouse at least 30 days before the election.
- The voters must approve the proposed amendment by a simple majority vote in a regular or special election.
- The governor, who has no veto power in the process, proclaims the amendment.

Points to Ponder

State law, as well as federal law, requires the secretary of state to publish explanatory statements twice for each proposed constitutional amendments in English and Spanish in Texas newspapers. Typically, these notices were published in both languages in the English-language press. In 2003, however, the U.S. Department of Justice and the Texas secretary of state entered into an agreement whereby only a Spanish-language version of the explanatory notice would be mailed to each registered voter with a Hispanic surname instead of publishing the notice in Spanish in the newspapers. The purpose of the agreement was to provide an efficient and economical method of reaching monolingual Spanish speakers. Nevertheless, many bilingual Texans with Hispanic surnames were upset when they received this communication. They believed that government officials should not infer or assume that people with Hispanic surnames are unable to read English, or for that matter that they are fluent in Spanish.

The Texas Legislature decides whether a proposed amendment will be submitted to the voters in the November general election of an even-numbered year or in a special election scheduled for an earlier date. The 77th Legislature submitted 19 proposed amendments to voters in November 2001, and it placed an additional amendment before voters in November 2002.[13] In contrast, the 78th Legislature proposed 22 amendments in its 2003 regular session, and it submitted all of them to the voters in September of that year. (Table 2.1 provides data on amendments proposed and adopted in each decade from 1879 through 2004.)

With the increasing influence of interest groups in the legislative process, there have been efforts to give Texans the powers of **initiative** and **referendum**. If adopted, the initiative process would bypass the legislature and allow individual Texans or groups to gather signatures required for submitting proposed constitutional amendments and statutes (ordinary laws) to direct popular vote. The referendum process would allow Texas voters to gather signatures to challenge and potentially overturn statutes enacted by state lawmakers. Currently, voters in 18 states are empowered to propose and enact their own laws; and in 28 states they can propose constitutional amendments.[14] Since 1997, however, there have been no serious legislative efforts to amend the Texas Constitution in order to authorize the initiative and referendum processes at the state level.

Constitutional Revision

Attempts to revise Texas's Constitution of 1876 began soon after its adoption. A legislative resolution calling for a constitutional revision convention was introduced in 1887 and was followed by others. Limited success was achieved in 1969, when an amendment removed 56 obsolete constitutional provisions. Not since the 1970s, however, have major efforts been made to revise the state's constitution.

Table 2.1 Texas Constitution of 1876: Amendments Proposed and Adopted, 1879–2004

Decade	Number Proposed	Number Adopted	Decade	Number Proposed	Number Adopted
1870s	1	1	1940s	35	22
1880s	15	7	1950s	43	37
1890s	15	9	1960s	84	56
1900s	20	11	1970s	67	42
1910s	35	10	1980s	99	84
1920s	46	15	1990s	81	64
1930s	45	32	2000s	42	42
			Totals	628	432

Source: Texas Legislative Council

The Revision Efforts of the 1970s

The most comprehensive movement to achieve wholesale **constitutional revision** began in 1971. In that year, the 62nd Legislature adopted a joint resolution proposing an amendment authorizing the appointment of a study commission and naming the members of the 63rd Legislature as delegates to a constitutional convention. Except for the Bill of Rights, any part of the Texas Constitution of 1876 could be changed or deleted. Submitted to the voters in 1972 as a proposed constitutional amendment, the resolution was approved by a comfortable margin of more than a half million votes (1,549,982 "yes" to 985,282 "no").

A six-member committee (composed of the governor, the lieutenant governor, the speaker of the House, the attorney general, the chief justice of the Texas Supreme Court, and the presiding judge of the Court of Criminal Appeals) selected 37 persons to serve as members of the Constitutional Revision Commission. The commission prepared a draft constitution based on opinions and information gathered at public hearings conducted throughout the state and from various authorities on constitutional revision. One-fourth the length of the present constitution, the completed draft was submitted to the legislature on 1 November 1973.

On 8 January 1974, members of both houses of the Texas Legislature met in Austin as a **constitutional revision convention**. Previous Texas constitutions had been drafted by convention delegates popularly elected for that purpose. When the finished document was put to a vote, the result was 118 for and 62 against. Thus, the two-thirds majority of the total membership needed for final approval lacked only 3 votes. (A total of at least 121 votes for approval was required.) Attempts to reach compromises on controversial issues proved futile.

Perhaps there has been no better demonstration of the politics surrounding Texas constitution making than the Constitutional Convention of 1974. First, the convention was hampered by a lack of positive political leadership. Governor Dolph Briscoe maintained a hands-off policy throughout the convention. Lieutenant Governor Bill Hobby similarly failed to provide needed political leadership, and the retiring speaker of the House, Price Daniel Jr., pursued a nonintervention course. Other members of the legislature were distracted by their need to campaign for reelection.

The primary reason the convention failed to agree on a proposed constitution was the phantom "non-issue" of a right-to-work provision. A statutory ban on union shop labor contracts was already in effect. Adding this prohibition to the constitution would not have strengthened the legal hand of employers to any significant degree. Nevertheless, conservative, anti-labor forces insisted on this provision, and a pro-labor minority vigorously opposed it. The controversy aroused much emotion and at times produced loud and bitter name calling among delegates on the floor and spectators in the galleries.[15]

Stung by widespread public criticism of the 1974 convention's failure to produce a proposed constitution for public approval or rejection, the 64th Legislature resolved to submit a proposal to Texas voters. In 1975, both houses of the legislature agreed on a constitutional revision resolution comprising 10 articles in 8 sections to be submitted to the Texas electorate in November. The content of the articles was essentially the same as that of the final resolution of the unsuccessful 1974 convention.

The revision proposed in 1975 represented years of work by men and women who were well informed about constitution making. Recognized constitutional authorities evaluated the concise and orderly document as one of the best-drafted state constitutions ever submitted to American voters. Although new and innovative in many respects, the proposal did not discard all of the old provisions. In addition to retaining the Bill of Rights, the proposed constitution incorporated such basic principles as limited government, separation of powers, and bicameralism (a two-house legislature).

Nevertheless, Texas voters demonstrated a strong preference for the status quo by rejecting each proposition. Voters in 250 of the state's 254 counties rejected all eight proposals. A mere 23 percent of the estimated 5.9 million registered voters cast ballots, meaning that only about 10 percent of the state's voting-age population participated in this important referendum. When asked to explain the resounding defeat of the eight propositions, Bill Hobby, then lieutenant governor, responded, "There's not enough of the body left for an autopsy."

Recent Revision Attempts

After the revision debacle of 1975, two decades passed before another attempt to revise the constitution was made in 1995. Senator John Montford (D-Lubbock) drafted a streamlined constitution that incorporated many of the concepts contained in the failed 1975 proposal. Montford's plan also called for a voter referendum every 30 years (without legislative approval) on the question of calling a constitutional revision convention. But Montford resigned from the Texas Senate to become chancellor of the Texas Tech University System in 1996; and with such issues as tax changes, welfare reform, and educational finance pressing for attention, the 75th Legislature did not seriously consider constitutional revision in 1997.

Another attempt to revise the constitution was launched in 1998 by Senator Bill Ratliff (R–Mount Pleasant) and Representative Rob Junell (D–San Angelo). With assistance from San Angelo State University students and others, they prepared a complete rewrite of the much-amended 1876 document.[16] Subsequently, Ratliff and Junell introduced another draft for consideration by the 76th Legislature in 1999. It did not muster enough support for serious consideration in committee and never received a floor vote in either legislative chamber. This proposal would have trimmed the 80,000-word document to about 19,000 words. Significant changes included expanding powers of the governor, repealing the current partisan election method of

POINT
COUNTERPOINT

Should the Texas Constitution Be Rewritten?

THE ISSUE

Over the past several decades, proponents and opponents to a wholesale constitutional rewrite have debated the merits of the issue. The opponents continue to argue for the status quo, whereas the proponents argue that now, more than ever before, a rewrite is necessary. An editorial by the *Dallas Morning News* in 2003 stated that since this is a new century, the leadership of the Texas Legislature should "lead the way on a renewed effort to give the state a new and streamlined constitution." Some of the arguments that have been raised are as follows:

Arguments For Rewriting the Constitution

1. It is excessively long and outdated.
2. Voter turnout for constitutional amendment elections tends to be very low.
3. Voters are asked to make decisions on complex proposals that are not (or cannot be) adequately summarized in brief explanatory statements.
4. Expanding the powers of the government would better serve the needs of Texans.

Arguments Against Rewriting the Constitution

1. Despite its flaws, the Texas Constitution is still a functioning document.
2. The amendment process allows changes when needed.
3. Special interests would in all likelihood control constitutional revision.
4. A comparison of state constitutional revision attempts suggests that constitutional revision can be a high-risk endeavor and does not assure success.[17]

selecting state judges, and increasing salaries of the House speaker and the lieutenant governor.[18]

With redistricting and budgeting issues dominating the regular session in 2001, the 77th Legislature gave constitutional revision little attention. Similarly, with a budget crisis and congressional redistricting at hand, wholesale constitutional revision was not on the agenda for the 78th Legislature in 2003.

Piecemeal Revision and Turnout for Voting on Amendments

Since extensive constitutional reform has proved to be futile, Texas legislators have sought to achieve some measure of government reform by other means, including legislative enactments and piecemeal constitutional amendments. In 1977, for example, the 65th Legislature enacted into law two parts of the 1975 propositions defeated at the polls. One established a procedure for reviewing state administrative agencies; the other created a planning agency within the Office of the Governor. In 1979, the 66th Legislature proposed six amendments designed to implement parts of the constitutional revision package rejected in 1975. Three were adopted by the voters and added to the Texas Constitution. They accomplished the following:

▪ Established a single property tax appraisal district in each county (discussed in the chapter "Local Governments")
▪ Gave criminal appellate jurisdiction to 14 courts of appeals that formerly had exercised civil jurisdiction only
▪ Allowed the governor restricted removal power over appointed statewide officials[19]

Proposals for important constitutional changes in recent years have been unsuccessful in the House and the Senate. For example, during the regular session of the 77th Legislature in 2001, Representative Rob Junell (D–San Angelo) submitted a proposal that was considered and won approval by the House Select Committee on Constitutional Revision. Among other items, the proposal would have changed the terms of office for state senators and House members. It would also have created a Texas Salary Commission to set salaries for elected and appointed officials of the executive, judicial, and legislative branches. This proposal, however, died because it was never brought up for a floor vote in the House.[20]

Part of the problem with piecemeal revision relates to the low voter turnout that is typical in odd-numbered years for constitutional amendment elections. Roughly 8.3 percent of Texas voters participated in the 1999 election—about 950,000 of the state's 11.4 million registered voters. Statewide turnout in the 2001 special constitutional election for voting on 19 proposed amendments was less than 7 percent. This amounted to merely 800,000 of Texas's 12 million registered voters. In 2002, given the gubernatorial contest and other competitive races, turnout was higher (36 percent), but only a single amendment was on the ballot. A year later, despite the controversy surrounding some of the 22 proposed amendments, voter turnout in this special election dropped to 12 percent (under 1.5 million voters).

The Texas Constitution: A Summary

Chiefly because of its length, complete printed copies of the Texas Constitution are not readily available to the public. Until publication of its Millennium Edition (2000–2001), the *Texas Almanac* was the most widely used source for the text of this document. That edition and the editions for 2002–2003 and 2004–2005, however, refer persons seeking the text of the Texas Constitution to the Internet. (See this chapter's "Internet Resources.")

Although *Practicing Texas Politics: A Brief Survey* does not include the entire text of the Texas Constitution, each chapter looks to Texas's basic law for its content. The rest of this chapter presents a brief synopsis of the document's 17 articles.[21]

The Bill of Rights

Eleven of the 30 sections of Article I, the Texas Constitution's **Bill of Rights**, provide protections for people and property against arbitrary governmental actions. Guarantees such as freedom of speech, press, religion, assembly, and petition are included. The right to keep and bear arms, prohibitions against taking of property by government action without just compensation, and forbidding impairment of the obligation of contract are also incorporated. Most of these rights found in the Texas Constitution are also protected under the U.S. Constitution. Thus, with their basic rights guaranteed in both national and state constitutions, Texans, like people in other states, have a double safeguard against arbitrary governmental actions.

Thirteen sections of the Texas Constitution's Bill of Rights relate to the rights of persons accused of crimes and to the rights of individuals who have been convicted of crimes. For example, one section concerns the right to release on bail, another prohibits unreasonable searches and seizures, and a third declares that "the right to trial by jury shall remain inviolate." These provisions are closely related to similar language in the national Bill of Rights.

With regard to some rights, the Texas Constitution is even more protective than the U.S. Constitution. For example, attempts nationwide to add the proposed Equal Rights Amendment (ERA) to the U.S. Constitution failed between 1972 and 1982 (even though the amendment was approved by the Texas Legislature). Nevertheless, the **Texas Equal Legal Rights Amendment (ELR)** was added to Article 1, Section 3, of the Texas Constitution in 1972. It states: "Equality under the law shall not be denied or abridged because of sex, race, color, creed or national origin." This constitutional amendment was proposed and adopted after several unsuccessful attempts dating back to the 1950s.[22]

Additional protections in the Texas Constitution include prohibitions against imprisonment for debt, outlawry (the process of putting a convicted person outside of the protection of the law), and transportation (punishing a convicted citizen by banishment from the state). Monopolies are prohibited by a provision of the Texas Bill of Rights but not by the U.S. Constitution. Likewise, an additional set of rights was added by a constitutional amendment in 1989 that guarantees the "rights of crime victims." (See Chapter 9, "Laws, Courts, and Justice.")

Constitutional interpretation of the Texas Constitution by the Texas Supreme Court has also provided additional rights, such as the court's interpretation of Article VII, Section 1, requiring the state legislature to provide support and maintenance for an efficient system of free public schools. In other words, the state legislature was required to create a more equitable public school finance system.

Three sections contain philosophical observations that have no direct force of law. Still stinging from what they saw as the "bondage" years of Reconstruction, the angry delegates to the constitutional convention of 1875 began their work by inserting this statement: "Texas is a free and independent state, subject only to the Constitution of the United States." They also asserted that all political power resides in the people and is legitimately exercised only in their behalf and that those people may at any time "alter, reform, or abolish their government." To guard against the possibility that any of the rights guaranteed in the other 28 sections would be eliminated or altered by the government, Section 29 proclaims that "everything in this 'Bill of Rights' is excepted out of the general powers of government, and shall forever remain inviolate."

The Powers of Government

Holding fast to the principle of limited government, the framers of the Constitution of 1876 firmly embedded in the state's fundamental law the familiar doctrine of **separation of powers**. In Article II, they assigned the lawmaking, law-enforcing, and law-adjudicating powers of government to three separate branches, identified as the legislative, executive, and judicial departments, respectively.

Article III is titled the Legislative Department. Legislative powers are vested in the bicameral legislature, composed of a House of Representatives with 150 members and a Senate with 31 members. A patchwork of more than 60 sections, this article provides vivid testimony to more than 125 years of amendments directly affecting the legislative branch. For example, in 1936, an amendment added a section granting the Texas Legislature the authority to levy taxes to fund a retirement system for public school, college, and university teachers. Today, public school teachers and personnel employed by public universities and community colleges benefit from pension programs provided by the state.

Article IV, the Executive Department, states unequivocally that the governor "shall be the Chief Executive Officer of the State" but then provides for the sharing of executive power with four other popularly elected officers who are independent of the governor: the lieutenant governor, the attorney general, the comptroller of public accounts, and the commissioner of the General Land Office. (The state treasurer was originally included in this list, but a constitutional amendment abolished the office.) With this and other provisions for division of executive power, the Texas governor is considered by some observers to be no more than first among equals in the Executive Department.

Through Article V, the Judicial Department, Texas joins Oklahoma as the only states in the country with two courts of final appeal: one for civil cases (the Supreme Court of Texas) and one for criminal cases (the Court of Criminal Appeals). Below these two supreme appellate courts are the courts authorized by the Texas Constitution and created by the legislature: the intermediate appellate courts (14 courts of appeals) and hundreds of courts of original jurisdiction (district courts, county courts, and justice of the peace courts).

Suffrage

Article VI, titled **Suffrage** (the right to vote), is one of the shortest articles in the Texas Constitution. Prior to 1870, states had the definitive power to conduct elections. Since that time, amendments to the U.S. Constitution, acts of Congress, and rulings by the U.S. Supreme Court have vastly diminished this power. Within the scope of current federal regulations, the Texas Constitution establishes qualifications for voters, provides for registration of citizens for voting, and governs the conduct of elections. In response to changes at the federal level, this article has been amended to abolish the payment of a poll tax or any other form of property qualification for voting in the state's elections, and to change the minimum voting age from 21 to 18.

Local Governments

The most disorganized part of the Texas Constitution concerns units of **local government**: counties, municipalities (cities), school districts, and other special districts. Although Article IX is titled Counties, the provisions concerning county government are scattered through four other articles. Moreover, the basic structure of county government is defined not in Article IX on counties but in Article V on the judiciary. Article XI on municipalities is equally disorganized and inadequate. Only four of the sections of this article relate exclusively to municipal government. Other sections concern county government, taxation, public indebtedness, and forced sale of public property.

Along with counties and municipalities, the original text of the Constitution of 1876 referred to school districts but not to other types of special-district governments. Authorization for special districts, however, crept into the Texas Constitution with a 1904 amendment that authorizes the borrowing of money for water development and road construction by a county "or any defined district." Thereafter, special districts have been created to provide myriad services, such as drainage, conservation, urban renewal, public housing, hospitals, and airports.

Other Articles

The nine remaining articles also reflect a strong devotion to constitutional minutiae. Titles of these articles are as follows: Education, Taxation and Revenue, Railroads, Private Corporations, Spanish and Mexican Land Titles, Public Lands and Land Office, Impeachment, General Provisions, and Mode of Amendment.

Looking Ahead

The Constitution of 1876 was written by a convention composed largely of Democrats; and, until recently, amendments were proposed by Democrat-controlled legislatures. Now that Texas Republicans dominate both houses of the legislature and have a record of winning statewide elections by large majorities, will GOP leaders launch a drive for a convention that would write the state's eighth constitution?

Later chapters will demonstrate how the Texas Constitution affects the structure, functions, and procedures of the three branches of the state's government; the operation of political parties and interest groups within the state; and the financial arrangements for state and local units of government in Texas.

It is important to note that counties, municipalities, and special districts do not derive their powers and responsibilities from the federal government. Rather, these low-level governments receive their legal authority from state constitutional provisions and/or acts of the Texas Legislature. The chapter "Local Governments" examines the structure and operation of these various forms of local government.

☆ Chapter Summary ☆

- The American federal system features a division of powers between a national government and 50 state governments. Powers not delegated (nor implied, as interpreted by federal courts) to the federal government are reserved to the states or to the people under the Tenth Amendment. A balance of power between the national and state governments has evolved over time.

- The Texas Constitution is the fundamental law that sets forth the powers and limitations of the state's government. Texas has had seven constitutions, each reflecting the political situation that existed when the document was drafted. The Constitution of 1876 has endured despite its excessive length, confusion, and statutory detail.

- Today's Texas Constitution is the country's second longest and, at the end of 2004, had 432 amendments. Most amendments are statutory in nature, so the document resembles a code of laws.

- Changing the Texas Constitution requires an amendment proposed by a two-thirds majority vote of the members in each legislative chamber and approved by a simple majority of the state's voters in a general or special election. Although there have been efforts to revise the Texas Constitution, only piecemeal revisions have occurred.

- The Texas Constitution is composed of 17 articles. Included are the Bill of Rights, an article on suffrage, articles on the three branches of state government, and provisions concerning the powers of state and local governments.

Key Terms

Tenth Amendment	constitutional amendment
national supremacy clause	process
delegated power	initiative
implied power	referendum
constitutional guarantee	constitutional revision
privileges and immunities	constitutional revision
full faith and credit clause	convention
reserved power	Bill of Rights
federal grant-in-aid	Texas Equal Legal Rights
devolution	Amendment (ELR)
block grant	separation of powers
constitutional history	suffrage
Texas Grange	local government
Texas Constitution of 1876	

Discussion Questions

1. How does Texas's constitutional history continue to influence Texas's present-day constitution and government?
2. What were your initial impressions of some of the constitutional amendments that have been considered or proposed by the Texas Legislature? Are these the kinds of issues that should be placed in the Texas Constitution?
3. In your opinion, should the Texas Constitution be rewritten?
4. What recommendations would you offer to the state legislature for revision of the Texas Constitution?

Internet Resources

FindLaw: U.S. Constitution: **www.findlaw.com/casecode/constitution**
National Governors Association: **www.nga.org**
Texas Constitution: **www.capitol.state.tx.us/txconst/toc.html**
Texas Legislature Online: **www.capitol.state.tx.us**
Texas Office of State-Federal Relations: **www.osfr.state.tx.us**
Texas Office of the Secretary of State: **www.sos.state.tx.us**
Texas State Historical Association Online: **www.tsha.utexas.edu**

Notes

1. David B. Walker, *The Rebirth of Federalism* (New York: Chatham House, 2000), p. 260.
2. See *Garcia* v. *San Antonio Metropolitan Transit Authority*, 469 U.S. 528 (1985).
3. See *U.S. Term Limits* v. *Thornton*, 514 U.S. 115 (1995).
4. See *Kimel* v. *Florida Board of Regents*, 528 U.S. 62 (2000); *Alden* v. *Maine*, 527 U.S. 706 (1999); and *Seminole Tribe v. Florida*, 517 U.S. 44 (1996).
5. See *Frew* v. *Hawkins, Commissioner, Texas Health & Human Services*, No. 02-628, Supreme Court of the U.S. 14 January 2004. See also Carlos Guerra, "High Court Orders Texas to Honor its Word—and Pay Up," *San Antonio Express-News*, 15 January 2004.
6. See *United States* v. *Lopez*, 514 U.S. 549 (1995).
7. See Sanford F. Schram, "Introduction: Welfare Reform: A Race to the Bottom?" *Publius: The Journal of Federalism* 28 (Summer 1998): 1–8. (Special issue: "Welfare Reform in the United States: A Race to the Bottom?" edited by Sanford F. Schram and Samuel H. Beer.)
8. For a four-part study examining the impact of the federal law, refer to "No Child Left Behind: A Federal-State Level Look at the First Year" at <www.civilrightsproject.harvard.edu>.
9. For a more detailed account of early Texas constitutions, see John Cornyn, "The Roots of the Texas Constitution: Settlement to Statehood," *Texas Tech Law Review* 26:4 (1995): 1089–1218. The author served as a member of the Supreme Court of Texas and as the state's attorney general before being elected to the U.S. Senate in 2002.
10. See Leobardo F. Estrada, F. Chris Garcia, Reynaldo Flores Macias, and Lionel Maldonado, "Chicanos in the United States: A History of Exploitation and Resistance," in *Latinos and the Political System*, edited by F. Chris Garcia (Notre Dame, Ind.: University of Notre Dame Press, 1988), pp. 28–64.
11. Janet Elliott, "Low Turnout Is Expected Despite Advertising Blitz," *Houston Chronicle*, 3 September 2003. See also Max B. Baker, "Tempers Flare at Rally: Groups Clash Over Move to Limit Damages," *Fort Worth Star-Telegram*, 6 September 2003.
12. "Voters Approve 22 Constitutional Amendments," *Interim News*, No. 78-1 (Austin: House Research Organization, Texas House of Representatives, 3 December 2003): 7.
13. *Constitutional Amendments Proposed for November 2001 Ballot,* Focus Report No. 77-12 (Austin: House Research Organization, Texas House of Representatives, 12 August 2001); and *Constitutional Amendment on November 2002 Ballot,* Focus Report No. 77-24 (Austin: House Research Organization, Texas House of Representatives, 23 August 2002).
14. Thomas R. Dye, *Politics in States and Communities*, 11th ed. (Upper Saddle River, N.J.: Prentice Hall, 2003), pp. 40–44.

15. Texas has a right-to-work law that was enacted in 1947 by the 50th Legislature.
16. See Jim Lewis, "Getting Around to a New Constitution," *County* (January/February 1999): 11–13. For a profile of Representative Rob Junell and his collaboration with Senator Bill Ratliff, see Janet Elliott, "Maverick in the Middle," *Texas Lawyer* (January 1999): 19–20.
17. For a review of constitutional revision attempts by various states, see James M. Burns et al., *State & Local Politics: Government by the People*, 11th ed. (Upper Saddle River, N.J.: Prentice Hall, 2004), pp. 47–50.
18. For the text of the Ratliff-Junell draft constitution, refer to Texas Legislature Online at <www.capitol.state.tx.us> and search by bill number for the 76th Regular Session, HJR1 or SJR1.
19. For an analysis of amendments proposed between 1976 and 1989, see James G. Dickson, "Erratic Continuity: Some Patterns of Constitutional Change in Texas Since 1975," *Texas Journal of Political Studies* 14 (Fall–Winter 1991–1992): 41–56.
20. For the text of Junell's constitutional proposal, refer to Texas Legislature Online at <http://www.capitol.state.tx.us> and search by bill for the 77th Legislature, HJR 69.
21. For a more detailed analysis of the contents of the Texas Constitution, see Janice C. May, *The Texas State Constitution: A Reference Guide* (Westport, Conn.: Greenwood Press, 1996); and George D. Braden, *Citizen's Guide to the Texas Constitution* (Austin: Texas Advisory Commission on Intergovernmental Relations, 1972).
22. For details concerning the struggle for ELR, see Rob Fink, "Hermine Tobolowsky, the Texas ELRA, and the Political Struggle for Women's Equal Rights," *Journal of the West* 42 (Summer 2003): 52–57; and Tai Kreidler, "Hermine Tobolowsky: Mother of Texas's Equal Legal Rights Amendment," in *The Human Tradition in Texas,* edited by Ty Cashion and Jesús de la Teja (Wilmington, Del.: SR Books, 2001), pp 209–220.

SELECTED READING

★

Of Rutabagas and Redeemers: Rethinking the Texas Constitution of 1876*

Patrick G. Williams

Like other southern states, Texas produced a constitution in the wake of Reconstruction. Many constitutional convention delegates, some of whom were members of the Grange, sought to redeem the states of the Confederacy from Republican domination accompanied by hard times for farmers. This reading throws new light on the politics of delegates who drafted Texas's current state constitution.

Rutabaga Johnson and the Grange

By November 24, 1875, the final day of a convention during which Redeemer Democrats scrapped Texas's Reconstruction-era constitution and remade the state's organic law, delegate John Johnson was ready to strut a bit. According to newspaper reports, the Collin County farmer, nicknamed "Rutabaga" by citified journalists, crowed to the convention that "he had carried every point he had started out with when he left his county. They had 'fit' the opposition carefully and beaten them. There were thirty-six lawyers in that body, but they had been superior to them. They had beaten the talent of the Convention all along the line." Rather than simply mimicking England's reigning monarch in referring to himself with plural pronouns, Johnson appeared to be speaking for a faction—a faction that many of his contemporaries associated with the Texas Patrons of Husbandry, or Grange. It was widely believed that delegates identified with the order, whom the same citified journalists accordingly dubbed "Rutabagas," had dominated the proceedings.[1]

From that day to this, scholars have tended to accept such estimates of the convention at face value, perpetuating the whole or in part "Rutabaga" Johnson's understanding of events. The Texas constitution written in 1875 and ratified in 1876 has been taken to represent the triumph of an agrarian bloc within the convention and within the Democratic Party over a more developmentally oriented and cos-

*"of Rutabagas and Redeemers: Rethinking the Texas Constitution of 1876" by Patrick G. Williams from the *Southwestern Historical Quarterly* 106:2 (2002): 230–253. Reprinted by permission of Texas Comptroller of Public Accounts. Patrick G. Williams is assistant professor of history at the University of Arkansas, Fayetteville, and associate editor of the *Arkansas Historical Quarterly*.

mopolitan wing. It has been described as a "Granger product" and even the "master work" of the Texas Grange, and the convention is understood to mark the victory of an agrarian-dominated (even "protopopulist") rank and file dedicated to reining in government. Even accounts that shy away from such broad-brush characterizations have stressed the influence of Grangers on delegates otherwise representing the interest of farmers, on essential components of the constitution. Like-minded agrarians voting as a bloc have been seen as chiefly responsible for the constitution's explicit, and grudging, limits on tax rates, official salaries, and the state debt. They reduced governors' terms to two years and made legislative sessions biennial, forbade expenditure of public money to promote railroad construction and immigration, provided for state regulation of corporations, and refused to abridge universal manhood suffrage. It has at least been implied that in defining the state's power to cultivate economic development and provide for the well-being of its citizenry, these agrarians thereby steered the convention toward the more tight-fisted and less energetic of the alternatives before it.[2]

An Agrarian Myth?

Yet a close examination of the convention proceedings and the post-Reconstruction context in which constitution-making took place simply does not bear out the reigning characterizations of a remorselessly minimalistic constitution made by a farm bloc. To filch a phrase from Richard Hofstadter, this image of the delegates and their work turns out to be something of an agrarian myth, and it is a myth that has proved as persistent, though surely not as noxious, an element of our understanding of Texas's history as the "carpetbagger myth" that Randolph Campbell has done such good work in destroying. Were the analytical shortcomings bound up in this agrarian myth merely a localized infection of the scholarly literature on the Texas constitution, they would still be of some consequence. Though written in the immediate aftermath of Reconstruction, the Constitution of 1876 (while much amended) remained the law of the land in Texas even 125 years later, and mistaken notions about how it was made cannot but hinder proper understanding of how the state has been governed. Yet the myth and the misunderstandings it embraces have not been confined to the specialized literature but have reached into works of far broader ken. It has found its way into textbooks and the foremost reference sources for Texas history and government. Elements of the myth can be detected in important studies of the postbellum era carried out by some of the most talented students of Texas history, demonstrating the dangers that even the best scholars face in having to rely on a flawed monographic literature when it comes to matters that are not the primary subject of their research.[3]

The agrarian myth has also insinuated itself into some of the broader accounts of postbellum southern politics that communicate the experience of the state to many non-Texans and nonspecialists in Texas history. These include such landmark studies as Michael Perman's *The Road to Redemption: Southern Politics, 1869–1879*, which sees in the 1875 convention the "rout" of business-minded "New South"

Texans by agrarian Democrats, and J. Morgan Kousser's very influential *The Shaping of Southern Politics: Suffrage Restriction and the Establishment of the One-Party South, 1880–1910*, which assigns to Grangers the credit (at least among Democrats) for defeating a poll tax limitation on the franchise in Texas. If the received wisdom as to the Constitution of 1876 has infected a broader regional scholarship, challenging the agrarian myth might, by the same measure, not only help clarify certain important episodes and developments in Texas history but also help sharpen the political taxonomy of the postbellum South. The example of Texas's Redeemer convention should caution historians against assigning a single label, such as "agrarian," to diverging, even conflicting, tendencies and warn them away from reducing the struggles among Democrats to simple factionalism between a handful of cohesive interest groups when something more complex was almost certainly taking place.[4]

Like many myths, the myth of an agrarian constitution was not fashioned from whole cloth. It was a well-publicized fact that fully half the members of the Democratic delegation to the constitutional convention—in other words, well over 40 percent of that overwhelmingly Democratic body—belonged to the Patrons of Husbandry, the national farm organization that had established itself in Texas in 1873. And a meaningful portion of these Grange delegates did, indeed, prove more likely than Democrats unaffiliated with the order to vote for greater restrictions on public spending and stricter limitations on government powers and against a poll tax aimed at disfranchising certain voters. This doubtlessly accounts for the perception among many contemporary observers that a "Rutabaga" Granger bloc had manhandled the constitution-making process. Yet the like-mindedness of some among the Grange delegates is a point that the sometimes hysterical reporting of Texas newspapers (most particularly the *Austin Daily Democratic Statesman*) and the generations of scholars that relied on such reportage clearly made entirely too much of. For, upon closer inspection, the portrait of a bloc voting among Grangers that allowed farm representatives to be prime movers in the passage of the constitution's most essential features requires so much qualification as to render the document's status as a specifically agrarian artifact dubious indeed.[5]

Defeat of a Poll Tax Requirement

Perhaps the most commonly told tale about the 1875 proceedings identifies Grangers as the Democrats responsible for the defeat of a requirement that citizens pay a poll tax as a prerequisite for voting. J. Morgan Kousser's is only the most prominent of a number of accounts that contend, in Kousser's words, that "almost every Democrat who joined the fourteen Republicans in opposition to the tax was a member of the Grange." In offering the argument, Kousser cites Seth S. McKay's *Making the Texas Constitution of 1876*. Alwyn Barr does as well, in making the same claim in *Reconstruction to Reform: Texas Politics, 1876–1906*. Nothing better illustrates how an old, weak link in the historiographical chain can confound the best efforts of fine scholars. For to support what would become an influential argument

McKay, in turn, cited nothing more than the October 8, 1875 edition of the *Austin Daily Democratic Statesman*, a paper that gave every evidence of being decidedly overwrought on the subject of Grange influence over the convention.[6]

What sealed the fate of efforts at the convention to restrict the right to vote were the concerns of delegates from securely Democratic counties that a poll tax would unduly burden their own overwhelmingly white, rural constituents. In the end, these concerns outweighed any impulse they might have felt to contain the power of African American voters in the state's relative handful of black-minority counties. But to identify the concern to preserve the franchise of the hardscrabble yeomanry with Grange delegates exclusively, or even primarily, is problematic in the extreme. A number of Democratic delegates central to the scuttling of a poll tax restriction on the franchise—including the man who introduced the substitute striking the tax from the suffrage article, and others who argued passionately against disfranchisement—were not Patrons. In fact, fourteen non-Granger Democrats opposed the poll tax on the most definitive vote—as many as supported it. At the same time, while a significant majority of the Democrats identified as Grangers did indeed vote against the poll tax, Grangers also made up nearly half (thirteen of twenty-eight) of the delegates supporting disfranchisement, including two of the men most active in the cause of suffrage restriction, John Reagan and John Whitfield. The key to voting on this issue seems not to have been Grange (or any other economic interest group) affiliation, but instead the size of the non-Democratic vote in delegates' home districts. The greater tendency of Grange delegates to vote against suffrage restriction is most likely to be attributed to the greater tendency of Grangers to come from securely Democratic, white-majority counties.[7]

The Texas constitution's affirmation of the state's right to regulate railroads, as well as the regulatory provisions actually written into the document, have also often been attributed to the Grangers. However, the railroad measures were not introduced by a Granger, the committee majority that reported them was evenly divided between Patrons and non-Patrons, and a substantial majority of non-Grange Democrats joined Grangers in supporting the railroad article. . . .[8]

A Complicated Compromise

To say the Texas constitution was not an agrarian document, either in being framed by a farm bloc or in representing the most restrictive of politically possible outcomes, hardly tells us enough about what it was. Nor does the simple assertion that the constitution was a complicated compromise born of complicated proceedings. It will continue to be the task of historians to seek out economic, social, and cultural bases for the political divisions in postbellum Texas. But if they should not be satisfied with simply throwing up their hands and surrendering themselves to the inscrutability of the past, neither should they accept conceptualizations that betray the complexity of events, that make a straightforward clash of two antagonists out of what was, in fact, a protracted free for all, a battle royal in which the combatants made friends and enemies with serial abandon. We most likely err if we expect greater orderliness in past politics than we find in the middle of our own day.

Notes

1. Seth S. McKay (ed.), *Debates in the Texas Constitutional Convention of 1875* (Austin: University of Texas, 1930), 459 (quotation); Seth S. McKay, *Making the Texas Constitution of 1876* (Philadelphia: n.p., 1924), 178. The *Austin Daily Democratic Statesman* appears to have coined this "rutabaga" appellation, which, by comparing farm delegates to a variety of turnips, seems intended to suggest that they were unappetizing products of the soil.
2. McKay, *Making the Texas Constitution of 1876*, 185 (1st quotation); Ralph Smith, "The Grange Movement in Texas, 1873–1900," *Southwestern Historical Quarterly* (cited hereafter as SHQ), 42 (Apr., 1939), 310 (2nd quotation); John S. Spratt, *The Road to Spindletop: Economic Change in Texas, 1875–1901* (Dallas: Southern Methodist University Press, 1955), 12–13; John Mauer, "State Constitutions in a Time of Crisis: The Case of the Texas Constitution of 1876," *Texas Law Review*, 68 (June 1990), 1623 (3rd quotation), 1640; Ben Procter, *Not Without Honor: The Life of John H. Reagan* (Austin: University of Texas Press, 1962), 210; David McComb, *Texas: A Modern History* (Austin: University of Texas Press, 1989), 98; John Anthony Moretta, *William Pitt Ballinger: Texas Lawyer, Southern Statesman, 1825–1888* (Austin: Texas State Historical Association, 2000), 215–217; Dale Baum and Robert A. Calvert, "Texas Patrons of Husbandry: Geography, Social Contexts, and Voting Behavior," *Agricultural History*, 63 (Fall, 1989), 49, 51.
3. Richard Hofstadter, *The Age of Reform: From Bryan to FDR* (New York: Knopf, 1955), 23–59; Randolph Campbell, "Carpetbagger Rule in Reconstruction Texas: An Enduring Myth," *SHQ* 97 (Apr., 1994), 587–596; Robert Calvert and Arnoldo De Leon, *The History of Texas* (2nd ed.; Wheeling, Ill.: Harlan Davidson, 1996), 163–164; Rupert Richardson, *Texas: The Lone Star State* (2nd ed.; Englewood Cliffs, N.J.: Prentice Hall, 1958), 221, 223; Wilbourn E. Benton, *Texas: Its Government and Politics* (2nd ed.; Englewood Cliffs, N.J.; Prentice-Hall, 1966), 39–44; Kenneth R. Mladenka and Kim Quaile Hill, *Texas Government: Politics and Economics* (Monterey, Calif.: Brooks/Cole Publishing Co., 1986), 92–93; Alwyn Barr, *Reconstruction to Reform: Texas Politics, 1876–1906* (Austin: University of Texas Press, 1971), 25, 113, 204. The article on the Constitution of 1876 in *The New Handbook of Texas* states, "In the convention the Grange members acted as a bloc in support of conservative constitutional measures." Joe E. Ericson and Ernest Wallace, "Constitution of Association, 1876," in Ron Tyler, et al. (eds.), *The New Handbook of Texas* (6 vols.; Austin: Texas State Historical Association, 1996), II, 289. See also John W. Mauer, "Constitution Proposed in 1874," ibid., III, 279.
4. Michael Perman, *The Road to Redemption: Southern Politics, 1869–1879* (Chapel Hill: University of North Carolina Press, 1984), 191, 203–204, 205

(quotations); J. Morgan Kousser, *The Shaping of Southern Politics: Suffrage Restriction and the Establishment of the One-Party South, 1880–1910* (New Haven: Yale University Press, 1974), 200.

5. A contemporary document, Walsh & Pilgrim's *Directory of the Officers and Members of the Constitutional Convention of the State of Texas, A.D. 1875* (Austin: Democratic Statesman Office, 1875), identified thirty-seven of the seventy-six Democratic delegates as Grangers. Two Democrats not listed as Patrons in that source—F. J. Lynch and W. D. S. Cook—identified themselves as members of the order on the floor of the convention. McKay (ed.), *Debates,* 190, 207. J. E. Ericson, "The Delegates to the Convention of 1875: A Reappraisal," *SHQ* 67 (July 1963), 22–27, gives a figure of thirty-eight Grangers without identifying them or assessing their influence on the convention.

6. Kousser, *Shaping of Southern Politics,* 200 (quotation): Barr, *Reconstruction to Reform,* 204. McKay's original statement was "The Democratic opponents to the majority report making a poll tax qualification for suffrage came almost entirely from the Grangers." *Making the Texas Constitution of 1876,* 97–98. Similar claims as to the Grange role in defeating the poll tax can be found in Baum and Calvert, "Texas Patrons of Husbandry," 49; Calvert and De Leon, *History of Texas,* 148–149; Mauer, "State Constitution in a Time of Crisis," 1644; Lawrence D. Rice, *The Negro in Texas 1874–1900* (Baton Rouge: Louisiana State University Press, 1971), 22–23. McKay's statement and the credence it has been given is all the more curious considering that elsewhere in the book he cites a fairly convincing contemporary argument against Grange responsibility for the defeat of the poll tax. McKay, *Making the Texas Constitution of 1876,* 135.

7. The median Republican percentage of the 1873 gubernatorial vote had been 40 percent in the home counties of Democrats voting for the poll tax but only 21 percent in the home counties of Democratic delegates opposing it. The Republican median in Grange-represented counties was about 22 percent, but it was approximately 33 percent in counties represented by non-Grange Democrats. For convention action on the poll tax, see *Journal of the Constitutional Convention of the State of Texas Begun and Held at the City of Austin, September 6, 1875* (Galveston: "News" Office, 1875), 29, 60,142, 238, 304–310, 328–330, 405–406, 697–698, 785; McKay (ed.), *Debates,* 167–190. For the 1873 gubernatorial vote by county, see Mike Kingston, Sam Attlesey, and Mary Crawford, *The Texas Almanac's Political History of Texas* (Austin: Eakin Press, 1992), 58–61.

8. *Journal of the Constitutional Convention,* 89–90, 376–378, 605, 716, 796–797. On the final passage of the proposed railroad article, thirty-three Grangers voted for it and only one against, while eighteen non-Grange Democrats supported it and eight opposed.

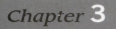
★
LOCAL GOVERNMENTS

Life for most Texans is linked to daily hassles that include motor vehicle traffic on increasingly congested roads, streets, and freeways. (See the cartoon that begins this chapter.) Whether home is a rural community (like Cotulla in South Texas), a suburb (like Carrollton, north of Dallas), or a big city (like Houston), most Texans demand transportation facilities and other governmental services delivered in a timely and effective manner. To see how individuals influence local government in constructive ways in order to receive these services requires an understanding of both governmental structures and political processes.

Cities (municipalities), counties, and special districts are separate, legal entities that are identified as grassroots governments. With 254 counties and more than 1,200 cities, Texas leads California, Florida, New York, and bordering U.S. and Mexican states in numbers of these local governments. Whether paving streets, conducting elections, combating crime, or providing mass transit systems, local governments and their policymakers directly affect the quality of life for all Texans.

Overview of Grassroots Problems

Who are the policymakers for grassroots governments? What differences do their decisions make in our daily lives? Answering these questions first requires an understanding of American federalism, discussed in the chapter "Federalism and the Texas Constitution." Texas's local governments, like those of other states, are at the bottom rung of the governmental ladder. Cities, counties, and special-district governments are creatures of the state of Texas.

Because more than 80 percent of all Texans reside in cities, the fast-paced metropolitan scene has become the center of attention. Residents of these heavily populated urban and suburban areas have immediate concerns: high crime rates, decaying infrastructures (streets, roads, and bridges), ineffective public schools, and, since September 11, 2001, the threat of terrorism.

Texas cities are also becoming increasingly diverse. Many African Americans and Latinos are seeking to obtain adequate public services and to gain access to local power structures long dominated by Anglos. "Suburban sprawl," "inner-city decay," and "white flight" are not mere jargon in social science literature. Determining how Texas's local governments should deal with these problems so that all communities receive equal access to public services is a challenge that drives most policy debates for policymakers, political scientists, and community activists at the grassroots level.

Opportunities to participate in local politics begin with registering and then voting in local elections. (See the chapter "The Politics of Elections and Parties" for voter qualifications and registration requirements under Texas law.) Some citizens may even seek election to a city council, county

How Do We Compare . . . in Number of Cities and Counties?

Comparing Number of Cities and Counties, 2002

Most Populous U.S. States	Number of Cities	Number of Counties	U.S. States Bordering Texas	Number of Cities	Number of Counties	Mexican States Bordering Texas	Number of Cities	Number of Counties (Municipios)
California	477	38	Arkansas	496	75	Chihuahua	220	67
Florida	406	67	Louisiana	303	64[a]	Coahuila	165	38
New York	477	58	New Mexico	102	33	Nuevo León	127	51
Texas	1,202	254	Oklahoma	596	77	Tamaulipas	193	43

Source: U.S. Department of Commerce and Instituto Nacional de Estadistica, Geografía e Informática de México (www.inegi.gob.mx), "Numero de Localidades y Población por Tamaño de Localidad, 2000."

[a]Louisiana is divided into parishes rather than counties.

commissioners court, school board, or other policymaking body. Short of winning public office, however, an individual may become politically active through homeowners' associations, neighborhood associations, other community or issue-oriented organizations, voter registration drives, and election campaigns of candidates seeking local offices. Unfortunately, despite the numerous ways to get involved in local politics, it is common to find fewer than 10 percent of a community's qualified voters participating in a local election. But voter interest increases when people understand that they can solve grassroots problems in Texas only through political partici-pation. By gaining influence in city halls, county courthouses, and special-district offices, individuals and groups may address grassroots problems through the democratic process.

Municipal Governments

Perhaps no level of government influences the daily lives of citizens more than **municipal** (city) **government**. Whether taxing residents, arresting criminals, collecting garbage, providing public libraries, or repairing streets, municipalities determine how millions of Texans live in more than 1,200 incorporated communities established by law. Knowing how and why pub-lic policies are made at city hall requires an understanding of the organiza-tional and legal framework within which municipalities function.

Legal Status of Municipalities Powers of city governments are outlined and restricted by municipal charters, state and national constitutions, and statutes. There are two legal classifications of cities in Texas: **general-law cities** and **home-rule cities**. A community with a population of 201 or more may become a general-law city through a charter prescribed by a general law enacted by the Texas Legislature.[1] But a city of more than 5,000 people may be incorporated as a home-rule city, with a locally drafted charter that is adopted, amended, or repealed by majority vote in a citywide election. Once chartered, a general-law city does not automatically become a home-rule city just because its population rises above 5,000, nor does home-rule status change when a population declines to 5,000 or less. Local voters must decide the legal designation of their city, but the Texas Legislature reserves the right to change a home-rule city's government.

At the start of 2005, there were more than 350 home-rule cities and close to 900 general-law cities in Texas. The principal advantage of home-rule cities is greater flexibility in determining their structures and forms of municipal government. Citizens draft, adopt, and may revise their city's charter through a citywide election. The charter establishes powers of municipal officers, sets salaries and terms of offices for council members and mayors, and spells out procedures for passing, repealing, or amending **ordinances** (city laws). In 2001, the voters of Houston approved a contentious city charter amendment banning the city council from offering benefits, such as health insurance, to same-sex domestic partners of city workers.

Some cities, such as Austin, provide a process for removing elected officials through a popular vote. This process is referred to as recall. In 2004, for example, voters in Kingsville (south of Corpus Christi) recalled their mayor and two council members. Along with initiative and referendum, recall is restricted to home-rule cities in Texas government. An initiative is a citizen-drafted measure proposed by a certain number or percentage of qualified voters. If approved by popular vote, an initiative becomes law without city approval, whereas a referendum repeals an existing ordinance. Ballot referenda and initiatives require voter approval and, depending on city charter provisions, may be binding or nonbinding on municipal governments. Contentious issues sometimes arise, such as in 1999, when Houston voters defeated by 54 percent to 46 percent an initiative that would have repealed the city's rules for hiring women and minorities and for awarding city contracts to them, or in 2000, when San Antonio voters approved an initiative allowing fluoridation of their drinking water.

Forms of Municipal Government

Four principal forms of municipal government operate in the United States and Texas: strong mayor-council, weak mayor-council, commission, and council-manager. There are many variations of these four forms. The council-manager form prevails in more than 80 percent of Texas's home-rule cities, and variations of the mayor-council system operate in many general-law cities.

Citizens often ask, "How do you explain the structure of municipal government in my town? None of the four models accurately depicts our government." The answer lies in home-rule flexibility. For instance, Brownsville and Harlingen in the Rio Grande Valley have a mayor and city commission structure. Various combinations of the forms discussed in the following sections are permissible under a home-rule charter, depending on community preference, provided they do not conflict with state law.

Strong Mayor-Council   Among larger American cities, the **strong mayor-council form** continues as the predominant governmental structure. Among the nation's ten largest cities, only Dallas and San Antonio operate with a structure (council-manager) other than some variation of the strong mayor-council system. In New York, Chicago, Philadelphia, Detroit, Boston, and St. Louis, the mayor is the chief administrator as well as the political head of the city. Houston and El Paso have the strong mayor-council form of government, but most of Texas's larger home-rule cities have chosen other forms of government. Perhaps this is due to a dislike for so-called machine or ward-heeling politics, a style that once characterized the strong mayor-council form in some northern cities and frequently resulted in corrupt municipal administrations. In Texas, cities operating with the strong mayor-council form have the following characteristics:

■ A council composed of members elected from single-member districts
■ A mayor elected at large, with power to appoint and remove department heads
■ Budgetary power (for example, preparation and execution of a plan for raising and spending city money) exercised by the mayor, subject to council approval before the budget may be implemented
■ Veto power over council actions given to the mayor

Houston has a variation of the strong mayor-council form that features a powerful mayor aided by a citizens' assistance office and an elected controller who is responsible for the budget (see Figure 3.1). This arrangement allows the mayor to delegate much administrative work to the chief of staff, whom the mayor appoints and may remove. Duties of the chief of staff include coordinating the activities of city departments, the mayor's office, and council members' offices.

Weak Mayor-Council   As the term **weak mayor-council form** implies, this model of local government gives limited administrative powers to the mayor, who is popularly elected along with members of the city council, some department heads, and other municipal officials. A city council has power to override the mayor's veto. The mayor's position is weak because the office shares appointive and removal powers over municipal government personnel with the city council.

Instead of being a chief executive, the mayor is merely one of several elected officials who are responsible to the electorate. Significantly, none of the 10 largest cities in Texas has the weak mayor-council form of municipal government. Although some small general-law and home-rule cities in Texas and other parts of the country operate under the weak mayor-council plan, the trend is away from this form. Conroe, for example, a city with a population of about 37,000 in Montgomery County north of Houston, has a weak-mayor council form of government.

Figure 3.1 Strong Mayor-Council Form of Municipal Government: City of Houston

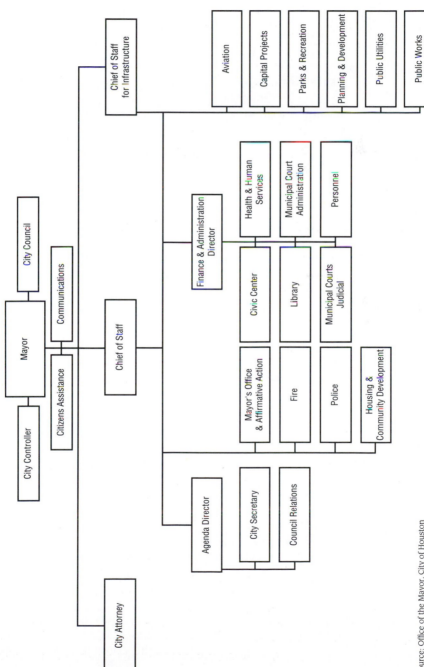

Source: Office of the Mayor, City of Houston

Commission Today, none of Texas's home-rule cities operates under a pure **commission form** of municipal government, in which each commissioner administers a department. This form does not provide a single executive but relies instead on elected commissioners constituting a policymaking board. Although first approved by the Texas Legislature for Galveston, following a destructive tidal wave that demolished that city in 1900, the commission form is no longer popular.

Each department (for example, public safety, finance, public works, welfare, or legal) is the responsibility of a single commissioner. Most students of municipal government are critical of the commission form because it has a dispersed administrative structure that lacks a chief executive. Texas municipalities with a variation of the commission form of government designate a city secretary or another official to coordinate departmental work. By state law, some general-law cities, such as Gorman (in Eastland County), have a commission form of government.

Council-Manager Most home-rule cities in Texas follow the **council-manager form** (sometimes termed the commission-manager form). This structure has the following characteristics:

▪ A mayor, elected at large, who is the presiding member of the council
▪ City council or commission members elected at large or in single-member districts
▪ A city manager who is appointed by the council (and can be removed by the council) and is responsible for budget coordination

When the cities of Amarillo and Terrell adopted the council-manager form in 1913, a new era in municipal administration began. (See Figure 3.2 for the council-manager form used by the city of San Antonio.) The mayor and city council make decisions after deliberation and debate on policy issues such as taxation, budgeting, annexation, and provision of services. City councils rely on their managers for preparation of annual budgets and policy recommendations. Once a policy is made, the city manager's office directs an appropriate department to implement it. Typically, city councils hire professionally trained managers. Successful applicants usually possess graduate degrees in public administration and can earn competitive salaries. City managers for Dallas, Austin, and San Antonio are among the highest paid in the country. Dallas's city manager, for instance, earns an annual salary of more than $263,000. Obviously, there is a delicate relationship between appointed managers and elected council members.

In theory, the council-manager system attempts to separate policymaking from administration. Councils are not supposed to "micromanage" departments. Practice demonstrates, however, that elected leaders experience difficulties in determining where to draw the line between administrative oversight and meddling in departmental affairs. Nevertheless, about 220 Texas home-rule cities are governed under the council-manager form of government.

Figure 3.2 Council-Manager Form of Municipal Government: City of San Antonio

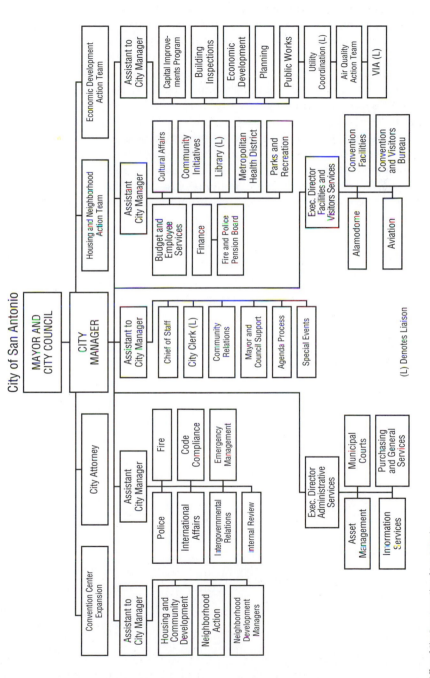

City of San Antonio

(L) Denotes Liaison

Source: Office of City Secretary, City of San Antonio

Municipal Politics

Elected mayors and city councils are focal points of policymaking. No longer controlled by wealthy elites, council members increasingly reflect Texas's cultural diversity. Mayoral and city council races can become quite competitive, especially when open seats arise. In 2001, Gus Garcia was elected as Austin's first Latino mayor and completed the term. Betty Flores was elected as Laredo's first Latina mayor in 1998, close to 250 years after the founding of that city.[2]

All Texas cities conduct state-mandated **nonpartisan elections**, in which candidates are listed on the ballot without party label. Aspirants to a city council or mayoral position are endorsed and supported by community groups, but party politics is becoming an important factor in some municipal elections. As a result of U.S. Census figures for 2000, Texas's city council districts had to be redrawn because of shifts in population within cities and between districts. Under federal law, a city's council districts must have approximately the same population, and any changes in districting must be approved by the U.S. Department of Justice.

There are two basic types of municipal elections: the **at-large election**, in which all council members are elected on a citywide basis, and the **single-member district election**, in which all voters cast a ballot for a candidate who resides within their district. Municipal politics has been influenced by two significant developments: emergence of single-member districts for city councils and rising expectations for equitable representation by African Americans and Latinos.

Studies on voting behavior by political scientists provide evidence that racial minorities have difficulty winning in at-large elections. This is primarily due to racially polarized voting (voters casting ballots for candidates of their own race) that favors Anglo candidates in a district that elects more than one council member. Single-member districts, in contrast, provide a system whereby some districts potentially have a majority of minority voters, thereby increasing the chance of a Latino or African American candidate being elected to the city council. Prompted by lawsuits, several municipalities have adopted single-member districts or a mixed system of at-large and single-member districts. As scholars point out, minorities have better opportunities in single-member districts to elect their own candidate; thus, both specific local and citywide interests are represented.[3]

Some Texas municipalities use **cumulative voting** to increase African American and Latino representation on city councils. In this election system, voters may cast one or more of the specified number of votes for one or more candidates in any combination. Only whole votes may be cast and counted in a city where cumulative voting is used. For example, if there are eight candidates vying for four positions on the city council, a voter may cast two votes for Candidate A, two votes for Candidate B, and no votes for the other candidates. By the same token, a voter may cast all four votes for Candidate A. In the end, the candidates with the most votes are selected to fill the four positions. Since racial minority voters tend to be a numerical minority in some communities, it is more likely under this system that their preferred candidate will be elected.

Five of the largest Texas cities operate with a single-member district system of representation or some combination of single-member and at-large election systems. Each council member in Dallas (14), San Antonio (10), Fort Worth (8), and El Paso (6) is elected from a single-member district. Houston has 5 council members elected at large (citywide) and 9 from single-member districts. With the increased use of single-member districts, the ethnic and racial composition of city councils has become more diverse.

Some cities, such as Austin, use a **place system** to elect council members. Under this structure, candidates file for a numerically designated place. Those who file for the same place run against one another. Voters throughout the city can vote in each place contest. The mayor is elected at large and presides over council meetings that are usually held weekly. Charters of most cities allow the mayor to vote on any matter before the council, but El Paso's mayor has only a tie-breaking vote. In some cities, the mayor is chosen by (and is a member of) the city council. In 2002, Dallas city council member Laura Miller was elected to replace Mayor Ron Kirk. He was that city's first African American mayor, but later stepped down and ran unsuccessfully for a seat in the U.S. Senate.

Home-rule cities may also determine whether **term limits** should be instituted for their elected officials. Beginning in the 1990s, many cities, such as San Antonio and Houston, amended their charters to institute term limits for their mayor and city council members. Houston has a limit of three 2-year terms for its mayor. In 2003, Houston's first African American mayor, Lee Brown, was term-limited after serving three terms. The race to elect the city's next mayor attracted nine candidates, forcing a runoff between an Anglo Democrat and former state chairman for the Texas Democrat Party, Bill White, and a Cuban American Republican and former city council member, Orlando Sanchez. In one of the most expensive electoral contests in Houston's history, White won the election with a wide margin. San Antonio has a limit of two 2-year terms for its mayor and city council members. (See this chapter's Selected Reading, "'Extreme' Term Limits—San Antonio Style," for a discussion of the impact of restrictive term limits on that city's government by its former city manager, Alexander Briseno.) In a charter reform election in May 2004, San Antonio voters defeated provisions that would have increased terms and paid professional salaries to city officials.[4]

Use of single-member districts has altered the power structures in Texas's cities and has changed municipal service agendas. Coupled with increasing minority populations in these cities, single-member districts have forced the white, male, business-oriented network of power brokers to "cut the pie" to make municipal government more responsive to today's demographic and economic realities.

POINT
COUNTERPOINT

Should Term Limits Be Instituted for City Council Members and the Mayor?

THE ISSUE

Municipal term limits are increasingly common within the Term Limits Movement. According to U.S. Term Limits (www.termlimits.org), Texas currently has about seventy cities with term limits. There are strong arguments for and against term limits. The following are some examples of the more common arguments.

Arguments For Instituting Term Limits

1. Long tenure tends to encourage corruption.
2. Term limits facilitate new approaches to solving public problems.
3. Turnover assures election of citizen public officials instead of professional office-seekers.

> "Local limits transform political culture from one of entrenched careers to one of progression and citizen representation."
> —Danielle Fagre, former research director for the U.S. Term Limits Foundation

Arguments Against Instituting Term Limits

1. Turnover does not guarantee better or more honest leaders.
2. Short tenure does not assure productivity and effectiveness.
3. Limitations on consecutive terms deprive cities of experienced leadership.

> "As an organization dedicated to protecting and enhancing the role of citizens in our representative democracy, the League strongly opposes term limits. . . ."
> —Becky Cain, President of the National League of Women Voters

Municipal Services

Traffic safety, consumer protection, pollution control, tree preservation, city planning, building safety, annexation, and zoning restrictions are examples of some of the affairs that municipalities regulate. Zoning ordinances, for instance, regulate the use of land for residential and commercial purposes. Changing a residential area into a commercial zone often brings increased traffic and crime. (Interestingly, Houston remains the only city among Texas's 10 largest municipalities without zoning authority.)

Protection of the homeless, elderly services, job-training programs, and delinquency prevention are examples of the services that cities may provide. Competing demands for municipal services often result in controversy, thus requiring city councils to make difficult decisions. Other controversies arise when city governments consider providing services not typically performed, or decide to cut back certain services because of budgetary restraints.

San Antonio City Council conducts a meeting in the summer of 2004. (Photo courtesy of Scott Schrader, Media Specialist, St. Mary's University)

Municipal Government Revenue

What Texans want most from their local governments are public services, programs, and facilities that protect the health, safety, and welfare of people but are paid for with low taxes. Although city hall is often a favorite target of frustrated taxpayers, the Texas Legislature receives its share of pressure because of strict statutory and constitutional limitations on cities.

Taxes Texas municipalities are constitutionally empowered to levy general property taxes and miscellaneous occupation taxes (further discussed in Chapter 8, "Bureaucracy, Public Policies, and Finance"). However, Governor Rick Perry's proposal in April 2004 to institute a cap on homestead appraisals and to require voter approval for any changes in local property tax revenue may substantially change the way city governments are financed.

Municipal property taxes vary among Texas cities. In 2004, for example, the city of Austin collected 45.97 cents per $100 valuation, whereas Fort Worth collected 86.5 cents. In addition, voters must authorize increases in city sales taxes. Under Texas law, cities may ask voters to approve a one-eighth cent sales tax (for a cumulative total of 1 percent) for services or projects such as mass transit, economic development, public safety, and street maintenance. The hotel occupancy tax is another important source of revenue, especially for cities in which tourism or major sports events (e.g., Super Bowl in Houston and Final Four in San Antonio in 2004) make up a large part of the local economy.

Fees Texas municipalities may levy fees for issuing beer and liquor licenses, as well as for granting building and development permits. Authorized to operate municipal courts, cities also obtain revenue from court costs, fines, and forfeitures for violations of laws. This revenue may be substantial, especially if traffic regulations are enforced vigorously. Texas cities may charge a franchise fee based on the gross receipts of public utilities (for example, telephone and cable TV companies operating within municipal jurisdictions). Trailing only property and sales tax revenues, franchise fees are steadily growing as a significant revenue source for the state's major cities.

Texas municipalities are authorized to own and operate water, electric, and gas utility systems. If a city decides to offer one or more of these services instead of depending on investor-owned companies, it may collect revenues large enough to permit profits or payments in lieu of taxes, which are transferred to general funds. Charges also are levied for such services as sewage treatment, garbage collection and disposal, hospital care, and use of city recreation facilities. A user fee may mean that a service requires only a small subsidy from a city's general revenue fund, or perhaps no subsidy at all.

Bonds Taxes and fees normally produce enough revenue to allow Texas cities to cover day-to-day operating expenses. Money for capital improvements (such as construction of city buildings), park projects (such as picnic areas and rest rooms), and emergencies (such as damage resulting from flooding) often must be obtained through the sale of **municipal bonds**. The Texas Constitution allows cities to issue bonds in any amount, provided they annually assess and collect sufficient revenue to pay the interest and retire the principal without exceeding legal tax limits. Cities are authorized to issue general obligation bonds and revenue bonds, but any bond issue must be approved by the voters. General obligation bonds are redeemed out of a city's property tax revenue. Revenue bonds are backed by and redeemed out of revenue from the property or activities (such as airports and convention centers) financed by sale of the bonds.

Property Taxes and Tax Exemptions Heavy reliance on taxation of home and business property (based on appraised value) places a burden on many Texas communities. Not only do municipal governments rely on the property tax as their major revenue source, but so do counties and most special districts, including those that operate public schools and community colleges.

To offset somewhat the burden of higher taxes resulting from reappraisals of property values, local governments (including cities) may grant homeowners a 20 percent homestead exemption on the assessed value of their homes. Cities may also provide an additional homestead exemption for veterans, the disabled, and homeowners 65 years of age or older (for example, exemption for senior citizens on the first $65,000 of their home value).

In 2001, the 77th Legislature proposed a constitutional amendment allowing property tax exemptions for travel-trailer owners. This measure was intended to benefit "Winter Texans" who travel from areas with colder climates to South Texas during the winter. Approved by the voters, the amendment inadvertently imposed a new property tax for school districts to collect. In effect, these districts could place a property tax on trailers that were exempt from other taxation. To correct the problem, a constitutional amendment exempting travel-trailer owners from property taxes was proposed by the 78th Legislature and approved by voters in 2003. At the same time, other relevant constitutional amendments were approved that affect potential local revenue. Texans voted to allow cities, counties, and community college districts to permanently cap or freeze property taxes for senior citizens 65 or older (irrespective of the wealth of property owners) and for the disabled. If a city votes to implement the cap on property taxes, it risks losing millions of dollars in tax revenue, particularly as baby boomers approach retirement. Implementing the cap can occur by action of a city council or by voter approval. In 2004, Selma (northeast of San Antonio) was the first city in Bexar county to implement this cap.

Because of pressure against raising property tax rates, municipal governments sometimes refrain from increased spending, cut services or programs from their budgets, or find new revenue sources. Typically, city councils are forced to opt for one or more of the following actions:

- Create new fees or raise fees on services such as garbage collection
- Impose hiring and wage freezes for municipal employees
- Cut services (such as emergency medical) that are especially important for inner-city populations
- Contract with private firms for service delivery
- Improve productivity, especially by investing in technology

Generating Revenue for Economic Development

Appropriations by state and federal lawmakers are shrinking as sources of municipal revenue, especially for economic development. Foremost among inner-city problems are dilapidated housing, abandoned buildings, and poorly maintained infrastructure (such as sewers and streets). This neglect blights neighborhoods and contributes to social problems, including crime and strained racial relations. Texas cities do have the local option of a half-cent sales tax for infrastructure upgrades, such as paving or repaving streets and replacing inadequate sewage disposal facilities.

Following a national trend, some Texas cities are opting for an innovative revenue-raising plan to attract development and businesses in order to stimulate local economies. The legislature authorizes municipalities to create **tax reinvestment zones (TRZs)** by providing temporary **tax abatements** (eliminating property taxes on increased value for a specified time limit) or **tax increment financing (TIF)**. The TIF process involves cities that dedicate zones for redevelopment through tax incentives for developers and businesses to build and locate in blighted inner-city areas. Tax abatements "freeze" commercial and residential property tax valuations for developers and businesses within a designated zone for a specified time limit. The incremental property taxes on the increased values from the investment are then dedicated to paying for public improvements (such as streets, drainage, and parks) in the zone. This reduces development costs and provides an incentive for reinvestment. The drawback, however, in offering such financial incentives is the immediate loss of revenue growth. Cities that include operating TRZs are Houston, Dallas, Fort Worth, Austin, San Antonio, and El Paso.

Counties

Article IX of the Texas Constitution is titled Counties, although it says little about county government. The county is an administrative arm of the state, created to serve its needs and purposes. State supervision of county operations, however, is minimal. As an agent of the state, each of the 254 Texas counties (more than any other state) issues state automobile licenses, enforces state laws, registers voters, conducts elections, collects some state taxes, and helps administer justice. In conjunction with state and federal governments, the county conducts health and welfare programs, maintains records of vital statistics (such as births and deaths), issues various licenses, collects fees, and provides a host of other public services.

Texans tend to regard the county's governmental functions as exclusively local. Most people cannot distinguish between functions performed for the county and those conducted for the state. For example, the county sheriff and county judge enforce and administer state law. These officials are therefore state functionaries, yet they are elected by the voters of the county and are paid from the county treasury.

Structure and Operation

Texas counties have the same basic governmental structure, as mandated by the state constitution, despite wide demographic and economic differences between rural and urban counties. (Figures 3.3 and 3.4 contrast the most populous Texas county, Harris, with 3,400,578 residents in 2000, and the least populous, Loving County, with 67 residents in that year.)

The Texas Constitution provides for the election of four county commissioners, county and district attorneys, a county sheriff, a county clerk, a district clerk, a county tax assessor-collector, a county treasurer, and constables, as well as judicial officers, including justices of the peace and a county judge. All elected county officials serve four-year terms.

Figure 3.3 Harris County Government (County Seat: Houston)

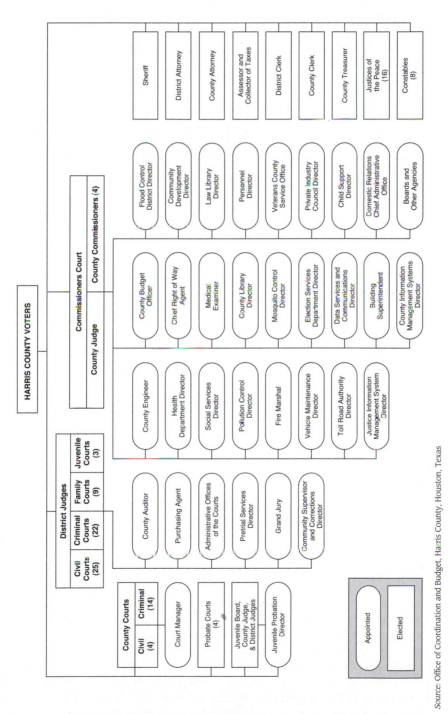

Source: Office of Coordination and Budget, Harris County, Houston, Texas

Figure 3.4 Loving County Government (County Seat: Mentone)

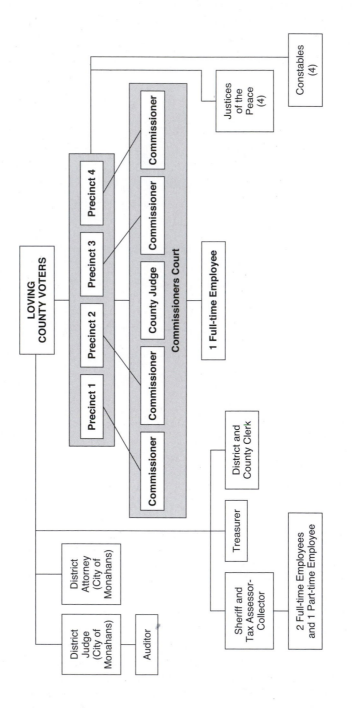

Source: County Clerk's Office, Loving County

Commissioners Court   Policymaking is performed by many county officials, but mainly by a body called the **commissioners court**. Its members are the county judge, who presides, and four elected commissioners. The latter serve staggered four-year terms so that two commissioners are elected every two years. Each commissioner is elected by voters residing in a commissioner precinct. Boundary lines for a county's four commissioner precincts are set by its commissioners court. Precincts must be of substantially equal population as mandated by the "one-man, one-vote" ruling of the U.S. Supreme Court in *Avery* v. *Midland County* (1968). As required for city council districts, redistricting must be done for county commissioners courts every ten years after U.S. Census data become available. Following the 2000 census, county redistricting battles centered on party power, such as in Bexar County (San Antonio) and Travis County (Austin), as well as increasing Latino representation, as in Harris County (Houston).[5]

The term "commissioners court" is actually a misnomer, because its functions are administrative rather than judicial. The court's major functions include the following:

- Adopting the county budget and setting tax rates (within constitutional limitations)
- Providing jails and building and maintaining county roads and bridges
- Operating a courthouse
- Administering county health and welfare programs
- Administering and financing elections (all general and special elections—national, state and local), as well as selecting type of ballot to be used

Beyond these functions, a county is free to decide whether to enter other programs authorized, but not required, by the state. Commissioners may establish and operate county hospitals, libraries, parks, airports, museums, and other public facilities. In addition to their collective responsibilities, commissioners court members may have individual duties, such as serving as road and bridge administrator in a precinct.

County Judge   Major responsibility for administrative operations of the commissioners court is vested in a **county judge**. For example, in "wet" counties the county judge issues licenses for the sale of alcoholic beverages. In a judicial capacity, the judge in most counties hears cases in county court but is not required to be a lawyer. (See Chapter 9, "Laws, Courts, and Justice," for more information on county judges, justices of the peace, and constables.) The judge also fills vacancies within the commissioners court, is authorized to perform marriages, and serves as a notary public (an individual who certifies documents, takes sworn statements, and administers oaths).

County Attorney and County Sheriff   The **county attorney** represents the state in civil and criminal cases. Nearly fifty counties do not elect a county attorney because the functions of that office are performed by a resident district attorney. Other counties elect a county attorney but share the services of a district attorney with two or more neighboring counties.

Bexar County Commissioners Court conducts a meeting. Seated (L-R) are commissioners Thomas F. Adkisson and Lyle T. Larson, county judge Nelson Wolff, and commissioners Paul Elizondo and Robert Tejeda. (Photo courtesy of Scott Schrader, Media Specialist, St. Mary's University)

The **county sheriff**, as chief law enforcement officer, is charged with keeping the peace in the county. In this capacity, the sheriff appoints deputies and is in charge of the county jail and its prisoners. In a county with a population of less than 10,000, the sheriff may also serve as tax assessor-collector, unless that county's electorate votes to separate the two offices.

County Clerk and County Tax Assessor-Collector A **county clerk** keeps records and handles a variety of paperwork chores for both the county court and the commissioners court. In addition, the county clerk files legal documents (such as deeds, mortgages, and contracts) in the county's public records and maintains the county's vital statistics (birth, death, and marriage records). Responsibility for administration of elections also extends to the county clerk, who certifies each candidate for a place on the general election ballot and prepares the ballot (unless the county has an administrator of elections).

Another county office receiving considerable statewide attention is that of the **county tax assessor-collector**, which, partially at least, is a misnomer. Since the adoption of a state constitutional amendment in 1982, the boards of **county tax appraisal districts** are charged with assessing property values in each county. Thus the county tax assessor–collector no longer makes assessments. Issuing certificates of title and collecting state license fees for

---

Points to Ponder In the 2002 general election, Bexar County was the last county in the nation to count its votes because of a complicated ballot that caused problems. Optical scanning of ballots was delayed because a two-sheet ballot (printed front and back on the first sheet) was held together with a paper clip. For the constitutional amendment election of 2003, Bexar County was one of the first counties in the state and in the nation to use the touch-screen ballot method of voting.

---

motor vehicles are important functions of the office. The county tax assessor-collector also serves as voting registrar, unless a county creates an election administrator with those duties.

Other County Officers The **county treasurer** receives and pays out all county funds authorized by the commissioners court. If the office is eliminated by constitutional amendment (as in Tarrant and Bell counties), the county commissioners assign treasurer duties to the **county auditor**. A county of 10,000 or more people must have a county auditor, who is appointed by the district court judge or judges having jurisdiction in the county. The auditing function involves checking the account books and records of all officials who handle county funds. Although not a required officer for some counties, the **county surveyor** is a constitutionally prescribed elected officer who draws no salary but is paid by contract to conduct specific surveys of land within the county.

County Finance

Increasing citizen demands for services and programs impose on most counties an ever-expanding need for money. Just as the structure of county governments is frozen in the Texas Constitution, so is the county's power to tax and, to a lesser extent, its power to spend.

Taxation The Texas Constitution authorizes county governments to collect taxes on property. Although occupations may also be taxed, none of the counties implements that provision. Money collected from the basic property tax is distributed among four funds in each county treasury. These are designated as general revenue, permanent improvements (such as new office buildings), road and bridge, and jury funds. The commissioners court may impose additional property taxes, but only after statutory authorization by the Texas Legislature and approval by a majority of the county's qualified voters. Counties and other taxing units may grant temporary tax exemptions on certain property.

A commissioners court may grant tax abatements (reductions or suspensions) on taxable property, reimbursements (return of taxes paid), or tax increment financing (TIF) to attract or retain businesses. For instance, in 2003 Bexar County offered a $22 million tax abatement for a Toyota factory to be built for producing pickup trucks in San Antonio. This tax abatement ensures that the company need not pay property taxes for a ten-year period.

The offer was part of a complex incentive package put together by officials of the city, the local school district, and the state, as well as the San Antonio's natural gas and electric power service company. Once operational, the factory is expected to create 1,800 high-paying jobs and foster economic development in the region.[6]

Revenues from Nontax Sources Special laws allow the issue of **county bonds**, subject to voter approval. Revenue from the sale of bonds is used for capital outlays such as payment for a new county courthouse or county jail. County indebtedness is limited by the Texas Constitution to 35 percent of a county's total assessed property value.

As additional sources of income, counties may impose fees for permitting the sale of liquor, wine, and beer. Counties also receive a percentage of the state's tax receipts on sales of liquor. Texas statutes allow each county to share in revenues obtained from state motor vehicle registration and license fees, motor fuel taxes, motor vehicle sales taxes, fees for issuing certificates of title for motor vehicles, and fines for violations of traffic regulations (speeding) that occur in unincorporated areas (outside city limits).

Federal grants-in-aid are another source of county revenue, but this source has continued to shrink with block grant funding. Typically, the U.S. Congress makes counties eligible to receive any and all aid extended to cities and towns, including grants for construction of hospitals, airports, and public housing. For counties that have military installations, grants of federal money increase.

Despite various revenue sources, Texas counties, like other units of local government, are pressured to raise property taxes or to balance their budgets by eliminating or reducing some programs and services. Although administrative costs and demands for expanded public services continue to increase, sources of county revenue are not expanding.

Expenditures Although county expenditures are restricted by legal requirements and state administrative directives, patterns of spending vary considerably from county to county. The county judge, auditor, or budget officer prepares the budget, but the commissioners court is responsible for final adoption of an annual spending plan. Maintenance of county roads and bridges continues to require the largest expenditures in rural counties throughout Texas.

Counties do not have complete control over their spending, because state and federal statutes and administrative directives require that certain county services be furnished and that regulatory activities be conducted. Thus, counties are required to raise and spend funds for some purposes dictated by state authorities, not by county commissioners. Examples include social services, medical care for poor people, and mental health programs. With state funding tightened in 2003 in order to avoid new state taxes, counties had to absorb more costs, such as providing indigent healthcare and legal representation. Early in 2004, about 165 county commissioners courts adopted resolutions protesting unfunded state mandates and cuts in state funding for Medicaid and the Children's Health Insurance Program (CHIP). In addition, counties are seeking a constitutional amendment to ban unfunded mandates.

County Government Reform

Two basic problems underlie any organizational or power changes in county government: (1) the government structure established in the Texas Constitution and (2) voter apathy toward local governments in general and county government in particular. Media coverage can do much to overcome the latter problem. Only a home-rule amendment to the Texas Constitution giving counties more autonomy can address the other problem. Texas is one of only a few states that do not grant home-rule status to counties. A county government, for instance, cannot pass ordinances unless authorized by the Texas Legislature. In 2001, the 77th Legislature passed a law giving counties some authority to regulate land use, such as new subdivision developments.

Border Counties

There has been unprecedented growth of population and economic development in Texas's counties along and near the Rio Grande over the past few years, chiefly because of the North American Free Trade Agreement (NAFTA). According to the 2000 census, Hidalgo County (Edinburg and McAllen) and Webb County (Laredo) were among the fastest-growing counties in Texas and in the United States.

More than 40 counties in the Mexican border area between El Paso and Brownsville are considered some of the most impoverished places in the country. Among serious issues facing these counties are the poverty rates and the growth of **colonias** (depressed housing settlements that are often without running water or sewage systems). It is estimated that there are currently about 1,800 colonias in the U.S.-Mexican border region. A majority of the colonias are located in Cameron County (Brownsville) and Starr County (Rio Grande City). Colonias, however, are not exclusive to the U.S.-Mexican border region. In 2002, a "colonia-like" district was identified in Colorado County (Alleyton), suggesting that this problem is expanding to other parts of Texas. More than 1 million Texans live under substandard conditions in these settlements.[7]

Some efforts have been made to deal with problems of the colonias. In 1999, for instance, legislation was passed allowing counties to establish planning commissions and giving county officials the authority to conduct inspections of subdivisions. Texas's Office of the Secretary of State created the Texas Plan, which promises running water and wastewater connections for 32 colonias by 2006. Nevertheless, evidence indicates that the program has been scaled back. Some federal funding has been provided to counties with colonias to develop water and sewer services. Moreover, in 2001 the 77th Legislature created The Border Affairs Committee. Among other things the committee initiated a constitutional amendment authorizing general obligation bonds to fund development of roads and streets within colonias. Subsequently, this proposal was approved by Texas voters.[8] After September 11, 2001, the federal government also allocated antiterrorism funds to border counties.

In the 2003 regular legislative session, House Speaker Tom Craddick pushed for a renamed committee, the Border and International Affairs Committee, to focus on this underserved region. Yet deliberation over issues affecting the border area did not receive the level of legislative attention and state funding that it had received in 2001. In fact, because of the anti-tax attitude in the state legislature, advocates for the border counties fear that the area's serious educational and medical needs, among other issues, will continue to be neglected.[9]

Special Districts

Among local governmental units, the least known and least understood are special-district governments. They fall into two basic categories: school districts and noneducation special districts. Created by an act of the legislature or, in some cases, by local ordinance (for example, establishing a public housing authority), a special district usually has one function and serves a specific group of people in a particular geographic area. Special districts must be classified as units of government because they have the following characteristics:

■ An organized existence
■ A governmental character (for example, many exercise taxing power)
■ Substantial independence from other units of government

Public School Districts

Citizen concerns over public education cause local school systems to occupy center stage among special-district governments. More than 1,000 Texas **independent school districts (ISDs)**, created by the legislature, are governed by popularly elected, nonsalaried boards of trustees.

Given the nonsalaried status of the office, why would citizens seek membership on a school board? The answer lies in the many powers and duties conferred on these boards by the Texas Legislature. One of their most important powers is authority to set a district's property tax rate.

Under the share-the-wealth school finance plan established by the Texas Legislature in 1993, taxable property cannot be taxed at a rate higher than $1.50 per $100 of its assessed valuation. (Some districts are exempt from this cap if they had a higher cap prior to 1993.) The cap was designed to provide an equalized funding system. In addition, more than 100 of the state's most wealthy districts must share their tax revenues with poorer districts under this plan. (For further discussion, see Chapter 8, "Bureaucracy, Public Policies, and Finance.") Growing resistance to this fixed cap (already met by more than four hundred school districts),[10] and legal challenges by wealthy property districts, led the Texas Legislature in 2003 to discontinue the existing school finance plan. A special session of the state legislature in April of 2004 failed to authorize a new school finance plan. Nevertheless, Governor Perry insists that such a plan for funding public education must be enacted.

Beginning in 1995, school boards have also been given increased local autonomy. State policy directives, however, are administered by the Texas Education Agency; and it is authorized to take control of school districts that fail to meet state standards. More recently, under President Bush's "No Child Left Behind" policy, school boards are being required to meet national standards in testing students, as well as to provide tutoring and other services. Some federal funding for implementing this policy has been provided. (For a discussion of education policy, see Chapter 8, "Bureaucracy, Public Policies, and Finance.")

Junior or Community College Districts

Another example of a special district is the **junior college or community college district**, which offers two-year academic programs beyond high school, as well as various technical and vocational programs. Each district is governed by a college board with the financial responsibilities of setting property tax rates, issuing bonds (subject to voter approval), and adopting an annual budget. Operated by 50 districts (some with two or more campuses) and three Lamar University units, Texas's 75 public junior or community colleges enroll more than 500,000 students. (See Figure 3.5 for the locations of these districts.)

Unlike fully supported state universities and technical colleges, all public two-year colleges are in part funded by local property taxes, as well as by state appropriations and student tuition and fees. Community colleges also receive some financial support from federal aid and miscellaneous sources, such as private donations to fund scholarships. A recent study commissioned by the Texas Association of Community Colleges found that community colleges stimulate the local economy and are critical to a region's economic development. The study also found that community colleges help the state to improve the health of Texans and to reduce crime, welfare costs, and unemployment.[11]

Points to Ponder

A recent study found that students who attend college increase their total earnings. Specifically, for every full-time year in college, students can expect to earn an additional $3,826 per year while employed. For every college-credit hour completed, average earnings increase $117 per year.

Noneducation Special Districts

As if over 1,200 municipalities, 254 counties, 1,040 school districts, and 50 community/junior college districts were not enough local governments for Texas taxpayers to bear, numerous **noneducation special districts** have been created. Each carries out a special function. Heading the list of these special districts are more than 1,000 water or utility districts and hundreds

Figure 3.5   Texas Community, Technical, and State Colleges

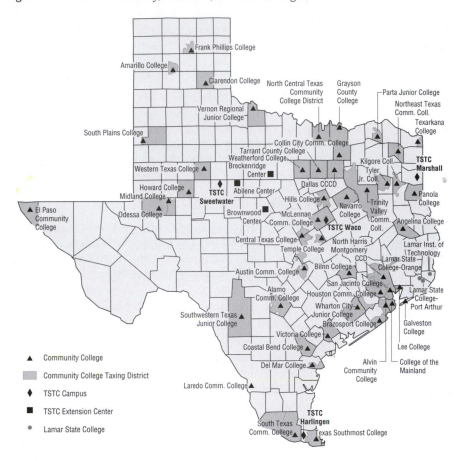

Source: Texas Higher Education Coordinating Board (www.thecb.state.tx.us)

of municipal utility districts, housing authorities, water conservation districts, library districts, and hospital districts. Mass transit authorities provide public transportation for cities in seven metropolitan areas: Austin, Corpus Christi, Dallas, El Paso, Fort Worth, Houston, and San Antonio. (Local voters determine whether a city establishes or joins a mass transit authority.)

Texas actually leads the nation in the number of municipal utility districts. Special districts often overcome heavy restrictions placed on municipalities and counties by the Texas Constitution. The state's greatest concentration is in the Houston area, where more than 400 municipal utility districts (MUDs) operate in Harris county and in adjoining counties.

In addition, special-district governments may raise revenue with property taxes, sales taxes, revenue bonds (subject to voter approval), and various fees, depending on statutory directives. Mass transit authorities, such as

Houston's Metro and Dallas's DART, rely on a l percent sales tax as their principal funding source. In 2003, Houston voters approved a proposition authorizing revenue bonds to extend Houston's light rail transportation system, which began operation in January of 2004.

Metropolitan Areas

More than 80 percent of Texas's people live in 22 metropolitan areas. Ringing large Texas cities are rapidly growing suburban communities with municipal and special-district governments that further fragment local governance. An ever-tightening economic squeeze on residents caused by escalating property taxes underlies many metropolitan problems. Scholars often debate the merits of special-district governments to address regional issues related to transportation, education, pollution, crime, and housing.

How will metropolitan areas be governed in the future? Given legal and political impediments to any comprehensive overhaul of existing governmental structures, quick and easy answers to this question are unrealistic. Entrenched officeholders, particularly county politicians, resist efforts to merge their duties with those of municipal officials. Long-range solutions must begin with an understanding of how and why urban problems transcend existing governmental boundaries.

Councils of Governments

Looking beyond city limits, county lines, and special-district boundaries requires expertise from planners who think regionally. In 1966, the legislature created the first of twenty-four regional planning bodies known as **councils of governments (COGs)** or, in some areas, planning/development commissions/councils. (See Figure 3.6.)

COGs perform regional planning activities and provide services requested by member governments or as directed by federal and state programs or mandates. These councils are not intended to usurp local autonomy of any governmental unit. Governmental membership in a COG is voluntary. Often, because of stringent guidelines for federal grants, COG expertise is required. Through review-and-comment procedures, local officials join with COGs to draft and implement state-funded and federally funded programs. The procedures involve a COG's evaluation of grant proposals submitted by member governments. For example, if a city wants to create an antipollution program or a program to control traffic congestion, a COG would determine how to implement the plan and evaluate its impact on surrounding cities.

Some critics of COGs argue that these regional forums are the first step toward **metro government**, which currently exists in Toronto, Ontario; Miami, Florida; Nashville-Davidson County, Tennessee; and, on a smaller scale, Portland, Oregon. Metro government results in consolidation of existing local governments within an urban area under one umbrella authority.

Figure 3.6 Texas Association of Regional Councils (COGs)

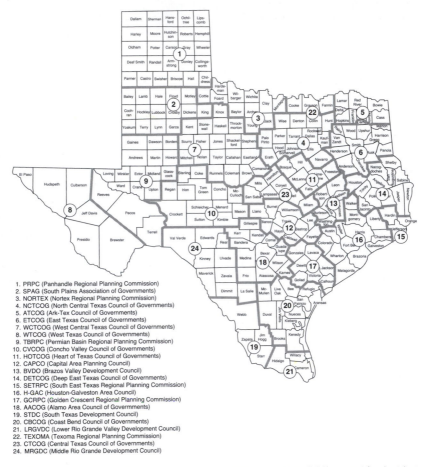

1. PRPC (Panhandle Regional Planning Commission)
2. SPAG (South Plains Association of Governments)
3. NORTEX (Nortex Regional Planning Commission)
4. NCTCOG (North Central Texas Council of Governments)
5. ATCOG (Ark-Tex Council of Governments)
6. ETCOG (East Texas Council of Governments)
7. WCTCOG (West Central Texas Council of Governments)
8. WTCOG (West Texas Council of Governments)
9. TBRPC (Permian Basin Regional Planning Commission)
10. CVCOG (Concho Valley Council of Governments)
11. HOTCOG (Heart of Texas Council of Governments)
12. CAPCO (Capital Area Planning Council)
13. BVDO (Brazos Valley Development Council)
14. DETCOG (Deep East Texas Council of Governments)
15. SETRPC (South East Texas Regional Planning Commission)
16. H-GAC (Houston-Galveston Area Council)
17. GCRPC (Golden Crescent Regional Planning Commission)
18. AACOG (Alamo Area Council of Govermments)
19. STDC (South Texas Development Council)
20. CBCOG (Coast Bend Council of Governments)
21. LRGVDC (Lower Rio Grande Valley Development Council)
22. TEXOMA (Texoma Regional Planning Commission)
23. CTCOG (Central Texas Council of Governments)
24. MRGDC (Middle Rio Grande Development Council)

Source: Office of the Governor, State Planning and Regions (www.governor.state.tx.us/divisions/tracs/planning/view)

Municipal Annexation

Aside from COG services, other means of coping with future development and addressing metropolitan problems tend to produce inadequate, cosmetic solutions. The main approach is municipal annexation.

In an attempt to provide statewide guidelines for home-rule cities grappling with suburban sprawl, the Texas Legislature enacted a municipal annexation law in 1963. This statute allows home-rule cities to annex territory beyond their corporate limits, with the following restrictions:

- Generally, territories annexed during a calendar year may not exceed 10 percent of a city's area as of January 1 and, depending on the city's population, must be within one-half mile to five miles of the city limits.

▪ When the unincorporated area is annexed, the city must provide services (for example, water and sewer) for the area, or the annexed area's residents can petition a state district court for deannexation. (Exceptions are general-law cities that must provide unincorporated areas with water and sewer services before annexation.)

▪ A suburban municipality adjoining the central city may be annexed by the central city, but only after voter approval in both the central and suburban communities.

Once annexed, the city can levy property taxes on these new subdivisions. Controversies usually occur when city councils adopt ordinances annexing unincorporated areas, thus depriving residents in subdivisions of an opportunity to determine whether or not they want to be annexed. To protect property owners from unwanted annexation, legislators passed a state law in 2001 that requires cities to have an annexation plan for three years before annexation can become effective. This law also allows the county to appoint a panel to negotiate a plan to determine the types and extent of services provided for residents in an area to be annexed. The law, however, does not prevent targeted areas from ultimately being annexed. Residents and developers often oppose annexation because it may mean more taxes, more government regulation, and shared responsibility for big-city problems.

Looking Ahead

Practice of local politics in Texas is as disjointed as the organizational structures of grassroots governments that attempt to deliver services. City hall politics, county politics, school board politics, and other special-district politics present a bewildering array of governments to frustrated taxpayers who are already skeptical and often cynical about politics in general. To whom, then, do grassroots residents turn for answers? How can a sense of community and cooperation be developed within Texas's complex urban areas? Answers to these and related questions must begin with more citizen involvement.

Greater freedom for grassroots governments gives rise to hope that Texas's local governments can become more regionally oriented. Increased voter registration, especially in central cities, may unlock doors that block political and economic progress. Aided by single-member districts, newly empowered African Americans and Latinos are changing political agendas.

Citizens must take advantage of opportunities to participate in politics at every level of government—local, state, and national. That first step toward building individual political efficacy (self-empowerment) is essential for democracy to flourish. The next chapter, "The Politics of Elections and Parties," describes how citizens can vote and work through political parties to affect party primaries and general elections.

☆ Chapter Summary ☆

▪ There are two legal classifications of municipalities in Texas: general-law cities and home-rule cities.

▪ Large municipalities have home-rule charters that spell out the structures and powers of individual cities.

▪ Four principal forms of municipal government operate in Texas: strong mayor-council, weak mayor-council, commission, and council-manager.

▪ Nonpartisan state-mandated elections for members of city councils and commissions are key features of Texas politics.

▪ Two basic types of election systems operate in Texas municipalities: at-large systems and single-member district systems.

▪ County governments have organizational structures and powers restricted by the Texas Constitution. Counties provide an array of services, conduct elections, and enforce state laws.

▪ Policymaking is performed by various county officials, but primarily by the commissioners court, which is comprised of the county judge and four elected commissioners.

▪ Multiple special-district governments are separate legal entities providing services that include public schools, community colleges, and mass transit systems.

▪ Metropolitan areas constitute the most formidable challenge for Texans trying to cope with rising property taxes and escalating needs for governmental service.

Key Terms

municipal government	place system
general-law city	term limits
home-rule city	municipal bond
ordinance	economic development
strong mayor-council form	tax reinvestment zone (TRZ)
weak mayor-council form	tax abatement
commission form	tax increment financing (TIF)
council-manager form	county
nonpartisan election	commissioners court
at-large election	county judge
single-member district election	county attorney
cumulative voting	county sheriff

county clerk	independent school district
county tax assessor-collector	(ISD)
county tax appraisal district	junior college or community
county treasurer	college district
county auditor	noneducation special districts
county surveyor	council of governments (COGs)
county bond	metro government
colonia	

 ## Discussion Questions

1. What is the form of municipal government for your hometown?
2. What are the advantages or disadvantages of one form of municipal government over another?
3. What recommendations would you offer to the state legislature to ensure equal funding for students attending Texas's public schools?
4. Give the arguments supporting and opposing term limits. What is your position on this issue?

Internet Resources

Austin city government: **www.ci.austin.tx.us**
Dallas city government: **www.dallascityhall.com**
El Paso city government: **www.ci.el-paso.tx.us/council**
Fort Worth city government: **www.fortworthgov.org**
Houston city government: **www.cityofhouston.gov**
San Antonio city government: **www.ci.sat.tx.us**
State Comptroller's Report on the Border: **www.cpa.state.tx.us/border/**
Texas Association of Counties: **www.county.org**
Texas Association of Regional Councils: **www.txregionalcouncil.org**
Texas Municipal League: **www.tml.org**
Texas State Data Center: **www.txsdc.utsa.edu**

Notes

1. See "Local Government Code," Sections 1.001–140, Chapters 6–8, *Vernon's Texas Codes Annotated* (St. Paul, Minn.: West Group, 1999).
2. See Sonia R. Garcia, Valerie Martinez-Ebers, Irasema Coronado, Sharon Navarro, and Patricia Jaramillo, *Politicas: Latina Trailblazers in*

the Texas Political Arena (University of Texas Press, forthcoming), which provides biographical essays on the first Latina elected public officials in Texas.

3. See Robert Bezdek, David Billeaux, and Juan Carlos Huerta, "Latinos, At-Large Elections, and Political Change: Evidence from the Transition Zone," *Social Science Quarterly* 81 (March 2000): 207–225. (Special issue: "Hispanics in America at 2000," edited by Benigno Aquirre, Robert Lineberry, and Edward Murguia.)

4. William Pack, "Three 3-year Terms on Ballot," *San Antonio Express-News*, 27 February 2004; and Greg Jefferson and William Pack, "3 of 4 Charter Changes Trounced," *San Antonio Express-News*, 16 May 2004.

5. Steve Brewer, "Redrawing of Precincts May Be Easy: Hispanic Could Be Member of Court," *Houston Chronicle*, 21 April 2001. See also Steve Brewer, "Hispanics Draw Lines on County Remapping," *Houston Chronicle*, 22 August 2001; Tom Bower, "County Redistricting May Shift Party Balance," *San Antonio Express-News*, 18 April 2001; and Alex Taylor, "Rise of Republicans Complicates Travis Redistricting Effort," *Austin American-Statesman*, 5 August 2001.

6. Tom Bower, "Toyota Incentives Gets County's OK," *San Antonio Express-News*, 21 May 2003.

7. Alison Gregor and W. Gardner Selby, "Census Finds Border Still Dirt-Poor," *San Antonio Express-News*, 27 May 2002. See also Armando Villafranca, "Not Suitable for Living," *Houston Chronicle*, 5 November 2001.

8. James Pinkerton, "Colonias Eager for Improvements," *Houston Chronicle*, 10 December 2001.

9. Peggy Fikac, "Border Braces for More Pain," *San Antonio Express-News*, 26 May 2003. See also Nancy Flores, "Colonia Effort Dries Up," *San Antonio Express-News,* 5 January 2004.

10. Cindy Horswell, "School Struggles with Tax Caps," *Houston Chronicle*, 22 September 2002. See also Janet Jacobs, "More Districts Maxing Out on Tax," *Austin American-Statesman*, 18 June 2002.

11. Kjell A. Christopherson and M. Henry Robison, "The Socioeconomic Benefits Generated by 50 Community College Districts in Texas: Executive Summary," commissioned by the Texas Association of Community Colleges, CC Benefits, Inc., 2002.

SELECTED READING

★
_____

"Extreme" Term Limits—San Antonio Style

Alexander E. Briseno*

Limiting the number of terms an elected official can serve in office is not an uncommon practice. In San Antonio however, the city charter's provision for term limits is among the most restrictive in the country and can be considered "extreme." This provision's impact on governance bears review after more than ten years of application.

Political Climate

To understand what instigated term limits in San Antonio, it is necessary to review the city's political environment in the late 1980s and early 1990s. This was a challenging period for San Antonio as well as most cities in Texas. The economy was suffering: banking, construction, and oil and gas industries were in disarray; unemployment rates were increasing; and real estate property values were decreasing. The impact on the city of San Antonio was daunting due to increasing demands for services while facing declining or stagnant revenues. City officials responded by adopting "bad news, bad news" budgets that reduced service levels while raising the property tax rate high enough to recover lost revenues due to lower property values and still generate a net revenue increase.

A number of other controversial issues (e.g., labor negotiations, a perceived doomed stadium, and a surface water project) muddied the political landscape and deepened divisions in the ongoing community debate. Ultimately, a taxpayers "watchdog" group organized petition drives that successfully garnered enough signatures to force elections in 1990 and 1991 on three major issues, including an amendment to the city charter limiting the terms for members of the city council.

The term limits provision allows an individual to be elected twice to the office of mayor or council member during his or her lifetime and then be prohibited from running for election again. As a result, 39 council members and four mayors served on San Antonio's 11-seat governing body between 1991 and 2001. By comparison, during the prior 10 years, 15 council members and 2 mayors occupied those same seats. This turnover has had a a significant effect on the community's governance.

_____

*"Extreme Term Limits—San Antonio Style" by Alexander E. Briseno. Reprinted by permission of Alexander E. Briseno. Alexander Briseno was San Antonio's city manager for almost 11 years until retiring in March of 2001. He currently serves as an appointed professor of Public Service in Residence at St. Mary's University, San Antonio, and works as a municipal consultant.

City Council Service
After Term Limits

Newly elected council members come into office from diverse backgrounds, with varying levels of life experience, and sometimes with a limited understanding of municipal government. Each, wittingly or unwittingly, evolves through progressive phases of learning, adapting, executing, campaigning, and completing— sometimes on an ongoing basis.

Local government in San Antonio is a complicated business. Within three months of taking office, council members are presented with a proposed consolidated annual budget of up to $1.5 billion that finances a full array of municipal services for almost 1.2 million residents. These services are delivered by more than 12,000 employees on a 24/7 basis. The city government must manage an array of basic city services (e.g., public safety), operate enterprises (e.g., garbage collection, airports, and convention facilities), and enhance the quality of life and well-being of the residents (e.g., libraries, parks, and social services). The city government is also actively engaged in stimulating economic activity and investment as well as the revitalization of decaying neighborhoods. To accomplish this, a strong revenue stream must be managed and financed by a complex assortment of taxes, fees, fines, rents, contracts, and other charges for services. In this context, new council members are responsible for making policy decisions and must learn as much as possible about the intricacies of governance to assure high-quality, responsive, and sufficient municipal services. This learning process is best achieved over time as issues arise and are addressed. At least one to two years of experience is necessary to be minimally effective.

A new council member must also adapt to conducting business in a different and very public environment. Getting to know the other 10 members of the council, their strengths and weaknesses, goals and priorities, and personalities is critical to being able to forge coalitions that result in success. Familiarity with procedures for initiating policy direction, accounting for expenses, complying with ethics and election laws, contracting, and countless other activities is also important. Moreover, city business must be conducted in the light of public scrutiny actively monitored by multiple media sources; neighborhood, community, and business groups; and opponents and supporters alike. This adaptation phase is rarely concluded since the variables are dynamic and evolutionary.

During their first term, council members must then execute or "deliver" to set the stage for reelection. Sometimes uninformed campaign rhetoric of expanded services, more efficiency, and "no increased taxes" demands adherence, although it is often difficult to achieve in reality. As a consequence of two-year terms, "making an impact" within six to 18 months is highly desirable. Frequently, elections based on a "change" agenda create conflict when implementation attempts are initiated. Intensive and sometimes frustrating, the execution phase is a prerequisite to a reelection campaign.

A year to 18 months after taking office, council members should be gearing up for the next election: organizing supporters, discouraging opponents, and soliciting campaign contributions. Then they must wage a three- to six-month reelection campaign with countless meetings, rallies, and speeches. Finally, council members must achieve all this while handling the persistent responsibilities of city business and while still learning, adapting, and executing. The campaign phase, if successful, completes the first two years in office and leads to a new term.

The final two years in office are punctuated by endeavors to complete the initiatives undertaken in the first term or promised during the campaign. Returning council members are now "veterans" who guide the recently elected freshmen and serve in leadership capacities on city council committees. With two opportunities for reviewing and approving the city budget and its implicit work program under their belt, these veterans are more effective in addressing pressing municipal issues and executing their commitments. However, this effectiveness is sometimes short-lived: within a year their attention becomes focused on who will succeed them, and they become potentially "lame ducks" and unaccountable to the voters.

This is not the case if they are ambitiously seeking higher office, such as the mayor's seat or state and county positions. Nevertheless, their effectiveness is frequently diminished by election calendars that may force them to resign their council seats as early as six months into their second term. Therefore, "extreme" term limits can produce officeholders who only serve as little as 30 months of their potential 48-month tenure. Their successors are appointed by the city council, creating a different breed of unelected new council member. Indeed, among the 39 San Antonio city council members who served from 1991 to 2001, eight were first appointed to the office, two of whom were never elected.

This final completion phase, marked by lameduck stature or pursuit of higher office, caps the progression, with varying levels of success, through the other phases of learning, adapting, executing, and campaigning. Together these phases reflect the overall context for city council service under the term limits provision.

Impact on Governance

But what are the results? What has been the impact of term limits on governance in San Antonio? Since 1991, it appears the community has experienced short-term, disjointed policy direction with limited overall vision. In addition, sources of influence have often shifted, and community leadership development has been challenged.

Continuity in completing multi-year phased projects or policy initiatives has been diminished. Each two-year council cycle witnesses from four to as many as eight council members elected for the first time. Bound by the pressure to make their own mark in order to get reelected, they infrequently focus on continuing the work or projects of their predecessors, sometimes leaving the investment in engineering designs and program plans on the shelf. Programs and projects that render short-term, positive, or visible results are pushed to the top of the list.

As policy priorities shift, long-term planning efforts drag on for years and can best be completed by advocate council members who may rise to the mayor's office. For example, the comprehensive revision of the Master Plan, a policy guide for community growth and development that was raised as an issue in the mayoral campaign of 1991, was not effectively completed until the approval of the rewrite of the Unified Development Code in 2001. Annual goal-setting sessions have generated top-echelon priorities in many diverse areas, such as youth programs, international trade, sidewalks, crime prevention, and infrastructure maintenance. Although new perspectives and ideas can be beneficial, these periodic shifts in municipal priorities drain resources and reduce their effectiveness in making a lasting impact with comprehensive strategies. This myopic, truncated vision through a four-year window ultimately can hamper San Antonio's ability to reach its potential for a better quality of life for all of its residents.

Term limits has generated a policy arena often filled with uncertainty and struggles for power and influence. Some observers see the power shifting to the bureaucracy, augmented by the strength of continuity and institutional knowledge and resistant to change. However, this view has nurtured skepticism among incoming elected officials that borders on mistrust and detonates teambuilding between policymakers and the city employees who execute their policies. Indeed, council members are often leery of municipal professionals' recommendations, forcing staff personnel to invest significant time and energy revalidating themselves every two years. Burdened by this lack of confidence in staff input, new council members are frequently vulnerable to the counsel of others seeking influence on policy decisions. Campaign contributors, contractors, special-interest groups, and lobbyists gain audiences and input that, although predictable in a political environment and sometimes valid, may outweigh the judgment of the city's own professional cadre and can result in policy decisions flavored by private gain at the expense of the public good.

Moreover, the policy arena is further scrambled as term-limited council members vie for an edge in the anticipated competition for the mayor's chair, the only option for continued municipal elected service after two terms. Policy agendas and supportive coalitions are juggled for months prior to the election as potential candidates poise themselves for the mayor's race. Conflicts lace policy decisions as campaign positions are staked out, and frequently policy decisions are postponed or hurried to satisfy political strategies. Indeed, the turmoil fueled by San Antonio's "extreme" term limits appears to have a questionable cumulative impact on governance in the community.

The inherent turnover mobilized by the term limits provision has also challenged the community's ability to renew its leadership talent pool. This continuous demand for new elected official talent has been aggravated by minuscule council pay ($20 per meeting) and demanding mayoral and council district responsibilities. Experienced midcareer individuals with family obligations are often reluctant to offer their candidacy for public service in this environment. Consequently, leadership options are sometimes inordinately skewed toward inexperienced, yet well-meaning and enthusiastic elected officials who are restricted from fully realizing their leadership potential before term limits force them out of office. Council members are elected, go through a learning process in the context of the conditions outlined above, become more effective, and then move out of office to other endeavors before the community can maximize the value of their newly developed expertise. The cycle is then repeated, further depleting the reservoir of willing and capable potential leaders. Outgoing council members interested in further elected public service are then thrust into the competition for county or state legislative seats, further complicating the governance scenario at other levels. Ultimately, this guaranteed turnover of leadership may be detrimental to the community.

Conclusion

Indeed, with more than 10 years of application, the current city charter provision limiting elected service in the positions of mayor and council member to two 2-year terms—with a subsequent lifetime prohibition of running for these offices—has had a significant impact on San Antonio's governance. It has fostered a challenging maze to maneuver in order for elected officials to become effective in their already difficult policy making role for cities. The community's vision has frequently narrowed to immediate fixes at the expense of nurturing comprehensive, long-term strategies for San Antonio's future. Struggles for power and influence often mark the decision-making process, sometimes minimizing the public good. Finally, the community's leadership talent pool is confronted with the constant need for reinvigoration.

Although term limits are common in government and periodic replacement of entrenched incumbents can inject fresh ideas into policy development, San Antonio's "extreme" term limits are frequently counterproductive. Given the electorate's apparent support for limiting elected service, a longer period of up to eight years, with the potential to return after an intermittent absence, may prove more effective. Indeed, in the spring of 2004, San Antonio voters overwhelmingly rejected a proposed charter amendment extending term limits to three 3-year terms (for a total of nine years) with the option to serve again after sitting out one term. Unfortunately, maintaining the status quo may only serve to jeopardize San Antonio's future!

*T*he fundamental principle on which every representative democracy is based is participation in the political process by the people. Yet, even as the right to vote in the twentieth century was extended to almost every citizen 18 years of age or older, participation declined throughout the century's final decades and into the twenty-first century. Citizen participation through elections and political parties, and the impact of that participation, are the subjects of this chapter. Ben Sargent's cartoon notes that even self-proclaimed patriots may not take time to vote.

Voting

The U.S. Supreme Court has declared the right to vote to be the "preservative" of all other rights.[1] For most Texans, voting is their principal political activity. For many, it is their only exercise in practicing Texas politics. Casting a ballot brings individuals and their government together for a moment and reminds people anew that they are part of a political system. We begin the study of the electoral process in the Lone Star State by focusing on voters and voting.

Obstacles to Voting

The right to vote has not always been as widespread in the United States as it is today. **Universal suffrage**, by which almost all citizens 18 years of age and older can vote, did not become a reality in Texas until the mid-1960s. Although most devices to prevent people from voting have been abolished, their legacy remains.

Adopted after the Civil War (1861–1865), the Fourteenth and Fifteenth Amendments to the U.S. Constitution were intended to prevent denial of the right to vote due to race. But for the next 100 years, African American citizens in Texas and other states of the former Confederacy, as well as many Latinos, were prevented from voting by one barrier after another—legal or otherwise. For example, the white-robed Ku Klux Klan and other lawless groups used terrorist tactics to keep African Americans from voting. Most of the Klan's activities were focused in northeast Texas. At least 20 counties, extending from Houston north to the Red River, experienced some form of Klan terror.[2]

Literacy Tests   Beginning in the 1870s, as a means to prevent minorities from voting, some counties in Texas began requiring prospective voters to take a screening test that conditioned voter registration on a person's literacy. Texans who could not pass these **literacy tests** were prohibited from registering. Other counties required constitutional-interpretation or citizenship-knowledge tests to deny voting rights. These tests usually consisted of difficult and abstract questions concerning a person's knowledge of the U.S. Constitution or understanding of issues supposedly related to citizenship. In no way, however, did these questions measure a citizen's ability to cast an informed vote.

Grandfather Clause Another device enacted by southern states to deny suffrage to minorities was the **grandfather clause**. It provided that persons who could exercise the right to vote prior to 1866 or 1867, or their descendants, would be exempt from educational, property, or tax requirements for voting. Because African Americans had not been allowed to vote prior to the adoption of the Fifteenth Amendment in 1870, grandfather clauses were used along with literacy tests to prevent African Americans from voting while assuring this right to many impoverished and illiterate whites. The United States Supreme Court decision in *Guinn* v. *United States* (1915) declared the grandfather clause unconstitutional because it violated equal voting rights guaranteed by the Fifteenth Amendment.

Poll Tax Beginning in 1902, Texas required that citizens pay a special tax, called the **poll tax**, to become eligible to vote. The cost was $1.75 ($1.50, plus $.25 that was optional with each county). For the next 62 years, many Texans—especially low-income persons, including disproportionately large numbers of African Americans and Mexican Americans—frequently failed to pay their poll tax during the designated four-month period from October 1 to January 31. This, in turn, disqualified them from voting during the following 12 months in party primaries and in any general or special election. As a result, African American voter participation declined from approximately 100,000 in the 1890s to about 5,000 in 1906. With ratification of the Twenty-Fourth Amendment to the U.S. Constitution in January 1964, the poll tax was abolished as a prerequisite for voting in national elections. Then, in *Harper* v. *Virginia State Board of Elections* (1966), the U.S. Supreme Court invalidated all state laws that made payment of a poll tax a prerequisite for voting in state elections.

All-White Primaries The so-called **white primary**, a product of political and legal maneuvering within the southern states, was designed to deny African Americans and some Latinos access to the Democratic primary.[3] Following Reconstruction, Texas, like most of the South, was predominately a one-party (Democratic) state. Between 1876 and 1926, the Republican Party held only one statewide primary in Texas. By contrast, the Democratic primary was the main election in every even-numbered year.

   White Democrats nominated white candidates, who almost always won the general elections. The U.S. Supreme Court had long held that the Fourteenth and Fifteenth Amendments, as well as successive civil rights laws, provided protection against public acts of discrimination, but not against private acts. In 1923, the Texas Legislature passed a law explicitly prohibiting African Americans from voting in Democratic primaries. When the U.S. Supreme Court declared this law unconstitutional, the legislature enacted another law giving the executive committee of each state party the power to decide who could participate in its primaries. The State Democratic Executive Committee immediately adopted a resolution that allowed only whites to vote in Democratic primaries. This practice lasted from 1923 to 1944, when the U.S. Supreme Court declared it unconstitutional in *Smith* v. *Allwright*.[4]

Racial Gerrymandering   Gerrymandering is the practice of manipulating legislative district lines to underrepresent persons of a political party or group. "Packing" black voters into a given district or "cracking" them to make black voters a minority in all districts both illustrate **racial gerrymandering**. Today this term is associated with the creation of "majority-minority" districts that allow more racial minorities to elect candidates of their choice. In *Shaw* v. *Reno* (1993), the U.S. Supreme Court condemned two extremely odd-shaped, black-majority districts in North Carolina. (For more on gerrymandering in Texas, see the Selected Reading at the end of the chapter titled "The Legislature.")

Diluting Minority Votes   Creating **at-large majority districts** (each electing two or more representatives) can prevent an area with a significant minority population from electing a representative of its choice. Under this scenario, the votes of a minority group can be diluted when combined with the votes of a majority group, but federal courts have declared this practice unconstitutional where representation of ethnic or racial minorities is diminished.[5]

Democratization of the Ballot

In America, successive waves of democratization have removed obstacles to voting. To promote and protect voting nationwide, in the later half of the twentieth century the U.S. Congress enacted important voting rights laws.

Federal Voting Rights Legislation   The Voting Rights Act of 1965 expanded the electorate and encouraged voting. As amended in later years, this law (together with federal court rulings):

- Abolishes use of all literacy tests in voter registrations
- Prohibits residency requirements of more than 30 days for voting in presidential elections
- Requires states to provide some form of absentee or early voting
- Allows individuals (as well as the U.S. Department of Justice) to sue in federal court to request that voting examiners be sent to a particular area

The Voting Rights Act of 1975 also established new federal policies designed to increase voter turnout among Native Americans and Latinos. For example, states with a significant percentage of Spanish-speaking residents, such as Texas, must use bilingual election materials.

In 1993, Congress passed the National Voter Registration Act, or **motor voter law**, which simplified voter registration by permitting registration by mail, or at welfare, disability assistance, and motor vehicle licensing agencies or at military recruitment centers. The new procedures allow persons to register to vote when they apply for, or renew, drivers' licenses or visit a public assistance office. Texas citizens can also apply for voter registration or to update their voter registration data by mail, using an appropriate state or federal voter registration form. In addition to registration by mail, motor vehicles offices and voter registration agencies are required to provide voter registration services to applicants. If citizens believe their voting rights have been violated in any way, federal administrative and judicial agencies such as the U.S. Department of Justice are available for assistance.

Amendments to the U.S. Constitution have also expanded the American electorate. The Fifteenth Amendment prohibits the denial of voting rights because of race; the Nineteenth Amendment precludes denial of suffrage on the basis of gender; the Twenty-Fourth Amendment prohibits states from requiring payment of a poll tax or any other tax as a condition for voting; and the Twenty-Sixth Amendment forbids setting the minimum voting age above 18 years.

In Texas, as in other states, determining voting procedures is essentially a state responsibility. All election laws currently in effect in the Lone Star State are compiled into one body of law, the **Texas Election Code**.[6] In administering this legal code, however, state and party officials must protect the voting rights guaranteed by federal law.

Qualifications for Voting   To be eligible to vote in Texas, a person must meet the following qualifications:

- Be a native-born or naturalized citizen of the United States
- Be at least 18 years of age on election day
- Be a resident of the state and county for at least 30 days immediately preceding election day
- Be a resident of the area covered by the election on election day
- Be a registered voter for at least 30 days immediately preceding election day
- Not be a convicted felon (unless sentence, probation, and parole are completed)
- Not be declared mentally incompetent by a court of law[7]

Most adults who live in Texas meet the first four qualifications for voting, but registration is required before a person can vote. Anyone serving a jail sentence as a result of a misdemeanor conviction or not finally convicted of a felony is not disqualified from voting. The Texas Constitution, however, bars from voting anyone who is incarcerated, on parole, or on probation as a result of a felony conviction and anyone who is "mentally incompetent as determined by a court." A convicted felon may vote immediately after completing a sentence or following a full pardon. (For examples of misdemeanors and felonies, see Table 9.2 in the chapter "Laws, Courts, and Justice.)

Voter registration is intended to determine in advance whether prospective voters meet all the qualifications prescribed by law. Most states, including Texas, use a permanent registration system. Under this plan, voters register once and remain registered unless they change their mailing address and fail to notify the voting registrar within three years or lose their eligibility to register in some other way. Because the requirement of voter registration may deter voting, the Texas Election Code provides a number of voter registration centers in addition to those sites authorized by Congress under the motor voter law. Texans may also register at local marriage license offices, in public high schools, with any volunteer deputy registrar, or in person at the office of the county voting registrar. Some counties have officials whose sole responsibility is election administration. In other counties, it is one of many responsibilities of the tax assessor-collector or (if designated by the county commissioners court) the county clerk. In 2004, less than 14 percent of the counties in Texas employed a full-time **elections administrator**.

Between November 1 and November 15 of each odd-numbered year, the registrar mails a registration certificate effective for the succeeding two voting years to every registered voter in the county. Postal authorities may not forward a certificate mailed to the address indicated on the voter's application form if the applicant has moved to another address; instead, the certificate must be returned to the registrar. This enables the county voting registrar to maintain an accurate list of names and mailing addresses of persons to whom voting certificates have been issued. Registration files are open for public inspection in the voting registrar's office, and a statewide registration file is available in Austin at the Elections Division of the Office of the Secretary of State.

The color of voter registration certificates mailed to eligible voters in November of odd-numbered years differs from the color of the cards sent two years earlier. The Office of the Secretary of State determines the color of voter registration certificates. Although voter registration certificates are issued after a person registers to vote, one can legally cast a vote without a certificate by providing some form of identification (such as a driver's license) and signing an affidavit of registration at the polls.

Two Trends in the Suffrage   From our overview of suffrage in Texas, two trends emerge. First, voting rights have steadily expanded to include virtually all persons, of both sexes, who are 18 years of age or older. Second, there has been a movement toward uniformity of voting policies among the 50 states. In fact, however, democratization of the ballot has been pressed on the states largely by the U.S. Congress, by federal judges, and by presidents who have enforced voting laws and judicial orders.

Now that nearly all legal barriers to the ballot have been swept away, the road to the voting booth seems clear for rich and poor alike, for historical minority groups as well as for the majority, and for individuals of all races, colors, and creeds. But universal suffrage has not resulted in a corresponding increase in voter turnout, either nationally or in Texas.

Voter turnout is the percentage of the voting-age population casting ballots. In Texas, turnout is higher in presidential elections than in nonpresidential elections. Although this pattern reflects the national trend, electoral turnout in Texas tends to be significantly lower than in the nation as a whole. But with Governor George W. Bush running for president in the 2000 election, Texas actually ranked above the national average in voter turnout at 44.3 percent. By contrast, the 2002 nonpresidential election yielded a 29.3 percent turnout in Texas. Few citizens believe their vote will determine an election outcome, but some races have actually been won by only a single vote. In local elections at the city or school district level, a turnout of 20 percent is relatively high. Among the five largest cities conducting city council elections in Texas in 2004, none yielded a turnout greater than 15 percent. These figures illustrate one of the greatest ironies in politics: that people are less likely to participate at the level of government in which they can potentially have the greatest influence.

Low citizen participation in elections has been attributed to the influence of pollsters and media consultants, voter fatigue resulting from too many elections, negative campaigning by candidates, lack of information about candidates and issues, and feelings of isolation from government. Members of Texas's 77th Legislature in 2001 determined that low voter turnout was caused by governmental entities holding too many elections. To cure "turnout burnout," they passed a bill that limits elections to four uniform election dates each year.[8] However, runoff elections, local option elections under the Alcoholic Beverage Code, bond or tax levy elections for school or college districts, emergency elections, elections to fill vacancies in the two chambers of the Texas Legislature and Texas delegation to the U.S. House of Representatives, recall elections, and other elections that are specifically exempted by statute can be held on non-uniform dates.[9]

People decide to vote or not to vote in the same way they make most other decisions: on the basis of anticipated consequences. A strong impulse to vote may stem from peer pressure, a perception of one's own self-interest, or a sense of duty toward one's country, state, local community, political party, or interest group. People also make personal decisions about whether to vote on the basis of cost measured in time, money, experience, information, job, and other resources.

Cultural, socioeconomic, and racial factors also contribute to the low voter turnout in the Lone Star State. As identified in Chapter 1, elements of Texas's political culture place little emphasis on the importance of voting.

Of all the socioeconomic influences on voting, education is by far the strongest. Statistics clearly indicate that as educational level rises, people are more likely to vote, assuming all other socioeconomic factors remain constant. Educated people usually have more income and leisure time for voting; moreover, education enhances one's ability to learn about political parties, candidates, and issues.

Income strongly affects voter turnout. Texas ranks sixth in the nation in the percentage of its population living in poverty. People of lower income often lack access to the polls, information about the candidates, or opportunities to learn about the system. Income levels and their impact on electoral turnout can be seen in the 2002 general election. For example, Starr County, with a median household income of $16,504, had a turnout of less than 23 percent of its registered voters. By contrast, Collin County, with a median income of $70,835, experienced a turnout of more than 40 percent of its registered voters.

Although far less important than education, gender and age also affect voting behavior. In the United States, women are slightly more likely to vote than men. Young people (ages 18–25) have the lowest voter turnout of any age group. The highest voter turnout is among middle-aged Americans (ages 40–64). Race and ethnicity also influence voting behavior. The turnout rate for African Americans is still substantially below that for Anglos. African Americans tend to be younger, less educated, and poorer than Anglos. Although Latino voter turnout rates in Texas are slightly below the state average in primaries and general elections, findings by scholars indicate that the gap is narrowing. Still, African Americans and Latinos in Texas vote at a rate that is approximately 65 percent of the state average.

Voting Early: In Person and by Mail   Opportunities to vote early in Texas are limited to in-person **early voting**, voting by mail, facsimile machine voting (for military personnel and their dependents in combat zones), and electronic voting for astronauts on space flights. Texas law allows voters to vote "early"—that is, during a 17-day period preceding a scheduled election or first primary and for 10 days preceding a runoff primary. Early voting ends, however, four days prior to any election or primary. In less-populated rural counties, early voting is done at the courthouse; in more populous urban areas, the county clerk's office accommodates voters by maintaining branch offices for early voting. Polling places are generally open for early voting on weekdays during the regular business hours of the official responsible for conducting the election. If requested by 15 registered voters within the county, polling places must also be opened on Saturday or Sunday.

Registered voters who qualify may vote by mail during an early voting period. Voting by mail has been available to elderly Texans and those with physical disabilities for decades. Today, anyone meeting the following qualifications can vote by mail-in ballot:

- Will not be in his or her county of residence during the entire early voting period and on election day
- Is at least 65
- Is or will be physically disabled on election day, including those who expect to be confined for childbirth on election day
- Is in jail (but not a convicted felon) during the early voting period and on election day
- Is in the military or a dependent of military personnel and has resided in Texas[10]

Since early voting was first used in 1998, the percentage of early voters has consistently been about 20 percent in the general elections. Although such measures make voting easier, at least one study indicates that states with longer early voting periods have experienced a greater decline in voter turnout than states with more restrictive election laws.[11]

POINT
COUNTERPOINT

Online Voting as a Means to Increase Voter Turnout[12]

ISSUE

National voter turnout has decreased from 63 percent of the voting-age population in 1960 to approximately 51 percent in 2000. Declining participation at the polls increasingly frustrates public officials and interest groups. A proposal to increase voter turnout that is gaining support in many circles is online voting, in which voters will be able to cast ballots from the comfort of their own homes or offices. Such proposals include voting from home via secure e-mail, from home or another location through a Web link to the ballot, and from a traditional polling place with Internet access.

Arguments For Online Voting

1. *Convenience will increase turnout.* If people could vote from their home computers, inclement weather or long lines at the polls would not deter people from voting. Additionally, online voting at home would improve access dramatically for disabled voters. It also has the potential to attract many more voters in the 18-to-34 age group, those most likely to use technology.
2. *More informed electorate.* The Internet is the fastest and easiest way for people to gain access to information about candidates and their campaigns. The Internet strengthens representative government by bringing candidates closer to the voters than could a 30-second television commercial and would provide more information about candidates and their policy positions.
3. *Quickest, cheapest, and most efficient way to administer elections.* Online voting would reduce the number of geographic polling places and consolidate the counting process. Currently, Texas's decentralized election system involves more than 3,200 separate local jurisdictions, each of which can use its own voting system. Ninety counties still use paper ballots that are counted by hand. Adopting a uniform system of online voting will make tabulation more efficient.

Arguments Against Online Voting

1. *Would create a disadvantage for those without access to technology.* The "digital divide" — the gap between technological haves and have-nots — could widen and online voting could discourage from voting people who do not have access to a computer or who are not computer-savvy. It discriminates against minority and low-income voters, who are not as likely to have access to the Internet.
2. *Integrity of election will be lost.* Security breaches and fraud could threaten the integrity of elections conducted online. Election officials must determine that each person trying to vote is eligible, that each person gets only one vote and that the vote is secret, and that tabulation is accurate. Online voting systems would require each voter to have a digital signature. Such technology is expensive, and questions about funding need to be addressed. Texas now has more than 11 million registered voters, each of whom would need a digital signature.

(continued on next page)

POINT

COUNTERPOINT

3. *Could not prevent unlawful electioneering*. Texas has laws prohibiting election-eering within a certain distance of a polling place. Voters may take voting material but not campaign material into a polling place. Someone could vote online while viewing a candidate's web site.

   Online voting would not ensure a higher turnout. Voter turnout has decreased even with such initiatives as The National Voter Registration Act of 1993 and the changes in early voting requirements. There is no assurance that online voting would increase turnout. Also, some believe that requiring at least some minimal effort to vote helps ensure that those voting will have made some attempt to cast an informed ballot.

Source: Abridged and adapted from Rita Barr, "Voting on the Internet: Promise and Problems," *Interim News* 76-3 (Austin: House Research Organization, Texas House of Representatives, 16 March 2000):1–5.

Electoral Politics

The electoral process includes the nomination and election of candidates through primary, general, and special elections. Administering these elections is the responsibility of party, state, and county officials.

Primaries

Political parties conduct **primary elections** to select their nominees for public office. Among the states, party primaries are held every two years. Presidential primaries occur every four years and provide a means for Democrats and Republicans to select delegates to their parties' national conventions, where candidates for president and vice president are nominated. Other primaries occur every two years, when party members go to the polls to choose candidates for the U.S. Congress and for many state, district, and county offices.

Development of Direct Primaries   A unique product of American political ingenuity, the **direct primary** was designed to provide a nominating method that would avoid domination by party bosses and allow wider participation by party members. This form of nomination permits party members to choose their candidates directly at the polls. For each office (except president and vice president of the United States and some local officials), party members select by popular vote the person they wish to be their party's candidate in the **general election**, in which candidates of all parties compete. An absolute majority of the vote (more than 50 percent) is required for nomination. When Texas's first primary fails to produce such a majority, a **runoff primary** is held a month after the first primary to allow party members to choose a candidate from the first primary's top two vote-getters.

Four basic forms of the direct primary have evolved in America. Most states use some form of **closed primary**, which requires voters to declare a party affiliation when registering to vote. They must show party identification when voting in a primary election and can only vote in the party primary for which they are registered. Other states use an **open primary**, which does not require party identification of voters. At the polls, voters can choose a ballot for any party, regardless of their party affiliation.

A few states use a **nonpartisan blanket primary**. In this type of primary, all voters receive the same ballot, on which is printed the names of all political party nominees and **independent candidates**. Louisiana conducts a form of blanket primary, commonly referred to as a **jungle primary**. Here, there are no party primaries. Candidates from all parties run in a single election, which is actually the general election. If a candidate receives more than 50 percent of the vote, he or she is declared the winner. If no candidate receives more than 50 percent, the names of the top two vote-getters appear on the general election ballot 30 days later. This was the case with the election of Governor Kathleen Babineaux Blanco, a Democrat who defeated Republican Bobby Jindal in 2003.

A criticism of the open, blanket, and jungle primaries is that they give voters of one party an opportunity to sabotage the primary election of another party. This can occur when voters who normally affiliate with one party try to nominate a "fringe" candidate from the other with little chance of victory in the general election. This is especially true with the blanket and jungle primaries. Open primaries at least restrict voters to voting for candidates of the same party, but blanket and jungle primaries allow voters to choose any candidate from any party for any office.

Texas Primaries   Texas political parties have had the opportunity to conduct primary elections since the enactment of the Terrell Election Law of 1905. Prior to this act, various practices had been used to select a party's nominees for public office. The Texas Democratic Party has held primaries since 1905. The Republican Party did not begin conducting primary elections until 1926. In 1996, for the first time in Texas history, the Republican Party held a primary election in all 254 counties of the state.

In Texas, bonds of party loyalty loosen at general election time. Beginning in the early 1950s, it became common practice in Texas for persons to participate in the primaries of the Democratic Party and then legally cross over to vote for Republican candidates in the general election. **Crossover voting** is evidence of a long-term trend toward voter independence of traditional party ties. Historically, Texas Republicans were more likely to engage in crossover voting. As the number of Republican candidates increased, the number of crossover Republican voters correspondingly declined. Today, Democrats in Republican-dominated counties (such as Collin, Denton, Midland, Montgomery, and Williamson) are likely to participate in crossover voting.

The Texas Election Code requires voters to identify their party affiliation at the time of voting, making Texas a combination of a closed primary

⭐ **How Do We Compare . . . in Types of Primaries?**

Most Populous U.S.States	Primary Type	U.S. States Bordering Texas	Primary Type
California	Closed	Arkansas	Open
Florida	Closed	Louisiana	Jungle
New York	Closed	New Mexico	Closed
Texas	**Combination (open/closed)**	Oklahoma	Closed

state and an open primary state. Voter registration certificates are stamped with the party name when voters participate in a primary. Qualified voters may vote in the primary of any party, so long as they have not already voted in another party's primary or convention in the same year. The primary ballot contains the following restriction: "I am a Democrat (Republican) and understand that I am ineligible to vote or participate in another political party's primary election or convention during this voting year."[13] Violation of a party pledge is a misdemeanor offense punishable by a fine of $500.

Administering Primaries In most states, political parties sponsor and administer their own primaries. The Texas Election Code allocates this responsibility to each political party's county executive committee. Political parties whose gubernatorial candidate received 20 percent or more of the vote in the preceding general election must nominate all of their candidates in direct primaries conducted in even-numbered years. In 2004, the first primaries and runoff (second) primaries were held on the second Tuesdays in March and April, respectively. But 20 other states conducted their presidential primaries earlier than Texas. As a result, by the date of Texas's first Republican and Democratic Party primaries (9 March), President George W. Bush and U.S. senator John Kerry were already their party's de facto nominees for president.

A law passed by the 78th Texas Legislature requires that Texas's first and runoff primaries in 2006 and subsequent years will be conducted a week earlier—on the first Tuesdays of March and April. But some Texans argue that too much time elapses between March primaries and the November general elections. They explain that the electorate has little interest in early primaries and has lost all interest by November.

Individuals who want to run in a direct primary for their party's nomination for a multicounty district office or a statewide office must file the necessary papers with their party's state chair. That official certifies the names of these persons to each county chair in counties in which the election is administered. Prospective candidates desiring to have their names placed on the primary ballot for a county or precinct office must file with the county chair of their party. County executive committees for each political party supervise the printing of primary ballots. If the parties conduct a joint primary, the county clerk administers the election, unless the county has an elections administrator. If each party conducts its own primaries, county chairs arrange for voting equipment and polling places in the precincts. With the approval of the county executive committee, the county chair obtains supplies and appoints a presiding judge of elections in each precinct. Together with the state executive committee, the county executive committee determines the order of names of candidates on the ballot and **canvasses** (that is, confirms and certifies) the vote tally for each candidate.

Financing Primaries   Major expenses for administering party primaries include renting facilities for polls (the places where voting is conducted), printing ballots and other election materials, and paying election judges and clerks. In recent years, approximately 30 percent of the cost of holding Texas primaries has come from filing fees paid by candidates. For example, candidates for the office of U.S. senator pay $4,000, and candidates for governor and all other statewide offices pay $3,000. Candidates for the Texas Senate and the Texas House of Representatives pay $1,000 and $600, respectively.[14]

In lieu of paying a fee, a candidate may file a nominating petition containing a specified number of signatures of people eligible to vote for the office for which that candidate is running. A candidate for statewide office must obtain 5,000 signatures. Candidates for district, county, or precinct office, and for offices of other political subdivisions, must obtain either 500 signatures or the equivalent of 2 percent of the area's votes for all candidates for governor in the last general election, whichever is less. Although second (or runoff) primaries are usually less expensive, the average expenditure per voter is greater because voter turnout tends to be lower. In 2004, the cost of primaries was over $15 million and exceeded state appropriations. To save money, the Texas secretary of state issued a memo to all county chairs, suggesting cost-saving measures such as consolidating polling locations and conducting jointly administered primary elections.

Elections

A clear distinction must be made between general elections and party primaries. General elections determine which candidates will fill government offices. These electoral contests are public and are conducted, financed, and administered by state and county governments. Primary elections are party functions that allow party members to select nominees to run against the candidates of opposing parties in a general election. This distinction between general elections and party primaries is valid even though the U.S. Supreme Court ruled primaries to be of such importance in the selection of general election candidates that they are subject to government regulation.

Thus, even though the state regulates and largely finances primaries, they serve only as a means for political parties to nominate candidates. The general election ballot also includes the names of independent candidates; write-in candidates; and candidates who were nominated by party convention, because their political party was not required by law to select party nominees in a primary election.

General Elections   Throughout the United States, the date prescribed by federal law for congressional elections is the first Tuesday following the first Monday in November of even-numbered years (for example, 2 November 2004 and 7 November 2006). Presidential elections take place on the same day in November every four years (for example, 2004 and 2008). The presidential election of 2004 was of special interest to Texans, because George W. Bush, the incumbent president and nominee of the Republican Party, was a former governor of Texas. His Democratic opponent was U.S. Senator John Kerry of Massachusetts.

In Texas's general elections involving candidates for state, district, and county offices, the candidate who receives a plurality (the largest number of votes) in a contest is the winner. Even if no candidate wins a majority, because of votes received by third-party or independent candidates, the state does not hold a runoff election. Elections for governor and other statewide officers serving terms of four years are scheduled in the off year. These **off-year** or **midterm elections** are held in November of the even-numbered years between presidential elections (for example, 2006). Along with most other states, Texas follows this schedule to minimize the influence of presidential campaigns on the election of state and local officials. Elections to fill offices for two-year or six-year terms must be conducted in both off years and presidential years.

Special Elections   Early in 2004, **special elections** were called to fill two vacancies in the Texas Senate. A District 1 vacancy resulted from the retirement of Senator Bill Ratliff (R-Mount Pleasant), who criticized his party and objected to increased partisan bickering in the Senate. He was replaced by Kevin Eltife (R-Tyler). Teel Bivins (R-Amarillo), a major fund raiser for President Bush, resigned from the Senate seat for District 31 when he was appointed United States ambassador to Sweden. Kel Seliger (R-Amarillo) was elected to replace Bivins.

In addition to participating in special elections to fill vacancies in U.S. congressional and state legislative offices, Texans vote in special elections to approve proposed state constitutional amendments, act on local bond issues, and, occasionally, elect members of city councils and school boards. If no candidate obtains a majority in a special election, a runoff contest between the top two contenders must be conducted to obtain a winner. Vacancies in state judicial and executive offices are filled by gubernatorial appointment until the next general election and do not require special elections.

Administering Elections

The Texas Constitution authorizes the legislature to provide for the administration of elections. State lawmakers, in turn, have made the secretary of state the chief election officer for Texas but have left most details of administering elections to county officials.

Voting Precincts The basic geographic area for conducting national, state, district, and county elections is the **voting precinct**. Each precinct usually contains between 100 and approximately 2,000 registered voters. Texas has more than 8,500 voting precincts, drawn by the 254 county commissioners courts (county judge and 4 commissioners). When a precinct's population exceeds a number prescribed by the Texas Election Code (3,000, 4,000, or 5,000, depending on the county's population), the commissioners court must draw new boundaries.[15] Citizens vote at polling places within their voting precincts or, if voting precincts have been combined for an election, at a polling place convenient to voters in each of the combined voting precincts. Municipal precincts must follow the boundary lines of county-designed voting precincts adjusted to city boundaries. Subject to this restriction, municipal and special-district voting precincts are designated by the governing body of each city and special district, respectively.

Election Officials Various county and political party officials participate in the administration of elections. The county clerk or elections administrator prepares general- and special-election ballots based on the certification of candidates by the appropriate authority (the secretary of state for state and district candidates and the county clerk or elections administrator for local candidates). The county election commission consists of the county judge, county clerk or elections administrator, sheriff, and chairs of the two major political parties. Commission responsibilities include selecting polling places, printing ballots, and providing supplies and voting equipment.

County commissioners courts appoint one **election judge** and one alternate judge, each from different political parties, to administer elections in each precinct for a maximum term of two years. Furthermore, each county's commissioners court canvasses and certifies election results. Each election judge selects as many clerks as will be needed to assist in conducting general and special elections in a precinct. Clerks must be selected from different political parties. In city elections, the city secretary appoints election judges.

Voting Systems In general elections, Texas uses five voting systems: paper ballot, manually operated voting machine, optical scan (like Scantrons), punch-card, and direct-record electronic (or touchscreen). In every county, the county commissioners court determines which system will be used. Each has advantages and disadvantages with regard to such matters as ballot and equipment costs, ease of use by voters, accuracy of counting, labor cost, and time required to count the votes. For example, paper ballots are relatively cheap and easy to use, but counting is a slow, laborious, and error-prone process. Some sparsely populated counties continue to use paper ballots, which must be counted by hand. Voting machines and some optical scan and direct-recording electronic voting systems automatically count each vote as the ballot is cast. Punch-card devices and some optical scan systems are electronically counted on delivery to the county clerk's office after the polls close. Purchase and storage of mechanical and electronic voting equipment are expensive, but such equipment can reduce the cost of conducting elections when many voters are involved.

After the controversial 2000 presidential election, in which the state of Florida and the U.S. Supreme Court questioned the accuracy of punch-card ballots, both federal and state elected officials evaluated different voting systems. A study conducted by the Office of the Secretary of State of Texas revealed that the 14 Texas counties (including Harris County [Houston]) that used punch-card ballots had much higher overvotes (in which voters selected more than one candidate for the same office) than counties using any other balloting method. Likewise, these counties had much higher undervotes (in which voters did not clearly select any candidate for a specific office).[16] In testimony before the House Elections Committee, then Secretary of State Henry Cuellar emphasized the need to replace punch-card ballots with more accurate equipment but urged caution in abandoning the system quickly. Although legislators and Cuellar preferred prohibiting the use of punch-card ballots, replacement cost was a factor. Harris County estimated the cost of replacing its punch-card ballot equipment at $20 million. Balancing cost and the need for more accurate voting systems, the Texas Legislature required counties to phase out the punch-card equipment. No new punch-card tabulating machines could be purchased after September 2001, except for early-voting purposes. Further, chads (the small pieces of paper that are punched out of the ballot) must be removed from tabulating machines before each election.

On machine and punch-card ballot forms, a list of parties for straight-party-ticket voting appears first, followed by lists of candidates for national, state, district, and local offices, in that order. (Figure 4.1 shows a sample machine ballot used in the 2002 general election.) Punch-card ballots have space for names of write-in candidates on a detachable portion of the ballot card. A list of all write-in candidates who have filed an appropriate declaration is posted in each polling place on the day of election. The name of one of these candidates may be written in to indicate the voter's selection in the appropriate contest.

In some instances, candidates for nomination or election to an office may request a recount of ballots if they believe vote tabulations are inaccurate. Texas law is specific on how election officials determine a voter's intent if a punch-card ballot was used, but not punched through. Only one recount is allowed.[17] The Texas Election Code also provides detailed procedures for settling disputed elections. Since the 1960s, several changes in voting procedures have been made to encourage full, informed participation in elections.

As a result of the 1975 extension of the federal Voting Rights Act, registration and election materials used in all counties must be printed in both

Figure 4.1 Sample Portion of Election Ballot for Harris County, Texas, 2002

GENERAL AND SPECIAL ELECTIONS
ELECCIONES GENERAL Y ESPECIAL
HARRIS COUNTY, TEXAS
CONDADO DE HARRIS, TEXAS
November 05, 2002 - 05 Noviembre 2002

Straight Party
Votar por Todos los Candidatos de un Solo Partido Político
- ☐ Republican Party — *Partido Republicano* — REP
- ☐ Democratic Party — *Partido Democrático* — DEM
- ☐ Libertarian Party — *Partido Libertariano* — LIB
- ☐ Green Party — *Partido Verde* — GRN

United States Senator
Senador de los Estados Unidos
- ☐ John Cornyn — REP
- ☐ Ron Kirk — DEM
- ☐ Scott Lanier Jameson — LIB
- ☐ Roy H. Williams — GRN
- ☐ Write-In *Voto Escrito*

United States Representative, District 7
Representante de los Estados Unidos, Distrito Núm. 7
- ☐ John Culberson — REP
- ☐ Drew Parks — LIB
- ☐ Write-In *Voto Escrito*

United States Representative, District 8
Representante de los Estados Unidos, Distrito Núm. 8
- ☐ Kevin Brady — REP
- ☐ Gil Guillory — LIB

United States Representative, District 9
Representante de los Estados Unidos, Distrito Núm. 9
- ☐ Paul Williams — REP
- ☐ Nick Lampson — DEM
- ☐ Dean L. Tucker — LIB

United States Representative, District 18
Representante de los Estados Unidos, Distrito Núm. 18
- ☐ Phillip J. Abbott — REP
- ☐ Sheila Jackson Lee — DEM
- ☐ Brent Sullivan — LIB

United States Representative, District 22
Representante de los Estados Unidos, Distrito Núm. 22
- ☐ Tom DeLay — REP
- ☐ Tim Riley — DEM
- ☐ Gerald W. "Jerry" LeFleur — LIB
- ☐ Joel West — GRN

United States Representative, District 25
Representante de los Estados Unidos, Distrito Núm. 25
- ☐ Tom Reiser — REP
- ☐ Chris Bell — DEM
- ☐ Guy McLendon — LIB
- ☐ George Reiter — GRN

United States Representative, District 29
Representante de los Estados Unidos, Distrito Núm. 29
- ☐ Gene Green — DEM
- ☐ Paul Hansen — LIB

United States Representative, District 31
Representante de los Estados Unidos, Distrito Núm. 31
- ☐ John R. Carter — REP
- ☐ David Bagley — DEM
- ☐ Clark Simmons — LIB
- ☐ John S. Peterson — GRN
- ☐ R.C. Crawford — IND

Governor
Gobernador
- ☐ Rick Perry — REP
- ☐ Tony Sanchez — DEM
- ☐ Jeff Daiell — LIB
- ☐ Rahul Mahajan — GRN
- ☐ Write-In *Voto Escrito*

Lieutenant Governor
Gobernador Teniente
- ☐ David Dewhurst — REP
- ☐ John Sharp — DEM
- ☐ Mark David Gessner — LIB
- ☐ Nathalie Paravicini — GRN

Attorney General
Procurador General
- ☐ Greg Abbott — REP
- ☐ Kirk Watson — DEM
- ☐ Jon Roland — LIB
- ☐ David Keith Cobb — GRN

Comptroller of Public Accounts
Contralor de Cuentas Públicas
- ☐ Carole Keeton Rylander — REP
- ☐ Marty Akins — DEM
- ☐ Bowie Ibarra — LIB
- ☐ Ruben L. Reyes — GRN

Comptroller of the General Land Office
Comisionado de la Oficina General de Terrenos
- ☐ Jerry Patterson — REP
- ☐ David Bernsen — DEM
- ☐ Barbara A. Hernandez — LIB
- ☐ Michael B. McInerney — GRN

Commissioner of Agriculture
Comisionado de Agricultura
- ☐ Susan Combs — REP
- ☐ Tom Ramsay — DEM
- ☐ Vincent J. May — LIB
- ☐ Jane Woodward Elioseff — GRN

Railroad Commissioner
Comisionado de Ferrocarriles
- ☐ Michael L. Williams — REP
- ☐ Sherry Boyles — DEM
- ☐ Nazirite R. Flores Perez — LIB
- ☐ Charles L. Mauch — GRN

Chief Justice, Supreme Court
Juez Presidente, Corte Suprema
- ☐ Tom Phillips — REP
- ☐ Richard G. Baker — DEM
- ☐ Eugene J. Flynn — LIB

English and Spanish. Texas voters can also take voting guides, newspaper endorsements, and other printed material into the voting booth. In 1999, the Texas Legislature passed a series of laws ensuring disabled voters access to polling places and the opportunity to cast a secret ballot.

Party Structure

Although neither the U.S. Constitution nor the Texas Constitution mentions political parties, these organizations are an integral part of the American governmental process. A **political party** can be defined as a combination of people and interests whose primary purpose is to gain control of government by winning elections. Whereas interest groups (covered in the following chapter) tend to focus on influencing governmental policies, political parties concentrate on nominating and electing candidates for public office. Parties are complex, loosely regulated organizations, chiefly concerned with the recruitment, nomination, and election of individuals to governmental office. In Texas, as throughout the United States, the Democratic and Republican parties are the two leading political parties. State election laws have contributed to the continuity of the two-party system. These laws specify that a general election is won by the candidate who receives the largest number of votes (a plurality) without a runoff. Third-party candidates have little chance of winning an election by defeating the two major-party nominees.

American political parties exist on four levels: national, state, county, and precinct. In part, these levels correspond to the organization of the federal system of government in the United States. Whereas a corporation is organized as a hierarchy, with a chain of command that makes each level directly accountable to the level above it, a political party is organized as a **stratarchy** in which power is diffused among and within levels of the party organization.[18] Each major party is loosely organized, so that state and local party organizations are free to decide their positions on party issues. State- and local-level organizations operate within their own spheres of influence, separate from one another. Although these levels of the two major parties are encouraged to support national party policies, this effort is not always successful. As mandated by the Texas Election Code, Texas's two major parties are alike in structure. Each has permanent and temporary organizational structures (see Figure 4.2).

Temporary Party Organization

The **temporary party organization** consists of primaries and conventions in which members of the major political parties select candidates for public office. Conventions elect state-level party officers. Primary election voting periods may also include runoff voting. Conventions are scheduled at the precinct level, the county and state senatorial district level, and the state

Figure 4.2 Texas Political Party Organization

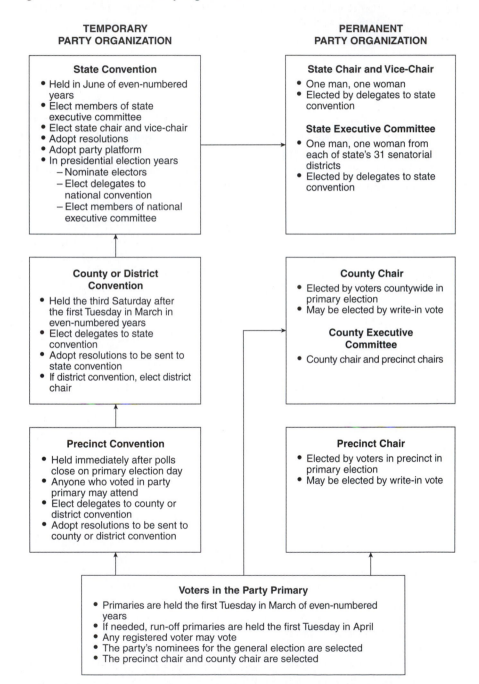

level. Each convention lasts for only a limited amount of time: from less than an hour to one or two days. These events are temporary because they are not ongoing party activities.

At the state level, conventions select party leaders who were chosen by delegates elected at the local level. Rules of the state Democratic and Republican parties mandate that party policy be determined at their conventions. This is done by passing resolutions, in both local and state conventions, and adopting a platform at the state conventions. A party's **platform** is a document that sets forth the party's position on current issues. In presidential election years, conventions on all levels select delegates who attend a party's national convention. Here candidates are chosen for president and vice president of the United States. All Texas political conventions must be open to the media, according to state law.

Precinct Conventions   In Texas, **precinct conventions** are conducted every even-numbered year on the first Tuesday in March, which is the first primary day. At the lowest level of the temporary party organization, these conventions (both Democratic and Republican) assemble in almost all of the state's voting precincts. Precinct conventions start immediately after the polls close that evening and last approximately 30 minutes to two hours. Usually, precinct conventions are sparsely attended. By state law, any individual who voted in the party primary is permitted to attend and participate in that party's precinct convention as a delegate. Delegates will elect a chairperson to preside over the convention and a secretary to record the proceedings. The main business of the precinct convention is to elect delegates to the county or district convention. Under long-standing rules of both the Democratic and Republican parties, precinct conventions have been authorized to elect one delegate to the county (or district) convention for every 25 votes cast in the precinct for the party's gubernatorial nominee in the last general election. Faced with decreasing participation at their conventions, however, the Texas Democratic Party, beginning in 2000, lowered this number to 15. Delegates to a party's precinct convention are allowed to submit and debate resolutions. These resolutions express the positions of precinct convention participants on any number of issues, ranging from immigration, to abortion, to the national debt. If adopted, a resolution will be submitted to a county or district convention for consideration.

County and District Conventions   State law requires that both **county conventions** and **district conventions** occur 11 days after the precinct conventions. These conventions are always held on a Saturday and usually last three or more hours. District conventions, rather than a single-county convention, are held in heavily populated counties (such as Harris, Dallas, and Bexar) that have more than one state senatorial district. Delegates to a party's county or district convention elect a chairperson to preside over the convention and a secretary to record the proceedings. The main business of county and district conventions is to elect delegates to the state convention.

Under party rules for the Republican Party, county and district conventions may select one delegate to the state convention for every 300 votes cast in the county or district for the party's gubernatorial nominee in the last general election. Since 2000, Democrats select one delegate for each 180 gubernatorial votes cast. Under Republican Party rules, all delegate candidates are submitted by the county or district convention's committee on nominations for approval by the county or district convention participants. Rules of the Democratic Party allow state delegates to be selected by precinct delegations. If all state delegate positions are not filled in this manner, the county or district convention's nominations committee proposes the remaining state delegates, subject to selection by the county or district convention delegates. County and district convention delegates consider resolutions submitted from the party's precinct conventions. The resolutions adopted at this level the go to the party's state convention for its consideration.

State Conventions   In June of even-numbered years, each Texas political party must hold a biennial **state convention** to conduct party business. State conventions occur over a two-day period. Delegates to a party's state convention elect a chairperson to preside over the convention and a secretary to record the proceedings. Additionally, delegates conduct the following tasks:

- Certify to the secretary of state the names of party members nominated in the March and April primaries for Texas elective offices (or by convention if no primary was held)
- Write the rules that will govern the party
- Draft and adopt a party platform
- Adopt resolutions regarding issues that are too specific to be included in the party platform
- Select members of the party's state executive committee

In presidential election years, the June convention delegates also perform the following three functions:

1. Elect delegates to the national presidential nominating convention (the total number for Texas is calculated under national party rules)
2. Elect members from Texas to serve on the party's national committee
3. Elect a slate of potential presidential electors to cast Texas's electoral votes if the party's ticket wins a plurality of the state's popular presidential vote

Texas is allowed 34 electoral votes. A state's electoral vote equals the number of its members in the U.S. Congress (for Texas, 32 representatives and 2 senators).

Selection of National Convention Delegates

Selection of delegates to a national party convention depends on their support for particular candidates for the party's presidential nomination. In a **presidential preference primary**, rank-and-file party members are permitted to vote directly for the presidential candidates of their choice. In states like Texas where primaries are used, voting is by precinct. Delegates to the party's national convention are chosen according to the results of the primary vote. The respective national conventions nominate the parties' candidates for president and vice president.

In many states, parties select delegates to a national convention in **caucuses**. Party members assemble in caucuses at the respective precinct, county, and state levels. Here they choose national convention delegates who either are pledged to support a particular presidential candidate or are uncommitted.

Democratic Selection   Texas Democrats combine the two delegate-selection plans in a primary-caucus plan. At each of the conventions in presidential years, participants must identify their presidential preferences. Individuals may indicate they are uncommitted and do not want to pledge their support to any candidate. Presidential candidates are awarded delegates to local and state conventions in proportion to the number of their supporters in attendance. In 2004, John Kerry won overwhelming support by the 232 Texas delegates to the national Democratic convention. National delegates include those selected by state senatorial district, those selected on an at-large basis, and **superdelegates** (unpledged party and elected officials).

Republican Selection   The Republican Party selects national delegates from the results of the presidential preference primary. Some Republican delegates are chosen by congressional district caucuses (three from each district in 2004). Others are chosen on an at-large basis by the entire convention. Any presidential candidate who wins 50 percent or more of the popular vote in the primary in a particular congressional district or statewide is entitled to all of the district or at-large delegates, respectively. A nominating committee selects all at-large delegates. State convention delegates approve all national delegates. George W. Bush won all 138 Texas delegates in 2004.

Permanent Party Organization

Each major political party in the United States consists of thousands of virtually autonomous executive committees at local, state, and national levels. For both Democrats and Republicans, these executive committees nationwide are linked only nominally. At the highest level, each party has a national committee. In Texas, the precinct chairs, together with the county, district, and state executive committees, comprise the permanent organization of the state parties. The role of the **permanent party organization** is to recruit candidates, devise strategies, raise funds, distribute candidate literature and information, register voters, and turn out voters on election day.

Precinct Chair   The basic party official in both the temporary and permanent party structures in Texas is the **precinct chair**, who is elected by precinct voters in the party primaries for a term of two years. Duties and responsibilities of a party's precinct chair include registering and canvassing voters within the precinct, distributing candidate literature and information, operating phone banks within the precinct on behalf of the party and its candidates, and getting people to the polls. If both parties are evenly matched in strength at the polls, the precinct chairs become more vital in getting people out to vote. A precinct chair is an unpaid party official who also arranges for the precinct convention and serves on the county executive committee. These positions often go unfilled in more populous counties that have one hundred or more precincts.

County and District Executive Committees A **county executive committee** is composed of all the precinct chairs and the county chair, who is elected on a countywide basis by party members in the primaries. The county chair heads the party's organization at the county level. County executive committees conduct primaries and arrange for county conventions. At the local level, the **county chair** is the key party official, serving as the party's chief strategist within that county. Duties of the county chair include recruiting local candidates for office, raising funds, establishing and staffing the party's campaign headquarters within the county, and serving as the local spokesperson for the party. The Texas Election Code also provides for a **district executive committee** composed of the county chairs from each county in a given district (senatorial, representative, or judicial). District executive committees rarely meet except to nominate candidates to fill a district vacancy when one occurs.

State Executive Committee For each major political party, the highest permanent party organization in the state is the **state executive committee**. As mandated by state law, an executive committee is composed of one man and one woman from each of the 31 state senatorial districts, plus a chair and a vice chair, one of whom must be a woman. For both the Democratic and Republican parties, a state executive committee with 64 members is elected at the party's state convention. On that occasion, delegates from each of the 31 senatorial districts choose two members from their district and place these names before the convention for its approval. At the same time, convention delegates choose the chair and vice chair at large. In addition to the 64 statutory members of the party's state executive committee, party rules may allow "add-on" members. An add-on member may represent recognized statewide auxiliary organizations within the party such as women's groups, racial groups, House and Senate caucus chairs, youth groups, and county chairs associations.

The party's state chair works with the party's state executive committee to recruit candidates for statewide and district offices, plan statewide strategies, and raise funds for the party at the state level. Additionally, the state executive committee of each party must canvass statewide primary returns and certify the nomination of party candidates. It also conducts the state convention, promotes party unity and strength, maintains relations with the party's national committee, and raises some campaign money for party candidates (although most campaign funds are raised by the candidates themselves).

Political Democracy

Today's politics in the Lone Star State reflects Texas's political history. Traditions based on centuries of political experience and culture influence current attitudes toward parties, candidates, and issues. Nevertheless, Texans' changing demands and expectations have forced revisions in party platforms and affected the campaigns of candidates for public office. Political parties cannot remain static and survive, nor can politicians win elections unless they are in step with the opinions of the voting majority. Increasing competition between Texas's Democratic and Republican parties has brought more women, Latinos, and African Americans into the state's political system. As a result of this competitiveness, party politics has become more democratic and more nationalized. Compared with the politics of earlier years, Texas politics today is more partisan (party centered). But internal feuding (factionalism) among competing groups exists within both the Democratic and Republican parties.

Ideology

Since the 1930s, the terms *liberal* and *conservative* have meant more to many Texas voters than the names of political parties. In view of long-standing ideological differences between liberals and conservatives, this terminology must be explained. These ideological labels almost defy definition, however, because meanings change with time and circumstances. Furthermore, each label has varying shades of meaning for different people. In Texas, because of the influences of the individualistic and traditionalistic cultures, both Democrats and Republicans tend to be conservative. But the Republican Party organization is dominated by right-wing conservatives, whereas the Democratic Party is influenced (but not dominated) by left-wing liberals. Despite the use of right-left terminology throughout the United States, the Texas Legislature has not traditionally used partisan or ideological criteria for assigning floor seats on the right and left sides of House and Senate chambers.

Conservatism   In its purest form, modern conservative doctrine envisions ideal social and economic orders that would be largely untouched by government. According to this philosophy, if all individuals were left alone (the doctrine of laissez-faire) to pursue their self-interests, both social and economic systems would benefit, and the cost of government would be low. **Conservatives**, therefore, are generally opposed to government-managed or government-subsidized programs such as assistance to poor families with dependent children, unemployment insurance, and federal price support programs for the benefit of farmers producing commodities such as cotton and wheat. Today's fiscal conservatives give the highest priority to reduced taxing and spending; on the other hand, social conservatives (such as those associated with the Christian Coalition) stress the importance of their family values, including opposition to abortion and homosexuality. They support school vouchers to provide government-funded assistance to parents who choose to send their children to private schools, especially church-affiliated schools.

Attempting to distance himself from more extreme conservative Republicans, President George W. Bush used the phrase "compassionate conservatism" to describe his political philosophy when he ran for governor of Texas in 1998 and for the presidency in 2000 and 2004. Bush insists that he is "a conservative who puts a compassionate face on a conservative philosophy."[19] His ideology is sometimes described as **neoconservatism** because he is fiscally conservative but does allow for a limited governmental role in solving social problems.

Liberalism **Liberals** favor government regulation of the economy to achieve a more equitable distribution of wealth. Only government, liberals insist, is capable of guarding against pollution of air, water, and soil by corporations and individuals. Liberals claim that government is obligated to aid the unemployed, alleviate poverty (especially for the benefit of children), and guarantee equal rights for minorities and women. Liberalism seeks a limited role for government involvement with regard to other social issues, especially those related to issues of morality or religion. Liberals are more likely to oppose mandatory prayer in public schools, government subsidies for religious institutions, and any church involvement in secular politics. Many Texas Democrats have a **neoliberal** ideology. This position incorporates a philosophy of less government regulation of business and the economy while adopting a more liberal view of greater government involvement in social programs.

Both Texas liberals and conservatives are often ideologically inconsistent. A conservative may oppose government subsidies, such as welfare assistance for individuals, but support similar payments to corporations. Liberals may support pollution control laws for corporations but oppose antipollution measures that require installation of emission control devices for their own automobiles. Frequently, individuals who have extreme conservative or liberal ideologies accuse moderates of being ideologically inconsistent.

An Overview of Texas Political History

From the time that political parties developed in Texas until the 1960s, the Lone Star State was dominated primarily by one political party: the Democratic Party. In the 1970s and 1980s, Texas moved toward a competitive two-party structure. However, by the 1990s and into the twenty-first century it appears that the state has become a one-party state again, with the Republican Party in control.

1840s to 1870s: The Origin of the Party System   Prior to the admission of Texas into the Union in 1845, its political parties had not fully developed. Political factions during the years that Texas was an independent republic tended to coalesce around personalities. The two dominant factions were the pro–(Sam) Houston and anti-Houston groups. Even after the Lone Star State's admission into the Union, these two factions remained. By the 1850s, the pro-Houston faction began referring to itself as the Jackson Democrats (Unionists), whereas the anti-Houston faction called themselves the Calhoun Democrats (after South Carolina senator John C. Calhoun, a states' rights and proslavery advocate). In the course of the Civil War, Texas politics became firmly aligned with the Democratic Party.

During the period of Reconstruction that followed the Civil War (1865–1873), the Republican Party controlled Texas politics. The Reconstruction acts passed by the United States Congress purged all officeholders with a Confederate past. Congress also disenfranchised all Southerners who had ever held a state or federal office before secession and later supported the Confederacy. In Texas, any man who had ever been a mayor, a school trustee, a clerk, or even a public weigher was denied the right to vote.[20] Republican governor Edmund J. Davis was elected in 1869 during this period of Radical Reconstruction. The Davis administration quickly became the most unpopular in Texas history. During his tenure in office, Davis took control of voter registration and appointed over 8,000 public officials. From the Texas Supreme Court justices to the state police to city officials, Davis placed Republicans in office throughout the state. Davis's administration is best remembered for its corruption, graft, and excessive taxation. Following Davis's defeat for reelection in 1873 by a newly enfranchised electorate, Texas voters did not elect another Republican governor for more than one hundred years.

1870s to 1970s: A Dominant One-Party System   From the end of Reconstruction until the 1970s, Texas and other former Confederate states had a one-party identity in which the Democratic Party was strong and Republican Party weak. During those years (when a gubernatorial term was two years), Democratic candidates won 52 consecutive gubernatorial elections, and Democratic presidential nominees carried the state in all but 3 of the 25 presidential elections.

During the latter part of the nineteenth century, Democrats faced a greater challenge from the Populist Party than they did from Republicans. The Populist (or People's) Party was formed in Texas as an agrarian-based party, winning local elections throughout the state. From 1892 to 1898, their gubernatorial nominees received more votes than did Republicans. Although its ideas remained influential in Texas, the Populist Party became less important after 1898. Rural Texans continued to be active in politics, but most farmers and others who had been Populists shifted their support to Democratic candidates. In large measure, the Populist Party declined because the Democratic Party adopted Populist issues such as government regulation of railroads.[21]

In the early twentieth century, the Democratic Party strengthened its control over state politics. Having adopted Populist issues, Democratic candidates faced no opposition from Populist candidates. Over the next five decades, two factions emerged within the Democratic Party: conservatives and liberals. Fighting between these two factions was often as fierce as between two separate political parties. By the late 1940s and early 1950s, Republican presidential candidates began enjoying greater support from the Texas electorate. With the backing of conservative Democratic governor Alan Shivers, Republican presidential nominee Dwight D. Eisenhower successfully carried Texas in 1952 and 1956. In order to bolster support for Eisenhower, Shivers secured both the Democratic and Republican nominations for governor. Supporters of Governor Shivers began referring to themselves as "Shivercrats."

Points to Ponder In the gubernatorial election of 1952, Democratic nominee Alan Shivers received more votes than did Republican nominee Alan Shivers by a three-to-one margin.

Evidence of the growing strength of the Texas GOP (Grand Old Party, a nickname that the Republican Party adopted in the 1870s) was sharply revealed in 1961 with the election to the U.S. Senate of Texas Republican John Tower, a political science professor at Midwestern State University in Wichita Falls. Originally elected to fill the vacancy created when Lyndon Johnson left the Senate to become vice president, Tower became the first Republican to win statewide office in Texas since 1869 and won successive elections until his retirement in 1984.

1970s to 1990s: An Emerging Two-Party System　Beginning in the late 1940s, a majority of conservative Democrats began to support the national Republican ticket. However, at the state and local levels, the Democratic Party remained firmly in control. Three decades later, however, the Republican Party began enjoying greater electoral support. No longer was the winner in a Democratic primary assured of victory in the general election contest in November. When Bill Clements was elected governor of the Lone Star State in 1978, he became the first Republican to hold that office since Reconstruction. In the 1980s, GOP voters elected growing numbers of candidates to the U.S. Congress, the Texas Legislature, and county courthouse offices. And they began to dominate local politics in suburban areas around the state.

The Republican Party continued to make substantial gains throughout the 1990s. With the Republican victory of U.S. senatorial candidate Kay Bailey Hutchison in the 1993 special election, the Texas GOP began a series of "firsts." Hutchison's victory included two firsts. She was the first woman to represent Texas in the U.S. Senate, and, for the first time in modern history, Texas was represented by two Republican senators.

The elections of 1994 were a preview of future elections. Elected governor in 1990, Democrat Ann Richards was unable to win reelection despite her personal popularity. Republican George W. Bush (who received more than 53 percent of the vote and strong support from Anglo and suburban voters) beat Richards in the 1994 gubernatorial race. At the same time, Senator Hutchison easily defeated her Democratic opponent. Democrats holding four executive offices (lieutenant governor, attorney general, comptroller of public accounts, and commissioner of the general Land Office) defeated their Republican challengers. However, Republican incumbent agriculture commissioner Rick Perry had a 1-million-vote margin of victory over his Democratic opponent, and all six Republican statewide candidates below him on the ballot won. These victories gave Republicans two Railroad Commission members, two more Supreme Court justices, and two more Court of Criminal Appeals judges. Republicans also won many lower-level judgeships. For the first time, they gained control of the 15-member State Board of Education. Active support by members of the Christian Coalition resulted in Republican victories in three of the six contested races for seats on this board.

In 1996, for the first time since the primary system was established, Republican primaries were conducted in all 254 Texas counties. More of the Lone Star State's voters participated in the Republican primary than the Democratic primary. In addition, Republican victories continued in the general election of that year, as all statewide Republican candidates won. Republicans now held all three positions on the Texas Railroad Commission and gained three more Court of Criminal Appeals judgeships and four more positions on the Texas Supreme Court. Republican presidential candidate Bob Dole carried the state over President Bill Clinton. The 1992 election had made Clinton the first Democratic president elected without carrying Texas. By 1996, Clinton was certain that he could be elected without Texas's electoral votes, so his campaign effort focused on closely contested states where he was more likely to win. This decision demonstrates the acceptance by national Democratic candidates that Texas is a Republican state and that its electoral votes may not be needed for a Democratic presidential victory.

The 1998 elections gave Republicans control of all statewide offices but one. Texas Supreme Court justice Raul Gonzalez was the lone Democrat in statewide office when he announced his retirement in December 1998. Then the GOP sweep was complete when Governor Bush appointed a Republican to replace Gonzalez. In 1998, Bush was so popular that he received endorsements from more than 100 elected Democratic officials and almost 70 percent of the vote in the gubernatorial election. When the prospect of a Bush presidential bid in 2000 seemed likely, Republican lieutenant gubernatorial nominee Rick Perry campaigned on the issue that a Republican should succeed Governor Bush if he resigned to become president. The 1998 elections allowed Republicans to retain control of the Texas Senate and to increase their representation in the state House of Representatives, although they did not gain control of the latter chamber.

Table 4.1 Growth of Republican Officeholders

Year	U.S. Senate	Other Statewide	U.S. Congress	Texas Senate	Texas House	County Offices	District Offices	School Board*	Total
1974	1	0	2	3	16	53	?	—	75+
1976	1	0	2	3	19	67	?	—	92+
1978	1	1	4	4	22	87	?	—	119+
1980	1	1	5	7	35	166	?	—	215+
1982	1	0	5	5	36	191	79	—	317
1984	1	0	10	6	52	287	90	—	446
1986	1	1	10	6	56	410	94	—	578
1988	1	5	8	8	57	485	123	5	692
1990	1	6	8	8	57	547	170	5	802
1992	1	8	9	13	58	634	183	5	911
1994	2	13	11	14	61	734	216	8	1,059
1996	2	18	13	17	68	938	278	9	1,343
1998	2	27	13	16	72	1,108	280	9	1,527
2000	2	27	13	16	72	1,233	336	10	1,709
2002	2	27	15	19	88	1,443	362	10	1,966

Source: Courtesy of the Texas Republican Party. Reprinted by permission.
*State Board of Education.

2000 to 2004: Republican Dominance By mid-2004, it appeared that Texas was becoming a one-party state again (see Table 4.1). In 2000, Texas Republicans focused their attention on national elections. Governor Bush's candidacy for the presidency was enhanced by his ability to maintain the backing of social conservatives within his party while at the same time gaining support from minority voters, women, and some Democrats. National Republican leaders seeking an electable candidate found Bush's 1998 gubernatorial victory and his inclusive strategy appealing. Although Bush did not announce that he would seek the Republican presidential nomination until after the Texas Legislature completed its 1999 regular session, Republican leaders streamed to Austin during the session. More than one-fourth of Texas Democrats told pollsters they would vote for Bush for president.

In the closest presidential election of modern times, Governor Bush defeated Democratic nominee Al Gore by four electoral votes (271 to 267). After controversial recounts and protracted court battles over Florida's 25 electoral votes, George W. Bush was ultimately declared the victor in mid-December 2000. In the Lone Star State, Bush received 3,795,262 votes (59.3 percent) to Gore's 2,428,187 votes (37.7 percent), giving Bush Texas's 32 electoral votes. For the third straight election, all statewide Republican candidates won, including U.S. senator Kay Bailey Hutchison, who became the first candidate in Texas history to receive more than 4 million votes. Democrats did not even have candidates in most statewide contests or in many local races. In fact, the Libertarian Party and Green Party each had more candidates for statewide office than the Democratic Party in 2000. Of the nine statewide offices up for election in 2000, the Democratic Party fielded candidates in only three contests. By contrast, the Libertarian Party ran candidates in seven of the nine races, and the Green Party had candidates in five.

After the dismal performance of Democratic candidates in the 1998 elections, Texas Republican chair Susan Weddington advised Democrats to "turn out the lights, [because] the Democrat[ic] party [was] definitely over." As early as 2000, potential gubernatorial candidates began to solicit campaign contributions for the 2002 election. Governor Rick Perry established the Century Council. To belong, donors pledged to donate or raise $100,000 each for Perry for the 2002 campaign.[22] Some Democrats encouraged Tony Sanchez, a Laredo businessman with a fortune of more than $600 million and a strong supporter of George W. Bush, to seek the office. Sanchez, a political newcomer, brought two major assets to the campaign: a Latino surname and an ability to fund more than $50 million from his own resources for the gubernatorial campaign.

In September 2001, Phil Gramm announced his retirement from the U.S. Senate. Following Gramm's announcement, Texas Attorney General John Cornyn declared that he would seek the Republican nomination to succeed Gramm. Several Democrats also filed for Gramm's Senate seat; but Dallas mayor Ron Kirk, an African American, emerged as the Democratic Party's nominee. To complete the Democratic line-up of candidates for the top three state offices, former comptroller John Sharp was nominated for Lieutenant Governor.

Sanchez, Kirk, and Sharp were dubbed the "dream team," because of their expected appeal to Latino, African American, and Anglo voters. They ran with a full slate of candidates for other statewide offices (including popular Austin mayor Kirk Watson for attorney general, state senator David Bernsen for commissioner of the General Land Office, and state representative Tom Ramsay for commissioner of agriculture). Thus, Texas Democrats presented their strongest field of candidates in 20 years. Many political analysts believed that the multiracial Democratic ticket would significantly increase minority turnout and help Democrats reclaim several statewide offices. However, on election night, the dream quickly turned into a nightmare as the GOP swept all statewide races, including contests for seats on the state's highest courts. The anticipated increase in voter turnout to support Tony Sanchez, Ron Kirk, John Sharp, and other Democratic candidates never materialized.

As a result of the 2002 election, Republicans increased their control over the Texas Senate from a 1-seat majority to a 7-seat majority (19 to 12). And for the first time since Reconstruction, the GOP gained control of the Texas House of Representatives, winning 88 of 150 seats. Thus the stage was set to elect a Republican as speaker of the Texas House at the beginning of the 78th regular legislative session in January 2003.

With Republicans firmly in control of both houses of the Texas Legislature, U.S. representative Tom DeLay (R-Sugar Land) was determined that his job as U.S. House majority leader in Washington would be made easier with more Republican-dominated congressional districts in his state. After a contentious regular legislative session early in 2003, and three special sessions called by the governor later that year, new congressional districts were finally crafted by DeLay and the state legislature. Their work ensured that after the 2004 election Texas would have a large Republican majority in its delegation to the U.S. House of Representatives for the first time since Reconstruction. (For a discussion of the Democratic Party's continued decline and inability to attract candidates in the 2004 election, see this chapter's selected reading, "AWOL.")

Electoral Trends

Some political scientists interpret recent polling and election results as evidence that there has been a **dealignment** of Texas voters. These scholars explain that the large percentage of Texans who claim to be independent voters have abandoned allegiance to any political party (especially the Democratic Party) but tend to vote for Republican candidates. Other political scientists assert that the rising tide of Republican electoral victories throughout the 1990s and into the twenty-first century demonstrates that many Texans have switched their political affiliation and loyalty to the Republican Party in a **realignment** of voters.

Republican candidates carried Texas in 9 of the 13 presidential elections between 1952 and 2000, including the last 6 elections in that period. Republican candidates also won 5 of 7 gubernatorial elections between 1978 and 2002. Because the GOP dominates statewide elections, intra-party competition among Republicans has increased. In 2004, Texas Comptroller of Public Accounts Carole Keeton Strayhorn and U.S. senator Kay Bailey Hutchinson emerged as potential competitors with Governor Rick Perry for the Republican gubernatorial nomination in 2006. Strayhorn was particularly critical of Perry's proposal for resolving the state's school finance problem, positioning herself as a leading critic of the governor within his party.

Texas GOP strongholds are in West Texas, the Panhandle–South Plains, some small towns and rural areas in East Texas, the Dallas–Fort Worth Metroplex, and the suburbs of Houston, San Antonio, and Austin. With the exception of Democratic El Paso, West Texas Republicanism is predominant from the Permian Basin (Midland-Odessa) through the Davis Mountains and the German Hill Country. This West Texas region, like the Panhandle–South Plains area to the north, is populated primarily by conservative farmers and ranchers, along with people connected with the oil and gas industry in Midland, Odessa, and other parts of the Permian Basin.

Although the Democratic Party has been unsuccessful in statewide election contests in recent years, it still controlled a majority of county offices in 2004. Democratic voting strength is concentrated in El Paso, South Texas, parts of East Texas, the Golden Triangle (Beaumont, Port Arthur, and Orange), portions of the diverse Central Texas region, and the lower-income neighborhoods of larger cities. **Straight-ticket voting** for all Democratic candidates on the general election ballot has declined, however, as fewer Texans (especially those in rural East Texas) choose to remain "yellow-dog Democrats." This term has been applied to people whose party loyalty is said to be so strong that they would vote for a yellow dog if it were a Democratic candidate for public office.

Republican expansion has strengthened partisan competition throughout the state and has diminished the intensity of factional politics within the Democratic Party. Nevertheless, Democrats are divided by many interests and issues.

Third Parties

Americans commonly apply the term *third party* (or minor party) to any political party other than the Democratic or Republican Party. Both in the United States and in Texas, third parties have never enjoyed the same success as the two major parties. Major parties' success is measured in their ability to win elections. By this measure, minor parties are unsuccessful. However, their success can better be measured by their ability to make the public aware of their issues, get the major parties to adopt those issues, and/or force the major parties to bring them into a coalition. When judged by these measures, third parties in Texas have enjoyed modest success.

During the 1890s, the Populist Party successfully promoted agricultural issues and displaced the Republicans as the "second" party in Texas.[23] In the 1970s, La Raza Unida elected a few candidates to local offices in South Texas (principally Crystal City and Zavala County offices) and forced the Democratic Party to begin to address Latino concerns. In the 1990s, Ross Perot's Reform Party had organizations in many areas in the state. Over the last 20 years, the Libertarian Party (a party that advocates minimizing the performance of government at all levels while maximizing individual freedom and rights) has nominated candidates for national, state, and local offices throughout Texas. In addition to these parties, other parties have nominated candidates and increased public awareness of their issues: the Greenback Party (late nineteenth century), the Prohibition Party (late nineteenth and early twentieth centuries), the Socialist and Socialist Labor parties (early twentieth century), the Progressive Party (early to mid-twentieth century), and the Green Party (starting in the late twentieth century). The Green Party has advocated environmental protection and government reform policies. In 2000, Green Party presidential candidate Ralph Nader received 2.2 percent of the popular vote in Texas. In 2002, the Green Party fielded candidates for U.S. senator, governor, lieutenant governor, attorney general, comptroller, land commissioner, agriculture commissioner, railroad commissioner, and several statewide judgeships and congressional seats. However, Green candidates (like Libertarians) won no elections and rarely received more than 3 percent of the vote. Ralph Nader failed to get on the general election ballot as an independent candidate in 2004. He did not submit 64,076 petition signatures to the secretary of state by the May 10 deadline.

Racial/Ethnic Politics

Race and ethnicity are factors that strongly influence Texas politics and shape political campaigns. Almost 45 percent of Texas's total population is composed of Latinos (chiefly Mexican Americans) and African Americans. Politically, the state's principal ethnic and racial minorities wield enough voting strength to decide any statewide election and determine the outcomes of local contests in areas where their numbers are concentrated. Large majorities of Texas's African American and Latino voters participate in Democratic primaries and vote for Democratic candidates in general elections. However, an increasing number of African Americans and Latinos claim to be politically independent and do not identify with either the Republican or Democratic Party.

Latinos

Early in the twenty-first century, candidates for elective office in Texas and most other parts of the United States recognize the potential of the Latino vote. Most Anglo candidates use Spanish phrases in their speeches, advertise in Spanish-language media (television, radio, and newspapers), and voice their concern for issues important to the Latino community (such as bilingual education and immigration). Candidates for the 2000 and 2004 presidential nomination from both major political parties included appearances in Latino communities and before national Latino organizations, such as the League of United Latin American Citizens (LULAC) and the National Council of La Raza, as a part of their campaign strategy. These appearances recognize the political clout of Latinos in the Republican and Democratic presidential primaries as well as in the general election.

Although Mexican Americans have played an important role in South Texas politics throughout the twentieth century, not until the 1960s and early 1970s did they begin to have a major political impact at the state level. Founded in 1969 by José Angel Gutiérrez of Crystal City and others, the Raza Unida Party mobilized many Mexican Americans who had been politically inactive. It attracted others who had formerly identified with the Democratic Party. By the end of the 1970s, however, Raza Unida had disintegrated. According to Ruben Bonilla, former president of LULAC, the main reason Raza Unida did not survive as a meaningful voice for Texas's Mexican American population was "the maturity of the Democratic Party to accept Hispanics."

In the 1980s, Mexican American election strategy became more sophisticated as a new generation of college-educated Latinos sought public office and assumed leadership roles in political organizations. Among Latinos elected to statewide office in the 1980s and 1990s were Democrat Raul Gonzalez (the first Latino elected to statewide office in Texas), who served on the Texas Supreme Court from 1986 until 1999; Democrat Dan Morales, the state's attorney general for two terms from 1991 through 1998; and Republican Tony Garza, elected to the Texas Railroad Commission in 1998. After President Bush appointed Garza U.S. ambassador to Mexico in 2002, Governor Perry replaced him on the commission with Victor Carrillo early in 2003. Just as the political party affiliation of Latino elected officials is divided, so too is the Latino electorate.

Although Latinos are more likely to vote for Democratic candidates, Republican candidates, such as George W. Bush, have succeeded in winning the support of many Latino voters. Successful GOP candidates emphasize family issues and target heavily Latino areas for campaign appearances and media advertising. Bush also selected several Latinos for high-profile positions, most notably secretary of state (Tony Garza and Al Gonzales) and Supreme Court justice (Al Gonzales). Gonzales resigned from the Texas Supreme Court in 2001 to become White House counsel to President Bush. Many political observers believe he will be the first Latino appointed to the U.S. Supreme Court. Governor Rick Perry also appointed a Latino secretary of state, Democrat Henry Cuellar, who served from 2001 to 2002.

As a result of the votes Bush received in the 1998 gubernatorial election, Democrats no longer assume they have the support of Latino voters in statewide electoral contests. The voting behavior of Latinos indicates they respond to candidates and issues, not to a particular political party. Often, successful Republican candidates distance themselves from their party, especially in the Latino community. In one 1998 commercial that appeared on Spanish-language television stations, Governor Bush highlighted the support he received from Democrats but never identified himself as a Republican. Although both national and state Republican Party platforms discourage bilingual education and urge stricter immigration controls, Republican candidates frequently do not endorse these positions.

Many members of the Democratic Party believe it is important to have Latino nominees for high-level statewide offices in order to attract Latino voters to the polls. They argue that since the majority of Latinos are more likely to support Democratic candidates, a higher voter turnout will result in the election of more Democrats to office. In 2002, Laredo businessman Tony Sanchez Jr. became the first Latino candidate to be nominated for governor by a major party in Texas. Challenged for the Democratic nomination by former Texas attorney general Dan Morales, on 1 March 2002 the two men held the first Spanish-language gubernatorial debate in U.S. history. By 2004, there were 37 Latinos serving in the Texas Legislature; and of the 5,200 elected positions in Texas, more than 1,900 were held by Latinos.

The sheer size of the Latino population causes politicians to solicit support from this group. Latino voters can represent the margin of victory for a successful candidate. Lower levels of political activity than in the population at large, however, both in registering to vote and in voting, limit the impact of the Latino electorate.

African Americans

In April 1990, the Texas State Democratic Executive Committee filled a candidate vacancy by nominating Potter County court-at-law judge Morris Overstreet, an African American Democrat, for a seat on the Texas Court of Criminal Appeals. Because the Republican candidate, Louis Sturns, was also African American, this historic action guaranteed the state's voters would elect the first African American to statewide office in Texas. Overstreet won in 1990 and again in 1994. He served until 1998, when he ran unsuccessfully for Texas attorney general. Governor Bush appointed Republican Michael Williams to the Texas Railroad Commission in 1999. This African American commissioner was elected to a six-year term in 2002.

The appointment of Justice Wallace Bernard Jefferson to the Texas Supreme Court in 2001 increased the number of African Americans in statewide offices to three. Justice Jefferson is the first African American to serve on the court. He and another African American, Dale Wainwright, were elected in 2002 to six-year terms on that court. In 2002, former Dallas mayor Ron Kirk became the first African American nominated by either major party in Texas as its candidate for United States senator. Although unsuccessful in the general election, Kirk's candidacy was seen by many political observers as an important breakthrough for African American politicians.

Since the 1930s, African American Texans have tended to identify with the Democratic Party. With a voting-age population in excess of 1 million, they constitute about 10 percent of the state's potential voters. As demonstrated in recent electoral contests, approximately 80 percent of Texas's African American citizens say that they are Democrats, and only 5 percent are declared Republicans. The remainder are independents. More than 90 percent of the state's African Americans of voting age support Democratic candidates and tend to remain with the Democratic Party regardless of income. From 1971 to 2004, African Americans increased their membership in the Texas Legislature from 3 to 16. By 2004, more than 500 elective offices in Texas were held by African Americans.

Women in Politics

Texas women did not begin to vote and hold public office for three-quarters of a century after Texas joined the federal Union. Nevertheless, in 1990, Texas female voters outnumbered male voters, and Ann Richards was elected governor. Through 1990, however, only four women had won a statewide office in Texas, including two-term governor Miriam A. ("Ma") Ferguson (1925–1927 and 1933–1935). Mrs. Ferguson owed her office to supporters of her husband, Jim, who was impeached and removed from the governorship in 1917. After 1990, the number of women elected to statewide office increased dramatically.

Female candidates were also successful in winning an increasing number of seats in the Texas Legislature—from 2 in 1971 to 36 in 2003. This total dropped to 35 after the death of Representative Irma Rangel (D-Kingsville). The expanded presence of women in public office is changing public policy. Increased punishment for family violence and sexual abuse of children, together with a renewed focus on public education, can be attributed in large part to the presence of women in policymaking positions.

In the early 1990s, Texas women served as mayors in about 150 of the state's towns and cities, including the first 4 in population (Houston, Dallas, San Antonio, and El Paso). As mayor of Dallas (1988–1991), Annette Strauss was fond of greeting out-of-state visitors with this message: "Welcome to Texas, where men are men and women are mayors." In 2004, women were mayors in some of the largest Texas cities: Beaumont, Dallas, Del Rio, Denton, Euless, Flower Mound, Killeen, Laredo, Plano, Sherman, and Waco. In fact, Dallas, was the largest city in America with a woman mayor.

The impact of women's voting power was evident in both 2000 and 2002, when women led all candidates on either ticket in votes received. With her reelection to the U.S. Senate in 2000, Republican Kay Bailey Hutchison became the first person to receive more than 4 million votes, and in 2002 Carole Keeton Rylander received over 2.8 million votes in her reelection as state comptroller. Rylander later changed her name to Strayhorn, following her marriage in early January 2003. However, despite their electoral victories in Texas and elsewhere across the nation, fewer women than men seek elective public office. There are several reasons for this situation, chief of which is difficulty in raising money to pay campaign expenses. There are, however, other reasons that discourage women from seeking public office. Although women are enjoy increasing freedom, they still shoulder more responsibilities for family and home than men do (even in two-career families). Some mothers feel obligated to care for children in the home until the children finish high school. Such parental obligations, together with age-old prejudices, deny women their rightful place in government. Yet customs, habits, and attitudes do not remain static; new opportunities for women in public service are expanding accordingly.

Political Campaigns

Elections in Texas fill national, state, county, city, and special-district offices. With so many electoral contests, citizens are frequently besieged by candidates seeking votes and asking for money to finance their election campaigns. It is through the democratic election process, however, that Texans have an opportunity to influence public policymaking by expressing preferences for candidates and issues when they vote.

Conducting Campaigns in the Twenty-First Century

Campaigns are no longer limited to speeches by candidates on a courthouse lawn or from the rear platform of a campaign train. Today prospective voters are more likely to be harried by a barrage of campaign publicity involving television and radio broadcasting, newspapers, billboards, yard signs, and bumper stickers. Moreover, voters will probably encounter door-to-door canvassers, receive political information in the mail, be asked to answer telephone inquiries from professional pollsters or locally hired telephone-bank callers, receive information by e-mail, and be solicited for donations to pay for campaign expenses.

Nonissue Campaigns   Only a minority of Texans, and indeed other Americans, are actively concerned with politics. But even among those interested in political affairs, there is a growing impatience with current styles of campaigning. Character and political style have become more important than issues. A candidate's physical appearance and personality are increasingly important, because television has become the primary mode of campaign communication.

Importance of the Media   Since the days of W. Lee "Pappy" O'Daniel, the media have played an important role in Texas politics. In the 1930s, O'Daniel gained fame as a radio host for Light Crust Flour and later his own Hillbilly Flour. On his weekly broadcast show, the slogan "Pass the biscuits, Pappy" made O'Daniel a household name throughout the state. In 1938, urged by his radio fans, "Pappy" ran for governor, attracting huge crowds. With a platform featuring the Ten Commandments and the Golden Rule, he won the election by a landslide.[24] In the 1970s, television and radio ads were a regular part of every gubernatorial and U.S. senatorial candidate's campaign budget. By the 1980s and 1990s, candidates from the top of the ballot to the local city council and school board used radio to reach potential voters. With the exception of smaller media markets and local cable providers, many "middle of the ballot" candidates have found television time to be cost-prohibitive.

Today, with over 12 million potential voters in 254 counties, Texas is by necessity a media state for political campaigning. To visit every county personally during a primary campaign, a candidate would need to go into 4 counties per day, five days a week, from the filing deadline in January to the March primary date. Such extensive travel would leave little time for speechmaking, fundraising, and other campaign activities. Although some candidates for statewide office in recent years have traveled to each county in the state, none won an election. Therefore, Texas campaigners must rely more heavily on television and radio exposure than candidates in other states.

Most Texas voters learn about candidates through television commercials that may range in length from 15 seconds for a **sound bite** (a brief statement of a candidate's campaign theme) to a full minute. Ads allow candidates to structure their messages carefully and avoid the risk of a possible misstatement that might occur in a political debate. Therefore, the more money a candidate's campaign has, the less interest the candidate has in debating an opponent. Usually the candidate who is the underdog (the one who is behind in the polls) wants to debate.

Points to Ponder

The father of western swing music, Bob Wills was one of the original Light Crust Doughboys who worked for W. Lee O'Daniel. (© Bettman/CORBIS)

Candidates are relying increasingly on the Internet to communicate with voters. But the benefit of low cost must be balanced against problems unique to the medium of web sites and electronic mail. Issues include limited access and use of computers by the population that votes (those 40 to 65 years old), consumer resistance to "spam" (electronic junk mail), "blogging" (creating weblogs), "cybersquatting" (individuals other than the candidate purchasing domain names that are similar to the candidate's name and then selling the domain name to the highest bidder), and hyperlinks to inappropriate web sites. In the 2002 mayoral election in Plano, incumbent Jeran Akers purchased the "patforplano" domain name to prevent his opponent, Pat "Pat for Plano" Evans access. However, the negative press that this generated contributed to Akers's loss in a closely contested election.

Mudslide Campaigns Following gubernatorial candidate Ann Richards's victory over Jim Mattox in the Democratic runoff primary of April 1990, one journalist reported that Richards had "won by a mudslide." This expression suggests the reaction of many citizens who were disappointed, if not infuriated, by the candidates' generally low ethical level of campaigning and by their avoidance of critical public issues. But when character became more important as a voting consideration in the 1990s, negative campaigning became more prominent.

The 2002 campaigns featured ads by U.S. Senate candidates claiming that the other had illegal or unethical ties with the failed energy giant Enron Corporation. Also, there were ads by attorney general candidates blaming the other for the high cost of insurance. However, the Texas gubernatorial campaign produced a new low in mudslinging. With less than two weeks remaining in the campaign, Tony Sanchez released a Texas Department of

Public Safety tape showing Rick Perry abusing his power of office, after his driver was pulled over for speeding, by asking a female state trooper, "Why don't you just let us get on down the road?" Less than one week prior to the election, Perry countered with the "Kiki" ad. The commercial featured two drug enforcement agents claiming that the drug lords who orchestrated a hit on federal drug agent Enrique "Kiki" Camarena had laundered their drug money through Tesoro Savings and Loan, a financial institution that Sanchez once owned. One political observer noted that this was the turning point in the campaign: "It was brutally negative, even by the standards of this bitterly partisan election season."[25]

Campaign Reform

Concern over the shortcomings of American election campaigns has given rise to organized efforts toward improvement at all levels of government. Reformers have ranged from a single citizen to members of the U.S. Congress and large lobby groups. Reform issues include eliminating negative campaigning, increasing free media access for candidates, and regulating campaign finance.

Eliminating Negative Campaigning   The Markle Commission on the Media and the Electorate has concluded that candidates, media people, consultants, and the electorate are all blameworthy for the increase in negative campaigns. Candidates and consultants, wishing to win at any cost, employ negative advertising and make exaggerated claims. The media emphasize poll results and the horserace appearance of a contest rather than basic issues and candidate personalities that relate to leadership potential. Voters must be the corrective force for reform. Because the bottom line of campaign reform involves educating citizens, little can be achieved quickly.

Increasing Free Media Access   Certainly a candidate for statewide office in Texas cannot win without first communicating with a large percentage of the state's voting population. As noted previously, television is the most important communication tool and the most expensive. One group supporting reform in the area of media access is the Alliance for Better Campaigns (**www.bettercampaigns.org**). So long as paid media advertising is a necessary part of political campaigns and media outlets generate a significant source of revenue from political campaigns, fundraising will remain important in electoral success.

Campaign Finance

On more than one occasion, President Lyndon Johnson bluntly summarized the relationship between politics and finance: "Money makes the mare go." Although most political scientists would state this fact differently, it is obvious that money is needed to pay the necessary expenses of election campaigns. The 1990 gubernatorial campaign established a record of $45 million spent on the primary and general election races combined, including more than $22 million by Midland oilman Clayton Williams. He narrowly lost to Ann Richards, who spent $12 million. However, that record was shattered by the 2002 gubernatorial election. Tony Sanchez's and Rick Perry's campaigns spent a combined record of more than $95 million. Sanchez outspent Perry by more than two to one ($67 million to $28 million) in the race for governor. Despite his big spending, Sanchez lost by 20 percent.[26] Even though $95 million establishes a new record for spending in a Texas race, it does not establish a national record. New York's 2002 gubernatorial contest, which cost an estimated $148 million, ranks first, followed by California's gubernatorial races in 1998 ($130 million) and 2002 ($110 million).

Many Texans are qualified to hold public office, but relatively few can afford to pay their own campaign expenses (as presidential candidates Ross Perot and Steve Forbes and gubernatorial candidates Clayton Williams and Tony Sanchez did) or are willing to undertake fundraising drives designed to attract significant campaign contributions by others (as George W. Bush has done in both his gubernatorial and presidential campaigns, and Governor Rick Perry has done in his campaigns for lieutenant governor and governor).

The need to raise large amounts of cash exists at local, state, and national levels. Successful Houston City Council candidates often require from $150,000 (for district races) to $250,000 (for at-large races), and mayoral candidates may need $2 million or more. In 2003, Houston businessman Bill White spent a record $8.6 million in his mayoral election, including $2.2 million of his own money. Some individuals and **political action committees (PACs)**, which are organizations created to collect and distribute contributions to political campaigns, donate because they agree with a candidate's position on the issues. The motivation of others, however, may be questionable. What these donors receive in return for their contributions is access to elected officials. Both politicians and donors argue that access does not mean donors gain control of officials' policymaking decisions. Yet others, such as former Texas House Speaker Pete Laney, attribute the decline in voter participation to a growing sense that average citizens have no voice in the political process because they cannot afford to make large financial donations to candidates.

Both federal and state laws have been enacted to regulate various aspects of campaign financing. Texas laws on the subject are relatively weak and tend to emphasize reporting of contributions. Federal laws are more restrictive, featuring both reporting requirements and limits on contributions to a candidate's political campaign by individuals and PACs.

In 1989, chicken magnate Lonnie "Bo" Pilgrim handed out $10,000 checks on the Senate floor, leaving the "payable to" lines blank, as legislators debated reforming the state's workers' compensation laws. Many were surprised to find that Texas had no laws prohibiting such actions. Two years later the Texas Legislature passed laws prohibiting political contributions to members of the legislature while they are in session, and in 1993 Texas voters approved a constitutional amendment establishing the **Texas Ethics**

Commission. Among its constitutional duties, the Texas Ethics Commission requires financial disclosure from public officials. However, unlike the Federal Election Campaign Act, Texas has no laws placing a limit on political contributions.

Further restricting the amount of money that can be contributed to campaigns is another area of possible reform. Efforts in this area, however, have been unsuccessful. In 2002, Congress passed the long-awaited **Campaign Reform Act**, signed into law by President Bush. This federal law includes the following reforms:

- It prohibits **soft money**—that is, donations made to national political parties.
- It increases individual **hard money** (or direct) contribution limits.
- It restricts corporations' and labor unions' ability to run "electioneering" ads featuring the names and/or likenesses of candidates close to election day.[27]

Plaintiffs such as Texas Congressman Ron Paul and others challenged the constitutionality of this act, claiming it was an unconstitutional restraint on freedom of speech. In 2003, in a sharply divided decision, the U.S. Supreme Court upheld the constitutionality of the "soft money" ban in *McConnell v. FEC*. Additional reform efforts include making contributor information more easily available to citizens. Candidates and treasurers of campaign committees are required to file periodically with the Texas Ethics Commission (**www.ethics.state.tx.us**). With limited exceptions, these reports must be made electronically. Sworn statements list all contributions received and expenditures made during designated reporting intervals. Candidates who fail to file these reports are subject to a fine.

During the 78th regular session in 2003, the Texas Legislature passed House Bill 1606 that was later signed into law by Governor Perry. Supported by such public interest groups as Common Cause Texas, Public Citizen, and Campaigns for People, this statute strengthens the Texas Ethics Commission, curbs conflicts of interest, and requires greater disclosure of campaign contributions. Specifically, the law requires officials of cities with more than 100,000 population and trustees of school districts with enrollments of 5,000 or more to disclose the sources of their income, as well as the value of their stocks and their real-estate holdings. Additionally, candidates for state political offices are required to identify employers and occupations of people contributing $500 or more to their campaigns, and publicly report "cash on hand." The measure also prohibits lawmakers from lobbying for clients before state agencies. "This bill eliminates several chronic ethics loopholes and gives the Ethics Commission some teeth," said Tom "Smitty" Smith, Texas director of Public Citizen, a government watchdog group. "It's a big step forward."[28]

In practice, both federal and state campaign finance laws have largely failed to cope with influence buying through transfers of money in the form of campaign contributions. It may well be that as long as campaigns are funded by private sources, they will remain inadequately regulated.

Looking Ahead

Under the freedom-of-speech guarantee in the First Amendment of the U.S. Constitution, Americans have a right to give money to the candidates of their choice. The U.S. Supreme Court has ruled that campaign contributions may be limited, but independent expenditures in support of a specific candidate may not. Furthermore, in *Buckley v. Valeo* (1976), the U.S. Supreme Court held that candidates may not be prohibited from spending their own money on their campaigns. In the face of these guaranteed rights, political parties are weakened in turn. When PACs can collectively contribute millions of dollars to a candidate for a statewide office, the candidate no longer needs to remain obligated to a party.

It is interesting to speculate on how candidates and voters would respond to or be affected by public funding of Texas elections. First, challengers would be placed on a more equal financial footing with incumbents. Private financing favors incumbents in raising campaign money. Texas legislators are well aware of this, and they will surrender their advantage only in the face of strong public pressure. Second, public funding would run counter to Texas tradition. The Lone Star State has never tried it, and many citizens are undisturbed by big-money domination of politics.

For the foreseeable future, Texas will continue to allow wealthy individuals and powerful interest groups to buy political favors from government under the guise of making campaign contributions. The "The Politics of Interest Groups," provides extensive coverage of interest groups.

☆ Chapter Summary ☆

- Nearly every citizen over the age of 18 can vote. One area of concern is how few eligible voters choose to exercise this right. There are three types of elections: party primaries, general elections, and special elections. Local government and political party officials administer elections.

- Political parties serve two functions: administering party primaries and conducting party conventions. These are activities of the party's temporary organization. The permanent party organization includes autonomous executive committees at the local, state, and national levels that direct party activities.

- Texas voters and political parties represent a variety of political ideologies, including conservatism and liberalism. The two major political parties are Republican and Democratic. A number of minor, or third, parties also often appear on general election ballots.

- Historically, Texas was a one-party state, dominated by the Democratic Party following Reconstruction through the 1960s. Beginning in the 1970s and 1980s, the state moved toward a competitive two-party structure. In the 1990s and into the twenty-first century, however, it appears that the state is becoming a one-party state again, with the Republican Party in control.

■ Recent elections reflect two major trends. The Republican Party now dominates statewide electoral contests. Democratic candidates are successful only in district and local races.

■ An increasing number of African Americans and Latinos have won office in recent years at both state and local levels of government. African American voters consistently favor Democratic candidates. Latino voters, although tending to favor Democratic candidates, have given strong support to some Republican candidates.

■ Gender-based politics became important during the final decades of the last century as women became more politically active and had a direct influence on public policy decisions. More women were elected to office from 1990 to 2004 than the total number elected prior to that time.

■ Political campaigns reflect the influence of the media (especially television), mudslide (negative) campaigning, and money. Both federal and state laws regulate election campaigns, with federal law requiring disclosure of donor information and limiting contributions. State law establishes reporting requirements. A possible solution to the influence of money on Texas politics is public funding of campaigns.

Key Terms

universal suffrage	jungle primary
literacy test	crossover voting
grandfather clause	canvass
poll tax	off-year or midterm election
white primary	special election
racial gerrymandering	voting precinct
at-large majority district	election judge
motor voter law	political party
Texas Election Code	stratarchy
voter registration	temporary party organization
elections administrator	platform
early voting	precinct convention
primary election	county convention
direct primary	district convention
general election	state convention
runoff primary	presidential preference primary
closed primary	caucus
open primary	superdelegate
nonpartisan blanket primary	permanent party organization
independent candidate	precinct chair

county executive committee	realignment
county chair	straight-ticket voting
district executive committee	third party
state executive committee	sound bite
conservative	political action committee (PAC)
neoconservatism	Texas Ethics Commission
liberal	Campaign Reform Act
neoliberal	soft money
dealignment	hard money

 Discussion Questions

1. Is the low voter turnout in Texas a problem? If so, how can this issue be addressed to increase voter participation?
2. Besides voting, what are some other ways a person can effectively participate in the system?
3. How has Texas's political culture been reflected in the development of political parties in the state? How is it reflected today?
4. In what ways does the structure of political parties in Texas encourage participation in partisan politics? In what ways does it discourage participation?
5. What challenges face the Democratic Party in Texas in the twenty-first century? What challenges face the state's Republican Party?
6. Can third parties be successful in Texas? How?
7. With the increasing political importance of women and of racial and ethnic minorities, how has Texas politics changed? What changes can we anticipate in the future?
8. What electoral reforms are suggested to improve all levels of government? Which of these reforms have the best chance of succeeding?

Internet Resources

Campaigns for Peoples: **www.campaignsforpeople.org**
Elections Division, Texas Secretary of State:
   www.sos.state.tx.us/elections/index.shtml
Green Party of Texas: **www.txgreens.org**
Independent Texans: **www.independenttexans.org**
Texas Democratic Party: **www.txdemocrats.org**
Texas Ethics Commission: **www.ethics.state.tx.us**
Texas Libertarian Party: **www.tx.lp.org**
Texas Reform Party: **www.texasreformparty.org**
Texas Republican Party: **www.texasgop.org**
Texas Young Republican Federation: **www.tyrf.org**
Young Democrats of Texas: **www.texasyds.org**

Notes

1. *Yick Wo* v. *Hopkins*, 118 U.S. 356, 370 (1886).
2. Christopher Long, "Ku Klux Klan," *The Handbook of Texas Online*, <www.tsha.utexas.edu/handbook/online/articles/view/KK/vek2.html>.
3. David Montejano, *Anglos and Mexicans in the Making of Texas, 1836–1986* (Austin: University of Texas Press, 1987), p. 143.
4. Other U.S. Supreme Court cases involving the Texas white primary are *Nixon* v. *Herndon* (1927), *Nixon* v. *Condon* (1932), and *Grovey* v. *Townsend* (1936). For more information on the history of the white primary in Texas, see Darlene Clark Hine, *Black Victory: The Rise and Fall of the White Primary in Texas* (Millwood, N.Y.: KTO Press, 1979).
5. For more information on racial gerrymandering and the use of at-large districts to disenfranchise minorities, see Christopher M. Burke, *The Appearance of Equality: Racial Gerrymandering, Redistricting, and the Supreme Court* (Westport, Conn.: Greenwood Press, 1999).
6. The Texas Election Code is a compilation of state laws that govern voter qualifications, procedures for nominating and electing party officials and government officials, and other matters related to suffrage and elections.
7. Office of the Texas Secretary of State. <http://www.sos.state.tx.us/>.
8. Sam Attlesey, "Bill Would Cut Election Dates to 4 Each Year," *Dallas Morning News*, 13 February 2001.
9. Tex. Elec. Code Ann. § 41.01 (2003).
10. Office of the Texas Secretary of State. <http://www.sos.state.tx.us/>.
11. Sam Attlesey, "Fewer Elections, More Votes?" *Dallas Morning News*, 17 May 1999.
12. This Point/Counterpoint is abridged and adapted from Rita Barr, "Voting on the Internet: Promise and Problems," *Interim News* 76 (3) (Austin: House Research Organization, Texas House of Representatives, 16 March 2000): 1–5.
13. Tex. Elec. Code Ann. § 172.086 (2003).
14. Tex. Elec. Code Ann. § 172.024 (2003).
15. Tex. Elec. Code Ann. § 42.006 (2003).
16. Office of the Secretary of State, "Under Vote_/_Over Vote State Averages." <http://www.sos.state.tx.us/>.
17. Dave McNeely, "Punch-Card Recount Law Helped GOP," *Austin American-Statesman*, 15 November 2000. See also Tex. Elec. Code Ann. § 127.130 (2003).
18. Samuel Eldersveld, *Political Parties: A Behavioral Analysis* (Chicago: Rand McNally, 1964).
19. Paul A. Gigot, "GOP's Clinton? George W. Bush Says No Way," *Wall Street Journal*, 30 October 1998.
20. T. R. Fehrenbach, *Lone Star: A History of Texas and Texans* (New York: Macmillan, 1999), p. 400.

21. Mike Kingston and Robert Piocheck, "A Brief Sketch of Texas History," *The Texas Almanac 2004–2005* (Dallas: Dallas Morning News, 2004), pp. 46–47.
22. Wayne Slater, "Governor Lines Up Millions in Pledges," *Dallas Morning News*, 25 February 2001.
23. For more information on the Grange in Texas, see Alwyn Barr, *Reconstruction to Reform: Texas Politics, 1876–1906* (Austin: University of Texas Press, 1971).
24. George N. Green, "O'Daniel, Wilbert Lee [Pappy]." *The Handbook of Texas Online* at <www.tsha.utexas.edu/handbook/online/articles/view/OO/fo'4.html>.
25. S. C. Gwynne, "Grand Illusion: Rich, Moderate, and Hispanic: For a While, Tony Sanchez Seemed Like a Competitive Candidate for Governor. Then the Smoke Cleared," *Texas Monthly*, December 2002, p. 46.
26. W. Gardner Selby, "Sanchez Campaign Fueled Record," *San Antonio Express-News*, 15 January 2002.
27. 2 U.S.C. § 431 (2002), The "Bipartisan Campaign Reform Act of 2002."
28. Quoted in "House Panel OK's Disclosure Rules," *Waco Tribune*, 17 April 2003.

SELECTED READING

───────────★───────────────────────────────────────

AWOL: The Texas Democrats Insist They've Still Got Some Fight Left in Them. So Why Are They Deserting the Battlefield?*

Evan Smith

Although the Texas Democratic Party claims to still be competitive in Texas elections, in recent years it has had few candidates file for high profile office. This article discusses the Texas Democratic Party's failure to field candidates for public office in 2004.

A few months ago, in the parking lot of the LBJ Library in Austin, I bumped into Ben Bentzin, the retired Dell Computer executive who ran unsuccessfully as a Republican for the Texas Senate in 2002. Ben and I are relentless kibitzers about politics, so I asked after his friend Michael McCaul, who is running for the U.S. House. One of the juicier fruits of last year's redistricting endgame was the creation of a new congressional district that stretches east from North Austin to suburban Houston; McCaul, a former federal prosecutor, was one of eight Republicans running for the seat in the March 9 primary. He told me that the race was going well: Another candidate had attempted to outflank McCaul on the right, but the likely outcome was that McCaul would decimate the guy and end up in a runoff with another of his rivals. (Which is exactly, come primary day, what happened.) Okay, I said innocently, but what happens in the fall? Which Democrat will the winner face? He grinned and replied, "There is none."

A No-show Election

Later that night, when I picked my jaw up off the floor, I wondered: How could the Democrats have permitted the Republicans to capture *without opposition* a new— that is, open—congressional seat, particularly when a nasty Republican primary would leave the eventual nominee bloodied and cash-strapped (which is also exactly what happened)? Beyond that, in how many other races had the Democrats decided to give up before the game began? The answer, I was surprised to learn, is way too many. In seventy races for the Texas Supreme Court, the Court of Criminal Appeals, the State Board of Education, the Texas Legislature, and the U.S. Congress, no Democrat will be on the ballot in November. The vast majority of the forfeits are in

*"AWOL: The Texas Democrats Insist They've Still Got Some Fight Left in Them, So Why Are They Deserting the Battlefield?" by Evan Smith. Reprinted with permission from *Texas Monthly*, May 2004.

races for the Texas House, where, of the 88 incumbent Republicans, 51 will waltz to victory without breaking a sweat. They include three of *Texas Monthly*'s Ten Worst Legislators of 2003—Joe Nixon and Beverly Woolley, both of Houston, and Robert Talton, of Pasadena—along with our lone pick for Dishonorable Mention, a certain Tom Craddick, of Midland. I always thought it was the obligation of the party out of power to run someone, anyone, even a guy in a chicken suit, against the sitting Speaker, if only to torment and distract him and hold him accountable. But apparently the Democrats couldn't even manage to do that.

Occasionally I give speeches around the state about Texas politics, and the question I'm always asked is, "Are the Democrats dead?" My standard answer is "no," partly because I'm a wishful thinker (democracy benefits from a lively debate over issues made possible by a two-party system, and nope, the two parties I'm referring to aren't the conservative Republicans and the moderate Republicans) and partly because I studied history (politics is cyclical—ask the Republicans who were wallowing in their minority party status as recently as a decade ago). But it's getting harder these days to answer anything other than "yes." Last year, the most substantive thing the Democrats did was flee Austin; what meaningful alternatives to the Republicans' cut-and-gut approach did they put before the people of Texas? (And why, right this minute, are they silent to the point of mute about school finance?) This year we have the Great No-show Election. And in two years, it appears, when the state's most powerful elective offices will again be up for grabs, the likelihood of the Democrats fielding a candidate who isn't a has-been, a sure loser, or a total unknown to the voters is slim. The only conclusion to be drawn is that the Democrats, if not dead, are on life support.

Not surprisingly, the Republicans agree with this analysis. "One of the main responsibilities of a political party is to put forward candidates and to give voters a choice," says Ted Royer, the spokesman for the Texas GOP. "Whenever you fail to do that, you're abdicating that responsibility." Surprisingly, although they're generally (a) smart and (b) realistic, few Democrats are willing to be as candid about their party's sorry state—at least publicly. Of the dozen or so former elected officials, kingmakers, and potential statewide candidates I talked to, only Ben Barnes, the ex-Speaker and lieutenant governor turned lobbyist and fundraiser, would criticize his brethren on the record. ("There's no one enunciating what we're for or against," Barnes says. "Unless there's someone out in front of the band, leading the parade, the party dies.") The rest offered, on background, a raft of excuses, justifications, recriminations, and what they insist, unconvincingly, are mitigating factors for this fall's dereliction of duty.

Mitigating Factors

The first of these was predictable, given the ideological makeup of the state: In many of the races in question, the Democrats can't possibly win, so why bother running? "Most of the seventy aren't competitive," says a Democrat who formerly held statewide office. "I don't even think you could keep Craddick busy. If Craddick went to Italy and stayed in Italy until November, he'd still get sixty-plus percent of the vote." This Democrat further argues that running candidates in can't-win districts purely for the sake of running could actually backfire, since it would drive up Republican turnout and cause problems for other Democrats in close races. "You put a bad candidate up for county commissioner," the ex-official says, "and you defeat your good candidate for county judge." And it works both ways: "When Rick Perry runs statewide, the last thing he wants is someone in a heavily Hispanic district ginning up a hot race and generating a lot of Democratic votes." Maybe all that's true, but it still reads like the Democrats are shrinking from a fight. (Gee, Santa Anna's army sure looks big. Not sure we can be "competitive." Guess we'll stay home.)

Another rationalization was a variation on the why-bother idea: Because of redistricting, the system is rigged to protect members of both parties, so the notion of a vigorous general election, however badly we might want one, is a sham. Even the late lieutenant governor Bob Bullock—a Democrat, it should be noted—took the path of least resistance when it came to creating safe seats for incumbents. "Toward the end of his career, Bullock was in the getting-people-reelected business rather than the serving-Texas business," says a prominent Democrat who's never run for office but might. Here the rationalizers have a point—to a point. Without a scandal for a story line, it is next to impossible for a challenger to defeat a better-known, better-funded incumbent in a district packed full of voters in the incumbent's party. The GOP acknowledges this too: While the Democrats haven't run candidates in 70 races this year, the Republicans have opted out of 45, mostly in nonwhite districts (the GOP's version of "noncompetitive"). But it's less of an issue when you're the majority. The minority, on the other hand, remains a minority unless it cracks the code. And first it has to try.

What about money? The Democrats I talked to say they don't have nearly enough of it and, given the catch-22-like conundrum of not being alive until they're alive, can't get any; short of finding another self-funder like Tony Sanchez, they can't possibly compete. So—once more with feeling—why run? Two words: Howard Dean, who launched a campaign for president against a wildly popular Republican at a time when the general belief was that the Democrats were dead and proceeded to raise $40 million, much of it from new donors, by running anyway.

Finally, there's the disarray of the party machinery, which everybody cites—and lays at the feet of poor Molly Beth Malcolm, who stepped down as state Democratic chair late last year after five and a half years in the post. She wasn't good at raising money, they say. She didn't recruit the kind of candidates who can win. She wasn't aggressive enough at "messaging" (a fancy word for the scorched-earth attacks that Karen Hughes used to level against the Democrats in the early nineties, when she was the GOP mouthpiece, Ann Richards was governor, and the Republicans were in the seemingly permanent minority). Malcolm categorically rejects the blame, but whatever happened in the past, she isn't the reason—no chair ever is—for the high number of no-shows this fall. It's the Democrats' deficit of ideas. Says Barnes: "We haven't shown the people of Texas solutions to their problems that are better than the Republican philosophy of 'Cut taxes, privatize everything, and have as little government as possible.'" Of course, it could be worse. Malcolm's successor, Charles Soechting, says that when he took the job four and a half months ago, the Democrats were planning on contesting only 11 of the 88 House seats. "I have to tell you," he says, "that I'm quite honestly very pleased with thirty-seven."

Why Democrats Should Have
Gone All Out in 2004

The shame of all this for the Democrats is that it didn't have to be. There were many reasons for the party to go all-out this year: the opportunity to benefit from divisive Republican primaries; the heavy Democratic turnout that will be generated by a close presidential election; the backlash against the Republican leadership, as manifested in Perry's low poll numbers (only a 40 percent approval rating) and the primary defeat of four so-called Craddick Democrats (with two more likely to lose their runoffs); the investigation of alleged campaign-finance violations by Craddick, Congressman Tom DeLay, and other Republicans and the prospect that a Sharpstown-style blitz of indictments could incite a throw-the-bums-out reaction by voters; the chance to groom young candidates for races in the future; the possibility that lightning could strike—you never know.

And, most of all, the looming specter of 2006, when the Republicans may be clawing each other's eyes out in primaries for governor, lieutenant governor, and several other top-tier offices. Any effort by the Democrats this year, even an unsuccessful one, might have inspired a crop of real rather than pretend candidates to make a play for control of the Legislature and the statehouse two years hence, and voters would have seen that reports of their death have been greatly exaggerated. Alas, there are seventy reasons to believe otherwise.

Chapter 5

THE POLITICS OF
INTEREST GROUPS

Sargent © *Austin American-Statesman*. Reprinted with permission of Universal Press Syndicate.
All rights reserved.

*A*s Ben Sargent's cartoon suggests, interest groups, such as the business lobby, have considerable influence in state government. Texas politicians need funding to finance their campaigns and to discourage others from running against them. Interest groups want favorable laws and policies from elected decision makers. Efforts by a well-financed group are usually productive, particularly if the group has helped to raise money for an election campaign.

Politics typically focuses on the nomination and election of individuals to public office. There is, however, much more to it than that. Politics is perhaps best understood as the process of influencing public policy decisions to protect and preserve a group, to achieve the group's goals, and to distribute benefits to the group's members. Organized citizens demand policies that promote their financial security, education, health, welfare, and protection.

Because government makes and enforces public policy decisions, it is not surprising that efforts are made to influence those officials who make and apply society's rules or policies. One important approach is through group action. History shows that people who organize for political action tend to be more effective in achieving their goals than persons acting alone.

Interest Groups in the Political Process

When attempting to influence political decisions or the selection of the men and women who make them, people usually turn either to political parties (examined in the chapter "The Politics of Elections and Parties") or to interest groups (the subject of this chapter).

What Is an Interest Group?

An **interest group** may be identified as a pressure group, special-interest group, or lobby. It is an organization whose members share common views and objectives. To promote their interests, such groups engage in activities designed to influence government officials and policy decisions. During the 2003 regular legislative session, the interest groups in action included the Independent Colleges and Universities of Texas (ICUT), which lobbied the legislature against cuts for the Texas Equalization Grants (TEG) and Texas Grants Scholarship Programs for college students, and the Texas Coalition to Abolish the Death Penalty, which continues to lobby actively for a moratorium on the death penalty. Entering the 2004 special legislative session on school finance, teachers and school boards associations supported funding increases to boost teacher salaries, as well as significant increases in state aid for other public education needs.

Political Parties and Interest Groups

Although political parties and interest groups both attempt to influence policy decisions by government officials, they differ in their methods. The principal purpose of party activity is to gain control of government to achieve party goals. In contrast, an interest group seeks to influence government officials (regardless of their party affiliation) to the advantage of the group. Interest groups try to influence policy decisions in the following ways:

- By using persuasion to mobilize their own members and supporters
- By attempting to sway public opinion
- By building coalitions with other groups, whose interests are identical or closely related, on one or more issues
- By obtaining access to key decision makers
- By influencing elections

Generally, an interest group wants government policies implemented in ways that benefit the group without necessarily placing its own members in public office. Economic groups (for example, the Texas Bankers Association) and social groups (such as the Texas Congress of Parents and Teachers) serve as vehicles to make their policy preferences known to government officials. As intermediaries for people who share common interests but reside throughout the state, interest groups in effect supplement the formal system of geographic representation used for electing many officeholders. In essence, such organizations provide an internal system of functional representation. They offer a form of protection for such groups as businesspeople, laborers, farmers, Roman Catholics, Latinos, teachers, physicians, and college students across the state. These groups are composed of people who have similar interests but may not constitute a majority in any city, county, legislative district, or state.

Factors Fostering Interest Group Formation

The growth and diversity of interest groups in the United States continue unabated. The rate of proliferation of interest groups in the country and within states has much to do with an increasingly complex society. Political scientists Burnett Loomis and Allan Cigler contend that these growing numbers, plus high levels of activity, distinguish contemporary interest group politics from previous eras.[1] There are a number of reasons interest groups proliferate in Texas and throughout the country.

Legal and Cultural Influences In *NAACP v. Alabama* (1958), the U.S. Supreme Court recognized the **right of association** as part of the right of assembly granted by the First Amendment of the U.S. Constitution. This decision greatly facilitated the development of interest groups, ensuring the right of individuals to organize into groups for political, economic, religious, and social purposes.

The nation's political culture has traditionally encouraged individuals to organize themselves into a bewildering array of associations—religious, fraternal, professional, and recreational, among others. Americans have responded by creating literally thousands of such groups. Social movements during the 1960s and 1970s also sparked interest group activity. New groups formed on issues surrounding civil rights, women's rights, and opposition to the Vietnam War.

Decentralized Structures of Governance   In a **decentralized government,** power is not concentrated at the highest level. Decentralization is achieved in two principal ways. First, the federal system divides power between the national government and the 50 state governments (as explained in the chapter "Federalism and the Texas Constitution"). In turn, each state shares its power with a wide variety of local governments, including counties, cities, and special districts. Second, within each level of government, power is separated into three branches or departments: legislative, executive, and judicial. This separation of powers is especially apparent at the national and state levels.

A decentralized structure increases the ability of interest groups to influence governmental activities. This structure provides different access points for groups to fight their battles at different levels of government and within different branches at each level. Dispersal of power within branches or departments of government enhances an interest group's chance of success. Divided power also makes public officials more vulnerable to the influence of interest groups.

Decentralized Party System and Deemphasized Ideologies   Two other factors have precipitated interest group activity: a decentralized political party system and deemphasized ideologies. First, the absence of unified and responsible political parties magnifies opportunities for influential interest group action. A lack of strong, organized political parties can particularly affect policymakers (both state and local). By contrast, a united, cohesive party can provide policymakers with a concrete agenda and political strength to resist pressure from well-organized interest groups. In recent years, Texas has experienced stronger party competition, which should produce more party unity, but interest groups still continue to exert heavy influence over the state's officials. Second, ideologies—well-developed systems of political, social, and economic beliefs—traditionally have not been strong factors in Texas politics. Many Texas voters do not typically act in accordance with their commitment to ideological beliefs. Conservative political ideas, however, have increased in importance for many Texans, especially supporters of Republican candidates. The Christian Coalition and similar organizations have spurred this new wave of political activism among social conservatives.

Organization of Interest Groups

As defined, an interest group is an organization of individuals who seek to influence government decisions, usually without trying to place the group's own members in public office. The organization provides members with information and benefits, and it generally tries to get them involved in the political process. Such a description suggests that any organization becomes an interest group when it influences or attempts to influence governmental decisions.

Organizational Patterns

There are almost as many **organizational patterns** as there are interest groups. This variety arises from the fact that, in addition to lobbying, most interest groups carry on nonpolitical functions of paramount importance to their members. A religious organization, for example, emphasizes charitable and spiritual activities, but on occasion it may undertake political activity.

Some interest groups are highly centralized organizations that take the form of a single controlling body without affiliated local or regional units. An example of such a centralized group currently operating in Texas is the National Rifle Association (NRA). Other groups are decentralized, consisting of loose alliances of local and regional subgroups. Their activities may be directed at either the local, state, or national level. Many trade associations (such as the Texas Association of Business and Chambers of Commerce) and labor unions (such as those affiliated with the American Federation of Labor–Congress of Industrial Organizations [AFL-CIO]) are examples of decentralized organizations active in Texas politics. Social organizations, including the National Women's Political Caucus and Common Cause, usually have both state and local chapters in Texas.

Membership and Leadership

Interest groups are composed chiefly of persons from professional and managerial occupations. They are individuals who already tend to have greater resources than most people possess. For instance, members are more likely to be homeowners with high levels of income and formal education who enjoy a high standard of living. Participation, especially active participation, varies. Many citizens are not affiliated with any group, whereas others are members of several. One study found that one of every four Americans is affiliated with three or more interest groups.[2]

An organized group of any size is usually composed of an active minority and a passive majority. As a result, decisions are regularly made by a small number of members. These decision makers may range from a few elected officers to a larger body of delegates representing the entire membership. Organizations generally leave decision making and other leadership activities to a few people. Widespread apathy among rank-and-file members and the difficulty of dislodging entrenched leaders probably account for limited participation in most group decisions.

Other factors influence **group leadership**. These include the financial resources of the group (members who contribute most heavily usually have greater weight in making decisions); time-consuming leadership duties (only a few people can afford to devote much of their time without compensation); and the personality traits of leaders (some individuals have greater leadership ability and motivation than others).

Classification of Interest Groups

The increasing diversity of American interest groups at the national, state, and local levels of government permits them to be classified in several ways. Not only can they be studied by organizational patterns but they can also be categorized according to the level or branch of government to which they direct their attention. Some groups exert their influence at all levels of government and on legislative, executive (including administrative), and judicial officials. Others may try to spread their views among the general public and may best be classified according to the subject matter they represent. Some groups do not fit readily into any category, whereas others fit into more than one.

Economic Groups

Many interest groups exist primarily to promote the economic self-interest of their members. These organizations are commonly known as **economic interest groups**. Traditionally, many people contribute significant amounts of money and time to obtain financial benefits. Thus, some organizations exist to further the economic interests of a broad group, such as trade associations. Others are created to protect the interests of a single type of business, such as restaurant associations. The Texas Association of Business and Chambers of Commerce is an example of a broader type of interest group, known as an umbrella organization. Then there are individual corporations, such as the bankrupt Enron Corporation (now operating on a very reduced scale as Prisma Energy International), that use the political process to promote the company's particular economic interests.

Business Groups   Businesspeople understand they have common interests that may be promoted by collective action. They were among the first to organize and press national, state, and local governments to adopt favorable public policies. **Business organizations** typically advocate lower taxes, a lessening or elimination of price and quality controls, and minimal concessions to labor unions. At the state level, business organizations most often take the form of trade associations (groups that act on behalf of an industry). Some of the many Texas trade associations are the

Texas Association of Builders, the Texas Good Roads and Transportation Association, and the newly formed Texas Coalition for Affordable Insurance Solutions. In past legislative sessions, Texas businesses and their representatives have generally succeeded in having many of their policy preferences enacted into law. Some reports indicate that the Texas Association of Business and Texans for Lawsuit Reform contributed more than $2.6 million to support Republican candidates in key legislative races in 2002. Subsequently, the GOP-controlled 78th Legislature passed several "business friendly" bills. One of these bills limited lawsuits against manufacturers, pharmaceutical companies, and retailers.[3]

Labor Groups Unions representing Texas workers are relatively active, but not as numerous or powerful as business-related groups. The state's **labor organizations** seek, among other goals, government intervention to increase wages, obtain adequate health insurance coverage, provide unemployment insurance, and promote safe working conditions.

Texans are traditionally sensitive to the potential political power of organized labor, especially since the enactment of a right-to-work law, but three industrial labor organizations are generally regarded as significant in Texas government. These are the Texas affiliates of the AFL-CIO (comprising approximately 60 percent of all Texas union members), Teamster locals, and the Texas Oil and Chemical Workers Union. For a highly industrialized state with a large population, union membership in Texas is small compared to that of other states. In 2003, there were slightly more than a half a million union members employed in Texas. This was only about one-fourth as many

AFL-CIO rally in Texas (Courtesy of Ed Sills, Director of Communications, Texas AFL-CIO)

as in New York, although Texas had 1.2 million more wage and salary work-ers than did New York.

Professional and Government Employee Groups

Closely related to economic interest groups are groups dedicated to further-ing the interests of a profession or an occupation.

Professional Groups Standards of admission to a profession or an occupa-tion and the licensing of practitioners concern **professional groups**. Exam-ples of Texas professional and occupational associations are the Texas Trial Lawyers Association, the Texas Health Care Association, and the Texas Society of Certified Accountants. In 1999, physicians won a significant vic-tory in the 76th Legislature when Texas became the first state to allow doc-tors to bargain collectively over fees and policies with health maintenance organizations (HMOs). In 2003, the Texas Medical Association (TMA) was successful in actively lobbying the passage of the constitutional amend-ment, Proposition 12, which authorized the state legislature to impose a $750,000 cap for noneconomic damages in medical malpractice cases.

Government Employee Groups Officers and employees of state and local governments organize to obtain better working conditions, higher wages, more fringe benefits, and better retirement packages. Teacher groups, for example, made some headway in the 76th legislative session. Senate Bill 5 allocated $2 billion to fund a $3,000 pay raise for every public school teacher, librarian, and registered school nurse in Texas. Building on their momentum, teacher groups successfully pushed a plan to fully or partially fund state-sup-ported health insurance for public school teachers and other school employ-ees, both active and retired. Teacher groups continue to lobby the legislature for a $5,000 salary increase that would place Texas teachers at par with the national salary average. In addition, when the 78th Legislature faced a bud-get crisis in 2003, teacher groups actively lobbied the legislature against cuts in education funding. These groups included the Texas State Teachers Asso-ciation (TSTA), Texas Federation of Teachers (TFT), Texas Association of Col-lege Teachers (TACT), and Texas Community College Teachers Association (TCCTA). According to the Texas State Teachers Association, 39 bills that the organization opposed were defeated in the 2003 legislative session.

Among state government employees, the largest group is the Texas Public Employees Association (TPEA). City government groups include the Texas City Management Association and the Texas City Attorneys Association. Through their organizational activities, **public officer and employee groups** resist efforts to reduce the size of state and local governmental bureaucracies (although not always with success). The County Judges and Commissioners Association of Texas and the Justices of the Peace and Con-stables Association of Texas, for example, have been instrumental in block-ing some measures designed to reform justice of the peace courts and county courts in Texas.

Social Groups

There is a wide array of **social interest groups**. These include racial and ethnic organizations, civil rights organizations, gender-based organizations, and religious-based organizations.

Racial and Ethnic Groups Leaders of **racial and ethnic groups** recognize that only through effective organizations can they hope to achieve their cherished goals. Some examples include eliminating racial discrimination in employment, improving public schools, increasing educational opportunities, and obtaining greater representation in state legislatures, city councils, school boards, and other policymaking bodies of government.

One formidable group, the National Association for the Advancement of Colored People (NAACP), is an effective social group. The organization has been successful in influencing public policies relating to school integration and local government redistricting. The NAACP also fought for hate crimes legislation that enhances penalties for crimes based on race, color, disability, religion, national origin, gender, or sexual preferences.[4]

In Texas, Latino groups, especially Mexican American organizations, are more numerous than African American groups. The oldest Latino group, the League of United Latin American Citizens (LULAC), was founded in 1929. (See this chapter's Selected Reading, "Unsung Hero of Civil Rights," for information on founder Alfonso S. Perales and his collection of papers.) LULAC has worked to achieve equal educational opportunities for Latinos, as well as full citizenship rights. The Mexican American Legal Defense and Education Fund (MALDEF) targets the courts in its efforts to obtain political equality for Latinos. These organizations have been instrumental in addressing inequitable funding allocations for public schools serving Latino children and for universities in South Texas. Following the census of 2000, several Latino-based organizations (including the William C. Velasquez Institute of San Antonio and the GI Forum) sought to influence state legislative and U.S. congressional redistricting.

Women's Groups The Women's Political Caucus of Texas is an example of a **women's organization** that promotes equal rights and greater participation by women in the political arena. The League of Women Voters of Texas is a nonpartisan organization advocating greater political participation and public understanding of governmental issues. It also assists voters in becoming more informed by publishing *The Texas Voters Guide*, which provides information about elections, candidates, and candidates' positions on various issues.

Religious-Based Groups The Christian Coalition is an example of a **religious-based group**. With millions of Texans identifying themselves as conservative Christians, the organization has emerged as one of the state's most influential political forces. It is an interest group that engages in political action, primarily within the Republican Party. Issues that have precipitated the Christian Coalition's entrance on the political scene are abortion, homosexuality, limits on prayer in public schools, and the decline of the traditional nuclear family.[5]

In 1995, Cecile Richards (daughter of former governor Ann Richards) played a leading role in organizing the Texas Freedom Network to oppose the Christian Coalition. Others created a similar group, the Texas Freedom Alliance. Both organizations watch the activities of right-wing conservatives, muster liberal and mainstream voters, and provide an alternative voice on current political issues.[6] The Texas Faith Network, also formed in 1996, calls on religious leaders statewide to resist Christian Coalition tactics intended to influence political conservatives (usually Republicans).

Another religious-based organization, the Texas Industrial Areas Foundation (IAF), operating in cities such as Dallas and in the Rio Grande Valley, supports increased funding for parent and teacher training and for making it easier for children to qualify for Medicaid benefits.[7] Valley Interfaith, made up primarily of churches and schools, has been successful in lobbying the Brownsville school district to increase wages for employees, and indirectly influencing other public institutions and companies to provide a living wage for their workers. In addition, sister organizations in San Antonio—Communities Organized for Public Service (COPS) and Metro Alliance—successfully lobbied the 77th Legislature to pass a bill that allows cities to use sales taxes to create job training and early childhood development programs.[8]

Public Interest Groups

Unlike most interest groups, **public interest groups** claim to promote the general interests of society rather than narrower private or corporate interests. Environmental, consumer, political participation, and public morality organizations are often identified as public interest groups.

Public interest organizations pursue diverse goals. Common Cause of Texas, for example, focuses primarily on governmental and institutional reform. It supports open-meeting laws, public financing of political campaigns, and stricter financial disclosure laws. Texans for Public Justice also supports efforts toward campaign finance reform, such as limitations on campaign contributions by political action committees and individuals.

Texas Power Groups

Texas legislators readily identify the types of interest groups they consider most powerful: business-oriented trade associations (oil and gas, chemical industry, and insurance), professional associations (physicians, lawyers, and teachers), and labor unions. Other groups wielding considerable influence include brewers, truckers, automobile dealers, bankers, and realtors.

There are a number of ways to determine which interest groups are **power groups**. For one, these groups maintain strong linkages with legislators (whose policy decisions affect group interests) and with bureaucrats (whose regulatory activities control the operations of group members). They are often considered repeat players in Texas politics, meaning they have been influencing politics over a long period of time.

Another indication of the power influence of groups is that they are likely to have their headquarters in Austin. More than 60 associations that are business related, for example, own a headquarters building in Austin. Others lease or rent buildings and office suites in the capital city. This proximity provides regular contact with state officials and gives the associations a path to influence in state government.[9]

Among the most influential business power groups operating in Texas are the Alliance for Responsible Energy Policy (representing the Texas Railroad Association), the Texas Mining and Reclamation Association, the Association of Electric Companies of Texas, ConnecTexas (which lobbies for the Texas Telephone Association), Southwestern Bell, GTE Southwest, and Texas Taxpayers and Research Association. Other powerful interest groups include the Texas Conference for Homeowners' Rights, the Texas Bankers Association, the Independent Bankers Association of Texas, and the Texas Credit Union League.

Another increasingly influential group is the Texas Medical Association (TMA). With a well-organized grassroots network, a skilled lobbying team, and more than 32,000 physicians licensed in Texas, TMA is one of Texas's most powerful professional groups. According to the TMA's figures, the group succeeded in passing as much as 90 percent of their agenda items in the late 1990s.[10]

Interest Group Activities

When interest groups urge their members and others to become actively involved, or even to consider running for public office, they are getting people to participate in the political process. Moreover, they also benefit from having their supporters serve in decision-making positions. Local property taxpayers' associations, for example, frequently put forward candidates for public school boards and municipal offices in an effort to keep property taxes at a minimum. Likewise, when organizations of real estate agents place their members in appointed positions on local planning and zoning commissions, they gain a distinct advantage.

Interest groups serve as an outlet for discussions concerning policy issues. In doing so, they define conflict and consensus. Conflict is the more usual outcome, because each group is bent on pursuing its own limited ends. This, in turn, leads to clashes with other groups seeking their own ends. Conflict becomes an even bigger problem when addressing controversial issues, such as school finance, abortion, and environmental protection.

In 2003, limiting medical malpractice awards was a contentious issue. During the regular legislative session, the 78th Legislature passed a constitutional amendment proposal (Proposition 12), authorizing the state legislature to limit noneconomic damages, such as for pain and suffering, in medical

Protesting radioactive waste policies in front of the Capitol in Austin. (Senate Media Services)

malpractice suits. Leading up to the popular election on the proposed amendment in September, groups representing HMOs, doctors, nurses, medical residents, hospital executives, insurance companies, and defense attorneys clashed over the issue with groups representing plaintiff attorneys, union leaders, consumers, environmentalists, racial and ethnic minorities, and senior citizens.

Because governments need support for their policies, interest groups seek to build that support, particularly for policies that are part of the group's goals and interests. For example, in 2003, the Texas Medical Association supported passage of Proposition 12, mentioned earlier. On a different issue, the Texas State Teachers Association openly opposed legislative efforts to adopt a pilot program for school vouchers that was considered in 1999. The 77th Legislature in 2001 and 78th Legislature in 2003 defeated similar proposals.

Techniques of Interest Groups

Political scientists know that interest groups use a wide range of techniques to influence policy decisions. These **interest group techniques** may be classified as lobbying, personal communication, favors and gifts, grassroots activities, electioneering, campaign financing by political action committees, and (in extreme instances) bribery and unethical practices.

During the special legislative session on school finance in 2004, numerous interests were represented by lobbyists. According to the Texas Ethics Commission, as reported in the *Dallas Morning News*, 61 lobbyists were hired by the alcohol and tobacco industry, 83 lobbyists were hired by the gambling industry, and 122 lobbyists were hired by school districts. Millions of dollars were spent to compensate these lobbyists.

Source: Dave Michaels, "Special Session's Winners: Lobbyists" *Dallas Morning News*, 9 May 2004.

Points to Ponder

Lobbying

Perhaps the oldest, and certainly the best-known, interest group tactic is **lobbying**. It is carried out by lobbyists, individuals who attempt to influence government decision makers on behalf of others. Lobbying is most often directed at legislators and the lawmaking process, although it is also practiced within state agencies. Not all lobbyists are full-time professionals. Most work for businesses and only occasionally go to Austin to speak to lawmakers about their concerns. There are also lobbyists who represent cities and counties.

In 2003, during the 78th regular session of the Texas Legislature, there were more than 1,600 registered lobbyists, outnumbering legislators by a margin of roughly nine to one.[11] Lobbyists are hired by a variety of interest groups and organizations through contracts. Identifying interest groups that hire lobbyists is one way to determine which interests are being represented before the state legislature and which are not. The first task of the lobbyist is to gain access to legislators and other government decision makers. Once the lobbyist has made personal contact with a legislator and captured the desired attention, he or she may use a variety of techniques to make the government official responsive to the group's demands, preferences, and expectations.

Personal Communication

One of the main lobbying techniques is personal communication. The immediate goal of lobbyists is to inform the legislators of their group's position on an issue. Because lobbyists are often experts in their field (or in some cases former state officials), their tool of influence is the information and research they convey to state legislators.

In addition, because the process requires careful strategy, the lobbyist chooses the most appropriate time and place to speak with an official and determines how best to phrase arguments designed to have a positive impact. For maximum effectiveness in using this technique, a lobbyist must select the proper target (for example, a key legislative committee chair, regulatory agency administrator, county commissioner, or city zoning board member). Successful lobbyists rely heavily on computers, calculators, pagers, cellular telephones, Internet communications, and other high-tech devices to store and communicate information. In fact, an important study of interest group politics in Texas has concluded that lobbying in the Lone Star State has shifted from an emphasis on personal argument to information-based communications.[12]

A former Texas legislator compared lobbyists to pharmaceutical salespeople who explain new medicines to doctors too busy to keep up with the latest developments. To perform their jobs effectively, successful lobbyists should clearly indicate the group they represent, define their interests, make clear what they want to do and why, answer questions readily, and provide enough information for politicians to make judgments. Successful lobbyists befriend as many legislators as possible, especially influential legislative leaders, and get to know their interests and needs. Lobbyists also put pressure on sympathetic legislators to influence other legislators.

Points to Ponder	There are currently no effective laws prohibiting former legislators (including former legislative officers) from becoming lobbyists and immediately lobbying former colleagues. During the 2003 regular session, ten former lawmakers from the 2001 regular session served as "revolving-door lobbyists." For instance, Senator Bill Ratliff (R-Mount Pleasant), a prominent legislator and former acting lieutenant governor, resigned in 2004 and joined his son's lobbying firm.

Favors and Gifts

Another lobbying technique involves providing favors for legislators and other government decision makers. Common favors include arranging daily or weekly luncheon and dinner gatherings; providing free liquor, wine, or beer; furnishing tickets for entertainment events, air transportation, and athletic contests; and giving miscellaneous gifts.

Grassroots Activities

Yet another influential technique is grassroots lobbying. Lobbyists rely heavily on pressure from a grassroots network of organization members and sympathizers. Interest groups will attempt to create an image of broad public support for a group's goals—mobilizing support when it is needed. They use such political campaign techniques as direct mailings, television and newspaper advertisements, and local group action. Recently, there has been a tendency to use the Internet as a forum for grassroots lobbying. The purpose of these communication methods is to generate information favorable to an interest group's cause and to spread it widely among legislators, other policymakers, and the general public. The Texas State Teachers Association (TSTA) and the National Rifle Association (NRA) are extremely effective at rallying grassroots support.

Electioneering

Participating in political campaign activities, or **electioneering**, is widespread among interest groups. These activities usually center on particular candidates, but may also revolve around issue advocacy. If a candidate who favors a group's goals can be elected, the group has a realistic expectation that its interests will be recognized and protected once the candidate takes office. Interest group participation in the election process takes a variety of forms. Publishing or otherwise publicizing the political records of incumbent candidates is one of the simplest and most common forms of interest group participation. Providing favored candidates with group membership information and mailing lists is another valuable contribution that helps candidates solicit money and votes. Groups may also allow candidates to speak at their meetings, thus giving them opportunities for direct contact with voters and possible media coverage.

During the gubernatorial race in 2002, publicly endorsing specific candidates was a strategy employed by various interest groups. For instance, Governor Rick Perry received endorsements from such groups as the Combined Law Enforcement Associations of Texas and the Texas Teamsters, while the Democratic gubernatorial candidate, Tony Sanchez, gained support from the Texas State Teachers Association (TSTA), the Texas AFL-CIO, and the Texas Medical Association (TMA).

Another type of group participation in electioneering involves getting out the vote—the favorable vote. Typically, this entails mailing campaign propaganda, making telephone calls to members, registering voters, transporting voters to the polls, and door-to-door canvassing (soliciting votes). Group members may also volunteer their time to the campaigns of sympathetic candidates.

Campaign Financing by Political Action Committees

Because political campaigns are becoming more expensive with each election, contributions from interest group members constitute an important form of participation. Although individuals continue to make personal financial contributions to candidates, there is a growing tendency for campaign funds to come from **political action committees** (PACs). Texas statutes prohibit political contributions by corporations and labor unions to individual candidates. These and other groups, however, may form PACs composed of their employees or members. PACs have the task of raising funds and distributing financial contributions to candidates who are sympathetic to their cause. A PAC may also influence political campaigns involving issues that affect the group's vital interests. Currently, there are no limits on what PACs (or individuals for that matter) can raise or spend in Texas.

PAC activities and their influence continue to increase, with more than 1,000 PACs reported in Texas in 2000.[13] During the presidential race of that year, Texas ranked third among the most populous U.S. states in overall PAC contributions. Reports prior to November's 2002 gubernatorial election note that PAC contributions were dominated by lawyers and lobbyists (accounting for 44 percent of the total), partisan PACs, ideological PACs (which

POINT
COUNTERPOINT

Should Campaign Contributions Be Regulated?

THE ISSUE

Most observers of Texas politics would agree that money plays a big role in political campaigns. There is less agreement on whether or not Texas needs strict campaign finance laws. The following are some of the most common arguments that address this issue.

Arguments For Regulating Campaign Contributions

1. Current federal law requires caps on all campaign contributions by individuals and PACs for federal elections.
2. Without a cap on campaign contributions, money will control politics, and wealthy individuals and PACs will have tremendous influence in public policymaking.

> "Wealthy individuals, businesses and lobby interests write the big checks that have thrown Lone Star democracy out of balance."
> —Quoted by Craig McDonald, Director for Texans for Public Justice

Arguments Against Regulating Campaign Contributions

1. Campaign contributions to political candidates are still considered a form of freedom of expression protected by the U.S. Constitution.
2. Campaign contributions to candidates and public officials only guarantee access, not policy outcomes.

> "It never ceases to amaze that people are so cynical they want to tie money to issues, money to bills, money to amendments."
> —Quoted by Tom DeLay, U.S. Representative

emphasize liberal or conservative leanings), as well as PACs representing labor, transportation, real estate, health, communications, and energy–natural resources. In all, these PACs spent more than $10 million.[14] Another report by Texans for Public Justice reveals that Republican candidate Rick Perry's largest contributions came from business interests, specifically those in the fields of energy–natural resources and finance. Tony Sanchez, the Democratic candidate, also received the majority of campaign contributions from business interests, including lawyers and lobbyists, and persons in the fields of finance and health.[15] Reports following the 2002 election show that legislative candidates and candidates for statewide office raised $127 million from donors (individuals, PACs and businesses). PACs and businesses provided $50 million in the form of political contributions.[16]

Perhaps the best indication of power among interest groups is the connection between the election campaign contributions of PACs and lobbying

☆ **How Do We Compare . . . in Total PAC Contributions for the 2002 Congressional Election?**

Most Populous U.S. States	Total Contributions[a]	Percentage Given to Democrats	Percentage Given to Republicans
California	$138,461,045	57	42
Florida	56,192,939	32	68
New York	109,014,574	63	37
Texas	**90,617,863**	**38**	**62**
U.S. States Bordering Texas			
Arkansas	1,779,341	12	88
Louisiana	$15,110,295	33	67
New Mexico	6,396,479	34	66
Oklahoma	9,920,462	34	66

Source: **www.opensecrets.org/states**.

[a]*Note:* Total PAC, soft dollar, and individual contributions to federal candidates and parties.

activities. It takes a coordinated effort on the part of an interest group to influence one part of the political process (the campaign) while also affecting policy decisions in another part (the legislative process). In this way, interest groups are able to exercise far greater control over the output of the Texas Legislature than their numbers would indicate.

Bribery and Unethical Practices

Bribery and blackmail, although not common in Texas, nevertheless have taken place in state and local government. There were, for example, some well-publicized scandals in the 1950s involving Texas legislators. In the 1970s, the Sharpstown Bank scandal rocked the legislature. House Speaker Gus Mutscher and others were convicted of conspiring to accept bribes for passing deposit-insurance bills as requested by Houston banker Frank Sharp. Following the scandal, the state legislature passed a law prohibiting speaker candidates from giving anything of value to a supportive legislator as a means to get elected as speaker. The law requires separate finance committees for election as a representative and for the speaker's race.

In February 1980, as revealed by an FBI investigation, House Speaker Billy Clayton accepted (but did not spend) $5,000 intended to influence the awarding of a state employee insurance contract. Because he had not cashed the checks, a federal district court found Clayton innocent of all bribery charges. In January 1981, he was elected to a fourth term as speaker of the House.

In 1991, five-time speaker Gib Lewis was indicted on two misdemeanor ethics charges by a Travis County grand jury. Rather than face the possibility of a trial subjecting him to a stiffer penalty, Lewis agreed to a plea bargain, was fined $2,000, and announced his decision not to seek reelection to the House of Representatives in 1992. Lewis became a very successful lobbyist.

In 2004, scrutiny centered on House Speaker Tom Craddick (R-Midland) and his involvement in the 2002 election that gave the GOP a House majority in the 78th Legislature. Reports by Texans for Public Justice found that Craddick was the biggest donor to a Republican leadership PAC that funded eight key House races.[17] In addition, in 2003 and 2004, Travis County district attorney Ronnie Earl and a succession of grand juries investigated use of corporate money to influence the outcome of legislative elections. Texans for a Republican Majority (TRM), a PAC founded under the influence of U.S. Representative Tom Delay (R-Sugar Land), was the center of the Travis County investigation.[18] Although corporations are restricted from directly contributing to a candidate's campaign, corporate funds may be used to assist with "administrative" expenses. The question remained whether or not these funds were, in fact, used for administrative expenses, or whether monies were used unlawfully to affect the outcome of electoral contests.

Regulation of Interest Group Politics

Prompted by media reports of big spending by lobbyists and a grand jury investigation into influence peddling, the 72nd Legislature created the eight-member **Texas Ethics Commission** to enforce new legal standards for lobbyists and public officials. This 1991 legislation increased the power of public prosecutors to use evidence that contributions to lawmakers by lobbyists and other individuals are more than mere campaign donations. The legislation also expanded disclosure requirements for lobbyists and legislators, and put a $500 annual cap on lobbyist-provided food and drink for a lawmaker. It also banned honoraria (gratuitous payments in recognition of professional services for which there is no legally enforceable obligation to pay) and lobby-paid pleasure trips (unless a legislator makes a speech or participates in a panel discussion). Despite these measures, however, there is no indication that campaign contributions from special interests have been reduced. Current laws are not very effective.

The ethics law defines any campaign contribution accepted with an agreement to act in the contributor's interest as a felony. The law also prohibits a candidate or official from receiving a contribution in the capitol building itself. The problem, however, is that it is difficult to prove a candidate has intentionally accepted a campaign contribution from a particular interest group in exchange for policy benefits.

Detailed records of political contributions and how this money is spent must be filed between two and seven times each year with the Texas Ethics Commission. These records are open to the public and are available on the commission's web site. Since 1999, electronic-filing law requires candidates for legislative and statewide office to file electronic campaign disclosure reports, so that this information can be made instantly available. Until recently, candidates who signed affidavits contending that they did not use computers to track campaign finances were exempt. Current law requires that all candidates file semiannual reports. In contested elections, however, candidates must file itemized contribution and expenditure reports every six months, thirty days, and eight days before the election. Contributions and expenditures in the last two days do not have to be disclosed until the next semiannual report is due. A study by Texans for Public Justice reports that 102 candidates raised $18.7 million in the primary election of 2002, with $1.7 million comprising late funds. The study also notes that more than $300,000 was contributed in the last two days prior to the election. Among the top donors were plaintiff attorneys, doctors, and the Republican National State Elections Committee.[19] The Ethics Commission also lists the names of lobbyists and their clients, as well as a range of payments received by each lobbyist. However, lobbyists themselves do not have to report exact dollar amounts for their contracts; the top end can range from $200,000 to as much as $5 million. Thus the commission's records do not give a complete picture.

In addition, the Texas Ethics Commission is authorized to hear ethics complaints against state officials, candidates for office, and state employees. Its budget allows about 60 reviews each year. Recent reports indicate that in the past decade 729 external sworn complaints were made to the commission. Reform advocates and others, however, contend that staff members are restricted from investigating complaints because of strict confidentiality rules that expose them to possible criminal prosecution, fines, and jail time.

With ineffective laws in place, questionable connections between lobbyists and legislators are largely unchecked. Governor Rick Perry drew criticism when he first took office after issuing a "strict" revolving-door lobby policy for his staff, preventing staff members from leaving their employment to become lobbyists. Shortly thereafter, however, he hired senior staff personnel who had been registered as lobbyists during the preceding legislative session. In *Texas Lobby Watch,* Texans for Public Justice concluded that special interests have entered the governor's office through a revolving back door.[20] Newly elected House Speaker Craddick received criticism from governmental watchdog groups when he hired lobbyists with ties to the insurance industry as members of his transition team.

The relationship between campaign contributions and policy decisions continues to be powerful. Sam Kinch (a retired political reporter and founder of the political newsletter *Texas Weekly*) and Anne Marie Kilday (a former capitol correspondent for Texas newspapers) conclude that not much has changed since creation of the Ethics Commission. The system is still set up to support incumbents.[21] All attempts to reform campaign finance were defeated in the 77th Legislature in 2001. Proposed reforms included contribution limits for individuals and PACs in legislative and statewide races, and full disclosure laws. As columnist Molly Ivins points out, "Texas is the Wild Frontier of campaign financing."[22]

How Do We Compare . . . in Campaign Finance Laws?

Most Populous U.S. States	Overall Rankings & State Score[a]	Registration of Lobbyists[b]	Allow Revolving-Door Lobbyists	Lobby Lists Updated
California	8 (71 score)	Yes	No	Daily
Florida	32 (55 score)	Yes	No	Daily
New York	5 (74 score)	Yes	No	Monthly
Texas	**12 (66 score)**	**Yes**	**Yes**	**Daily**
U.S. States Bordering Texas				
Arkansas	29 (56 score)	Yes	Yes	Daily
Louisiana	32 (55 score)	Yes	No	Monthly
New Mexico	26 (58 score)	Yes	No	Weekly
Oklahoma	42 (47 score)	Yes	(no information)	Daily

Source: **www.publicintegrity**.

[a]*Note:* The state's score is determined by the responses to a state survey. Scores of 60 to 69 are classified as barely passing.

[b]*Note:* The state requires lobbyists to fill out registration materials.

Following review of the Ethics Commission in 2002 by the Texas Sunset Advisory Commission (See Chapter 8 "Bureaucracy, Public Policies, and Finance"), the 78th Legislature in 2003 passed H.B. 1606, which renewed the Ethics Commission until 2015. First and foremost, the law strengthens the enforcement powers of the Texas Ethics Commission. The law also provides stricter disclosure requirements. For example, legislators must disclose the occupation and employer of large donors. Reports from elected officials concerning campaign cash on hand, as well as personal financial disclosure statements by municipal officers, are now required. New features include disclosure reports of lawyer-legislators who seek trial postponements during a legislative session, along with broadened requirements for disclosing conflicts of interest.[23]

Interest Group Power and Public Policy

The **political influence of interest groups** is determined by several factors. Some observers argue that a group with a sizable membership, above-average financial resources, knowledgeable and dedicated leadership, and a high degree of unity (agreement on and commitment to goals among the membership) will be able to exert virtually limitless pressure on governmental decision makers. Others point out that the extent to which the aims of an interest group are consistent with broad-based public beliefs or stem from issue networks greatly increases the probability that the group will be successful and wield significant power. They also observe that if interest groups are well represented in the structure of the government itself, their power will be enhanced materially. Also, it is noted that a structure of weak governments will ordinarily produce strong interest groups.

From a different point of view, others insist that factors external to the group are also highly relevant. Research indicates that a strong relationship exists between the larger socioeconomic conditions in a state and the power of interest groups. These findings have led some observers to conclude that states with high population levels, advanced industrialization, significant per capita wealth, and high levels of formal education are likely to produce relatively weak interest groups and strong political parties.

Texas is among the states with very strong interest groups and relatively weak political parties. Three circumstances explain why states such as Texas may not fit the expected pattern. First, many Texas interest groups identify with free enterprise, self-reliance, and other elements of the state's culture, and so they are readily accepted. Most Texans are predisposed to distrust government and its agents but to trust interest groups and their lobbyists.

Second, until recently, the century-long, one-party tradition in Texas rendered interparty competition negligible. The absence of strong parties and meaningful competition between them has made Texas government vulnerable to the pressures of strong interest groups and their lobbyists. Finally, the Texas Constitution of 1876 and its many amendments have created state and local governments that are beset by weak, uncoordinated institutions. Faced with a government lacking sufficient strength to offer any real opposition, interest groups often obtain decisions favorable to their causes.

Pinpointing Political Power

Assessing the political power and influence of interest groups in American government is difficult, and determining the extent of their power in Texas is especially complex. There is no simple top-down or bottom-up arrangement. Rather, political decisions (especially policy decisions) are made by a wide variety of individuals and groups. Some of these decision makers participate in local ad hoc (specific-purpose) organizations; others wield influence through statewide groups. Ascertaining which individuals or groups have the greatest influence often depends on the issue or issues involved.

The political influence of any interest group cannot be fairly calculated by looking at the distribution of only one political asset, whether it be money, status, knowledge, organization, or sheer numbers. Nevertheless, we may safely conclude that organized interest groups in Texas often put the unorganized citizenry at a great disadvantage when public issues are at stake.

Looking Ahead

Texas interest groups exert their influence over public policy decisions within local governments, the Texas Legislature, executive departments, the judiciary, and the state's bureaucracy. To be sure, students should be alert to evidence of interest group participation in all levels and branches of Texas government. No better illustration of the power of interest groups in Texas politics can be found than that wielded in the legislative process, which is the subject of the next chapter, "The Legislature."

☆ Chapter Summary ☆

- Interest groups act in the interests of their members to influence policy decisions made by government officials. There are various factors that foster interest group formation, such as legal and cultural reasons, a decentralized government and party system, as well as deemphasized ideologies.

- Involvement in an interest group provides members with information and opportunities to become active in the political process. Interest groups vary by organizational pattern, membership, and leadership.

- Generally, all interest groups at all levels of government can be classified according to their interests, members, and the public policies they advocate.

- Interest groups are involved in all types and areas of political activity. They serve various functions, which include recruiting candidates for public office, shaping consensus on issues, and providing an outlet for concerned citizens.

- To influence policy decisions, interest groups use several techniques, which include lobbying, personal communication, favors and gifts, grassroots activities, electioneering, campaign financing by political action committees (PACs), and in extreme cases resorting to bribery and unethical practices.

- An eight-member Texas Ethics Commission is charged with enforcing legal standards for lobbyists and public officials.

- There are various ways to gauge an interest group's potential for political influence, such as the group's size of membership, financial resources, quality of leadership, and the degree of unity among members.

- Interest group participation influences public policy at all levels and within each branch (legislative, executive, judicial) of Texas government, and it allows all members to become a part of the political process.

Key Terms

interest group
right of association
decentralized government
organizational pattern
group leadership
economic interest group
business organization
labor organization
professional group
public officer and employee
 group
social interest group

racial and ethnic groups
women's organization
religious-based group
public interest group
power group
interest group techniques
lobbying
electioneering
political action committee
Texas Ethics Commission
political influence of interest
 groups

 ## Discussion Questions

1. What interest groups are you familiar with? If you are not already a member of an interest group, would you consider joining one?
2. Do you think interest groups have too much power in Texas politics?
3. What recommendations would you offer to the state legislature to put more teeth in the Texas Ethics Commission?

Internet Resources

Common Cause Texas: **www.commoncause.org/states/texas**
League of Women Voters of Texas: **www.lwvtexas.org**
Professional Advocacy Association of Texas: **www.texasadvocacy.com**
Public Citizen/Texas: **www.citizen.org/texas**
Sierra Club, Lone Star Chapter: **texas.sierraclub.org**
Texans for Public Justice: **www.tpj.org/index.jsp**
Texas Community College Teachers Association: **www.tccta.org**
Texas Christian Coalition: **www.texascc.org**
Texas Ethics Commission: **www.ethics.state.tx.us**
Texas League of United Latin American Citizens: **www.txlulac.org**
Texas NAACP: **www.texasnaacp.org**
Texas Public Employees Association: **www.tpea.org**

Notes

1. Burdett Loomis and Allan Cigler, *Interest Group Politics* (Washington: Congressional Quarterly Press, 1998), p. 2.

2. Steffen W. Schmidt, Mack C. Shelley II, and Barbara A. Bardes, *American Government and Politics Today* (Belmont, Calif.: Wadsworth, 1997), p. 249.

3. Christy Hoppe, "Business Lobby Flexes Muscle in Legislature," *Dallas Morning News*, 12 April 2003.

4. Peggy Fikac, "Perry Signs Hate Crimes Legislation," *San Antonio Express-News*, 12 May 2001.

5. For recent information on the role of the Christian Coalition, see James Lamare, Jerry L. Polinard, and Robert D. Wrinkle, "Texas: Religion and Politics in God's Country," in *The Christian Right in American Politics: Marching Toward the Millennium*, edited by John C. Green, Mark J. Rozell, and Clyde Wilcox (Washington, D.C.: Georgetown University Press, 2003), pp. 59–78.

6. Peggy Fikac, "Alliance Formed to Monitor Radical Right," *Houston Chronicle*, 1 October 1995.

7. See Dennis Shirley, *Valley Interfaith and School Reform: Organizing for Power in South Texas* (Austin: University of Austin Press, 2002).

8. For a history of COPS, see Mark R. Warren, *Dry Bones Rattling: Community Building to Revitalize an American Democracy* (Princeton, N.J.: Princeton University Press, 2001).

9. H. C. Pittman, *Inside the Third House: A Veteran Lobbyist Takes a 50-Year Frolic Through Texas Politics* (Austin: Eakin Press, 1992), p. 219.

10. "Doctors' Orders: Medical Lobby Becomes a Powerhouse in Austin," *Wall Street Journal*, 19 May 1999.

11. "2003 Lobby Lists," Texas Ethics Commission, <www.ethics.state.tx.us/dfs/loblists.htm>.

12. Keith E. Hamm and Charles W. Wiggins, "Texas: The Transformation from Personal to Informational Lobbying," in *Interest Group Politics in the Southern States*, edited by Ronald J. Hrebenar and Olive S. Thomas (Tuscaloosa: University of Alabama Press, 1992), p. 180.

13. "Texas PACs 2000 Election Cycle: Texas PAC Facts" (October 2001), <www.tpj.org/publications/reports/index.html>.

14. "50 People, 30 Institutions Supply 26% of TX Political Money," *Lobby Watch* (4 October 2002), <www.tpj.org>.

15. "Two Studies Probe $66 Million That TX Gubernatorial Candidates Raised," *Press Releases* (2 October 2002), <www.tpj.org>.

16. For an extensive report on the role of money in the 2002 election, see "Money in PoliTex" (November 2003), <www.tpj.org/publications/reports/index.html>.

17. "Craddick-Tied PAC Cash Routed to Just 8 GOP House Candidates," *Lobby Watch* (2 April 2004), <www.tpj.org>.

18. W. Gardner Selby, "Probe of GOP Growing: Grand Jury Seeks Records from 7 Legislators, 2 Fund-Raisers," *San Antonio Express-News*, 22 February 2004.

19. "The Morning After: Last-Minute Contributions in Texas' 2002 Primary Elections" (October 2002), <www.tpj.org/publications/reports/index.html>.

20. "New Governor Hires Hired Guns as Hypes Lobby Ethics Code," *Lobby Watch* (5 January 2001), <www.tpj.org>.
21. See Sam Kinch, Jr. with Anne Marie Kilday, *Too Much Money Is Not Enough: Big Money and Political Power in Texas* (Austin: Campaigns for People, 2000).
22. Molly Ivins, "Who Let the PACs Out? Woof, Woof!" *Fort Worth Star-Telegram*, 18 February 2001.
23. "With Perry's Signature, Texas Campaign Law Will Get Boost They Need," *Austin American-Statesman*, 9 June 2003; Ginger Richardson, "Stronger Ethics Rules Hang on House Vote," *Fort Worth Star-Telegram*, 2 June 2003.

SELECTED READING

★
——

Unsung Hero of Civil Rights: "Father of LULAC" a Fading Memory*

Hector Saldana

Mexican American civil rights leader Alonso S. Perales is all but a fading memory for most students of Texas politics. Attempts, however, are being made to preserve his collection of papers for students and scholars. This reading sheds light on a Texas hero and on efforts to preserve Perales's papers for an archival collection in a university depository.

Though he was once hailed as the "Father of LULAC" and a civil rights giant, Alonso S. Perales today is a historical shadow figure, little more than a name frozen on an elementary school building on the West Side. Students pass by his portrait daily without much thought, says Perales Elementary School principal Dolores Mena. "The kids know what he looks like, but they don't know what he's done." "He was a most extraordinary man," recalls retired County Commissioner and Municipal Court Judge Albert Pena, a friend who says he is perplexed why such a historic leader is forgotten to a generation. "But he was very well known when I knew him." That was more than 40 years ago. Perales died in 1960 at the age of 61.

A self-made man, highly educated and erudite, Perales was a prolific writer of position papers and books on the second-class status of Mexican Americans, a newspaper columnist, a spokesman at rallies, a foreign diplomat and shaper of laws. He traveled the globe to promote his culture and to fight for its rights—"En defensa de mi raza." "He was the great intellectual of LULAC," says Ed Peña, former LULAC national president in Washington, D.C. "He was our Thomas Jefferson."

In the late 1920s, Perales founded the League of United Latin American Citizens in his image—working alongside other activist-philosophers such as J. T. Canales, Ben Garza, M. C. Gonzalez, Gus Garcia, Carlos Castañeda, George Sanchez and Jose Luz Saenz to shape its goals. Perales delineated that vision in a draft of LULAC bylaws: "To develop within the members of our race the best, purest and most perfect type of true, loyal citizen of the United States." "We are going to show the world that we have just and legitimate aspirations, that we have self-pride, dignity and racial pride; that we have a very high concept of our

American citizenship; that we have a great love of our country," Perales said in a 1943 radio address. . . .

And as politico Romulo Munguia notes, Perales had the wisdom, guts and skills to "fight the fight in English." Seventy-five years ago, he declared English "the official language" of LULAC and campaigned for Hispanics to be classified as "white" in the census—actions that rankle modern Latinos, many of whom accuse Perales of elitism in light of today's continuing struggle for equality. But the fiery speaker whose persuasive rhetoric often kept LULAC from splintering also considered certain Anglos the enemy, says one family member. Perales' language in 1929 is blunt: "We shall resist and attack energetically all machinations tending to prevent our social and political unification." He was the voice of calm, however. "We should pity and not despise those who are yet in darkness," Perales wrote. Perales was a bridge builder who never forgot where he came from, say those who knew him. His ideas were born of early struggle and poverty.

A dark-skinned Mexican American, Perales was born in Alice in 1898. Orphaned young, he picked cotton in the fields to earn a living and enlisted in the Army during World War I. Through guts and determination, and the belief that education could overcome other handicaps, he graduated with a law degree from George Washington University. He passed the Texas State Bar exam in 1925 and became an early civil rights lawyer in San Antonio.

"He was a poor kid that had nothing and it's hard to visualize how he got from this point to that point. He had a vision; he had a dream. I want to say he was like Martin Luther King—but he preceded Martin Luther King," says Carrizales. To his nephew and namesake, Alonso M. Perales, 77, his uncle was down-to-earth "and a real Tejano."

In 1931, *La Prensa* called Perales the one American that defends Mexicans. His early radio speeches made clear that Mexicans were "thirsty for justice" and a rightful place in the society they labored to support. By the mid-'40s, he had documented more than 150 towns in Texas with establishments that barred service to Hispanics and wrote about it in the book, "Are We Good Neighbors?" Throughout the '50s, Perales fought for a living wage for braceros. He opposed restrictive covenants that kept Mexican Americans out of certain neighborhoods; he fought the poll tax. His fight against segregation and for equal rights rivals the work of Martin Luther King, say historians and admirers. . . .

Yet for all his work on behalf of Mexican Americans, Perales has all but faded from collective memory. "We don't know how to take care of our heroes," says Dallas attorney Jose Angel Gutierrez, co-founder of La Raza Unida and a guiding light of the Chicano Movement of the '60s and '70s, about Perales' modern obscurity—which he considers a travesty. "[Perales'] history is there for those who seek it out," Houston attorney Alfred J. Hernandez says. "This is a deep story about *nosotros*." It's a story that can be found in a cache of Perales' personal documents—and that has yet to see the light of day.

Died Too Soon

They say that history belongs to those who write it. Perales' story rests in dozens of moldy boxes once coveted by his widow, a high-strung former opera singer who in later years vacillated between guarding that packaged legacy and threatening to burn the entire lot, says Perales' nephew. The boxes have collected dust since Perales died in 1960. When Marta Perales died a couple of years ago, heirs Raymond Perales and Martha Carrizales—Perales' adopted children—vowed to preserve their father's papers and restore his rightful image. But action has been slow. They eventually asked Henry Cisneros' politically savvy uncle, printer Ruben Munguia, to help sort mountains of pioneering material. . . .

It was Ruben Munguia's last great undertaking, his brother says. He worked meticulously sorting the delicate treasure of documents at his draft table at his Buena Vista Street print shop "because he liked to be around all the action," says Ruben Munguia's daughter Mary Perales. Since his death earlier this year, the project has languished. Brother and sister do what they can in their spare time. As Carrizales pores over reams of her father's delicate documents, she gushes, "It's like learning about a character in history." Perales' collection is voluminous. . . . Historian and University of Texas associate professor Emilio Zamora agrees and urged the family to deposit the papers at the Mexican American Library Program at the University of Texas because of its "unmatched historical value." In 2001, he wrote to Carrizales: "I honestly believe that Perales is the most important Mexican American leader of the 20th century." Zamora cites Perales' prominence as an author, diplomat and LULAC officer, and his ties to Latino organizations, civic service and civil rights activism. "Not only within the Mexican American community, but I think he's a major civil rights leader of the nation," Zamora says.

That the materials are still out of the hands of researchers is a serious issue, he says. There is also a fear that the integrity of the collection could be unintentionally undermined and lose research value. "Anyone who's involved in archival collection will tell you that a collection of that immense value has to be deposited somewhere and processed and then made available for researchers," Zamora says. His hope is that UT gets them ("It's the natural home," he says) because Perales' contemporaries are archived there. . . .

Not Really 'Radical'

"My mother was a radical and marched with Cesar Chavez," says Carrizales. "Of course, she could afford that. She was bourgeois. My father wouldn't have agreed with the '60s." Certainly Perales' words from the late '20s—"We shall oppose any radical and violent demonstration which may tend to create conflicts and disturb the peace and tranquility of our country"—had no place in the Chicano Movement. "He was a realist," says Chicano leader Gutierrez, who notes that the FBI's surveillance of LULAC started because of Perales' overseas activities. "It was very dangerous to be an activist Mexican at that time, very dangerous. You could lose your life, and people did. This was not a time to stand up and be radical, and what he was doing was perceived to be radical."

Zamora argues that Perales' great achievement was taking the cause of Mexican Americans to international forums. Perales spoke at international conferences; he appealed for nations to put pressure on the United States for Mexican American equal rights. Perales participated in founding meetings of the United Nations in

1945. "At that meeting, he again included the Mexican American in the deliberations of human rights," Zamora explains.

"He was an extraordinary man. If we had him today, I'm telling you, he'd be up in front. And he'd be shaking stuff," Zamora says. "He had conservative ideas, but some of his ideas for that time were pretty radical. He had so much courage and intellect. His stamina and sense of civic responsibility was just tremendous." Many say that the true value of the Perales papers is to put his "conservative" activism in perspective. "It was a very primitive democracy for us," LULAC historian Pena adds. "He was visible when there were very few (Mexican Americans) that were visible. . ."

He outlined his views in October 1931 in a position paper, "El Mexico Americano y la Politica del Sur Texas." "If we want to accelerate our political evolution, it's imperative that we change the system," wrote Perales, who argued that self-education on issues was more important than party affiliation.

In his eyes, pulling a voting lever blindly was akin to a sin: "It's one thing to vote and know what you're voting for, but it's another thing to do it because someone ordered you to do it and who to vote for," he wrote in Spanish. And though he fought against the poll tax, he urged Latinos to pay it and participate. Former Houston judge Hernandez says that Perales is responsible "for Mexican Americans coming of age" because he was willing to enter *un nido de viboras* (the viper's nest) of an often-racist Texas legal system. . . .

Lost History

It was only in the '70s that major universities became interested in collecting the papers of major Latino figures. In some cases, that was more than 50 years too late. "Man, I could tell you some stories that would make you cry about stuff we've lost," Zamora says from Austin. "We're lacking in the telling of the story because the historical record is not readily available," Zamora adds.

Sociologist and Mexican American studies expert Avelardo Valdez at the University of Houston says that Perales is "part of a constellation of lost figures" in the Mexican American experience. "It's highly significant and important that these kinds of papers are found, and that they be archived and that we have access to them," says Valdez, adding that the find will show "Perales' founding generation was much more progressive than our generation today. It took a lot of guts to be organizing political organizations in the 1920s and '30s in South Texas. . . ."

Carrizales says her ultimate dream is that researchers will restore her father's legacy. "He was an activist for human dignity—like Cesar Chavez, like Martin Luther King," Carrizales says. "He needs to be recognized, not glorified, for his efforts. History must do him justice. People need a full cup of information." Gutierrez says the Perales papers must be made public sooner rather than later. "It's a way to make him alive again," he said.

Chapter 6

THE LEGISLATURE

John Branch cartoon. Copyright © 2004 *San Antonio Express-News.* Reprinted with permission.

*A*fter many years of researching, observing, and writing about state legislatures, Professor Alan Rosenthal (Rutgers University) concluded: "Despite the popular perceptions that legislatures are autocratic, arbitrary, isolated, unresponsive, and up for sale, legislatures are in fact extraordinarily democratic institutions." He explained: "They have been becoming more democratic of late, so that a systematic shift from representative democracy to participatory democracy now seems to be under way."[1] After reading this chapter on the Texas Legislature, you can decide whether the shift is under way in the Lone Star State.

Traditionally, the Texas Legislature has been the most heavily criticized and ridiculed of the three branches of state government. (For example, see John Branch's cartoon ridiculing a long, windy Senate session.) Nevertheless, the work of our legislators is of vital importance, because they make laws that affect the life, liberty, and property of all persons in the state.

A Preliminary View

Lawmaking by an elected representative body with many members is a slow, frustrating, and often disappointing process. Moreover, most citizens are impatient with political tactics and procedural delays, even if their policy objectives are achieved. Usually, they are dissatisfied with the inevitable

Iman Moujahed Bakhach delivering invocation at the beginning of a daily session (18 March 2003) of the Texas House of Representatives (Texas House of Representatives Photography Department)

compromises involved in the process by which the Texas Legislature creates and enacts legislation.

At the beginning of each daily session in the House of Representatives and Senate, an invited member of the clergy calls legislators to prayer. On 18 March 2003, shortly before U.S. military forces entered Iraq, Iman Moujahed Bakhach of Fort Worth became the first Muslim to offer an opening prayer in the House. With an American flag pin on his suit, he prayed that Austin and all America would be made "a place of hope, peace, and security."[2]

In January 2003, at the beginning of the 78th regular session, 20 Texas senators and 51 representatives occupied offices in the Capitol. From the south side of this imposing Austin building—slightly taller than the U.S. Capitol in Washington, D.C.—legislators can gaze down Congress Avenue toward the Colorado River and the famous bridge that is home to millions of bats. From the north side of the Capitol, they can see the towering dormitories and academic buildings of the University of Texas at Austin—including the Darrell K Royal–Texas Memorial Stadium, where Big 12 football is played. The other 11 senators and 99 representatives in the 78th Legislature were housed on the top two floors in the four-story underground Capitol Extension. Their only view of the outside world was the patch of sky above the Central Court Open Air Rotunda, which is also the only place in the underground structure where a cell phone will operate.

Legislative Framework

In all of their state constitutions, Texans have entrusted enactment of bills and adoption of resolutions to popularly elected legislators. This is the essence of representative government. As in a majority of states, the lawmaking branch of Texas government is officially termed the legislature. Nebraska has a **unicameral** (single-chamber, or one-house) legislature. Texas and all 48 other states have **bicameral** (two-chamber, or two-house) lawmaking bodies that are similar to the U.S. Congress in Washington, D.C.

Points to Ponder

- A copy of the King James Bible (bearing desk number and state seal on its blue cover) is provided to each senator and representative.
- Some Texas legislators wear official rings (costing more than $600) and official lapel pins (costing more than $400) that they purchase at their own expense.
- To protect legislators and others, Department of Public Safety troopers patrol the Capitol and surrounding grounds with dogs that have been trained to sniff for explosives.
- Hung behind the House speaker's rostrum during legislative sessions is the original San Jacinto battle flag, on which is painted a partially barebreasted woman clutching a sword draped with a streamer proclaiming "Liberty or Death." When legislators are not in session, a reproduction of this flag is displayed, and the original is covered by a curtain.

Floor of the Texas House of Representatives as viewed from the gallery behind the speaker's podium (Texas House of Representatives Photography Department)

Visitors watch Senate proceedings from the gallery (Senate Media Services)

☆ **How Do We Compare . . . in State Legislative Seats?**

Most Populous U.S. States	Senate Seats	House Seats*	U.S. States Bordering Texas	Senate Seats	House Seats	Mexican States Bordering Texas	Unicameral Seats
California	40	80	Arkansas	35	100	Chihuahua	35
Florida	40	120	Louisiana	39	105	Coahuila	33
New York	62	150	New Mexico	42	70	Nuevo León	52
Texas	31	150	Oklahoma	48	101	Tamaulipas	32

Sources: *The Book of the States, 2003* (Lexington, Ky.: Council of State Governments, 2003), p. 113; and Gobiernos y Congresos Estatales de México (**www.cddhcu.gob.mx/virtual/gem/htm**).

*In California and New York, the more numerous chamber is called the Assembly.

Composition

In Texas and 40 other states, the larger legislative chamber is called the House of Representatives. Remaining states use the terms "assembly," "house of delegates," or "general assembly." In the 49 states with bicameral legislatures, the larger chamber ranges in size from 40 members in Alaska to 400 members in New Hampshire. Texas has 150 members in its House of Representatives. The smaller legislative chamber is called the Senate. Alaska has the smallest senate, with 20 members; Minnesota has the largest, with 67. The Texas Senate has 31 members.

Election and Terms of Office

Voters residing in representative and senatorial districts elect Texas legislators. Representatives are elected for two years; senators are usually elected for four years. Terms of office for members of both houses begin in January of odd-numbered years.

Senatorial redistricting occurs in the first odd-numbered year in a decade (for example, 2001). A new Senate is elected in the general election of the following year (for example, November 2002). In January of the next odd-numbered year (for example, 2003), Senators draw lots, using 31 numbered pieces of paper sealed in envelopes. The 16 who draw odd numbers get four-year terms, but the 15 who draw even numbers get only two-year terms. Subsequently, until after redistricting following the U.S. Census of 2010, approximately half of the senators (that is, 15 or 16) will be elected in each even-numbered year.

If a member of the legislature dies, resigns, or is expelled from office, the vacancy is filled by special election. A legislator may be expelled by a two-thirds majority vote of the membership of the legislator's chamber.

Sessions

A Texas law requires a **regular session** to begin on the second Tuesday in January of each odd-numbered year (for example, 11 January in 2005 and

9 January in 2007). In practice, these regular biennial sessions always run for the full 140 days authorized by the Texas Constitution (for example, through May 30 in 2005 and May 28 in 2007). Legislative sessions mean big money for many Austin businesses. Spending by legislators and lobbyists, along with people who work for them, boosts the Austin economy by more than $10 million during a regular session.

The governor may call **special sessions,** lasting no longer than 30 days each, at any time. Governor Perry called three special sessions on congressional redistricting in 2003 and one on school finance in 2004. During a special session, the legislature may consider only those matters placed before it by the governor. Such limits indicate a deep-seated popular distrust of legislators and a fear of change. Governor Bill Clements expressed his sentiments with the statement that "all kinds of bad things can happen when the legislature is in session."

Districting

Providing equal representation in a legislative chamber involves dividing a state into districts with approximately the same number of inhabitants. Population distribution changes constantly, owing to migration of people and to different birthrates and death rates. Therefore, the boundaries of legislative districts must be redrawn periodically to ensure equitable representation. Such **redistricting** can be politically painful to a legislator. It may take away territory that has provided strong voter support for a particular lawmaker; it may add to a legislator's district an area that produces little support and much opposition; or it may include within a new district the residences of two or more representatives or senators, only one of whom can be reelected to represent the district.[3]

Framers of the Texas Constitution of 1876 stipulated, "the legislature shall, at its first session after the publication of each United States decennial census, apportion the State into Senatorial and Representative districts." Nevertheless, in the decades that followed, the legislature sometimes failed to redivide the state's population and map new districts for legislators. Thus, some districts became heavily populated and greatly underrepresented; others experienced population decline or slow growth, resulting in overrepresentation.

In 1948, the inequities of legislative districting in Texas finally led to the adoption of a state constitutional amendment designed to pressure the legislature to remedy this situation. Under the amendment, failure of the legislature to redistrict during the first regular session following a decennial census brings the Legislative Redistricting Board into operation. This board consists of the following five ex officio (that is, "holding other office") members: lieutenant governor, speaker of the House of Representatives, attorney general, comptroller of public accounts, and commissioner of the General Land Office. The board must meet within 90 days after the legislative session and redistrict the state within another 60 days.

Although the legislature drew new legislative districts after the federal censuses of 1950 and 1960, the Texas Constitution's apportionment formulas for the Texas House and Senate discriminated against heavily populated urban counties. These formulas were not changed until after the U.S. Supreme Court held in *Reynolds* v. *Sims* (1964) that "the seats in both houses of a bicameral state legislature must be apportioned on a population basis." This "one person, one vote" principle was applied first in Texas by a federal district court in *Kilgarlin* v. *Martin* (1965).

For more than four decades, every redistricting measure enacted by the Texas Legislature has resulted in complaints about **gerrymandering**. This practice involves drawing legislative districts to include or exclude certain groups of voters, thus giving the political party in power an advantage in elections. Usually gerrymandered districts are oddly shaped rather than compact, as was the case with districts created under the guidance of Governor Elbridge Gerry for Massachusetts in 1812. Many state and federal court battles have been fought over the constitutionality of Texas's legislative districting arrangements. Use of RedAppl (Redistricting Application) software, which runs on each legislator's computer, allows persons drawing new districts to see the ethnic and racial characteristics of voters added to or removed from a district as boundaries change. Senate and House districts are posted on the Internet at **www.tlc.state.tx.us/research/redist/ redist.htm**. The RedViewer system allows Internet users to view district maps and population data.

Members of the Texas Senate have always represented **single-member districts**; that is, the voters of each district elect one senator. Redistricting according to the 2000 federal census provides for a population of about 673,000 in each senatorial district. Many of the 31 senatorial districts cover several counties. With 38 West Texas counties, District 28, where Lubbock is the largest city, has the most. A few big-city senatorial districts are formed from the territory of one county or part of a county. For example, Harris County, where Houston is located, has 8 senatorial districts or parts of districts that extend into adjoining counties. (See Figure 6.1.)

Until 1971, a Texas county with two or more seats in the House used **multimember districts** to elect representatives at large who represented the whole county. Thus, a voter in such a county could vote in all of the county's House races. In 1971, however, single-member districts were established in Harris, Dallas, and Bexar Counties. Four years later, the single-member districting system was extended to all other counties electing more than one representative. The change to single-member districts was largely a result of court actions. Today, all representatives are elected on a single-member-district basis. Election results demonstrate that single-member districts reduce campaign costs and increase the probability that more African American and Latino candidates will be elected. As a result of the 2000 federal census, redistricting provided each state representative district with a population of approximately 139,000. District 88, in the Panhandle region of West Texas, covers 19 counties; but

Figure 6.1   Texas State Senatorial Districts (used for electing state senators in 2002 and 2004)

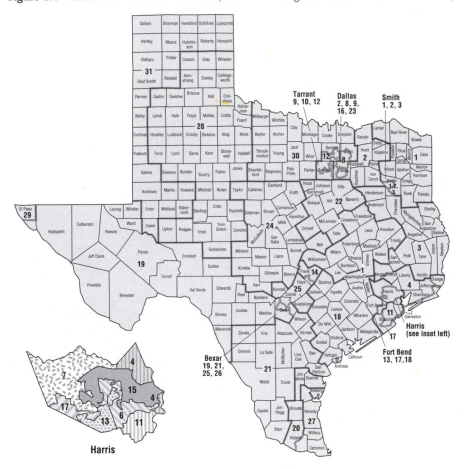

Source: Texas Legislative Council

densely populated Harris County has 22 districts or parts of districts. (See Figure 6.2.)

In the year following each federal census, the Texas Legislature is supposed to draw new district lines for its U.S. congressional districts (from which representatives to the U.S. House of Representatives are elected) and for its State Board of Education (SBOE) districts, to make the number of people in each district roughly equal. Results of the 2000 federal census indicated that each of Texas's 32 congressional districts should have a population of about 652,000, and each of its 15 SBOE districts should have a population of about 1.4 million.

In 2001, the Texas Legislature failed to pass a bill to redistrict Texas's seats in the U.S. House of Representatives. Likewise, the legislature failed to draw new district lines for the SBOE. Because congressional and SBOE districting does not fall within the jurisdiction of the Legislative Redistricting Board, and because Governor Perry was opposed to calling a special session of the

Figure 6.2 Texas State House Districts (used for electing state representatives in 2002 and 2004)

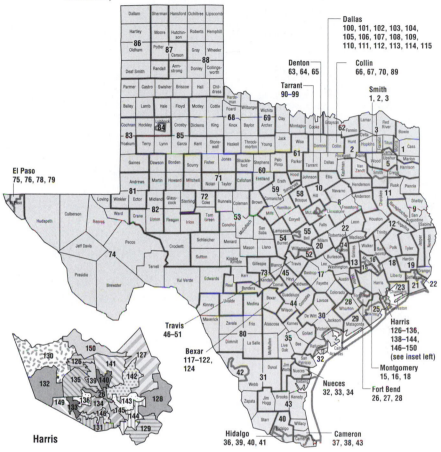

Source: Texas Legislative Council

legislature, it fell to federal judges to carry out these redistricting tasks before the 2002 elections.[4]

In November 2002, Texas Republicans won 15 U.S. House seats, while Democrats won 17. Wanting more GOP representation in Washington, U.S. House majority leader Tom DeLay (R-Sugar Land) insisted that the Texas Legislature should draw new districts in 2003. But in May 2003, near the end of the 78th regular session, 53 Democrats broke a House quorum by fleeing to Ardmore, Oklahoma. There, they stayed in a Holiday Inn until time ran out for voting on a redistricting bill in Austin. Subsequently, Governor Perry called three special sessions before congressional redistricting was accomplished. The first session ended without action in the Senate because the Democratic minority used that chamber's two-thirds rule to prevent a redistricting bill from being considered. Then, when they learned that the president of the Senate would not observe the two-thirds rule in a second session, 11 Democrats (but not Sen. Kenneth Armbrister from Victoria) fled

Representatives Martha Wong (R-Houston) and Debbie Riddle (R-Tomball) (© Bob Daemmrich Photography, Inc.)

to Albuquerque, New Mexico. Their flight prevented Senate action on a redistricting bill until Senator John Whitmire (D-Houston) returned to Austin. Then the other 10 Democrats (2 African Americans, 8 Latinos, and Anglo Eliot Shapleigh) returned also, and the redistricting bill was passed in the third special session. Court challenges followed, but in November 2004, Republicans were elected to 21 of the state's 32 congressional seats. (For more details concerning procedures and consequences of legislative and congressional redistricting in the Lone Star State early in the current decade, see this chapter's selected reading, "Redistricting and Electoral Results in Texas in the Twenty-First Century.")

Compensation

Many states pay legislators ridiculously low salaries (for example, an average of $300 per year in Rhode Island and $100 per year in New Hampshire). In contrast, members of California's assembly receive an annual salary of $99,000, and its senators are paid $120,000. Texas's legislators receive low pay, reasonable allowances, and a relatively generous retirement pension after a minimum period of service.

☆ **How Do We Compare . . . in Salary of Legislators?**
Annual Salary of Legislators for the Year of the Last Regular Session

Most Populous U.S. States	Annual Salary	U.S. States Bordering Texas	Annual Salary
California	Assembly $99,000	Arkansas	$12,796
	Senate $120,000	Louisiana	$16,800
Florida	$27,900	New Mexico	NA*
New York	$79,500	Oklahoma	$38,400
Texas	$7,200		

Source: The Book of the States, 2003 (Lexington, Ky.: Council of State Governments, 2003), pp. 86–87.

*Legislators in New Mexico receive mileage and a per diem allowance but are not paid an annual salary.

Pay and Per Diem Allowance

Originally, Texas legislators' salaries and per diem (daily) personal allowances during a regular or special session were specified by the state constitution and could be changed only by constitutional amendment. Thus, a 1975 amendment increased annual salaries from $4,800 to $7,200 for senators, representatives (including the speaker of the House), and the president of the Senate (the lieutenant governor). That amendment also increased their per diem allowance from $12 to $30. Since adoption of a 1991 amendment, however, the Texas Ethics Commission sets the per diem allowance and may recommend salary increases for legislators and even higher salaries for the speaker and the lieutenant governor. Such salary changes must be submitted to Texas voters for approval or disapproval at the next general election.

For the 78th Legislature, which convened in January 2003, the per diem allowance was $125 for senators, representatives, and the lieutenant governor. This amounted to a total of $17,360 per official for the 140-day regular session. (The maximum amount permitted as a federal income tax deduction by the Internal Revenue Service was $125 per day.) No salary increases had been recommended and approved, however, so in 2003 and 2004 all Texas legislators (including the House speaker) and the lieutenant governor still received an annual salary of only $7,200.

Contingency Expense Allowances

Each chamber authorizes contingency expense allowances for its members. For example, the House authorized every representative's operating account to be credited monthly, from January 2003 to January 2005, with $10,750 (the same amount authorized for the preceding two years). House members in the 78th Legislature could use money in this account to cover the cost of travel, postage, office operations, and staff salaries. Some representatives and senators use money from campaign contributions to supplement the salaries of their assistants.

During the regular session of the 78th Legislature, Senate committee chairs were restricted to not more than $32,000 per month for secretarial and other office staff salaries and for staff travel within Texas. Other senators, who were not assisted by committee employees, had the slightly higher maximum monthly allowance of $34,000, but this was $1,000 less than the maximum allowed during the 77th Legislature.

Retirement Pension

Under the terms of the State Employees Retirement Act of 1975, legislators contribute 8 percent of their salaries to a retirement fund. Retirement pay for senators and representatives amounts to 2.3 percent of a district judge's salary for each year served. As a result of an unpublicized amendment slipped into a state employee benefits bill passed in 1991, a legislator with 12 years of service may retire at age 50, or with 8 years of service at age 60. Thus, a legislator who serves 30 years becomes eligible for a pension of more than $70,000 per year. And a legislator who serves for 8 years becomes eligible for a pension of more than $18,000 per year. Of course, many legislators do not serve long enough to qualify for a pension.

Membership

Members of the Texas Legislature must meet specific state constitutional qualifications concerning citizenship, voter status, state residence, district residence, and age. Despite such restrictions, millions of Texans possess all the prescribed legal qualifications. As is true of the memberships in other state legislatures, however, the biographical characteristics of members of recent Texas legislatures suggest restricted opportunities for election to either of the two chambers.

Qualifications of Members

The Texas Constitution specifies that House and Senate members must be citizens of the United States, qualified Texas voters, and residents of the districts they represent for one year immediately preceding a general election. In matters of state residence and age, however, qualifications differ between the two chambers (see Table 6.1.).

A House candidate must have resided in Texas for two years before being elected, whereas a Senate candidate must have five years of state residence. To be eligible for House membership, a person must be at least 21 years of age; to serve in the Senate, a person must be at least 26. If there is a question concerning constitutional qualifications or a dispute over election returns, each legislative chamber determines who will be seated.

Table 6.1 Constitutional Qualifications for Membership in the Texas Legislature

Qualification	House	Senate
Citizenship	United States citizen	United States citizen
Voter status	Qualified Texas voter	Qualified Texas voter
Residence in district to be represented	1 year immediately preceding election	1 year immediately preceding election
Texas residence	2 years immediately preceding election	5 years immediately preceding election
Age	21 years	26 years

Source: Constitution of Texas, Art. 3, Secs. 6 and 7

Characteristics of Members

The typical Texas legislator is an Anglo Protestant male between 35 and 50 years of age, was born in Texas, is an attorney or a businessperson, and has served one or more previous terms of office. Such characteristics do not guarantee any predetermined reaction to issues and events, but legislators tend to be influenced by their experience and environment, both of which have policy consequences. Any study of the legislature must pay some attention to the biographical characteristics of legislators.

Gender Classification Anglo males continue to dominate the Texas Legislature, but their number has declined in recent years. At the beginning of the 62nd Legislature's regular session in January 1971, only one woman senator was listed on the legislative rolls. Thirty-two years later, when the 78th Legislature convened in January 2003, the number of women had increased to 36 (4 senators and 32 representatives). Two of the senators were Anglo Republicans; the other two were Latina Democrats. Twelve of the representatives were Democrats (6 Latinas and 6 African Americans), and 20 were Republicans (18 Anglos, 1 Latina, and 1 Asian American). Nevertheless, because about 51 percent of Texas's inhabitants and 53 percent of its registered voters are women, their representation in the legislature continues to be disproportionately low.[5]

Racial/Ethnic Classification Representation of racial/ethnic minorities increased substantially from the late 1960s through the early 1990s. Barbara Jordan, the first African American to be elected to the Texas Senate in the twentieth century, served from 1967 until she was seated in the U.S. Congress in 1973.

At the beginning of the regular session of the 78th Legislature in 2003, Senate seats were held by 2 African Americans and 7 Latinos. In the House, there were 14 African American representatives and 30 Latino representatives. Despite the fact that both African Americans and Latinos have been underrepresented in the Texas Legislature, total African American representation increased from 3 legislators in 1971 to 16 in 2003, and the number of Latino legislators grew from 12 to 37 during that 32-year period. Martha Wong (R-

Houston), Texas's second Asian American legislator, became a House member in 2003. The first was Thomas J. Lee (D–San Antonio, Jan. 1965–Jan. 1967).

Political Party Affiliation   In the election of 1960, no Republican won a seat in the 57th Legislature; 42 years later, 19 Republican senators and 88 Republican representatives were elected to serve in the 78th Legislature. Thus, between January 1961 and January 2003, the political division in the House shifted from a total of 150 Democrats and no Republicans to a majority of 88 Republicans and a minority of 62 Democrats. During that same period, the political lineup in the Senate changed from 31 Democrats and no Republicans to a minority of 12 Democrats and a majority of 19 Republicans. Since January 2003, when Republicans began operating with comfortable majorities in both the House and the Senate, there have been more party-line votes in each chamber. Such voting involves Democrats voting one way on an issue and Republicans voting the other way.

Most African American and Latino legislators have been Democrats. Like African American and Latino legislators, Republican legislators tend to reside in metropolitan areas. But whereas central-city residents usually elect African American and Latino lawmakers, Republican senators and representatives receive their strongest support from suburban voters. Because legislative districts in the area extending from South Texas to El Paso tend to have large numbers of Latinos in both rural and urban areas, voters in most of those districts elect Democrats who are Latinos.

Age   The minimum age qualifications set by the Texas Constitution are 26 years for senators and 21 years for representatives, but legislators are rarely under 30. In recent years, the average age of senators (mid-50s) has tended to be slightly higher than that of representatives (late 40s).

Occupation   Traditionally, Texas legislators have included a large number of attorneys, many business owners or managers, lesser numbers of real estate and insurance people, and some farmers and ranchers. Teachers, medical personnel, engineers, and accountants have held very few legislative seats, and laborers have held almost none.

Lawyer-legislators may receive retainers (payments) from corporations and special-interest groups, with the understanding that legal services will be performed if needed. In some cases, these retainer payments are intended to influence legislation rather than guarantee availability of legal counsel. It is also noteworthy that lawyer-legislators, some of whom represent defendants in courts, exercise a decisive influence in amending and revising the Penal Code and the Code of Criminal Procedure. Since 2003, a legislator may not represent a paying client before a state agency.

Individuals and corporations desiring to delay justice may seek the services of lawyer-legislators because these attorneys are entitled to obtain a continuance (that is, a postponement) of any case set for trial during a period extending from 30 days before to 30 days after a legislative session. As a result of blatant abuse of this privilege, a law was enacted that allows a judge to deny continuance when, within 10 days of the trial or any related legal proceeding, a lawmaker is hired to assist with a case. Since 2003, a legislator is required to disclose payment received for obtaining a continuance.

Education   In government, as in business, most positions of leadership call for college credentials. Thus, it is not surprising to find that nearly all members of recent Texas legislatures attended one or more institutions of higher education. Most of them could claim a bachelor's degree, and many had graduate degrees or professional degrees (especially in law).

Religious Affiliation   The Texas Constitution guarantees freedom of religion and prohibits use of public funds for the benefit of a sect or religious group. Since the era of the Texas Republic, Texans have tended to support separation of church and state, but this principle has become the subject of recent controversies. Because religion may play a critical role in the formulation of public policy, political analysts must take a legislator's denominational ties and church doctrines into consideration. These factors are especially important when considering legislation involving abortion, birth control, gambling, sale of alcoholic beverages, state aid to parochial schools, Sabbath observance, and other matters of vital concern to some religious groups but not others. The religious affiliation of each legislator is not a matter of record, but it appears that Catholic senators and representatives are most numerous, followed (in order) by Baptists, Methodists, and Episcopalians.

Legislative Experience   In a legislative body, experience is measured in terms of turnover (first-termers replacing experienced members) and tenure (years of service in a legislative chamber). Once elected, senators tend to remain in the Senate longer than representatives serve in the House. To some extent, this tendency is influenced by the fact that representatives are more likely to pass up opportunities for nomination and reelection to make a bid for a Senate seat or some other office.

   As a general rule, lawmakers do not become very effective until they have spent two or more years working with constituents, bureaucrats, lobbyists, fellow legislators, and other elected officials. Many Americans believe, however, that long legislative tenure should be discouraged if not prohibited. In the 1990s, unsuccessful efforts were made to propose term limits amendments to the Texas Constitution.

Powers and Immunities

Although bound by restrictions not found in many state constitutions, the legislature is the dominant branch of Texas government and the chief agent in making public policy. Through control of government spending, for example, legislators make state agencies and personnel—and, to some extent, units of local government—dependent on them. In addition to their constitutional powers, lawmakers enjoy certain immunities designed to allow them to function freely.

Legislative Powers

Using language reminiscent of George Orwell's *Animal Farm*, we may say that whereas all powers exercised by the Texas Legislature are, in a sense, legislative, some are more legislative than others. The more typical exercise of legislative power involves making public policy by passing bills and adopting resolutions. As explained below, each bill or resolution has a distinctive abbreviation that indicates the chamber of origin, and every legislative proposal is designated by a number indicating the order of introduction.

Simple Resolutions   Abbreviated H.R. (House Resolution) if introduced in the House and S.R. (Senate Resolution) if introduced in the Senate, a **simple resolution** involves action by one house only and is not sent to the governor. Adoption requires a simple majority vote (more than half) of members present. Matters dealt with by simple resolution include rules of the House and Senate, procedures for House and Senate operation, and invitations extended to nonmembers to address the chambers.

Concurrent Resolutions   After adoption by simple majority votes of members present in the House and in the Senate, a **concurrent resolution** (H.C.R. or S.C.R.) is sent to the governor, who has two options: sign it or veto it. Typical examples are resolutions requesting action by the U.S. Congress or information from state agencies, establishing joint study committees composed of senators and representatives, or granting permission to sue the state. An exception is the concurrent resolution to adjourn at the end of a legislative session; this measure does not require approval by the governor.

Joint Resolutions   Adoption of a **joint resolution** (H.J.R. or S.J.R.) requires approval by both houses, but the governor's signature is not necessary. Proposed amendments to the Texas Constitution are examples of joint resolutions requiring a two-thirds majority vote of the membership of each house. To date, all proposed amendments to the U.S. Constitution initiated by Congress, with the exception of the Twenty-First Amendment, have been submitted to state legislatures for ratification. The Texas Legislature ratifies a proposed U.S. constitutional amendment with a joint resolution adopted by simple majority votes of members present in both houses.

Bills   Before enactment, a proposed law is known as a **bill** (H.B. or S.B.). Each regular session brings forth an avalanche of bills, but less than half become law. In the regular session of the 78th Legislature in 2003, for example, 3,636 bills were introduced in the House and 1,956 in the Senate. Together, both chambers passed 824 House bills and 559 Senate bills. The governor vetoed 31 House bills and 17 Senate bills. He signed all of the 275 concurrent resolutions and allowed 14 bills to become law without his signature.[6]

For purposes of classification, bills fall into three categories: special, general, and local. A special bill makes an exception to general laws for the benefit of a specific individual, class, or corporation. Of greater importance are general bills, which apply to all people or property in all parts of Texas. To become law, a bill must pass by a simple majority of votes of members present in both the House and the Senate, but a two-thirds majority vote of the membership in each chamber is required to pass an emergency measure that will take effect as soon as the governor signs it. A local bill creates or affects a single unit of local government (for example, a city, county, or special district). Such bills usually pass without opposition if sponsored by all legislators representing the affected area.

Other Powers

Although the Texas Legislature exercises its principal powers by passing bills and adopting resolutions, the House and Senate have other important powers. Some of these relate only indirectly to the lawmaking function.

Constitutional Amendment Power   Both legislative chambers take part in proposing amendments to the Texas Constitution. A proposal is officially made when the joint resolution is approved by a two-thirds majority vote of the total membership of each house. (The constitutional amendment process is covered in detail in the chapter "Federalism and the Texas Constitution.")

Administrative Power   Most of the governor's appointments to boards and commissions that head state agencies must be submitted to the Senate and approved by at least two-thirds of the senators present. Thus, the Senate is in a position to influence the selection of many important officials. Moreover, the unwritten rule of **senatorial courtesy** requires that the Senate "bust" (reject) an appointment if the appointee is declared "personally objectionable" by the senator representing the district in which the appointee resides.

The legislature defines the responsibilities of state agencies and imposes restrictions on them through appropriation of money for their operation and through general oversight of their activities. One form of administrative supervision involves requiring state agencies to make both periodic and special reports to the legislature. The state auditor, who provides information concerning irregular or inefficient use of funds by administrative agencies, is appointed by (and serves at the will of) the Legislative Audit Committee. This six-member committee is composed of the speaker, the chair of the House Appropriations Committee, the chair of the House Ways and Means Committee, the lieutenant governor, the chair of the Senate Finance Committee, and a senator appointed by the lieutenant governor. Members elect the committee chair. Another important instrument of control over state administration is the legislature's Sunset Advisory Commission, which makes recommendations to the House and Senate concerning continuation, merger, division, or abolition of nearly every state agency within a 12-year period.

Investigative Power   To obtain information about problems requiring remedial legislation, the legislature may subpoena witnesses to testify, administer oaths, and compel submission of records and documents. Such action may be taken jointly by the two houses as a body, by one house, or by a committee of either house. Refusal to obey a subpoena may result in prosecution for contempt of the legislature, which is a misdemeanor offense punishable by a jail sentence of from 30 days to a year and a fine ranging from $100 to $1,000. Legislative investigations that led to reforms include probes of higher education in South Texas, rural health care delivery, and the insurance industry.

Impeachment Power   The House of Representatives has the power to impeach judges of hundreds of district courts, justices of the 14 state courts of appeals and the Supreme Court of Texas, and judges of the Texas Court of Criminal Appeals. The House may also impeach executive officers, such as the governor, the attorney general, the comptroller of public accounts, and the commissioner of the General Land Office. Impeachment power is rarely used, however.

   Impeachment involves bringing charges by a simple majority vote of House members present. It resembles the indictment process of a grand jury. Following impeachment, the Senate renders judgment after a proceeding that resembles a court trial. Conviction requires a two-thirds majority vote of the Senate membership. The only punishment that may be imposed is removal from office and disqualification from holding any other public office under the Texas Constitution. If a crime has been committed, the deposed official may also be prosecuted before an appropriate court like any other person.

Immunities

In addition to their constitutional powers, state senators and representatives enjoy legislative immunities conferred by the Texas Constitution. First, they may not be sued for slander or otherwise held accountable for any statements made in a speech or debate during the course of a legislative proceeding. Of course, this protection does not extend to remarks made under other circumstances. Second, they may not be arrested while attending a legislative session or while traveling to or from the legislature's meeting place for the purpose of attending, unless charged with "treason, felony, or breach of the peace."

Presiding Officers

Merely bringing 181 men and women together in the Capitol does not ensure the making of laws or any other governmental activity. If several people are to transact official business jointly, there must be organized effort. The Texas Constitution prescribes the basic organization of the legislature. For example, it designates the lieutenant governor as president of the Senate and provides for the election of a speaker to preside over the House of Representatives.

President of the Senate:
The Lieutenant Governor

The most important function of the lieutenant governor of Texas is to serve as **president of the Senate**. Just as the vice president of the United States is empowered to preside over the U.S. Senate but is not a member of that national lawmaking body, so too the lieutenant governor of Texas is not a member of the state Senate. The big difference between them is that the vice president seldom presides or becomes involved in daily Senate business, but the lieutenant governor presides over most sessions and plays a leading role in legislative matters.

Chosen by the people of Texas in a statewide election for a four-year term, the lieutenant governor is first in line of succession in the event of the death, resignation, or removal of the governor. When the governor is absent from the state, the lieutenant governor serves as acting governor and receives the gubernatorial salary, which amounted to nearly $350 per day early in 2005. Ordinarily, however, the lieutenant governor's salary is the same as those of senators and representatives: $7,200 per year, which amounts to less than $20 per day.

After Governor George W. Bush was elected U.S. president in 2000, Lieutenant Governor Rick Perry succeeded him in the state's highest executive office. Subsequently, members of the Senate elected Senator Bill Ratliff (R–Mt. Pleasant) as acting lieutenant governor to serve until January 2003.[7] Although Ratliff decided to seek election as lieutenant governor in 2002, he bowed out of the race because of the high cost of campaigning and was elected for another Senate term. Republican David Dewhurst, a multimillionaire who was serving as commissioner of the General Land Office, was elected and took office in January 2003.

As president of the Texas Senate, the lieutenant governor exercises the following important powers:

- Appoints all Senate committee chairs and vice chairs (but cannot remove them)
- Appoints Senate committee members
- Determines the Senate committee to which a bill will be sent after introduction
- Recognizes senators who wish to speak on the Senate floor or to make a motion (for example, to take up a bill out of order of calendar listing)
- Votes to break a tie vote in Senate
- Joint-chairs, with the speaker of the House, the Legislative Council (a research arm of the legislature)
- Joint-chairs, with the speaker of the House, the Legislative Budget Board
- Joint-chairs, with the speaker of the House, the Legislative Audit Committee

Given these powers (most of which have been granted by the Senate rather than the constitution), the lieutenant governor is perhaps the most powerful officer in the state, especially when the legislature is in session.

At the beginning of each session, the Senate elects a president pro tempore, who presides when the lieutenant governor is absent or disabled. At the end of a session, a new president pro tempore is named for the interim period. Customarily, on the basis of seniority—that is, years of cumulative service as a member of the Senate—the office is passed around among those senators who have not yet served as president pro tempore. By custom, the governor and lieutenant governor arrange to be absent from the state on the same day during the president pro tempore's term so that official can serve as governor for one day—an event that involves a swearing-in ceremony and celebration.

Speaker of the House

The presiding officer of the House of Representatives is the **speaker of the House**, a representative who is elected to that office for a two-year term in an open (not secret) vote by the House membership. Like the lieutenant governor in the Senate, the speaker controls proceedings in the House. Among the speaker's more important powers are the following:

- Appoints (but cannot remove) all chairs and vice-chairs of House substantive and procedural committees
- Appoints all members of House procedural committees
- Appoints House substantive committee members within limitations of the seniority rule, but this rule does not apply to the House Appropriations Committee
- Recognizes members who wish to speak on the House floor or to make a motion
- Assigns bills and resolutions to House committees
- Joint-chairs, with the lieutenant governor, the Legislative Council
- Joint-chairs, with the lieutenant governor, the Legislative Budget Board
- Joint-chairs, with the lieutenant governor, the Legislative Audit Committee

House rules authorize the speaker to name another representative to preside over the chamber temporarily. The speaker may also name a member of the House to serve as permanent speaker pro tempore for as long as the speaker desires. A speaker pro tempore performs all the duties of the speaker when that officer is absent.

Because of the speaker's power, filling this House office involves intense political activity. Lobbyists make every effort to ensure the election of a sympathetic speaker, and potential candidates for the position begin to line up support several months or even years before a speaker's race begins. Long before election of a speaker, anyone aspiring to that office will attempt to induce House members to sign cards pledging their support. House rules, however, prohibit soliciting written pledges during a regular session. Once elected, a speaker usually finds it easier to obtain similar pledges of support for reelection in future regular sessions.

A candidate for speaker must file with the Texas Ethics Commission before receiving loans or contributions and before spending money on a

Speaker Tom Craddick and seven of the 78th Texas Legislature's twenty Republican women serving in the House of Representatives (Texas House of Representatives Photography Department)

speaker's race. Money from regular political contributions may not be spent in a campaign to win this House office. It is customary for speaker candidates to visit members in their districts for the purpose of gaining and keeping their support.

When 88 Republicans won House seats in November 2002, it was apparent that the GOP would capture the speaker's office for the first time in more than 130 years. On 14 January 2003, House members elected Tom Craddick (R-Midland) as presiding officer in the House by a vote of 149-1. After casting the only dissenting vote, Representative Lon Burnam (D–Fort Worth) stated that he liked Craddick but explained, "I don't like the way he votes. I don't like his sense of ethics."[8] As did his three immediate, long-tenured predecessors (Bill Clayton, 8 years; Gib Lewis, 10 years; and Pete Laney, 10 years), Craddick appointed both Republicans (28) and Democrats (12) as committee chairs—but not Burnam!

Although Craddick named Democrats to chair nearly one-third of all committees, his professed dedication to bipartisanship wore thin as the 78th regular session progressed. Party differences over the state budget and congressional redistricting were the two most divisive issues during that session, but party-line votes on other issues were common. Nationwide publicity given to the flights of Democratic representatives to Oklahoma and senators to New Mexico embarrassed and angered the speaker. They fled from Texas to break quorums in the two chambers and thus delay action on a congressional redistricting plan for electing more Republicans to the U.S. House of Representatives. By the end of the third special session in 2003, bipartisanship was dead; and partisan conflict over school finance raged during the fourth special session, which was called in April 2004. Ronnie Earle, Travis County's Democratic district attorney, contributed to Craddick's discomfort when he launched a grand jury investigation of Craddick's involvement in transmitting questionable campaign funds to some Republican legislative candidates in 2002.[9]

Committee System

Presiding officers determine the committees to which bills will be referred. (See Table 6.2 for committee titles and numbers of members for House and Senate committees in the 78th Legislature.) In addition, and of special importance, is their power to appoint committee members as well as designate all committee chairs and vice chairs. Because both House and Senate committees play important roles in the fate or fortune of all bills and resolutions, selection of committee members goes far toward determining the amount and type of legislative output during a session. Consequently, lobbyists attempt to influence committee selection. Permanent staff personnel are available to assist legislators with committee work on a continuing basis. Usually, they also work on interim study committees created to examine legislative issues between regular sessions. The presiding officers appoint members of all specially created committees.

House Committees

Until January 2003, House rules provided for a limited seniority system for all **substantive committees**, each of which considers bills and resolutions relating to the subject identified by a committee's name (for example, elections or transportation). At that time, the rules were changed to give Speaker Craddick authority to appoint a chair for budget and oversight for each of 27 substantive committees. These budget and oversight chairs serve on the important Appropriations Committee. Headed by a chair and a vice chair appointed by the speaker, this 29-member committee handles budget legislation. A maximum of half the membership for other substantive committees—exclusive of the chair and the vice chair—is based on seniority. When a regular session begins, each representative, in order of seniority, designates three committees in order of preference. A representative is entitled to become a member of the committee of highest preference on which there is a vacant seniority position. The speaker appoints other committee members. Seniority does not apply to membership on the six **procedural committees**, each of which considers bills and resolutions relating primarily to an internal legislative matter (for example, calendars or House administration). The speaker appoints all members of procedural committees.

Table 6.2 Texas House and Senate Committees, 78th Legislature,
January 2003–January 2005

House Committees (number of members) *Substantive Committees*	House Committees (number of members) *Procedural Committees*
Agriculture and Livestock (7)[a]	Calendars (11)
Appropriations (29)	General Investigating (5)
Border and International Affairs (7)	House Administration (11)
Business and Industry (9)[a]	Local and Consent Calendars (11)
Civil Practices (9)	Redistricting (15)
Corrections (7)[a]	Rules and Resolutions (11)
County Affairs (9)	
Criminal Jurisprudence (9)[a]	*Select Committees*
Defense Affairs and State-Federal Relations (9)[a]	Ethics (7)
Economic Development (7)[a]	Public School Finance (23)
Elections (7)[a]	State Health Care Expenditures (11)
Energy Resources (7)[a]	
Environmental Regulation (7)[a]	**Senate Committees**
Financial Institutions (7)[a]	**(number of members)**
Government Reform (7)	*Standing Committees*
Higher Education (9)[a]	
Human Services (9)[a]	Administration (7)
Insurance (9)[a]	Business and Commerce (9)
Judicial Affairs (9)[a]	Criminal Justice (7)
Juvenile Justice and Family Issues (9)	Education (9)
Land and Resource Management (9)[a]	Finance (15)
Law Enforcement (7)[a]	Government Organization (7)
Licensing and Administrative Procedures (9)[a]	Health and Human Services (9)
Local Government Ways and Means (7)	Infrastructure Development and Security (9)
Natural Resources (9)[a]	Intergovernmental Relations (5)
Pensions and Investments (7)[a]	International Relations and Trade (7)
Public Education (7)[a]	Jurisprudence (7)
Public Health (9)[a]	Natural Resources (11)
Regulated Industries (7)[a]	Nominations (7)
State Affairs (9)[a]	State Affairs (9)
State Cultural and Recreational Resources (7)[a]	Veterans Affairs and Military Installations (5)
Transportation (9)[a]	
Urban Affairs (7)[a]	
Ways and Means (7)[a]	

Sources: Texas Legislative Handbook, 2003-2004 (Austin: Texas State Directory Press, 2003); and Speaker Tom Craddick's news release, 29 April 2003, concerning the Select Committee on Public School Finance (**www.house.state.tx.us/news/release.php?id=262**).

[a]Budget and oversight chair is a member of the Appropriations Committee.

Representative Harold Dutton questions econonomist Milton Friedman at a meeting of the House Public Education Committee, 78th Regular Session, 18 March 2003 (Texas House of Representatives Photography Department)

Although substantive and procedural committees are established under House rules adopted in each regular session, the speaker independently creates **select committees** and appoints all members. He may do so at the beginning of a session, so that the House can work on emergency legislation before appointments for House substantive committees have been made. In January 2003, for example, Speaker Craddick created select committees on Ethics and on State Health Care Expenditures. He abolished the Ethics Committee in April 2004.

To ensure that representatives' efforts are not divided among too many committees, membership is limited to no more than two substantive committees. Chairs of the powerful Appropriations Committee (spending of state money), Ways and Means Committee (taxes), and State Affairs Committee (many of the important subjects that do not involve spending and taxing) may not serve concurrently on another substantive committee.

Senate Committees

Senate rules provide for **standing committees** (but do not identify them as substantive or procedural committees) and **special interim committees** (for studying important policy issues between sessions, such as the Legislative Oversight Committee on Higher Education in 2003–2004). The lieutenant governor, whose legislative title is president of the Senate, appoints all committee members and designates the chair and vice chair of each committee. This power of appointment also extends to the two 3-member standing subcommittees: Agriculture (within the Committee on Natural Resources) and [Military] Base Realignment and Closure (within the Committee on Veterans Affairs and Military Installations). Also appointed by the lieutenant governor is one 5-member standing subcommittee: Higher

Education (within the Committee on Education). A senator serves on a maximum of three standing committees and is restricted to holding not more than one standing committee chair. At the beginning of the 78th regular session in 2003, Lieutenant Governor David Dewhurst appointed Republicans to chair nine standing committees and Democrats to chair six.

Legislative Caucus System

With the House and Senate firmly controlled for several years by Speaker Gib Lewis (1983–1993) and Lieutenant Governor Bill Hobby (1973–1991), caucuses of like-minded members exercised limited influence on the Texas Legislature. Each of these presiding officers sought to absorb potential opponents within his team and to discourage caucuses—legislative organizations based on partisan, philosophical, racial, or ethnic interests. Later, however, these organizations increased in importance, but caucuses are prohibited from receiving public money and using state office space.[10]

Party Caucuses

Students of American national government are aware of the importance of the Democratic and Republican Party caucuses in both houses of the U.S. Congress. In state legislatures, one finds strong party caucus organizations whenever a strong two-party system prevails and party competition is keen. In the 1980s and 1990s, the growing importance of party caucuses in each chamber of the Texas Legislature was one indication that Texas was becoming a two-party state. The House Democratic Caucus was organized in 1981 with 37 members. In recent years, all Democratic legislators have been reported as belonging to their party's House or Senate caucuses. Under the leadership of Tom Craddick, the House Republican Caucus was organized at the beginning of the 71st regular session in 1989. Party caucuses take policy positions on important issues and promote unity among their members.

Racial/Ethnic Caucuses

In the U.S. Congress and in many state legislatures, racial and ethnic minorities organize and form voting blocs to maximize their power. Because African Americans and Latinos constitute significant minorities in the Texas Legislature, it is not surprising that they have formed caucuses for this purpose. Composed of African American senators and representatives, the Legislative Black Caucus concentrates on issues affecting African American Texans, such as the hate crimes bill that was enacted in 2001. In the 1980s, the House-based Mexican American Legislative Caucus (including some Anglo and African American members with many Latinos in their districts) successfully pushed legislation placing farm workers under state workers' compensation, unemployment compensation, and minimum wage protection. In the 1990s, pressure from this caucus produced larger appropriations for state universities in South Texas and the Mexican border area from El Paso to Brownsville and north to Corpus Christi and San Antonio. More recently, the caucus has been instrumental in obtaining authorization and funding for a school of pharmacy at Texas A&M University–Kingsville and for the Regional Academic Health Center to serve the Lower Rio Grande Valley. The Senate Hispanic Caucus includes a few Anglo and African American senators who have large numbers of Latino voters in their districts.

Ideological Caucuses

Two House-based ideological caucuses have emerged. A conservative organization attracts Republicans and conservative Democrats, and a liberal group appeals to many Democrats (including several who are also members of the Legislative Black Caucus and the Mexican American Legislative Caucus). As might be expected, the conservative and liberal caucuses reflect opposing views on taxing and spending as well as on public interest issues such as environmental protection, but a few representatives belong to both caucuses.

House Democratic Caucus chair Jim Dunnam and others from the group of 53 "Killer Ds" who returned to the Capitol on 16 May 2003, after breaking a House quorum by fleeing to Ardmore, Oklahoma (Newsmakers photo/CORBIS)

Organized in 1985, the Texas Conservative Coalition is composed of both Republicans and conservative Democrats. This organization owes its creation to an increased number of Republican legislators elected in the early 1980s and to dissatisfaction with education reforms and tax increases enacted during a special session in 1984. Membership in the Conservative Coalition reached 69 in 1993 and climbed to 93 in 1997, but by 2003 it had fallen to 79 (72 Republicans and 7 Democrats). Sixty-six were representatives, and 13 were senators. The Conservative Coalition Research Institute has a staff that does public policy research and works through the media to sell its ideas to the public.

Established in November 1993 with 42 charter members, the Legislative Study Group represents the liberal Democrats' response to the Texas Conservative Coalition. The Legislative Study Group has called for ethics throughout state government, campaign finance reform, consumer and environmental protection, long-term solutions to problems involving public safety, and various changes in Texas's systems of public education, health and human services, and criminal justice. Membership during the 78th regular session in 2003 was 45. All members were Democrats (43 representatives and 2 senators).

Procedure

Enacting a law is not the only way to get things done in Austin, but passing bills and adopting resolutions are the principal means whereby members of the Texas Legislature participate in making public policy according to detailed rules of procedure.

Rules

To guide legislators in their work, each chamber adopts its own set of rules at the beginning of every regular session, usually with only a few changes in the rules of the preceding session. Whether a bill is passed or defeated depends heavily on skillful use of House and Senate rules by sponsors and opponents.

The lieutenant governor and the speaker, who wield the gavel of authority in their respective chambers, decide questions concerning interpretation of rules. Because procedural questions may be complex and decisions must be made quickly, each chamber employs a **parliamentarian** to assist its presiding officer. Positioned on the dais immediately to the left of the lieutenant governor or speaker, this Senate or House expert on rules is ever ready to provide answers to procedural questions.

A Bill Becomes a Law

The Texas Constitution calls for regular sessions to be divided into three periods for distinct purposes. The first 30 days are reserved for the introduction of bills and resolutions, action on emergency appropriations, and the confirmation or rejection of recess appointments—appointments made by the governor between sessions. The second 30 days are meant to be devoted to consideration of bills and resolutions by committees. The remainder of the session, which amounts to 80 days because regular sessions always run the full 140 days allowed, is devoted to floor debate and voting on bills and resolutions. Throughout a session, action may be taken at any time on emergency matters submitted by the governor. Early in the regular session of the 78th Legislature, for example, Governor Perry declared reforms in homeowner insurance rates and medical malpractice to be emergency matters needing prompt legislative action.

Because the Texas Constitution allows each chamber to determine by a four-fifths majority vote its own order of business, the House has customarily permitted unlimited consideration of bills during the first 60 days. The Senate, however, suspends the constitutional rule on a bill-by-bill basis during the 60-day period. The Texas Constitution specifies that all revenue bills must originate in the House; other kinds of legislation may originate in either chamber.

Although the full process of turning a bill into a law is complex, certain basic steps are clearly outlined. The following paragraphs trace these steps from introduction to action by the governor. For our purposes, we will describe the path of a bill that originates in the House.[11] (The step numbers in Figure 6.3 will help you visualize the bill's progress.)

1. Introduction in the House   Any House member may introduce a bill by filing 13 copies (15 copies of every bill related to conservation and reclamation districts) with the chief clerk. This staff person supervises legislative administration in the House. Prefiling of bills by members and members-elect is allowed as early as the first Monday following the November general election (8 November in 2004 and 13 November in 2006) before a regular session begins in January, or 30 days before the start of a special session.

It is common practice for an identical bill, known as a **companion bill**, to be introduced in the Senate at the same time. This allows simultaneous committee action in the two chambers. A senator's sponsorship of a House bill is necessary if it is to be given serious consideration in the Senate. Likewise, a representative's sponsorship of a Senate bill is needed in the House.

2. First reading (House) and referral to committee   After receiving a bill, the chief clerk assigns it a number in order of submission and turns the bill over to the reading clerk for the first reading. The reading clerk reads aloud the caption (a summary of contents) and announces the committee to which the bill has been assigned by the speaker.

3. House committee consideration and report   Before any committee action, the committee staff must distribute to committee members a bill analysis that summarizes important provisions of the bill.[12] The committee

Figure 6.3 Route Followed by a House Bill from Texas Legislature to Governor (Prepared with the assistance of Dr. Beryl E. Pettus)

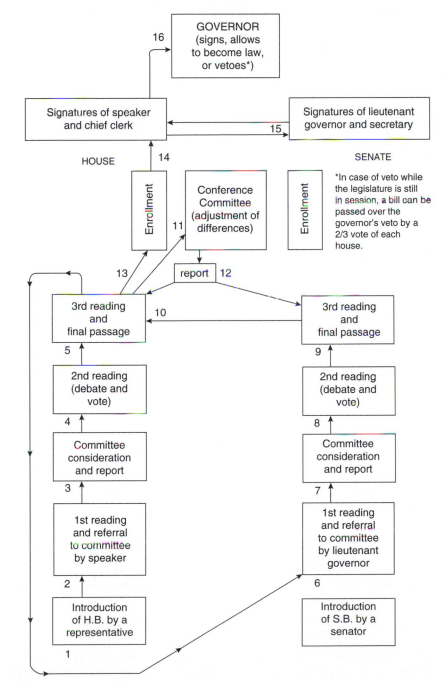

chair decides whether the bill needs a fiscal note (provided by the Legislative Budget Board) projecting the costs of implementing the proposed legislation for five years. It is also a responsibility of the committee chair to decide whether the Legislative Budget Board should prepare an impact statement for a bill that would change punishment for a felony offense, change the public school finance system, create certain water districts, affect or create a state fee or tax, or affect a retirement system for public employees.

As a courtesy to sponsoring representatives, most bills receive a committee hearing at which lobbyists and other interested persons have an opportunity to express their views. By a vote of two-thirds of committee members present, subpoenas may be issued to summon witnesses or require the submission of information. State employees may testify on proposed legislation if requested by a legislator. Proceedings are electronically recorded. Some hearings are tedious, time-consuming "dog-and-pony shows" involving many witnesses whose testimony may be of little value.

At the discretion of the committee chair, a bill may go to a subcommittee for a hearing, followed by submission of a written subcommittee report to the committee. If a majority of a committee's members decides that a bill should be passed, usually with proposed amendments, a favorable report is referred to the chief clerk.

Determining the order in which House bills are cleared for floor action is entrusted to two committees that conduct sessions that are open to the public, the press, and all representatives. These committees are the Local and Consent Calendar Committee and the Calendars Committee.

The Local and Consent Calendar Committee assigns three types of legislative proposals to the Local, Consent, and Resolutions Calendar:

1. Bills affecting a limited number of localities, districts, counties, or municipalities
2. Consent bills that are uncontested and not likely to face opposition
3. Noncontroversial resolutions other than congratulatory and memorial resolutions

The Calendars Committee is responsible for placing other House bills on three daily calendars:

1. *The Emergency Calendar* for bills needing immediate action and all taxing and spending bills
2. *The Major State Calendar* for nonemergency bills changing policy in a major field of government activity and having a major statewide impact
3. *The General State Calendar* for nonemergency bills having statewide application, but limited legal effect and policy impact

Within 30 days after receiving a bill, a calendars committee should decide by record vote whether to place the bill on a calendar for floor consideration. After the expiration of that period, any representative may introduce on the House floor a motion to place that bill on an appropriate calendar. When seconded by five representatives and adopted by a simple majority vote, the House may schedule the bill for floor action without approval of a calendars committee, but this procedure is seldom attempted.

4. Second reading (House)   Usually, the second reading is limited to caption only. The author of a bill, or the committee member reporting on behalf of the committee, has the privilege of beginning and ending floor debate with a speech of not more than 20 minutes. Other speakers are limited to not more than 10 minutes each, unless extra time is granted. A computer on the desk of each representative provides easy access to the text of amendments proposed during floor debate. After discussion ends and any amendments are added, a vote is taken on "passage to engrossment" (preparation of an officially inscribed copy). A quorum (the minimum number required to do business) is constituted when at least two-thirds of the House members (100 representatives) are present.

A record vote usually involves an electronic system. Votes are recorded and tallied as each representative presses the button on a desktop voting machine. This action turns on a light (green, yes; red, no; white, present but not voting) beside the representative's name on the two huge tote boards mounted on the wall behind (and to the right and left of) the speaker's podium. House and Senate journals list the record votes of members of the respective chambers.

If a "division vote" is taken, there is no official record of how each representative voted after the tote boards are cleared. Division votes have become common in recent years. This procedure makes it difficult for citizens to know how their representatives voted on many important issues. Newspaper editors and many other people throughout the state have demanded record votes in both the House and the Senate on virtually all bills and proposed constitutional amendments. To date, their demands have not been heeded by legislators who may want to be shielded from public scrutiny of their work.

House rules prohibit **ghost voting** (that is, pressing the voting button for an absent representative). In 1991, however, votes by one representative were recorded hours after his death from an overdose of crack cocaine. If a member calls for "strict enforcement" of House rules, the voting clerk locks the voting machine of each member who is absent.

Approval of a bill on second reading requires a simple majority vote. Such a House vote marks an important step in the enactment of any proposed bill. A motion may be made to suspend the rules by a four-fifths majority vote of members present and to give the bill an immediate third reading. Thus, an exception can be made to the constitutional rule that all bills must be read on three separate days, although an exception for the third reading is seldom made in the House. Occasionally (especially at the end of a session) some representatives engage in lengthy debate on a bill they do not oppose. Such action is intended to prevent the House from taking up another bill that they do oppose, but which would probably be approved if brought up for a vote. This delaying action is called **chubbing**.

POINT **COUNTERPOINT**

Should Record Votes Be Required on Bills and Amendments?

ISSUE

In an article published in the *Abilene Reporter News*, 3 April 2004, Scripps Howard reporter Monica Wolfson states: "[Texas] lawmakers make thousands of votes every session on a variety of legislation including second and third readings of bills, amendments to bills, adoption of conference committee reports and constitutional joint resolutions. In the 2003 legislative session the Texas House recorded 951 votes, an increase from 649 in 2001, but there were at least 3,200 votes that went unrecorded. The Texas Senate took 3,449 recorded votes, but at least 1,000 votes went unrecorded." Should the House and Senate be required to record votes?

Arguments For Requiring Record Votes

1. At an estimated expense of $330,000 for each regular session, including additional costs of printing and labor for daily journals, recorded votes will be worth the price ($50 per House vote and $100 per Senate vote).
2. Record votes are not too time-consuming; 41 state legislatures operate successfully with such a requirement.
3. The quality of debate will improve when legislators know that measures debated will be the subject of record votes.
4. Voters will be educated concerning the work of their legislators and will be able to cast informed votes when senators and representatives seek reelection.

> "It's poor governance to permit legislators to conceal their votes by failing to require that they be documented."
> — *Dallas Morning News* editorial, 29 April 2004

Arguments Against Requiring Record Votes

1. In a time of tight budgets, any additional expenditure is too much.
2. Time devoted to recording votes will reduce the amount of time available for more important matters.
3. Debate will be chilled when legislators worry about how every one of their votes could be the subject of politically motivated criticism.
4. Votes on most controversial measures are recorded, because any legislator can ask for a record vote if two other members support the request.

> Texas legislators like Rep. Roberto Gutierrez invariably insist that their votes should be recorded, but he warns: "If we were to go to a record vote on every vote, it could cost the state a great deal of money."
> — Quoted by Alma Walzer, "Groups Look to Change Legislature's Voting Method," *McAllen Monitor*, 8 June 2004

To limit legislative logjams and discourage uninformed voting in the final days of a regular session, House rules contain prohibitions against second and third readings for the following:

- Nonlocal House bills during the last 17 days
- Local House bills during the last 10 days
- Senate bills during the last 5 days

Other detailed restrictions apply to House actions on the 126th to 139th days of a regular session. On the 140th, or final, day, House voting is limited to correcting bills that have passed. The Senate has similar end-of-session restrictions on considering legislation.

5. Third reading (House)   On the third reading, a simple majority vote of members present is required to pass the bill. Amendments may still be added at this stage, but such action requires a two-thirds majority vote. Following the addition of an amendment, a new copy is made, checked over by the chief clerk, and stamped "Engrossed."

6. First reading (Senate)   After a bill passes on the third reading in the House, the chief clerk adds a statement certifying passage and transmits the bill to the Senate (where the original House number is retained). In the Senate, the House bill's caption is read aloud by the secretary of the Senate, who also announces the committee to which the bill has been assigned by the lieutenant governor. Unless a sponsor certifies that the bill has no effect on the Texas Public Information Act, the director of the Legislative Budget Board must compile an impact statement that indicates whether the proposed legislation would prevent access to a public record and thus violate the state's open records law.

7. Senate Committee Consideration and Report   Senate procedure differs somewhat from House procedure. A senator may tag any bill by filing a request with either the Senate secretary or the committee chair to notify the tagging senator 48 hours before a hearing will be held on the bill. A tag usually kills the bill if done during the last days of a session.

If a majority of the committee members wants a bill to pass, it is given a favorable report. Bills are listed on the Senate's Regular Order of Business in the order in which the secretary of the Senate receives them. Unlike the House, the Senate does not have calendar committees to control the flow of bills from standing committees to the Senate floor. At the beginning of each session, however, the Senate Administration Committee "parks" a blocking bill (called a "blocker")—on which floor action is not intended—at the head of the line. Bills arriving later are considered to be "out of order." A senator who desires to suspend the regular order for a bill must give notice of this intent by placing the bill on the Intent Calendar. Then a vote of two-thirds of Senators present and voting is required to bring the bill to the Senate floor for debate. This two-thirds rule enhances the power of a party or a bipartisan group that can control more than one-third of the votes, which would be 11 votes if all

31 senators were present and voting. In 2003, the blocker for the 78th regular session was S.B. 220, authorizing a county park beautification program.

8. Second reading (Senate)   As with second readings in the House, the Senate at this stage debates the bill, considers proposed amendments, and routinely puts the measure to a voice vote. A computer on the desk of each senator displays the texts of proposed amendments. Votes are registered as the roll is called by the secretary of the Senate, who is employed to supervise legislative administration in that chamber. Unless a senator holds up two fingers to indicate an intention to vote no, the presiding officer usually announces that the chamber unanimously approves the bill after only a few names are called. A computer-controlled board at the front of the chamber shows how each senator has voted. When a vote is taken, a quorum of 21 senators must be present. Only a simple majority is needed to pass a bill.

Custom permits a senator to speak as long as physical endurance permits, which on one occasion in 1977 amounted to 43 hours. Such **filibustering** is most effective when undertaken during the final hours of a session.

9. Third reading (Senate)   If passed on the second reading, a bill can have its third reading immediately, assuming the rules have been suspended (as is routinely done in the Senate) by the required four-fifths majority vote of members present. Amending a bill on the third reading requires a two-thirds majority vote of members present.

10. Return to the House   After passage by the Senate, a House bill is returned to the chief clerk of the House, who has the responsibility to supervise preparation of a perfect copy of the bill and deliver it to the speaker. When an amendment has been added in the Senate (as usually happens), the change must be voted on in the House. If the House is not prepared to accept the amended bill, the ordinary procedure is to request a conference. Otherwise, the bill will die unless one of the chambers reverses its position.

11. Conference committee   When the two chambers agree to send the bill to conference, each presiding officer appoints five members to serve on the **conference committee**. Attempts will be made to adjust differences and produce a compromise version acceptable to both the House and the Senate. At least three Senate members and three House members must agree before the committee can recommend a course of action in the two houses. The author of the House bill (usually but not necessarily) serves as conference committee chair.

12. Conference committee report   The conference committee's recommended settlement of questions at issue must be fully accepted or rejected by a simple majority vote in each chamber. Most are accepted. Both chambers, however, may agree to return the report to the committee, or, on request of the House, the Senate may accept a proposal for a new conference.

13. Enrollment   After a conference report has been accepted by both chambers, the chief clerk of the House prepares a perfect copy of the bill and stamps it "Enrolled."

14. Signatures of the Chief Clerk and Speaker   When the enrolled conference committee report is received in the House, the bill is read by number
only. Subsequently, it is signed by the chief clerk, who certifies the vote by
which it passed. Then the speaker signs the bill.

15. Signatures of the Secretary of the Senate and the Lieutenant Governor
Next, the chief clerk of the House takes the bill to the Senate, where it is read
by number only. With certification of the vote by which it passed, the bill is
signed by the secretary of the Senate and by the lieutenant governor.

16. Action by the governor   While the legislature remains in session, the
governor has three options: sign the bill; allow it to remain unsigned for 10
days, not including Sundays, after which time it becomes law without the
chief executive's signature; or, within the 10-day period, veto the measure
by returning it to the House unsigned, with a message giving a reason for
the veto. The Texas Constitution requires a vote of "two-thirds of the membership present" in the first house that considers a vetoed bill (in this case,
the House of Representatives) and a vote of "two-thirds of the members" in
the second house (in this case, the Senate) to override the governor's veto.[13]

   After a session ends, the governor has 20 days, counting Sundays, in
which to veto pending legislation and file the rejected bills with the secretary of state. A bill not vetoed by the governor automatically becomes law at
the end of the 20-day period. The governor's postadjournment veto is of
special importance because it cannot be overridden. However, relatively few
bills are vetoed. (See the chapter "The Executive" for information on Governor Perry's vetoes after the 77th and 78th Legislatures' regular sessions in
2001 and 2003.)

   Ordinarily, an act of the legislature does not take effect as a law until 90
days after adjournment, or even later if specified in the bill. Exceptions to
this rule include a general appropriations act (which takes effect when
approved) and a measure containing the provision that it will take effect
immediately or less than 90 days after adjournment. The latter is no longer
required to contain an emergency clause, but it must pass each house by a
two-thirds majority vote of the total membership (21 votes in the Senate and
100 votes in the House of Representatives).

Influences Within the Legislative Environment

In theory, elected legislators are influenced primarily, if not exclusively, by
their constituents. In practice, however, many legislators' actions bear little
relationship to the needs or interests of the "folks back home." To be sure,
Texas senators and representatives are not completely indifferent to voters,
but many of them fall far short of being genuinely representative. One problem is that large numbers of citizens are uninterested in most governmental
affairs and have no opinions about how the legislature should act in making

public policy. Others may have opinions but are inarticulate or unable to communicate with their legislators. Therefore, lawmakers are likely to yield not only to the influence of the presiding officers in the House and Senate, but also to pressure from the governor and other powerful political actors (especially lobbyists) seeking to win their voluntary support or force their cooperation.

The Governor

We have described the roles of legislative leaders and the governor's veto power. It is also necessary to point out that the ever-present threat of executive veto plays an equally important part in legislative behavior. Even though a bill is popular with many senators and representatives, it may not pass. Knowledge that the governor opposes the measure is often sufficient to discourage its introduction. If introduced despite the governor's opposition, it is likely to be buried in a committee, tabled (postponed without commitment to reconsider), or defeated on the floor of the House or Senate.

Each governor campaigns for office on a platform of promises and then feels compelled to promote certain policies after being elected. Thus, legislators must be influenced to ensure the success of the governor's plans for taxing, spending, building, and educating, among other things. And if there is any doubt as to what the governor wants, gubernatorial policies will be outlined in messages from time to time. Popular support for the chief executive's ideas will make opposition difficult, even though the people in a legislator's district may be adversely affected.[14]

Judges, the Attorney General, and the Comptroller of Public Accounts

An act that is politically expedient and even popular with constituents may conflict with provisions of the Texas Constitution or the U.S. Constitution. Thus, in their lawmaking, all legislators are influenced by what state and federal judges have done or could do about possible legislative action.

Usually, senators and representatives wish neither to spend time nor to invest political capital in legislative efforts that will be struck down by judicial decisions or opinions of the attorney general. Therefore, while a bill is being considered, the committee chair may turn to the attorney general for an opinion concerning its constitutionality.

By estimating how much money will be collected under current and projected revenue laws, the state comptroller exercises great influence because the legislature must keep state spending within the limits of anticipated revenue. For example, after an appropriation bill has passed the House and Senate, it goes to the comptroller. If the comptroller determines that sufficient revenue will be unavailable, the bill will not receive the comptroller's certification and cannot be enacted unless both houses approve it by a four-fifths majority vote.

Lobbyists

Lobbying as an interest group tactic is discussed in the chapter "The Politics of Interest Groups." Opinions vary concerning the influence of lobbyists on legislative behavior and public policy. In many minds, lobbying means corruption. Others see lobbyists as performing a useful role by supplying information and serving as links with organized groups of constituents. But it is a nagging fact that special-interest groups spend large amounts of money to induce legislative action (usually to kill a bill) that otherwise would not be taken on a legislator's own initiative or in response to requests by constituents. In fact, many bills are written by lobbyists and "carried" by cooperative legislators.[15]

Lobbyists are required to register with the Ethics Commission, and lobbying reports mandated by state law are made to that agency. Both lobbyists and political action committees (PACs) contribute directly to the campaign funds that cover legislators' election expenses and are used to pay for a wide range of political and officeholder activities.[16]

Research Organizations

Reliable information is essential to policymakers. Most Texas legislators depend heavily on information provided by their own staffs, administrative agencies, and lobbyists. In addition, legislators obtain information from three official research bodies:

- The Texas Legislative Council, **www.tlc.state.tx.us**
- The House Research Organization, **www.capitol.state.tx.us/hrofr/ hrofr.htm**
- The Senate Research Center, **www.senate.state.tx.us/src/index.htm**

Two of Texas's more important independent providers of public policy research and analysis are the following:

- The Center for Public Policy Priorities, **www.cppp.org**
- The Texas Public Policy Foundation, **www.tppf.org**

The Legislative Council   Authorizing special research projects by its staff is one of the functions of the Legislative Council, which is composed of the lieutenant governor (joint chair), the speaker of the House (joint chair), six senators appointed by the lieutenant governor, the chair of the House Administration Committee, and five representatives appointed by the speaker. The council offers support to legislators, other state officials, and the public in a number of areas. During the 78th regular session in 2003, the Legislative Council's executive director supervised about 450 employees, who provided bill drafting, legislative counseling, legislative research and writing, interim study committee research support, demographic and statistical data compilation and analysis, computer mapping and analysis, publications, and computer services.

The House Research Organization A bipartisan steering committee of 15 representatives—elected by the House membership for staggered four-year terms—governs the House Research Organization (HRO). Because the HRO is an administrative department of the House, the House Administration Committee provides the organization's operating funds. The HRO employed 16 staff personnel during the 78th regular legislative session in 2003, and about half that number worked during the interim between sessions.

The HRO produces reports on a wide variety of policy issues. Of special importance is its *Daily Floor Report* for each day the legislature is in session. This publication analyzes important bills to be considered, providing an objective summary of their content and arguments for and against each bill. After the close of a regular session, the staff publishes a report on the session's important bills and resolutions, including some that were defeated. (For example, see *Major Issues of the 78th Legislature* published after the 2003 regular session.)

The Senate Research Center Organized under the secretary of the Senate, the Senate Research Center succeeded the Senate Office of Bill Analysis. In addition to analyzing bills before the Senate, the center conducts research in diverse areas. Primarily, it responds to requests from Senate members for research and information. The lieutenant governor, however, as president of the Senate, also calls on the center's information and expertise. The center's periodic publications range from the semimonthly *Clearinghouse Update,* which presents brief accounts of issues facing Texas and the nation, to *Highlights of the . . . Legislature*, published after each regular session. Other publications produced by the center include *Budget 101: A Guide to the Budget Process in Texas* (January 2003), and *A Senate Guide to Ethics and Disclosure—78th Legislative Session* (January 2003).

The Center for Public Policy Priorities Founded in 1985 as an Austin office of the Benedictine Resource Center, the Center for Public Policy Priorities has been operating as an independent nonprofit organization since 1999. Its principal focus is on the problems of low- and moderate-income families in Texas. Legislators and other public officials have utilized its policy analysis on issues ranging from state taxation and appropriations to public education and health care access. Scott McCown, a former state district judge who dealt with some of Texas's most important public school finance cases, has served as the center's executive director since 2002.

The Texas Public Policy Foundation Established in 1989 in San Antonio, the Texas Public Policy Foundation (TPPF) has been heavily funded and influenced by its founder, Dr. James Leininger. He became wealthy as a manufacturer of hospital beds and has contributed heavily to campaigns of Governor Rick Perry and other conservative politicians. Claiming to be nonpartisan, the foundation announces that it is guided by concern for limited government, free enterprise, private property rights, and individual responsibility. With an aggressive marketing program, TPPF seeks to influence Texas government by policy research and analysis, and by recommending its findings to legislators and other policymakers, group leaders, media persons, and the general public. Brooke Leslie Rollins, a Texas A&M and University of Texas Law School graduate who served as Governor Perry's policy director, became president of TPPF in January 2003.

The Media

It is difficult to measure (or even estimate) the influence of newspapers, magazines, television, the Internet, and radio on legislative behavior. Legislators are aware that some of their activities will be publicized by the press (especially the *Austin American-Statesman* and other big-city newspapers), web sites created by special interest groups, radio and television broadcasts, and magazines such as *Texas Monthly* and the *Texas Observer,* along with newsletters and other publications produced for subscribers or members of special-interest groups. Thus, a legislator may be induced to work for or against a bill to avoid negative publicity or to earn favorable publicity. On some policy issues, lawmakers (as well as voters) may be impressed by reasoned opinions expressed in editorials, persuasive analyses from political columnists and commentators, reporters' news stories, postings by bloggers, and editorial cartoons such as those printed in *Practicing Texas Politics: A Brief Survey.*

Looking Ahead

In the Texas Legislature's 78th regular session in 2003 and subsequent special sessions in 2003 and 2004, neither the House nor the Senate distinguished itself in handling important public policy issues. Congressional redistricting distracted both representatives and senators from other matters for many months; disagreements over taxing and spending were sharp; and personal animosities developed. Will the influence of corporate money in Austin provoke widespread demand for change? The Lone Star State's political history reveals that significant reform and pressure for ethical conduct in government usually come only after a highly publicized scandal that arouses public indignation. Is such a scandal looming on the Texas political horizon?

The following chapter, "The Executive," presents more information concerning relations between the legislative and executive branches. In particular, it gives attention to the role of the governor and the other executive officials in making and implementing public policy.

☆ Chapter Summary ☆

- The Texas Legislature is composed of 31 senators elected for four-year terms and 150 representatives elected for two-year terms. Biennial regular sessions are limited to 140 days, and special sessions called by the governor are limited to 30 days. New legislative districts are drawn after each federal decennial census.

- Legislators must be U.S. citizens, qualified Texas voters, and residents of their district for one year. Minimum Texas residence is one year for representatives and two years for senators. Minimum age is 21 for representatives and 26 for senators.

- The lieutenant governor presides over the Senate, and the speaker presides over the House. They appoint committee members and name committee chairs and vice chairs for their respective chambers.

- Legislators form legislative caucuses with common interests. There are party caucuses for Democrats and Republicans, racial/ethnic caucuses for African Americans and Mexican Americans, and ideological caucuses for conservatives and liberals.

- Constitutional provisions and rules of the House and Senate control the detailed process whereby a bill is passed in both chambers. The governor may sign a bill, allow it to become law without signing, or veto it. A veto kills a bill unless the veto is overruled by a two-thirds vote in each chamber.

- Legislators are popularly elected, but they are influenced by the governor and other state officials, lobbyists, research organizations, and the media.

Key Terms

unicameral	president of the Senate
bicameral	speaker of the House
regular session	substantive committee
special session	procedural committee
redistricting	select committee
gerrymandering	standing committee
single-member district	special interim committee
multimember district	parliamentarian
simple resolution	companion bill
concurrent resolution	ghost voting
joint resolution	chubbing
bill	filibustering
senatorial courtesy	conference committee
impeachment	

Discussion Questions

1. Do you think that Texas's legislative redistricting process meets the needs of Texans, or do you believe that it should be changed?
2. Do you believe that the Texas Legislature should include equal numbers of men and women and should include members of different racial or ethnic groups in proportion to their populations?
3. Which state official has the most power to influence legislation, and how is this power used?
4. Which legislative caucus appears to work for legislation that you support or that you would like to see introduced?
5. Which steps in passing a bill are most critical in the legislative process?
6. How should the legislature regulate lobbying activities to ensure that freedoms are preserved but that the public interest is protected?
7. What role do research organizations play in lawmaking?

Internet Resources

Legislative Reference Library: **www.lrl.state.tx.us**
Conference on State Legislature: **www.ncsl.org**
Texas House of Representatives: **www.house.state.tx.us**
Texas Legislature Online: **www.capitol.state.tx.us**
Texas Media Watch: **www.texasmediawatch.com**
Texas Senate: **www.senate.state.tx.us**

Notes

1. Alan Rosenthal, *The Decline of Representative Democracy: Process, Participation, and Power in State Legislatures* (Washington, D.C.: CQ Press, 1998), p. x.
2. John Kirsch, "Lawmakers in Austin Hear Message of Hope, Peace," *Fort Worth Star–Telegram,* 19 March 2003.
3. For detailed treatment of redistricting, see *State and Federal Law Governing Redistricting in Texas* (Austin: Texas Legislative Council, March 2001); and Mark Monmonier, *Bushmanders and Bullwinkles: How Politicians Manipulate Electronic Maps and Census Data to Win Elections* (Chicago: University of Chicago Press, 2001).
4. See "New Districts in Place for 2002 Elections," *Interim News* No. 77-4 (Austin: House Research Organization, Texas House of Representatives, 14 January 2002), pp. 1–8.
5. See Nancy Baker Jones and Ruth Winegarten, *Capitol Women: Texas Female Legislators, 1923–1999* (Austin: University of Texas Press, 1999).

6. See *Major Issues of the 78th Legislature: Regular Session Focus Report No. 78-12* (Austin: House Research Organization, Texas House of Representatives, 6 August 2003), p. 1; bill statistics at <www.lrl.state.tx.us/legis/profile78.html>.

7. For more details concerning Ratliff's election as acting lieutenant governor, see Patricia Kilday Hart, "Bill Passes," *Texas Monthly,* February 2001, pp. 94, 102–104.

8. Quoted by R. A. Dyer, "Lone Dissent Marks Craddick's Swearing In," *Austin American-Statesman,* 15 January 2003.

9. See Patricia Kilday Hart, "Speakergate," *Texas Monthly,* May 2004, pp. 78, 95-97; and Jake Bernstein and Dave Mann, "Scandal in the Speaker's Office," *Texas Observer,* 27 February 2004, pp. 4–7, 18–19.

10. See Juan Elizondo, "Power in the Capital Shifts to Caucuses," *Austin American-Statesman*, 8 November 1999.

11. For a more detailed description of the lawmaking process, see *How a Bill Becomes a Law: 78th Legislature,* Focus Report No. 78-4 (Austin: House Research Organization, Texas House of Representatives, 23 January 2003).

12. For more information on how committees work, see *House Committee Procedures: 78th Legislature,* Focus Report No. 78-5 (Austin: House Research Organization, Texas House of Representatives, 23 January 2003).

13. As one authority explains, this difference in the two-thirds majorities required by Article IV, Section 14, represents "a mysterious error in the present constitution." See George D. Braden, *Citizens' Guide to the Proposed New Texas Constitution* (Austin: Sterling Swift, 1975), p. 15.

14. For contrasting accounts of relations between Governor Bush and the legislature, see George W. Bush, *A Charge to Keep* (New York: Morrow, 1999), pp. 110–131; and Molly Ivins and Lou Dubose, *Shrub: The Short But Happy Political Life of George W. Bush* (New York: Random House, 2000), pp. 84–106.

15. For a scholarly yet readable description of lobbying in the Lone Star State, see Keith E. Hamm and Charles W. Wiggins, "Texas: The Transformation from Personal to Information Lobbying," in *Interest Group Politics in the Southern States,* edited by Ronald J. Hrebenar and Clive S. Thomas (Tuscaloosa: University of Alabama Press, 1992), pp. 152–180.

16. For a study featuring interviews with 14 former Texas legislators, see Sam Kinch, Jr. with Anne Marie Kilday, *Too Much Money Is Not Enough: Big Money and Political Power in Texas* (Austin: Campaigns for People, 2000).

SELECTED READING

★

Redistricting and Electoral Results in Texas in the Twenty-First Century*

Lyle C. Brown and Jerry Wilkins

Two factors helped Texas Republicans elect large majorities for both chambers of the 78th Legislature that convened in Austin in January 2003: redistricting of the Texas House and Senate in 2001, and heavy contributions of corporate money to support GOP candidates in the 2002 election. But congressional districts drawn by federal judges in 2001 elected a Democratic majority in the Texas delegation to the U.S. House of Representatives in 2002. This caused U.S. Representative Tom DeLay to push successfully for congressional "re-redistricting" in his native state in 2003. At the same time, however, partisan warfare and grand jury investigations changed the face of Texas politics.

Seismic political shifts have jolted Texas in recent years. How did the impact affect legislative and congressional redistricting in the Lone Star State after 2000? And what were the electoral results?

Legislative and Congressional Redistricting in 2001

The story of redistricting in Texas in the first decade of the twenty-first century begins with the elections of November 2000. At that time, Texas voters elected a state House majority of 78 Democrats and a minority of 72 Republicans. Concurrently, they elected a state Senate majority of 16 Republicans and a minority of 15 Democrats. To fill Texas's 30 seats in the U.S House of Representatives, 17 Democrats and 13 Republicans were elected.

When the Texas Legislature convened in Austin for its 77th regular session in January 2001, one state constitutional responsibility was to redistrict the Lone Star State for electing all members of the state House and Senate in 2002. Despite its Democratic majority, the Texas House passed H.B. 150, which was expected to result in electing a Republican majority for that chamber in 2002. The Senate Redistricting Committee appoved the bill eight to nothing, but it died without a floor vote—perhaps because some Republicans feared the formation of a coalition of Democrats and West Texas Republicans that would reelect Pete Laney (D-Hale Center) to a sixth term as speaker at the beginning of the 78th Legislature's regular session in

*Lyle C. Brown is professor emeritus of political science at Baylor University. Jerry Wilkins is adjunct professor of public administration and urban studies at San Diego State University. This article was written especially for *Practicing Texas Politics: A Brief Survey.*

January 2003. Meanwhile, the Senate Redistricting Committee gave a favorable report for S.B. 499. This redistricting plan featured three GOP-leaning districts and sixteen that were solidly Republican, but it died without floor debate.

Because of redistricting failures by the Texas House and Senate, legislative redistricting chores were performed in the summer of 2001 by the Legislative Redistricting Board (LRB). Its five ex-officio members were acting Lieutenant Governor Bill Ratliff, Attorney General John Cornyn, Land Commissioner David Dewhurst, Comptroller of Public Accounts Carole Keeton Rylander (later Strayhorn), and Speaker Pete Laney, who was the only Democrat. Ratliff supported Laney on most issues, but they were outvoted 3 to 2 on the LRB's redistricting plans for both the state House and Senate.

When considered by the Civil Rights Division of the U.S. Department of Justice, as required by the federal Voting Rights Act, the House plan was found to be defective because minority voters in three districts would be adversely affected. Subsequently, a three-judge federal district court adopted a plan that was more acceptable to Texas Latinos. Nevertheless, the Mexican American Legislative Caucus and the Mexican American Legal Defense and Education Fund appealed to the U.S. Supreme Court but lost. Although challenged by Latinos, the Senate plan was given preclearance by the U.S. Department of Justice and approved by the three-judge panel; however, Judge John Hannah complained of political gerrymandering in both the Senate and the House plans.

During its regular session in 2001, the 77th Legislature was as unsuccessful in redistricting the state for electing members of Texas's congressional delegation as it was in redistricting for members of the Texas House and Senate. Because the LRB is not authorized to do congressional redistricting, a three-judge federal district court performed that task. The result was a redistricting plan providing new Republican-dominated districts in the Dallas and Houston areas for the two seats that Texas gained as a result of the state's population increase between 1990 and 2000. The other 30 districts were drawn to protect both Democratic and Republican incumbents.

Elections of 2002

As political parties and candidates prepared for primary and general election contests in 2002, Republican strategies were developed for electing a socially conservative, business-friendly GOP majority for the Texas House and for maintaining a similar majority in the Senate. Two important instruments of these electoral efforts were the Texas Association of Business (TAB), representing chambers of commerce throughout the state, and Texans for a Republican Majority, a political action committee (TRMPAC) modeled after Americans for a Republican Majority founded by U.S. Representative Tom Delay (R-Sugar Land).[1]

As president of TAB, former Texas House member Bill Hammond viewed the 2002 primaries and general election as steps toward a House GOP majority that would elect his friend Tom Craddick as Texas's first Republican speaker since the Reconstruction era. To do this, Hammond used his corporate contacts to raise big money, but it is a third-degree felony offense to give corporate funds directly to candidates. Hammond's strategy was to spend corporate contributions, such as those he solicited from the Texas insurance industry in August 2002, to "educate" voters by using TAB phone banks and direct mail for communicating positive or negative messages designed to affect voter behavior in selected districts.

A few weeks before the November 2002 election, lobbyist Mike Toomey began playing a major role in the effort to elect Republican legislative candidates. He was a member of TAB's governing board, former state representative, former chief of staff for governor Bill Clements, and long-time friend of Governor Perry. According to Austin journalist Laylan Copelin, Toomey raised funds for TAB's $1.7 million advertising campaign, supervised direct-mail efforts, and organized meetings attended by representatives of TRMPAC and Texans for Lawsuit Reform, business lobbyists and public relations specialists, and others who wanted to elect business-friendly legislators.[2]

As an example of TAB's operations, Representative Ann Kitchen (D-Austin) was targeted with negative "issue ads" mailed to voters in her district and by phone calls suggesting that Kitchen favored more government taxing and spending. Todd Baxter, her GOP opponent, denied that his election campaign was coordinated with TAB. As evidence that the defeated Democrats could have grounds for complaint, Hammond bragged that TAB "blew the doors off" the 2002 election by "educating" voters with 4 million mailings and spending $2 million on just 22 House contests and 2 Senate races. Hammond's boasting caught the attention of Travis County district attorney Ronnie Earle, who began a grand jury investigation.

Earle investigated TRMPAC, too. Organized by Tom DeLay on 1 September 2001, this political action committee received $50,000 in start-up money from Americans for a Republican Majority. Jim Ellis, one of DeLay's top aides, became director of the Texas PAC. Bill Ceverha, a lobbyist and former GOP member of the Texas House, was made treasurer; and John Colyandro, executive director of the Texas Conservative Coalition in 2004, was hired as executive director. How TRMPAC raised money that influenced the outcome of legislative elections in 2002 is documented in a typed memo obtained by the *Texas Observer* and first publicized by the *Houston Chronicle*. The memo features a list of executives with Houston businesses (e.g., Reliant Energy, Compass Bank, Maxxam, EOG Resources) who were visited on 9 September 2002 by Representative Beverly Woolley (R-Houston) and TRMPAC fund-raiser Susan Lilly. Beside the names of these business executives are notes that indicate amounts of money promised and legislative matters in which donors were interested. A total of $53,000 was pledged that day, and campaign finance records indicate the pledges were paid shortly thereafter. On 12 September 2002, Lilly and Representative Dianne Delisi (R-Temple) made similar fundraising efforts in Dallas netting $35,000; but their itinerary for that trip does not indicate the legislative interests of the Dallas executives they visited.

Results of the 2002 election caused most Republicans to be jubilant. GOP candidates won 88 of 150 state House seats and 19 of 31 Senate seats. At the same time, Republicans won the governor's race and all other statewide contests. Outcomes of congressional elections, however, were disappointing for DeLay and the GOP.

Across the Lone Star State, nearly 2,300,000 Republican votes were cast to elect fifteen U.S. representatives; but seventeen were elected with less than 1,900,000 Democratic votes. In part, these results were due to low voter turnout in Democrat-controlled districts with many Latino and African American residents. Furthermore, some Republican voters preferred incumbent Democratic representatives with seniority rather than less-experienced Republican candidates. (When seeking federal funds for projects within a congressional district, seniority helps to "bring home the bacon.")

Congressional "Re-redistricting" in 2003

Traditionally, congressional redistricting in Texas and other states is done only once each decade, unless a districting plan is found to violate the U.S. Constitution or a statute. Nevertheless, DeLay was determined that the Republican-controlled 78th Legislature would "re-redistrict" Texas in 2003; and Texas Attorney General Greg Abbott ruled that it had such authority. Lieutenant Governor David Dewhurst was not enthusiastic about drawing new congressional districts, but Tom Craddick (R-Midland) had been elected speaker of the House in January 2003. Craddick and Governor Perry agreed with DeLay. Nevertheless, a congressional redistricting bill failed to pass the House because 53 Democratic members broke the House quorum by fleeing to Ardmore, Oklahoma. They stayed there until time ran out for House action in the regular session that ended on 2 June 2003.

In the first special session lasting from 30 June to 28 July, GOP efforts to pass a congressional redistricting bill were thwarted by the Senate rule requiring a two-thirds majority to bring a bill to the Senate floor. Just before the second special session was called, eleven of the Senate's twelve Democrats escaped to Albuquerque, New Mexico, when it became apparent that Lieutenant Governor Dewhurst would dispense with the two-thirds rule for that session (28 July to 26 August). Eventually, Senator John Whitmire (D-Houston) deserted his colleagues in Albuquerque and returned to Austin. This paved the way for the third special session (15 September to 12 October), when the two-thirds rule was not used and a congressional redistricting bill was passed.

Democrats contended that Plan 01374C involved unconstitutional partisan and racial gerrymandering and violated the Voting Rights Act. Nevertheless, early in 2004 a three-judge federal district court sitting in Austin decided 2 to 1 to uphold the plan. Subsequently, the U.S. Supreme Court refused to prevent the plan's use while the Texas redistricting case was being appealed as *Jackson* v. *Perry*. At the earliest, the U.S. Supreme Court would decide in October 2004 whether it would hear plaintiffs' arguments in the case. Thus, the way was clear for using Plan 01374C to elect Texas's 32 U.S. representatives in November 2004.

Elections of 2004

Because his old Piney Woods district was dismembered by the new congressional redistricting plan, U.S. Representative Jim Turner (D-Crockett) did not seek reelection in 2004. Ralph Hall (D-Rockwall) saved his congressional skin by switching to the Republican Party and winning the District 4 nomination in the GOP's first primary. Chris Bell (D-Houston) was defeated in the Democratic Party's first primary by African American Al Green in District 9, a largely African American district. Democrats Eddie Bernice Johnson (Dallas, Dist. 30), Sheila Jackson Lee (Houston, Dist. 18), and Gene Green (Houston, Dist. 29) had no Republican opponents in November. Democrats Charlie Gonzalez (San Antonio, Dist. 20), Solomon Ortiz (Corpus Christi, Dist. 27), Silvestre Reyes (El Paso, Dist. 16), and Ruben Hinojosa (Mercedes, Dist. 15) had GOP opponents but won their general election contests. Five incumbents did not face opposition in the second Democratic primary: Max Sandlin (Marshall, Dist. 1), Nick Lampson (Beaumont, Dist. 2), Chet Edwards (Waco, Dist. 17), Charlie Stenholm (Abilene, Dist. 19), and Martin Frost (Arlington, Dist. 32). All but Edwards were defeated in November when they ran in districts that had been drawn to the advantage of Republican candidates. Frost's opponent was U.S. Representative Pete Sessions (R-Dallas). Incumbent Ciro Rodriguez (San Antonio, Dist. 28) was named winner over Henry Cuellar in the first Democratic primary, but a recount turned Rodriguez's victory by a margin of 145 votes into a 203-vote loss that he challenged unsuccessfully in court. Cuellar won the District 28 seat by defeating Republican Jim Hopson in November. In the first Democratic primary, Lloyd Doggett (Austin, Dist. 25) defeated Leticia Hinojosa in a predominantly Hispanic-populated, "fajita-strip" or "bacon-strip" district stretching 300 miles from Austin to the Rio Grande. In November, Doggett retained his congressional seat by beating Republican Rebecca Armendariz Klein. GOP candidates in Republican-friendly districts won the remaining seats in the Texas delegation.

As a result of congressional redistricting in 2003, Texas's Republican representation in the U.S. House increased in that year to 21 in 2005, while Democratic representation fell from 17 to 11. But at what risks and what costs did DeLay and others engineer their redistricting feats and electoral triumphs?

Legal Problems

Bill Hammond insists that TAB's use of corporate funding for mailouts and phone banks was a constitutional use of free speech because nobody was pressured to vote for or against any candidate. TRMPAC claims that its use of corporate contributions to raise funds, pay telemarketers and pollsters, evaluate candidates, organize events, and pay part-time executive John Colyandro were legitimate administrative expenses. Speaker Craddick became the subject of a Travis County grand jury investigation to determine if he violated state law when he became involved in delivering TRMPAC checks to 14 Republican candidates for House seats just before the November election in 2002. And Earle looked into a possible money laundering operation whereby TRMPAC sent $190,000 of corporate money to the Republican National Committee, which within two weeks contributed exactly $190,000 to seven GOP candidates for state House seats.

Charging that Earle's investigations were politically motivated, Republican Party chair Tina Benkiser filed an open records request that produced hundreds of documents. Among the DA's records that were released were five advance drafts of an article by Dave McNeely, a long-time columnist for the *Austin American-Statesman,* concerning Craddick, Hammond, and DeLay. With one of these drafts sent to Earle and assistant district attorney Gregg Cox, McNeely wrote, "Appreciate it if you each give it a read and then let's talk. Looking mostly to make sure I haven't screwed up anywhere or have some huge omission." Later, McNeely's long article, "Grand Old Politics," appeared in the 20 July 2003 issue of the *Austin American-Statesman.* The article's subheading declared: "Money paved the road to Republican dominance in the Legislature, and to no one's surprise, that road led straight to contributors' goals. But was it all legal?"

While Earle and a succession of Travis County grand juries conducted official investigations, researchers for the *Houston Chronicle* independently examined more than 10,000 pages of Republican and Democratic campaign records. A *Chronicle* article published on 25 April 2004 noted "no apparent violations of state laws" by the Texas Democratic Party. At the same time, it reported that in 2002 the Texas Republican Party raised $5.7 million from corporations and from national committees that solicit corporate donations. Most of these funds, according to the *Chronicle,* were then transferred to the Texas Republican Congressional Campaign Committee (TRCCC) and spent for nonadministrative purposes.

On 15 June 2004, Texas's congressional redistricting controversy became a national political issue. That was the day U.S. Representative Chris Bell announced he had filed a complaint with the U.S. House Committee on Standards of Official Conduct against House Majority Leader Tom DeLay. Seven years had passed since the committee's finding in another ethics case led the House to reprimand Speaker Newt Gingrich, fine him $300,000, and influence his departure from the U.S. Congress. Now Bell was striking back at DeLay, whose congressional redistricting scheme had forced Bell into a losing primary contest. His complaint charged that DeLay

■ accepted $25,000 for TRMPAC, from Westar, in return for promoting congressional legislation that would have benefited the Kansas-based energy company.
■ used the Republican National Committee to launder $190,000 in corporate contributions to benefit GOP legislative candidates in Texas
■ pressured federal agencies to locate Pete Laney's airplane and prevent its use to transport Texas representatives out of the state in an effort to prevent passage of a congressional redistricting bill.[3]

The bipartisan Committee on Standards of Official Conduct (5 Republicans and 5 Democrats) found Bell's complaint had merit. This meant that the committee would study it for a maximum of 45 days before deciding whether to undertake an investigation that could lead to fining DeLay or even expelling him from the House. Many Democrats and others were calling for appointment of an independent counsel to investigate Bell's charges against DeLay.

On 21 September 2004, DeLay's involvement with TRMPAC became national news when a Travis County grand jury returned indictments against three of DeLay's associates (Jim Ellis, John Colyandro, and Warren RoBold), seven corporations, and the Alliance for Quality Nursing Home Care. The corporations and the nursing home organization contributed to TRMPAC before the 2002 election. On 22 September 2004 it was revealed that Chris Winkle, CEO of Mariner Health Care, had given Speaker Tom Craddick the Alliance's $100,000 check for TRMPAC as they dined at Anthony's in Houston. Then on 27 September, Democrat Kirk Watson sued the Lawsuit Alliance of America, a Virginia-based "pro-gun, pro-police" organization that spent an estimated $1.5 million on attack ads favoring winner Gregg Abbott in the 2002 contest for the office of attorney general. Watson also sued John Colyandro, who served as Abbott's political adviser.

On 6 October, the U.S. House Committee on Standards of Official Conduct rebuked DeLay for participating with Weststar Energy Corporation executives in a golfing fund-raiser shortly after they contributed $25,000 to Texans for a Republican Majority and while an energy bill was before Congress. Although the ethics committee also criticized DeLay for seeking the Federal Aviation Administration's assistance in locating Speaker Pete Laney's private plane when Democratic legislators fled from Austin to Ardmore in 2003, it decided not to rule on Bell's money-laundering charge while legal actions were underway in Texas.

On 18 October, the U.S. Supreme Court ordered the three-judge federal district court to reconsider its earlier ruling. This action did not affect the November 2004 elections, but it guaranteed that the redistricting struggle would continue until 2005 or later.

What's Ahead?

The impact of Texas's congressional redistricting in 2003 will be felt in Austin and Washington for years to come. Although full details of the unfolding story cannot be spelled out in a few pages, this brief reading gives students a background for under-standing future media coverage of the following subjectss and related matters:

- Actions by federal courts regarding the case of *Jackson V. Perry;*
- Pleas, trials, and appeals resulting from Travis County grand jury indictments;
- Continuing grand jury investigations of TAB, TRMPAC, Speaker Tom Craddick, U.S. Rep. Tom DeLay, and others;
- Outcomes of civil suits by losing Democratic candidates in 2002;
- Legislative politics concerning Travis County district attorney Ronnie Earle's Public Integrity Unit and state regulations of campaign finance;
- Further action (or inaction) of the U.S. House Committee on Standards of Official Conduct in response to Chris Bell's complaint against Tom DeLay;
- DeLay's relations with Texas legislators and his Republican leadership role in the U.S. House of Representatives.

Notes

1. For biographical information and details concerning DeLay's involvement in Texas redistricting politics, see Lou Dubose and Jan Reid, *The Hammer, Tom DeLay: God, Money, and the Rise of the Republican Congress* (New York: Public Affairs Press, 2004).
2. Laylan Copelin, "GOP Heavyweight Toomey Led Key Ad Effort," *Austin American-Statesman,* 16 May 2004.
3. See Eunice Moscoso, "DeLay Targeted In Ethics Complaint," *Austin American-Statesman,* 16 June 2004; and Gary Martin, "DeLay Accused of Criminal Ethics Violations," *San Antonio Express-News,* 16 June 2004. For conflicting views, see U.S. Rep. Chris Bell, "DeLay Undermines Small 'd' Democracy," *Houston Chronicle,* 20 June 2004; and Rep. John Carter, "Bell's Frivolous Complaint Is a Bid to Demonize DeLay," *Austin American-Statesman,* 25 June 2004.

⭐

Chapter 7

THE EXECUTIVE

John Branch cartoon. Copyright © 2004 *San Antonio Express-News*. Reprinted with permission.

*I*n a book widely read by political scientists and others for more than two decades, Professor Larry Sabato (University of Virginia) asserts, "Governors as a class have outgrown the description 'good time Charlie.'"[1] He observes that they are concerned about their work, have new powers that give them influence in state and national councils, are skilled negotiators and coordinators in dealing with officials at state and national levels, and are trained, effective leaders. Readers of this chapter should decide whether the governor of Texas is a "good-time Charlie."

In April 2004, when faced with the need for additional revenue to finance public education, Governor Rick Perry proposed raising part of the money through a $1 increase per pack for the state cigarette tax, a $5 admission fee to places of so-called adult entertainment, and a state tax on video lottery terminals (slot-machines) at racetracks. Although many Texans reacted with disdain to some or all elements of Perry's revenue plan (see John Branch's cartoon), others supported it. News media throughout the state gave much publicity to Perry's proposal.

No other Texas officeholder is so widely recognized and receives as much media attention as the governor. Nevertheless, Article IV of the Texas Constitution establishes a multiheaded executive branch within which the governor shares power with other elected executive officials and with appointed members of numerous boards and commissions created by the legislature (see Figure 7.1). Unlike the Texas governor, the president of the United States is a strong chief executive who appoints with Senate approval, but removes independently, the department heads who form a cabinet.

Looking Back

Several of Texas's political traditions and institutions stem from the state's experiences after the Civil War. Even today, the state's executive structure shows the influence of anti-Reconstruction reactions against Governor E. J. Davis's administration (1870–1874). Numerous abuses of power by state officials reporting directly to Governor Davis explain why many Texans still distrust the "strong" executive model of state government.

Written after the end of Reconstruction, the Constitution of 1876 provides for election of the governor, lieutenant governor, attorney general, comptroller of public accounts, and commissioner of the General Land Office. In addition, the legislature has provided for election of a commissioner of agriculture. The secretary of state is the only constitutional executive officer who is appointed by the governor, with approval by the Senate.

Overview of the Governorship

Recent acts of the Texas Legislature have given the governor more power than was available to earlier governors, but Texas does not have a governor

Figure 7.1 The Structure of Texas Government (Important Agencies and Officials)

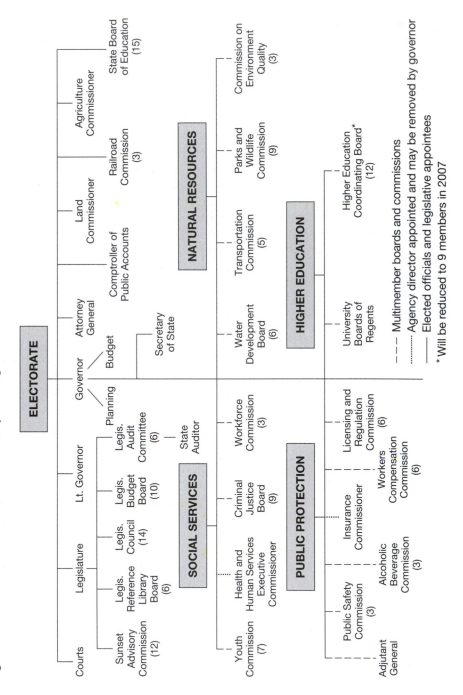

who merits the title "chief executive." Nevertheless, limited executive power does not discourage ambitious gubernatorial candidates who wage multi-million-dollar campaigns in their efforts to win this prestigious office.

Gubernatorial Politics

After pumping millions of dollars into an election campaign, the victorious gubernatorial candidate is obligated to reward some of the heavy contributors by appointing them to key policymaking positions. The practice of buying influence with campaign contributions permeates American politics, and Texas politics is no exception.

Before moving to the Governor's Mansion after Governor George W. Bush won the presidential election of 2000, Rick Perry demonstrated a mastery of campaign finance. In 1998, he raised more than $10 million to defeat Democrat John Sharp by 68,700 votes in a hard-fought contest for lieutenant governor. Key to Perry's 1.8 percent margin of victory was a $1.1 million loan obtained late in the campaign after being guaranteed by Dr. James Leininger, a wealthy San Antonio advocate of school vouchers and a founder of the conservative Texas Public Policy Foundation.[2]

In 2002, South Texas Democrat Tony Sanchez received more than 1.8 million votes while spending in excess of $67 million of campaign money on an unsuccessful effort to win the governorship. Multimillionaire Sanchez used his personal fortune to pay for most of his campaign expenses. Perry raised less than half the amount that Sanchez spent but was reelected with 2.6 million votes. In politics, money talks (even shouts, screeches, and screams), but Sanchez's defeat indicates that campaign finance is only one factor in a gubernatorial election.

Because of the state's budget crisis and the looming war with Iraq, perhaps the inauguration of Governor Perry and Lieutenant Governor David Dewhurst on 21 January 2003 should have been limited to speeches by these officials and a simple swearing-in ceremony. Perry and Dewhurst did deliver inaugural addresses that included pledges to balance the budget without new taxes, and Texas Supreme Court chief justice Tom Phillips used Sam Houston's Bible to administer oaths of office. But an inaugural committee composed of friends and supporters of the governor and lieutenant governor continued the Texas tradition of organizing a big inaugural celebration.

Following the speechmaking and oaths of office, a $5 barbecue lunch was served on the Capitol grounds to 12,000 hungry Texans. For this occasion, Eddie Dean's Catering prepared four tons of briskets, a ton of smoked turkey, and a ton of Earl Campbell Smoked Sausage links that would have stretched more than half a mile. Then there was an afternoon parade with 35 entries (including the Fightin' Texas Aggie Band, the Budweiser Clydesdales, and the Kilgore College Rangerettes). Finally, for 10,000 celebrants who had purchased $65 tickets, the big bash ended with an evening ball in the Austin Convention Center. Sale of barbecue and ball tickets covered less

Governor Rick Perry (Photo courtesy Office of the Governor)

than a third of the inaugural expenses. The balance was contributed by three categories of "underwriters": Gold, $50,000; Silver, $25,000; and Bronze, $10,000. On the evening before the inauguration, these 66 benefactors (mostly lobbyists and corporate executives) were honored with an appreciation dinner at the Bob Bullock History Museum. And on the following day, they received VIP seating at all inaugural events. State spending of $100,000 was authorized for the inauguration, but Perry and Dewhurst decided to demonstrate their dedication to economy in government by refusing to use this public money.[3]

Although some Texans opposed financing inaugural events largely with corporate contributions, others approved the policy that made this big celebration possible at relatively low cost to participants.[4] Because public opinion is greatly influenced by television and press coverage of gubernatorial activities, such as the inaugural celebration, well-orchestrated media relations are critical to the success of any governor. Lacking sufficient constitutional powers, a Texas governor must rely heavily on skills in personal relations, competent staff assistance from communications professionals, and talent for gentle persuasion as well as arm-twisting. Although arm-twisting is usually done without publicity, early in January 2003, Governor Perry made public statements about funding for a new medical school in El Paso and for expanding the Regional Academic Health Center in the Rio Grande Valley. According to an Associated Press report, the governor warned that such spending would depend on support by legislators in those areas for his plan to change the state's medical malpractice and liability laws.[5]

How Do We Compare . . . in Qualifications for the Office of Governor?

Most Populous U.S. States	Minimum Age Required	Length of State Residency Required	U.S. States Bordering Texas	Minimum Age Required	Length of State Residency Required
California	18 years	5 years	Arkansas	30 years	7 years
Florida	30 years	7 years	Louisiana	25 years	5 years
New York	30 years	5 years	New Mexico	30 years	5 years
Texas	**30 years**	**5 years**	Oklahoma	31 years	none

Source: *The Book of the States: 2003* (Lexington, Ky.: Council of State Governments, 2003), p. 185.

Election

Superimposed on constitutional prerequisites for minimum age (30 years), U.S. citizenship, and Texas residency (for 5 years immediately preceding the gubernatorial election) are numerous extralegal restraints on who is elected governor. Historically, a conservative-moderate mold for successful gubernatorial candidates seemed unbreakable. William P. Clements (in 1978 and 1986) and George W. Bush (in 1994 and 1998) partially broke tradition by becoming Texas's first and second Republican governors, respectively, since E. J. Davis. (See Table 7.1 for a listing of Texas governors since 1874.) As conservative businesspeople, Clements and Bush resembled most of their Democratic predecessors in the governor's office. But their Republicanism, and the fact that they had not previously held elective public office, represented a dramatic departure from the past.[6]

Republican Rick Perry entered the Governor's Mansion at the end of 2000 without having won a gubernatorial election. Unlike Clements and Bush, however, Perry had a record of government service. First elected to the Texas House of Representatives as a Democrat in 1984, he won two more terms in the House before switching parties. Subsequently, he was elected commissioner of agriculture in 1990 and again in 1994. Perry was the first Republican to serve in that office since its creation in 1907. In 1998, he became the first Texas GOP candidate to win a campaign for lieutenant governor since Reconstruction. Before becoming a state officeholder, this Texas A&M graduate (class of 1972) had served five years as an Air Force pilot before joining his father in the family's Haskell County farming and ranching operations in West Texas. During the 1990s, according to public records, Perry became wealthy through land deals in the Austin area.[7]

Compensation

Gubernatorial pay is determined by the Texas Legislature. For fiscal years 2004–2005, beginning on 1 September 2003, the annual salary for the governor remained unchanged at $115,345. Fringe benefits include allowances for staffing and maintaining the Governor's Mansion. This

Table 7.1 Governors of Texas Since 1874

Governor	Term	Distinction
Richard Coke	1874–1876	Present constitution was written
Richard B. Hubbard	1876–1879	First governor under Constitution of 1876
Oran M. Roberts	1879–1883	His "pay as you go" plan lowered taxes and reduced the state debt.
John Ireland	1883–1887	Ended the fence-cutting war in West Texas
Lawrence S. Ross	1887–1891	"Man of the people"—mediocrity in government
James S. Hogg	1891–1895	First governor born in Texas
Charles A. Culberson	1895–1899	Called a special session of the legislature that made prizefighting a felony offense
Joseph D. Sayers	1899–1903	Left U.S. Congress for the governorship
Samuel W. T. Lanham	1903–1907	Last Confederate veteran elected as governor
Thomas M. Campbell	1907–1911	First leftist in the governorship
Oscar B. Colquitt	1911–1915	Campaigned against Prohibition, advanced public education, and promoted prison and labor reforms
James E. Ferguson	1915–1917	Only governor to be impeached and convicted
William P. Hobby	1917–1921	Began an amicable era in Texas's relations with Mexico
Pat M. Neff	1921–1925	First governor to emphasize high cost of winning the governorship
Miriam A. Ferguson	1925–1927	First woman elected governor of Texas
Dan Moody	1927–1931	Laid the groundwork for creation of the Board of Pardons and Paroles
Ross S. Sterling	1931–1933	Imposed martial law in East Texas oil fields for six months
Miriam A. Ferguson	1933–1935	First governor to be reelected to a nonconsecutive second term
James V. Allred	1935–1939	Strong supporter of FDR's New Deal
W. Lee O'Daniel	1939–1941	Championed populist causes with extensive use of the radio
Coke R. Stevenson	1941–1947	First governor to break two-term tradition
Beauford H. Jester	1947–1949	First governor to die in office
Allan Shivers	1949–1957	Led Texas Democrats for Eisenhower and Republican Party in 1952 and 1956
Price Daniel, Sr.	1957–1963	First governor to seek a fourth elective term
John Connally	1963–1969	Creation of Higher Education Coordinating Board
Preston Smith	1969–1973	Began Goals for Texas program
Dolph Briscoe, Jr.	1973–1979	First governor to be elected to a four-year term (1975–1979)
William Clements, Jr.	1979–1983	First Republican governor elected in more than 100 years
Mark White	1983–1987	Led movement to reform public education
William Clements, Jr.	1987–1991	Reluctantly approved the biggest tax increase in Texas history
Ann Richards	1991–1995	Appointed record numbers of women, Latinos, and African Americans to high office

Table 7.1 Governors of Texas Since 1874 (continued)

Governor	Term	Distinction
George W. Bush	1995–2000	First governor elected as U.S. president
Rick Perry	2000–	Ascended from lieutenant governor after Governor Bush resigned in 2000 to become U.S. president; was elected to a four-year term in 2002

See "Chief Texas Administrative Officials" in successive editions of the *Texas Almanac* for a listing of Texas chief executives from the first Spanish governor, Domingo Terán de los Rios (1691–1692). Biographical sketches for Texas governors are printed in the *New Handbook of Texas,* 6 vols. (Austin: Texas State Historical Association, 1996).

imposing nineteenth-century building is located one block west of the Capitol grounds at 1010 Colorado Street in Austin.

The Texas Constitution forbids the governor and other executive officers (except the lieutenant governor) from holding any other civil or corporate office, and the governor may receive neither compensation nor the promise of pay for other employment after taking office. Nevertheless, governors do continue to own property and accumulate wealth while serving. To avoid the appearance of conflict between their personal economic interest and the public interest while in office, both Bush and Perry placed their assets in a blind trust (a legal arrangement whereby holdings are administered by others).

Succession

Should a governor die, resign (as did George W. Bush after he was elected to the U.S. presidency in 2000), or be removed from office, or should a governor-elect refuse to take office or be permanently unable to fill the office, a successor serves for the remainder of the governor's four-year term. The lieutenant governor heads the constitutional order of succession. Next in line is the president pro tempore of the Senate. After these two officials, the legislature has designated the following line of succession: speaker of the House, attorney general, and chief justices of the 14 courts of appeals in ascending numerical order, beginning with the chief justice of the First Court of Appeals and ending with the chief justice of the Fourteenth Court of Appeals, both of whom have their primary seats in Houston.

If the governor is temporarily unable to serve, is temporarily disqualified, or is impeached, the lieutenant governor exercises the powers of the governor's office until the governor becomes able or qualified to serve, or is acquitted of impeachment charges. The lieutenant governor becomes acting governor while the governor is absent from the state. By custom, the Texas governor and lieutenant governor arrange their schedules so that, on at least one occasion, both are conveniently out of state at the same time. In such circumstances, the president pro tempore of the Senate has the honor of becoming acting governor until the governor or lieutenant governor returns. Typically, the senator will host a day of festivities (largely financed by lobbyists) for supporters while serving temporarily as governor.

★   **How Do We Compare . . . in Governor's Compensation and Staff Size?**

Most Populous U.S. States	Governor's Annual Salary	Number of People Working in the Governor's Office	U.S. States Bordering Texas	Governor's Annual Salary	Number of People Working in the Governor's Office
California	$175,000	86	Arkansas	$71,738	39
Florida	$120,171	310	Louisiana	$95,000	119
New York	$179,000	203	New Mexico	$90,000	27
Texas	**$115,345**	**198**	Oklahoma	$101,040	34

Source: *The Book of the States: 2003* (Lexington, Ky.: Council of State Governments, 2003), p. 186.

Removal from Office

Impeachment by the House of Representatives and conviction by the Senate constitute the only constitutionally prescribed method of forcing a Texas governor from office before the end of a term. Article XV of the Texas Constitution states, "The power of impeachment shall be vested in the House of Representatives." Each article of impeachment (similar to a grand jury's indictment) must be approved by a simple majority vote of the House. To remove the governor, one or more impeachment articles must be approved by a two-thirds majority vote of the senators present.

The penalty for conviction on an impeachment charge is removal from office and disqualification from holding any other appointive or elective office at state or local levels in Texas, but such conviction does not bar the person from holding a federal office, such as U.S. senator or representative. Following removal, a former governor who has been ousted after violating a law may be tried and convicted in a regular criminal trial or may be subjected to a judgment rendered in a civil court.

Although all of Texas's state constitutions have provided for impeachment and removal of the governor, only Governor James E. "Pa" Ferguson has been impeached and removed. Ferguson's troubles stemmed from misuse of state funds and a personal feud with the University of Texas. After Ferguson vetoed all appropriations for the university, the House speaker called a special session of the legislature. The attorney general approved this action, although the Texas Constitution gives the power only to the governor to call special sessions. On 25 September 1917, the Senate convicted Ferguson on 10 articles of impeachment, one of which charged him with official misconduct. The other 9 articles involved violations of the state's banking laws and use of state funds for private gain. For example, he was convicted of causing state funds to be deposited at the Temple State Bank in accounts that did not pay interest. He then used the deposits as collateral for obtaining personal loans.

Reporting how University of Texas students and powerful alumni were outraged when Ferguson used his veto power on the state appropriation, one historian noted: "Soon after Ferguson's 'war' with the University, the Ex-Students' Association voted to remain an independent organization, outside the sphere of state control where it would be free to defend the University again if needed."[8] Grounds for removing governors or other officials in the executive branch are not stipulated in the Texas Constitution. Rather, impeachment proceedings are highly charged political affairs with legal overtones.

Staff

Even though the Texas governor's hands are often tied when dealing with the state bureaucracy, the chief executive's personal staff continues to function directly under gubernatorial supervision. A governor's success in dealing with lobbyists, legislators, journalists and other media people, and the general public depends largely on staff input and support.

The **Governor's Office** directs programs mandated by the legislature, such as statewide planning. Pressure for belt tightening in state government resulted in a reduction of staff from more than 300 at the end of Governor Ann Richards's term (January 1995) to less than 200 under Governor Rick Perry in 2004. Even that number dwarfs the 68 full-time employees who served under Governor John Connally (1963–1969).

The principal impetus for more personnel in the Governor's Office is an activist approach to statewide issues, ranging from coordination of criminal justice to administration of federal funds. Furthermore, a nationwide trend is personalizing this office, to give every interested citizen access to the governor or a staff member. Also, increasing emphasis is placed on intergovernmental relations involving cities, councils of governments, interstate councils, federal agencies, and international affairs (particularly matters involving Mexico). The governor of Texas appoints and removes staff members without legislative approval.

How much the governor's appointed assistants and unofficial advisers influence gubernatorial decisions is open to speculation. Protecting their chief is still a primary function of many staff assistants, particularly the press secretary and the assistant for board appointments. All Texas governors have placed close friends and political associates in these positions—persons who can be relied on for their loyalty to the chief executive. For example, Mike McKinney, Mike Toomey, and Rick Perry began serving in the House of Representatives in 1985. With two other conservative representatives, they became known as the "Pit Bulls" for their budget-cutting zeal. After Perry became governor, he appointed McKinney as his first chief of staff. Two years later, Toomey (then an influential lobbyist and former chief of staff for Governor Bill Clements) became Perry's second chief of staff.[9] Like other top staffers, and even some interns,[10] Toomey received a state salary and supplemental pay. He was replaced by Deirdre Delisi in September 2004.

COUNTERPOINT

Should Top Aides Receive Supplemental Pay from Campaign Funds?

ISSUE

"Pay Supplements to Top State Aides Let Lobby Buy Access, Critics Charge" is the title of journalist Ken Herman's article in the *Austin American-Statesman,* 9 August 2003. Explaining that annual salary supplements are paid from Governor Rick Perry's campaign fund, Herman provides the following data:

Aide	State	Supplement Salary
Mike Toomey, chief of staff	$135,000	$107,000*
Bill Jones, general counsel	$134,160	$13,842
Deirdre Delisi, deputy chief of staff	$84,000	$14,378
Eric Bearse, speechwriter	$77,400	$4,282

*Annualized calculation based on payments reported by Perry for the first six months of the year.
Source: Governor's Office and campaign finance reports.

Arguments For Supplemental Pay

1. Higher pay is needed to attract top talent to important jobs.
2. Supplemental pay is a bargain for taxpayers, because it does not come from the state treasury.
3. Top staff members do some political work, so it is appropriate that they should receive supplemental pay from campaign funds.

> "In a letter seeking money to supplement primarily the salary of one top staff assistant for comptroller Carole Keeton Rylander, fund-raiser Len Mertz explained, 'These professionals are necessary for the comptroller's office to provide the state of Texas with first-class service and would most likely not be in public service due to the disparity in wages compared with the private sector."
>
> —Quoted by Jay Root in "Campaign Raises Funds for Staffers,"
> *Fort Worth Star-Telegram,* 19 June 2004

Arguments Against Supplemental Pay

1. Texas can afford to pay whatever compensation is needed for personnel who assist elected officials.
2. State employees at all levels should be beholden to taxpayers alone and not beholden in part to big donors who contribute most of the campaign money raised by elected officials.
3. Supplemental pay for employees of the federal government is illegal, so this should be the model for Texas government.

(Continued on next page)

Powers of the Governor

The governor of Texas is inaugurated on the third Tuesday in January of every fourth year (16 January in 2007, and always in the odd-numbered year before a presidential election). In the inauguration ceremony, the governor swears "to cause the laws to be faithfully executed." Nevertheless, the governor has limited formal powers to carry out this responsibility. Whatever success a governor may achieve stems less from constitutional or statutory power than from personal ability to rally political groups and public opinion behind gubernatorial programs and to balance the ever-present demands of lobbyists. Powers of the governor may be classified as formal (executive, legislative, judicial) and informal.

Executive Powers

The governor's executive powers are used to:

- appoint—and in some cases remove—state officials
- deal with problems caused by civil disorder and natural disasters
- participate in state budget making and budget management
- announce policies by issuing executive orders
- make public proclamations for ceremonial and other purposes
- promote the economic development of Texas.

In some respects, the governor exercises executive powers like those wielded by heads of other large organizations (for example, university presidents, business CEOs, union leaders, or the U.S. president), but there are obvious differences. Of course, the executive powers of the governor of Texas resemble those of the country's other 49 state governors, but different state laws and state constitutions give some governors more executive powers while other governors get less.

Appointive Power Fundamental to the effective management of any organization is the chief executive's power to appoint subordinates who will be effective and loyal. Such **appointive power** is the most significant of the Texas governor's executive powers. The same laws that create administrative agencies allow a governor to appoint friends and political supporters to more than 2,000 positions on about 300 boards, commissions, and committees. The relationship between campaign contributions and gubernatorial appointments is documented in a recent study by Texans for Public Justice. According to this study, from 1995 to mid-2000, George W. Bush received $1.4 million in gubernatorial campaign money from 413 contributors whom he later appointed to 50 of the state's most important boards and commissions.[11]

Department heads appointed by the governor include the secretary of state; the adjutant general, who heads the Texas National Guard; the executive director of the Office of State-Federal Relations; the executive commissioner of health and human services; commissioners of education, insurance, and firefighters' pensions; and the chief administrative law judge of the State Office of Administrative Hearings (SOAH). House Bill 7, passed by the 78th Legislature in 2003 in its third special session, increases the appointive power of the governor significantly. It allows the governor, "notwithstanding other law," to designate and change the chairs of most state boards and commissions. The law also allows the governor to change designation of the chair of a board or commission from one member to another. Not affected by this law are the presiding officers of governing bodies of institutions of higher education and those that advise or report to statewide-elected officials other than the governor. All members of the governor's personal staff also are appointed.

Gubernatorial appointive power is not without certain legal and political limitations. The Texas Constitution requires that all appointees (except personal staff) be confirmed by the Senate with a two-thirds vote of senators present. This practice is known as "advice and consent," and it applies to the appointees of U.S. presidents and governors in most other states. Politics requires that the governor respect a tradition of senatorial courtesy by consulting with a prospective appointee's state senator before sending the candidate's name to the full Senate for confirmation. Politics also demands that the appointments director in the Governor's Office conduct a background check on the appointee to avoid any prospective embarrassment—as occurred when, for example, Governor Dolph Briscoe appointed a dead man to a state board.

Governors may try to circumvent the Senate by making **recess appointments** while the Senate is not in session. However, the Texas Constitution requires that all recess appointments be submitted to the Senate for confirmation within 10 days after it convenes for a regular or special session. Failure of the Senate to confirm a gubernatorial recess appointment prevents the governor from reappointing that person to the same position.

Another limitation on the governor's appointive power is that the members of most state boards and commissions serve for six years, with overlapping terms of office. Thus, a first-term governor must work with carryovers from previous administrations, even if such carryovers are not supportive of the new governor.

Due to the elective status of the three-member Railroad Commission (elected statewide) and the 15-member State Board of Education (elected from districts drawn by the legislature, or by a court if the legislature fails to act or draws districts that are unconstitutional), the governor lacks direct control over these agencies. But the governor appoints the chair of the State Board of Education from among board members.

The appointive power of the governor extends to filling vacancies for elected heads of the executive departments, members of the Railroad Commission and the State Board of Education, and judges (except those for county, municipal, and justice of the peace courts) until the next general election. Also, when a U.S. senator from Texas dies, resigns, or is removed from office before his or her term expires, the governor fills the vacancy with an interim appointee. That appointee serves until a successor is elected in a special election called by the governor. A vacancy in either house of the Texas Legislature or in the Texas delegation to the U.S. House of Representatives does not result in an interim appointment. Instead, the governor must call a special election to fill the position until the next regularly scheduled election.

Removal Power   In creating numerous boards and commissions, the legislature gives the governor extensive appointive power but no independent **removal power** over most state agencies. Lack of effective removal power greatly limits gubernatorial control over the state bureaucracy. The governor's independent removal power extends to members of the governor's staff and three statutory officials whose offices were created by the legislature: the executive director of the Department of Housing and Community Affairs, the executive commissioner of health and human services, and the insurance commissioner.

Elected department heads and their subordinates are not subject to the governor's removal power. Moreover, other than the executive commissioner for health and human services and the insurance commissioner, both of whom the governor appoints and can remove, the governor's hands are tied in directly removing most board and commission officials. The governor may informally pressure an appointee to resign or accept another appointment, but this pressure is not as effective as the power of direct removal. Governors may remove their own appointees with consent of two-thirds of the state senators present; however, this authority still falls short of independent removal power.

Military Power   The governor of Texas is commander in chief of the state's military forces: the Texas Army National Guard, the Texas Air National

Guard, and the Texas State Guard. Units of the Texas State Guard are available for service within the state when National Guard units are mobilized for federal service in time of war or national emergency. Early in July 2004, when about 2,000 Texas National Guard soldiers were on active duty, 3,000 others were mobilized to serve for at least 18 months.[12]

Acting under gubernatorial direction, the adjutant general (the state's highest-ranking military officer) may mobilize National Guard units to enforce state law, repel invasion, curb insurrection and riot, and maintain order in times of natural disasters, such as those resulting from tornadoes and floods. For example, National Guard personnel were sent to the Lufkin and Nacogdoches areas to help recover hazardous material from the space shuttle *Columbia*, which disintegrated over East Texas on 1 February 2003. The governor may declare **martial law** (temporary rule by the state's military forces and suspension of civil authority) if deemed necessary because of civil disorder, such as a riot that cannot be handled by local government.

Law Enforcement Power   In Texas, law enforcement is primarily a responsibility of city police departments and county sheriffs' departments. Nevertheless, the Texas Department of Public Safety, headed by the Public Safety Commission, is an important law enforcement agency. The governor appoints the commission's three members, although these appointments are subject to Senate approval. The director of public safety is appointed by the commission and oversees more than 7,000 personnel in the Department of Public Safety (DPS). Included among the department's responsibilities are highway traffic supervision, driver licensing, motor vehicle inspection, and criminal law enforcement in cooperation with local and federal agencies.

If circumstances demand swift but limited police action, the governor is empowered to assume command of the Texas Rangers, a division of DPS composed of a few more than 100 highly trained law enforcement personnel. In July 2004, Ranger membership included 115 men (93 Anglo, 15 Latino, 5 African American, 1 Asian American, 1 Native American) and 2 women (1 Anglo, 1 African American). The first woman Ranger was selected by DPS in 1993. Earl Pearson, who began his law enforcement career as a DPS Highway Patrol trooper in El Paso in 1975, became the first black Chief Ranger in 2004.

Budgetary Power   Gubernatorial **budgetary power** is subordinated in part to the legislature's prerogative of controlling the state's purse strings. By statutory requirement, the governor (assisted by personnel in the Governor's Office of Budget, Planning and Policy) and the Legislative Budget Board each should prepare separate budgets for consideration by the legislature. In 2003, a law was enacted requiring the distribution of the governor's budget to each legislator before delivery of the State of the State message. Traditionally, both the House and the Senate have been inclined to give greater respect to the Legislative Budget Board's spending proposals.

In the fall of 2002, Governor Perry announced his intention to present a detailed budget to the 78th Legislature early in 2003. Until the day before the legislature convened, he and his budget assistants were following the comptroller's earlier estimate that the state would experience a $5.1 billion short-fall for the 2004–2005 biennium. Then on 13 January, Comptroller Carole Keeton Strayhorn shocked Perry and others with a new estimate indicating that the shortfall would be $9.9 billion. Shortly thereafter, the Legislative Budget Board indicated that the gap would be $10.5 billion, and some legis-lators predicted it would be even higher. Subsequently, the governor ceased efforts to produce a detailed spending plan, and on 17 January he sent to the legislature a 400-page document filled with budget items followed by zeros. Perry explained that this "zero-based" budget would make legislators start from scratch and justify spending for every budget item. Later, in his State of the State address on 11 February, Perry made suggestions for spending reductions totaling about $9.5 billion.[13]

The governor's principal control over state spending comes from the con-stitutional power to veto an entire appropriations bill or individual budget items. In June 2003, for example, Governor Perry used the line–item veto to cut $81.1 million from the state budget for fiscal years 2004 and 2005. (See this chapter's reading, "Gov. Perry Signs $117 Billion State Budget and Uses Line-Item Veto Power to Eliminate $81 Million in Spending.")

Executive Orders and Proclamations One instrument of executive author-ity is the **executive order**. Between March 2001 and July 2004, Governor Perry issued 35 executive orders to set policy within the executive branch and to create or abolish various executive task forces, boards, commissions, and councils. In 2002, for example, he issued Executive Order 21, creating the Governor's Clean Coal Technology Council to advise him on preserving fuel diversity and on reducing emissions and increasing efficiency of coal-fired electric generation.[14] Another instrument of executive authority is the **proclamation**, an official public announcement. Proclamations are often used for ceremonial purposes (for example, proclaiming Pearl Harbor Remembrance Day or Disabilities Employment Awareness Month). Other uses include calling special elections and special sessions of the legislature, declaring a region to be a disaster area, and announcing the ratification of constitutional amendments.

Economic Development After a series of mismanagement problems within the Texas Department of Economic Development, Governor Perry sought direct control over efforts to attract investment from other states and coun-tries. In 2003, the 78th Legislature abolished the department and placed the state's economic development program within the Office of the Governor. This action was taken after failure to coordinate local and state efforts to persuade the Boeing Company to relocate its corporate headquarters from Seattle to the Dallas–Fort Worth area instead of Chicago. In an effort to pre-vent a similar occurrence, Governor Perry intervened directly in efforts to bring a Toyota plant to San Antonio. Finally, with a $133 million incentive package for Toyota and $28.5 million for an 8-mile rail spur and other infra-structure improvements, the Toyota Motor Company announced on 5 Feb-ruary 2003 that it would build a pickup truck plant in San Antonio.[15]

At Perry's urging, the 78th Legislature established the Texas Enterprise Fund by taking $295 million from the state's rainy day fund and using it to attract or retain industry in fiscal years 2004 and 2005. With approval of Speaker Craddick and Lieutenant Governor Dewhurst, by April 2004 about $195 million had been allocated to keep or create more than 9,000 jobs in Texas. Included were $40 million to keep Sematech in Austin; $35 million for Vought Aircraft Industries to consolidate two of its out-of-state facilities with operations in Dallas; $3.5 million for the Texas Energy Center at Sugar Land, near Houston; $50 million for engineering and computer science programs at the University of Texas at Dallas, as part of a deal for Texas Instruments to build a microchip factory nearby; and $5 million to the Citgo Petroleum Corporation to move its headquarters from Tulsa to Houston.[16]

To complement the Texas Enterprise Fund, Perry established TexasOne, a nonprofit, tax-exempt corporation with directors appointed by the governor. Its primary mission is to attract business from other states by marketing economic opportunities in Texas. Perry invited major companies and business-related groups to support the fund for three years with a range of annual tax-deductible contributions providing the following yearly benefits for donors:

1. $50,000 for quail hunting with the governor at "one of Texas's premier ranches," a luncheon at the Governor's Mansion, and a seat on the TexasOne Round Table to advise on the use of marketing funds
2. $25,000 for a TexasOne Round Table seat
3. $10,000 to have a donor's corporate logo placed on TexasOne marketing materials
4. $5,000 for marketing name recognition
5. $1,000 for an invitation to a business briefing hosted by Perry[17]

To recruit out-of-state companies, prospective contributors were informed that visiting executives would be given "red carpet treatment throughout; flight into Texas, limousine transportation, four-star hotel accommodations, reception on arrival evening with local and state leadership, one host assigned for each guest, tickets/box seats for event, personalized clothing (jackets, etc.) for each guest, gifts, etc."[18]

Legislative Powers

Perhaps the most stringent test of a Texas governor's capacity for leadership involves handling of legislative matters. The governor's **legislative power** is exercised through three major functions authorized by the Texas Constitution:

- delivering messages to the legislature
- vetoing bills
- calling special sessions of the legislature

However, the success of a legislative program depends heavily on a governor's ability to bargain with influential lobbyists and legislative leaders (particularly the speaker of the House of Representatives and the lieutenant governor).

Message Power   The Texas Constitution requires the governor to deliver a State of the State address at the "commencement" (beginning) of each regular session of the legislature, but this is not interpreted to mean the first day of a session. In 2003, Governor Perry delivered his State of the State address more than four weeks after the beginning of the 78th regular session. On occasion, the governor may also present special messages, either in person or in writing. A governor's success in using **message power** to promote a harmonious relationship with the legislature depends on such variables as the timing of special messages concerning volatile issues, the support of the governor's program by the chairs of legislative committees, and the governor's personal popularity.

Veto Power   The governor's most direct legislative tool is the power to veto legislation. A governor may veto a bill by returning it unsigned (with written reasons for not signing) to the chamber in which it originated. If the legislature is no longer in session, the vetoed bill is filed with the secretary of state. **Veto power** takes different forms. For example, the governor may kill one or more specific spending authorizations in an appropriation bill while permitting enactment of the remainder of the budget. This **item veto** (also called a line-item veto) places the governor in a powerful bargaining position with individual legislators in the delicate game of pork-barrel politics. That is, the governor may strike a bargain with a senator or representative in which the chief executive promises not to deny funding for a lawmaker's pet project (the pork). In return, the legislator agrees to support a bill favored by the governor. The legislature can override the governor's veto by a two-thirds majority vote in both houses, but overriding a governor's veto has occurred only once since the administration of Governor W. Lee O'Daniel (1939–1941). In 1979, the House and Senate overrode a veto by Governor Clements. The strong veto power that the Texas Constitution gives to the governor and the governor's informal power of threatening to veto a bill are formidable weapons for dealing with uncooperative legislators.

Both the governor of Texas and the president of the United States have the prerogative of neither signing nor vetoing a bill within 10 days (Sundays excepted) after its passage, thus allowing the measure to become law without executive signature. But if the president "pockets" a bill that is passed within 10 weekdays before congressional adjournment, such failure to act kills the measure. Although not possessing pocket-veto power, the governor of Texas may exercise a **postadjournment veto** by rejecting any pending legislation within 20 days after a session has ended. Because most bills pass late in a legislative session, the postadjournment veto is a powerful tool for the governor.

During the regular session of the 77th Legislature in 2001, Governor Perry vetoed only a few bills. But in what some critics termed the "Father's Day Massacre," he exercised 78 postadjournment vetoes at 9 P.M. on the last possible day to do so (17 June). Perry's total of 82 vetoes in 2001 set a record, surpassing 59 vetoes by Governor Bill Clements in 1989. Two years later,

Perry issued a total of 48 vetoes to kill bills passed during the regular session of the 78th Legislature.[19]

Special-Sessions Power　Included among the governor's powers is the authority to call special sessions of the legislature. The Texas Constitution places no limits on the number of special sessions a governor may call, but a special session is limited to 30 days. During a special session, the legislature may consider only those matters the governor specifies in the call or subsequently presents to the legislature. Exceptions to this limitation extend to confirmation of appointments and impeachment proceedings without gubernatorial approval. As with message power, a governor's success in using the power to call special sessions depends on timing and on rapport with legislative leaders. From 1991 through 1994, Governor Richards called four special sessions. Governor Bush called none, mainly because the state did not experience budget crises during his six years in office. In 2003, Governor Perry called three special sessions before a congressional redistricting bill was passed, as described in the reading at the end of the chapter "The Legislature." Then, in April 2004, he called an unsuccessful special session on school finance.

Judicial Powers

The governor exercises a few formal judicial powers. Included are powers to:

- fill vacancies on state (but not county or city) courts
- play a limited but outdated role in removing judges and justices
- perform acts of clemency to lighten sentences given to some convicted criminals

Appointment and Removal of Judges and Justices　More than half of Texas's state judges and justices first serve on district courts and higher appellate courts through gubernatorial appointment to fill a vacancy caused by a judge's death, resignation, or removal. For example, Wallace B. Jefferson became the first African American to serve on the Texas Supreme Court after Governor Perry appointed him to replace Justice Al Gonzales, who resigned to become White House Counsel for President Bush. According to Article XV, Section 8, of the Texas Constitution, the governor may remove any jurist "on address of two-thirds of each house of the Legislature for willful neglect of duty, incompetence, habitual drunkenness, oppression in office, or other reasonable cause which shall not be sufficient ground for impeachment." Governors and the legislature have not used this process for many years. They have left removal of state jurists to other proceedings and to voters. (See the chapter "Laws, Courts, and Justice" for a discussion of the disciplining and removal of judges and justices.)

Acts of Executive Clemency　Until the mid-1930s, Texas governors had extensive powers to undo or lessen punishment for convicted criminals through acts of clemency that set aside or reduced court-imposed penalties.

Exercise of these powers led to charges of corruption, which are illustrated by the story about a man who stepped on a foot of Miriam A. Ferguson (governor, 1925–1927 and 1933–1935) after they entered an elevator in the Capitol. According to this apocryphal tale, the man said to the governor, "Pardon me." Her response was, "You will have to ask Jim." Whether or not Ma Ferguson and her husband, James E. Ferguson (governor, 1915–1917) sold pardons has been hotly debated. Nevertheless, a constitutional amendment adopted in 1936 reduced the clemency powers of the governor and established the Board of Pardons and Paroles, which is now a division of the Texas Department of Criminal Justice.

Parole—the release of a prisoner before completion of a sentence on condition of good behavior—is granted by the seven-member Board of Pardons and Paroles, without action by the governor. However, the governor may perform various acts of executive clemency that set aside or reduce a court-imposed penalty through pardon, reprieve, or commutation of sentence. For example, on recommendation of the Board of Pardons and Paroles, the governor may grant a full or conditional pardon. A **full pardon** releases a person from all consequences of a criminal act and restores rights enjoyed by persons who have not been convicted of crimes. Under a **conditional pardon**, the governor may withhold certain rights, such as being licensed to practice a selected occupation or profession. Acting independently, the governor may also revoke a conditional pardon if the terms of that pardon have been violated.

The governor also independently may grant one 30-day **reprieve** in a death sentence case. A reprieve temporarily suspends execution of the penalty imposed by a court. Ann Richards refused all requests for reprieve from the 48 condemned men who were executed during her four years as governor. She did, however, grant one reprieve in the highly publicized capital murder case of Gary Graham, who later requested a second 30-day stay of execution from Governor Bush. However, a Texas attorney general's opinion advised that only one 30-day reprieve could be issued in any given case. One reprieve was granted in a death-penalty case while Bush served as governor, but 150 men and two women failed in their attempts to obtain stays of execution.[20] After becoming governor, Perry granted no reprieves in death sentence cases during his first three and one-half years in office.

The governor possesses two other clemency powers. If recommended by the Board of Pardons and Paroles, the governor may reduce a penalty through **commutation of sentence** and may remit (return) forfeitures of money or property surrendered as punishment. By mid–2004, Perry had granted one death–penalty commutation.

Informal Powers

The ability of a governor to sway public opinion and to direct or influence the actions of other government officials depends on more than constitutional powers or powers conferred by the legislature. Informal powers are not based on law but stem from a governor's popularity and on traditions, symbols, and ceremonies. Governor Rick Perry, who is a runner, uses his personal dedication to physical fitness to relate to Texans who share his interest and to challenge others to "fight the war on fat."[21]

In the eyes of most Texans, the governor's ceremonial office in the Capitol holds center stage. Although this room is used primarily for press interviews and public functions, its occupant is a symbol of the government of the Lone Star State. For routine work on a daily basis, the governor has another office in the Capitol, and staff members have offices in the State Insurance Building, located on San Jacinto Street, one block east of the Capitol.

Of course, a governor cannot accept all invitations to deliver speeches or participate in dedications, banquets, and other public events. Within the limits of time and priorities, however, every governor does attempt to play the role of chief of state. The breadth and depth of this role cannot be fully measured, but its significance should not be underestimated in determining a governor's effectiveness.

Media relations are important. Responding to journalists' demands for information requires an able press secretary, along with a governor's ability to make impressive speeches, to be at ease while communicating effectively in interviews with newspaper and television reporters, and to express his views in articles (perhaps written by staff members) published in newspapers (especially the big-city press).[22] Public involvement of family members may also be a source of support. Laura Bush, for example, enhanced her husband's image as a governor committed to improving education. Her First Lady's Family Literacy Initiative Program was especially designed to assist children from lower-income families living in disadvantaged neighborhoods.

Anita Perry, with bachelor's and master's degrees in nursing and 17 years of experience in various fields of nursing, is often referred to by her husband as First Nurse as well as First Lady. Her public speeches on topics such as Alzheimer's disease, breast cancer awareness, and prevention of family violence have been a source of support for Governor Perry. In addition, Anita Perry has worked with her husband to host the annual Texas Conference for Women, at which women from all parts of Texas, as well as other states, meet to consider a wide range of women's interests, such as health care, personal growth, and professional development. Late in 2003 Anita Perry made history when she began work as a $5,000 per month consultant for the Texas Association Against Sexual Assault. None of the wives of earlier governors were employed while a husband was in office.[23]

The Plural Executive

Politically, the governor of Texas is the state's highest-ranking officer, but in practice the governor shares executive power with other state officers. Although millions of Texans cannot readily identify by name the attorney general, the comptroller of public accounts, the land commissioner, and the agriculture commissioner, these elected executive officers oversee large departments with multimillion-dollar budgets. Set by the legislature, their annual salaries for fiscal years 2004 and 2005 remained unchanged at $92,217. Along with the governor, the lieutenant governor, and the appointed secretary of state, these state officials are referred to collectively as the **plural executive**.

Points to Ponder

Beginning in 1846, following annexation by the United States in 1845, Texas had the following numbers of state officials through June 2004:
- 62 governors
- 42 lieutenant governors
- 50 attorneys general
- 25 comptrollers of public accounts
- 28 commissioners of the General Land Office
- 10 commissioners of agriculture (office created by the legislature in 1907)
- 89 secretaries of state

Source: *Texas Almanac 2004–2005* (Dallas: Dallas Morning News, 2004), pp. 427–431; Office of the Commissioner of Agriculture; and web sites for the executive departments.

This structural arrangement contributes significantly to the state's long ballot, because these executive officials (except the secretary of state) are popularly elected to four-year terms with no limit on their reelection. There is no restriction on the number of terms a secretary of state may serve, although each new governor appoints his or her own. Elected department heads are largely independent of gubernatorial control; however, with the advice and consent of the Senate, the governor makes appointments to fill vacancies in these offices until the next general election. Unlike department heads in the federal government, those in Texas do not form a cabinet to advise the governor.

Lieutenant Governor David Dewhurst

Attorney General Gregg Abbott

Comptroller of Public Accounts Carole Keeton Strayhorn

Commissioner of the General Land Office Jerry Patterson

Commissioner of Agriculture Susan Combs

Secretary of State Geoffrey S. Connor

The Lieutenant Governor

Considered by some political observers to be the most powerful official in Texas government, the **lieutenant governor** functions less in the executive branch than in the legislative branch. The Texas Constitution requires the Senate to convene within 30 days whenever a vacancy occurs in the lieutenant governor's office. Senators then elect one of their members (as in the case of Bill Ratliff in 2000) to fill the office as acting lieutenant governor until the next general election.

The annual state salary for the office of lieutenant governor is only $7,200, the same as that paid to members of the legislature. Like legislators, the lieutenant governor may also hold a paying job in private business.

As president of the Senate, the lieutenant governor is the presiding officer for that chamber and exercises great influence on legislation. (See Chapter 6 "The Legislature.") Also, because the lieutenant governorship is regarded as a possible steppingstone to the governorship or other high positions, competition is intense among candidates for that office.

Many Texas lobbyists and members of the business community supported John Sharp, a Democrat and former comptroller of public accounts, in the 2002 race for lieutenant governor. But multimillionaire Republican David Dewhurst, the state's commissioner of the General Land Office at that time, won the November general election. To finance his campaign, Dewhurst used more than $10 million of his own money plus another borrowed $13 million. After his victory, Dewhurst recouped some of this money at fundraising events where Sharp's former supporters were able to "catch the late train" by making postelection contributions to Dewhurst.[24] As his chief of staff, Lieutenant Governor Dewhurst hired Bruce Gibson, who formerly served as Democratic state representative and assistant to former Lieutenant Governor Bob Bullock. Gibson was employed in the private sector as vice president for government and regulatory affairs by Reliant Energy.[25]

Dewhurst also signed on Chuck Anderson, former executive director of the Texas Christian Coalition, as another top staff assistant.[26] Some members of the lieutenant governor's staff receive pay from his unbudgeted officeholder account, to which money is contributed by political supporters.

The Attorney General

One of Texas's most visible and powerful officeholders is the **attorney general**. Whether suing tobacco companies, arguing affirmative action questions, or trying to resolve redistricting disputes, the state's chief lawyer is a major player in making many important public policy decisions. This officer gives advisory opinions to state and local authorities and represents the state in civil litigation.

With more than 4,000 employees, the Office of the Attorney General is asked for advice concerning the constitutionality of many pending bills. The governor, heads of state agencies, and local government officials also request opinions from the attorney general on the scope of their jurisdiction and the interpretation of vaguely worded laws. Although neither judges nor other officials are bound by these opinions, the attorney general's rulings are considered authoritative unless overruled by court decisions or new laws. Another power of the attorney general is to initiate quo warranto proceedings, which challenge an official's right to hold public office. Such action may lead to the removal of an officeholder judged guilty of official misconduct.

The election of Democratic candidate Dan Morales as attorney general in 1990 gave him the distinction of being the first Latino elected to head an executive department under the Texas Constitution of 1876. Morales's low-key style during his first term as attorney general (1991–1995) stood in sharp contrast to the high-profile lawsuits handled by his office, especially Texas's multibillion-dollar suit against the country's biggest tobacco companies. In 1994, Morales won a second term by defeating his Republican rival, Don Wittig, a Houston state district judge, but in 1998 he decided not to seek a third term. Morales unsuccessfully challenged Tony Sanchez for nomination as the Democratic Party's gubernatorial candidate in 2002. After losing the primary contest with Sanchez, he endorsed Republican candidate Rick Perry in the general election. Later, however, Morales pled guilty to federal charges of filing a false income tax return and committing mail fraud related to lawyer's fees for his friend, attorney Marc Murr, in Texas's $17.3 billion tobacco settlement. He was sentenced to imprisonment for four years.[27]

Morales was replaced by San Antonio attorney John Cornyn, a Republican and former Texas Supreme Court justice. When Cornyn decided to run for a seat in the U.S. Senate in 2002, Supreme Court Justice Greg Abbott was nominated by the Republican Party for the office of attorney general. In the November election of 2002, Abbott defeated Democrat Kirk Watson, a former Austin mayor. Before Abbott began his elected term in January 2003, Governor Perry appointed him to serve for a few weeks in that office following Cornyn's resignation in November 2002. At that time, Abbott declared that he was "philosophically very committed to open government" and that he would enforce the state's open records laws for the benefit of the public and the media. This statement was welcomed by the press and public interest groups that had complained about lack of access to information concerning government operations.[28]

The Comptroller of Public Accounts

One of the most powerful elected officers in Texas government is the **comptroller of public accounts**, the state's chief accounting officer and tax collector. After a biennial appropriation bill passes by a simple majority vote in the House and Senate, the Texas Constitution requires the comptroller's certification that expected revenue will be collected to cover all of the budgeted expenditures. Otherwise, an appropriation must be approved by a four-fifths majority vote in both houses. One of the comptroller's duties is to designate hundreds of Texas financial institutions (mostly banks, but also a few savings and loan companies and credit unions) to serve as depositories for state-collected funds.

Bob Bullock left the comptroller's post in 1990 to become lieutenant governor. Democrat John Sharp, a former state legislator and member of the Texas Railroad Commission, succeeded him. Sharp won a second term in 1994 when he defeated Republican Theresa Doggett. Sharp was succeeded by Carole Keeton Rylander. She resigned her Texas Railroad Commission seat to become Texas's first woman state comptroller after defeating Democrat Paul Hobby, son of former lieutenant governor Bill Hobby, in 1998. Four years later Rylander won another term by defeating Democratic candidate Marty Akins, a former lawyer, rancher, and All-American quarterback for the UT Longhorns. In January 2003, at the swearing-in ceremony for her second term, the self-styled "tough grandma" presented her third husband, announced that Strayhorn would be her new surname, and took personal pride in her weight loss of more than 100 pounds.[29]

During the legislature's 78th regular session in 2003, Strayhorn clashed with Governor Perry and legislative leaders concerning her budget estimates. Then, in the third special session, the legislature transferred the comptroller's school district audit and performance review programs to the Legislative Budget Board. In addition, the state auditor was given authority to review contested tax cases settled by the comptroller. This permits the auditor to compare the comptroller's campaign finance reports with tax settlements in order to determine if there is a relationship between tax refunds and political contributions. In 2004, Strayhorn was loud in her criticism of the Perry school finance plan and changes in the Children's Health Insurance Program (CHIP) that cut enrollment by more than 145,000 between September 2003 and July 2004. Many observers concluded that Strayhorn would seek the GOP nomination for governor in 2006.[30]

The Commissioner of the
General Land Office

Although less visible than other elected executives, the **commissioner of the General Land Office** is an important figure in Texas politics. Since the creation of the General Land Office under the Constitution of the Republic of Texas (1836), the commissioner's duties have expanded to include awarding oil, gas, and sulfur leases for lands owned by the state; serving as chairman of the Veterans Land Board; and sitting as an ex-officio member of other boards responsible for managing state-owned lands. With more than 600 employees, the General Land Office also oversees growth of the Permanent School Fund. It is financed by oil and gas leases, rentals, and royalties that annually provide more than $700 million for public school funding.

When Democrat Garry Mauro left the land commissioner's post to make an unsuccessful bid for the governorship in 1998, his decision afforded Republicans an opportunity to win a state office. Houston businessman David Dewhurst seized that moment. In winning his first political office, Dewhurst spent more than $5 million on his campaign and was helped by Governor George W. Bush's popularity.

After Dewhurst decided to run for lieutenant governor in 2002, lobbyist and former state senator Jerry Patterson became the GOP candidate for land commissioner. Patterson defeated the Democratic candidate, state senator David Bernsen. When he was sworn in on 3 January 2003, Patterson declared that he would serve out his term and seek reelection in 2006. Environmentalists were unhappy with Patterson's plan to increase oil and gas production by reducing drilling restrictions along the Gulf Coast, including the Padre Island National Seashore.[31] In November 2003, Patterson became involved in a controversy with Agricultural Commissioner Susan Combs about negotiations between Patterson and Rio Nuevo, Ltd., for the lease of rights to water under state-owned land in West Texas. Patterson insisted that such leasing and pipe line movement of water to other areas would bring millions of dollars into the Permanent School Fund, but Combs was concerned about the loss of water needed for agriculture and other purposes in that arid region.[32]

The Commissioner of Agriculture

By law, the **commissioner of agriculture** is supposed to be a "practicing farmer," but this criterion is vague enough to qualify anyone who owns or rents a piece of agricultural land. Name recognition by the state's voters (most of whom live in suburbs or central cities) is the principal requirement for winning the office.

In 1998, Susan Combs, a former state representative from Austin, became Texas's first woman to be elected agriculture commissioner. This state officer is responsible for enforcing agricultural laws and for providing service programs to Texas farmers, ranchers, and consumers. Control over the use of often-controversial pesticides is exercised through the Department of Agriculture's Pesticide Programs Division. This division restricts the use of high-risk chemicals and licenses dealers and commercial applicators as well as private applicators who use pest control chemicals on their own farms and ranches. Other enforcement actions of the department include inspections to determine the accuracy of commercial scales, pumps, and meters.

Combs won a second term by defeating Democrat Tom Ramsay in 2002. Subsequently, she gained widespread publicity with demands that Mexico repay its water debt by releasing more water into the Rio Grande. Other matters attracting her attention are childhood obesity and diabetes. Combs's response was to use her authority to ban sale of junk food and soft drinks in most of Texas's elementary schools.[33] In April 2004, Combs announced that she would seek the GOP nomination for state comptroller in 2006 if Carole Keeton Strayhorn were to run for another office.

The Secretary of State

The only constitutional executive officer appointed by the governor is the **secretary of state**. This appointment must be confirmed by a two-thirds vote of the Senate. The secretary of state serves a four-year term with no limitation on the number of reappointments.

George W. Bush's first secretary of state, and first Latino appointee, was Tony Garza, a former Cameron County judge. When the Brownsville attorney resigned to win a seat on the Texas Railroad Commission, he was succeeded as secretary of state by Houston attorney Al Gonzales. Later, Bush appointed Gonzales to fill a vacancy on the Supreme Court of Texas. Reaching out to Democrats, Bush chose Insurance Commissioner Elton Bomer, a former Democratic state representative from East Texas, as his third secretary of state. When Rick Perry succeeded Bush as governor, he appointed another Democrat, Representative Henry Cuellar from Laredo, to fill this office. After Cuellar resigned, Perry named Republican Gwyn Shea as secretary of state in January 2002. She resigned in July 2003 and was replaced by Geoffrey S. Connor. Before his appointment by Perry, Connor served for two years as assistant secretary of state.

The secretary of state oversees a staff of about 250 people and is the chief election officer of Texas. Principal responsibilities of the office include the following:

- Administering state election laws in conjunction with county officials
- Tabulating election returns for state and district offices
- Granting charters to Texas corporations
- Issuing permits to outside corporations to conduct business within Texas
- Processing requests for extradition of criminals to or from other states for trial and punishment

With these diverse duties, the secretary of state is obviously more than just a record keeper. How the office functions is determined largely by the occupant's relations with the governor.

Looking Ahead

Debate among Texas's academicians, journalists, politicians, and other interested citizens will continue to focus on appropriate power for the governor and other executive officials, as well as the best way to organize the executive branch of state government. In 1999, Republican senator (later acting lieutenant governor) Bill Ratliff and Democratic representative Rob Junell worked for a new constitution that would provide a cabinet structure to replace the state's system of elected executives. This proposal was "dead on arrival." Legislative support was weak, and neither Governor Bush nor Lieutenant Governor Perry weighed in with their support. At the beginning of 2003, Republicans were in control of all statewide executive offices and had comfortable majorities in both state legislative chambers. Nevertheless, none of the constitutional amendments proposed by the 78th Legislature was designed to affect the powers of the governor or other executive officials. As indicated above and in the chapter "Bureaucracy, Public Policies, and Finance," however, the 78th Legislature did take some steps to increase the governor's control over the state's administrative agencies. Future developments largely depend on whether the present executive structure can meet the needs of Texas's changing society and economy.

☆ Chapter Summary ☆

- Since 1876, Texas governors have held a weak constitutional office.
- Principal among the governor's prerogatives are extensive power to appoint members to the state's multiple boards and commissions, along with a strong veto power in dealing with the Texas Legislature.
- All governors must share executive power with the lieutenant governor and four elected department heads: the attorney general, state comptroller, land commissioner, and agriculture commissioner.
- The secretary of state is the only appointed executive department head provided for in the Texas Constitution.

Key Terms

Governor's Office	budgetary power
appointive power	executive order
recess appointment	proclamation
removal power	legislative power
martial law	message power

veto power	plural executive
item veto	lieutenant governor
postadjournment veto	attorney general
parole	comptroller of public accounts
full pardon	commissioner of the General
conditional pardon	Land Office
reprieve	commissioner of agriculture
commutation of sentence	secretary of state

 ## Discussion Questions

1. Is the governor compensated adequately?
2. Should changes be made in the governor's removal powers?
3. How does the governor exercise influence over legislation?
4. How does the governor exercise influence over judicial matters?
5. Should executive department heads be popularly elected or appointed by the governor?
6. Which executive department head appears to have the greatest potential for affecting your personal life and career?

Internet Resources

Office of the Attorney General: **www.oag.state.tx.us**
Office of the Comptroller of Public Accounts: **www.window.state.tx.us**
Office of the Governor: **www.governor.state.tx.us**
Office of the Lieutenant Governor:
    www.senate.state.tx.us/75r/ltgov/ltgov.htm
Office of the Secretary of State: **www.sos.state.tx.us**
Texas Department of Agriculture: **www.agr.state.tx.us**
Texas General Land Office: **www.glo.state.tx.us**

Notes

1. Larry Sabato, *Good-bye to Good-time Charlie*, 2d ed. (Washington, D.C.: CQ Press, 1983), p. 2.
2. Robert Bryce, "The Pols He Bought," *Texas Observer*, 5 February 1999, p. 11.
3. For two journalists' coverage of inaugural events, see Ken Herman, "Pomp and Promises," *Austin American-Statesman*, 22 January 2003; and Jay Root, "Perry, Dewhurst's Day in the Sun," *Fort Worth Star-Telegram*, 22 January 2003.

4. See George Kuempel, "Firms Help Pay the Tab, *Dallas Morning News*, 19 January 2003.

5. "Perry Links Funding for Medical Facilities to Reform Legislation," *Houston Chronicle*, 11 January 2003.

6. See Carolyn Barta, *Bill Clements: Texan to His Toenails* (Austin: Eakin Press, 1996); and Bill Minutaglio, *First Son: George W. Bush and the Bush Family Dynasty* (New York: Times Books, 1999).

7. Gordon Dixon, "Following the Leader," *Fort Worth Star-Telegram*, 16 December 2000; Bonnie Pfister, "Ranch-Country Republican Finds Gold in Austin Land Rush," *San Antonio Express-News*, 20 October 2002; and Patricia Kilday Hart, "It's Rick Perry's Party Now," *Texas Monthly*, October 2000, pp. 150–153, 163–167.

8. Jim Nicar, "A Summer of Discontent," *Texas Alcalde*, September/October 1997, p. 83.

9. For more about Toomey and other actors on the Texas political stage, see Patricia Kilday Hart, "The Enforcer," *Texas Monthly*, May 2003, pp. 128–131, 175–177; Wayne Slater and James Moore, *Bush's Brain: How Karl Rove Made George W. Bush Presidential* (New York: Wiley, 2003); and Lou Dubose, Jan Reid, and Carl Cannon, *Boy Genius: Karl Rove, the Brains Behind the Remarkable Triumph of George W. Bush* (New York: Public Affairs, 2003).

10. Mike West, "Group Raising Money for Perry Interns," *Austin American-Statesman*, 28 July 2004.

11. *Governor Bush's Well-Appointed Texas Officials* (Austin: Texans for Public Justice, 2000).

12. Toya Lynn Stewart, "3,000 in Texas Guard Called Up," *Dallas Morning News*, 9 July 2004.

13. Ken Herman, "Governor Unveils Budget Recipe," *Austin American-Statesman*, 12 February 2003.

14. For praise of this order, see David Sibley, "Perry's Coal Initiative Important Step," *Waco Tribune-Herald*, 27 January 2003. Sibley, a lobbyist and former state senator, played a leading role in lobbying for this executive order.

15. See T. A. Badger, "Perry Proposes $15 Million for Rails to Entice Toyota," *Fort Worth Star-Telegram*, 19 December 2003; and L. A. Lorek, "Luring Plant Was a Texas-Size Job," *San Antonio Express-News*, 9 February 2003.

16. See Jenalia Moreno and L. M. Sixel, "Citgo Headquarters Moving to Houston," *Houston Chronicle*, 27 April 2004; and Monica Wolfson, "Some Lawmakers Unhappy with State Enterprise Fund," *Wichita Falls Times Record News*, 2 April 2004.

17. See Ken Herman, "Lunch and Hunt with Perry for $150,000," *Austin American-Statesman*, 5 November 2003; Clay Robison, "Perry's Perks Go to Big Spenders," *Houston Chronicle*, 5 November 2003; and W. Gardner Selby, "Critic Pans Perry's Bid for Funds as 'Greedy and Seedy,'" *San Antonio Express-News*, 5 November 2003.

18. Quoted by Wayne Slater, "Perry Criticized for Soliciting Funds," *Dallas Morning News,* 5 November 2003.

19. See *Vetoes of the Legislature—77th Legislature,* Focus Report No. 77-10 (Austin: House Research Organization, Texas House of Representatives, 26 June 2001); and *Vetoes of the Legislature–78th Legislature,* Focus Report No. 78-11 (Austin: House Research Organization, Texas House of Representatives, 5 August 2003).

20. For a critical report on the 57 requests for reprieve that were considered and rejected by Governor Bush while Alberto R. Gonzales served as his legal counsel, see Alan Berlow, "The Texas Clemency Memos," *Atlantic Monthly,* July 2003, pp. 91–96. George W. Bush describes his clemency actions in *A Charge to Keep* (New York: Morrow, 1999).

21. William Pack, "Governor Fires 1st Volley in War on Fat," *San Antonio Express-News,* 21 November 2003.

22. For example, see Rick Perry, "A Look Behind the Headlines Reveals Texas' Bright Future," *Austin American-Statesman* 11 November 2003.

23. Ken Herman, "First Lady of Texas Takes a New Job," *Austin American-Statesman,* 7 November 2003.

24. Michele Kay and Gary Susswein, "Supporters Gave Millions in 'Late Train' Donations," *Austin American-Statesman,* 16 January 2003.

25. Dave McNeely, "Dewhurst Can Capitalize on Chief of Staff's Experience," *Austin American-Statesman,* 2 February 2003.

26. Molly Ivins, "Duck and Cover! They're Back!" *Fort Worth Star-Telegram,* 16 January 2003.

27. Janet Elliott, "Morales Ordered to Prison," *Houston Chronicle,* 1 November 2003.

28. Bob Richter, "AG Vows to Defend Open Records," *San Antonio Express-News,* 12 December 2002.

29. Gary Susswein, "Strayhorn Charges into Session," *Austin American-Statesman,* 8 February 2003.

30. Numerous articles have been published concerning the Strayhorn-Perry feud. For examples, see George Kuempel, "Senate Strips Comptroller of Duties," *Dallas Morning News,* 26 September 2003; Evan Smith, "One Ticked Off Grandma," *Texas Monthly,* December 2003, pp. 160-163, 206; and Ken Herman and Ben Wear, "Strayhorn Hurls Darts at Perry's School Plan," *Austin American-Statesman,* 20 April 2004.

31. April Castro, "Patterson Takes Reins as New Land Commissioner," *San Antonio Express-News,* 12 December 2002.

32. See Susan Combs, "Looking Out for Water," *Austin American-Statesman,* 25 October 2003; and Jerry Patterson's response, "Get the Facts Right on West Texas Water Deal," *Austin American-Statesman,* 3 November 2003.

33. See Kelley Shannon's two articles: "Seeking Change in School Snack Machines," *Dallas Morning News,* 26 August 2003; and "Agriculture Chief Eyes Move Up Ladder," *Dallas Mornig News,* 17 November 2003.

SELECTED READING

★ ───

*Gov. Perry Signs $117 Billion State Budget and Uses Line-Item Veto Power to Eliminate $81 Million in Spending**

On 22 June 2003, Governor Rick Perry signed House Bill 1, which authorizes the state budget for fiscal years 2004 and 2005; and he proclaimed his objections to individual items of appropriation that were vetoed. The following press release from the Office of the Governor outlines important spending provisions and line-item vetoes.

AUSTIN – Gov. Rick Perry today signed a $117 billion state budget that meets the needs of Texans and includes new tools for job creation without new taxes. Perry also used his line-item veto power to reduce the two-year spending plan by $81.1 million.

"This budget reflects the same fiscal discipline Texas families must show," Perry said. "We set priorities, separated wants from needs and stretched every dollar. We protected both the pocketbooks of Texas taxpayers and vital programs, increasing funding for public education and health care."

The governor used line-item vetoes to reduce the budget by $81.1 million, including:

- $7.4 million which had been appropriated to the State Aircraft Pooling Board. [For an example of a line-item veto, see the Appendix at the end of this press release for the item and the statement of Governor Perry's objection to it.]
- $2 million which had been appropriated to the Telecommunications Infrastructure Fund Board.
- $9.5 million which had been appropriated to the Higher Education Coordinating Board for the Advanced Research Program.
- $250,000 in FY 2005 which had been appropriated to the Higher Education Coordinating Board for the Parker Chiropractic College and the Texas Chiropractic College.
- $22.5 million which had been appropriated for the Texas Excellence Fund.
- $22.5 million which had been appropriated for the University Research Fund.

*Press Release, Office of the Governor of Texas, 22 June 2003 <www.governor.state.tx.us/divisions/press/pressreleases/PressRelease.2003-06-22.3707/view>.

- $6.6 million which had been appropriated to the Texas Wildlife Damage Management Service.
- $2.5 million which had been appropriated to the Criminal Justice Policy Council.
- $3 million which had been appropriated to the Texas Council on Environmental Technology.
- $451,237 which had been appropriated to the Board of Nurse Examiners.
- $2 million which had been appropriated to the Research and Oversight Council on Workers' Compensation.
- $2.4 million which had been appropriated for legislation that did not pass or was vetoed by the governor.

The line-item vetoes are in addition to two actions the governor announced Friday to balance the budget passed by lawmakers. Friday, the governor notified Comptroller Carole Keeton Strayhorn that he had eliminated more than $200 million in appropriations from House Bill 2425 and House Bill 3175. Those moves allowed the comptroller to certify the budget, paving the way for Perry to sign the bill by the June 22 deadline.

The state budget reduces general revenue spending by $2.6 billion over the previous biennium, while at the same time drawing down more federal funds. It allocates $1.1 billion in new funds for vital health care programs over and above the previous budget.

Eligibility for coverage under the Children's Health Insurance Program remains at 200 percent of poverty while increasing funding for Medicaid acute care coverage, HIV medications and children with special health care needs. The budget also includes an additional $172 million to help trauma care centers, as well as new dollars to increase the number of federally qualified health centers to provide care for an estimated 250,000 Texans statewide, many of whom are uninsured.

Other highlights of the budget include:

- Increasing public education funding by $1.2 billion, creating a new science initiative and allocating $324 million—a $56 million increase—for the TEXAS Grant Program.
- Establishing the $295 million Texas Enterprise Fund to assist the state's efforts to attract employers and create new jobs in Texas.
- Providing seed money to generate billions in bond funds for the Texas Mobility Fund to help build needed road, rail and public infrastructure projects.
- Funding the Texas Emissions Reduction Plan to bring the state's clean air plan into federal compliance and assure the continued flow of federal highway construction dollars to Texas.
- Significantly increasing funding for research carried out by public universities by allowing universities to retain 100% of their Indirect Cost Recovery for research purposes. Health-related institutions were also appropriated funds to increase their research into biotechnology initiatives.

The 2004-2005 budget will take effect at the beginning of the new biennium on Sept. 1, 2003.

Appendix

Excerpted from Governor Rick Perry's budget proclamation of 22 January 2004 is the following line-item veto and his stated objection to that item:

Aircraft Pooling Board	2004	2005
All items of appropriation	~~$3,741,068~~	~~$3,660,494~~

This veto action will eliminate the Aircraft Pooling Board. As I said in my State of the State Address, this agency underutilizes valuable state assets and is no longer needed. Operations of the Pooling Board can be conducted by outsourcing to commercial carriers and using charter planes. In addition, maintenance functions can be transferred to the Department of Public Safety through budget execution.

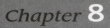

Chapter 8

BUREAUCRACY, PUBLIC POLICIES, AND FINANCE

Sargent © *Austin American-Statesman*. Reprinted with permission of Universal Press Syndicate.
All rights reserved.

*P*erhaps, the practice of Texas politics is no more intense than in the development, approval, and implementation of budgets. Who or which programs are favored in the budgeting process determines which policies, government agencies, and groups of individuals will thrive and which will diminish during a particular budget period (as illustrated by Ben Sargent's cartoon). Although the Texas Legislature adopts biennial budgets for gubernatorial approval, their development and implementation by government agencies and the lobbying efforts surrounding these activities by affected groups are ongoing.

Most of the work of Texas state government (public administration) is done by people who serve in departments headed by elected executive officials (covered in the chapter "The Executive") or who are employed by agencies headed by appointed boards and commissions (some of which are discussed in this chapter). Although often the subject of criticism or jokes about inefficiency, ineffectiveness, or laziness, these individuals are responsible for delivering governmental services to the state's residents. Some state employees prepare proposed budgets for their department or agency, and others implement approved budgets. Building strong relationships with legislators and their staff members is critical to agency success because an agency's existence, responsibilities, and funding are largely dependent on actions taken by the Texas Legislature.

Role of State Agencies

More than 200 boards, commissions, and departments implement state laws and programs in Texas. Some of these agencies were created in the Texas Constitution. Others were created by the legislature, either as directed by provisions of the state's constitution or independent of it. As problems emerge that elected officials believe government must address, they look to existing state agencies or create new ones to provide solutions. Sometimes, citizen complaints force an agency's creation. For example, citizen outrage at rising utility rates resulted in the creation of the Public Utilities Commission to review and limit those rates.

Not only do agencies depend on the state legislature for their creation and grants of power, they must also rely on this same body to provide funding. At least every 12 years, each agency must participate in a **sunset process** whereby the agency is systematically studied and then abolished, merged, reorganized, or retained. This examination is conducted by the Sunset Advisory Commission, composed of 10 legislators (5 from each chamber) and 2 public members. It has a staff of fewer than 30 employees. In 2004–2005, the commission reviewed 30 agencies, including the Texas Education Agency (discussed later in this chapter), the State Board of Acupuncture, and the Texas Lottery Commission (also discussed later in this chapter). The Sunset Advisory Commission makes recommendations to the legislature. Whether an agency lives or dies is determined by majority votes in both the Texas Senate and House of Representatives.

It is not surprising that regulated groups (often enjoying cozy relationships with friendly administrators and legislators) and state employees (fighting for their jobs) wage vigorous campaigns for preserving agencies and continuing business as usual. From 1979, the year the Sunset Advisory Commission was established, through 2003, fewer than 50 minor state boards and commissions had been abolished ("sunsetted"), approximately four per legislative session. In contrast, by use of the line-item veto, Governor Rick Perry abolished six agencies in one day in 2003 when he eliminated their funding in the state's budget.

Although people often think of government agencies as giant bureaucracies, they are in fact people charged with implementing public policy. The focus of this chapter is fourfold: how Texas treats its public employees; why selected policy areas—education, social services, and the economy—command significant legislative attention and appropriations; how Texas budgets money for government services; and what future demands there will be on state revenue. The influence of agencies and their funding extends to all who pay taxes, study for diplomas and degrees, purchase goods and services, breathe the state's air, drink its water, or live within its borders.

State Employees

With Internet web sites and telephone numbers (some of which are toll-free), most of Texas's state agencies are quite accessible. Many impatient citizens, however, want to interface with helpful human beings. That forces bureaucracies to hire and train personnel who are people-friendly, not just technocrats toiling at computers and shuffling papers.

Number

State government is Texas's biggest employer. When state college and university personnel are included, more than 296,000 Texans were drawing state paychecks for their full- or part-time labor at the end of August 2003. Calculated on a full-time equivalent (FTE) basis, whereby two half-time workers are counted as one employee, this total amounted to about 270,000 FTE employees. As a result of budget cutting for fiscal years 2004 and 2005, several thousand state employees lost their jobs or retired early. Each agency determines its own personnel policies, but the legislature sets salaries, wage scales, and other benefits. (See the Selected Reading at the end of this chapter for information about bureaucratic politics involving Carol Jones, a former director of governmental relations for the Texas Workforce Commission.)

How Do We Compare . . . in Number of State Employees?

Full-Time Equivalent State Employees (FTE) and Number per 10,000 Population

Most Populous U.S. States	Number of FTE Employees	Number per 10,000 of State Population	U.S. States Bordering Texas	Number of FTE Employees	Number per 10,000 of State Population
California	372,678	110	Arkansas	51,230	192
Florida	187,552	117	Louisiana	93,919	210
New York	252,099	133	New Mexico	47,839	263
Texas	268,637	129	Oklahoma	64,704	188

Source: *The Book of the States: 2003* (Lexington, Ky.: Council of State Governments, 2003), 460.

Compensation

Despite employee incentive options, state employee salaries remain low, and turnover is high (over 17 percent in fiscal year 2003, the most recent year for which information is available). Unlike federal and some local government employees, state workers do not have civil service protections. Additionally, salary increases are low. In fiscal year 2004, as an example, a newly hired word processing operator in the Texas Department of Criminal Justice received an annual salary of $17,532, with a maximum limit of $21,744, regardless of years of service.

Women hold more than half of the non-higher-education jobs in state government. Blacks and Latinos each account for about one-fifth of state personnel. Percentages for newly hired employees indicate that this pattern is not changing. (See Table 8.1.) Filling some high-tech positions has been a special problem, but downsizing in the private sector causes more workers with high-tech skills to seek public employment.

Education

In 2003, after a legislative hearing on health problems along the Mexican border, Representative Debbie Riddle (R-Tomball) asked an *El Paso Times* reporter, "Where did this idea come from that everybody deserves free education, free medical care, free whatever? It comes from Moscow, from Russia. It comes straight out of the pit of hell." Indeed, education and social services are controversial in Texas.

Public Schools

Approximately 1,040 independent school districts (ISDs) shoulder primary responsibility for delivery of educational services to more than 4 million students. (See the chapter "Local Governments.") These districts are heavily influenced by ethnic/racial politics (especially within large cities) and by socially

Table 8.1 Texas Minorities and Women in Non-Higher-Education State Employment, Fiscal Year 2002

Job Category	New Hires				Agency Workforce			
	Number	Black (%)	Hispanic (%)	Female (%)	Number	Black (%)	Hispanic (%)	Female (%)
Administration	816	8.70	15.19	49.38	4,936	8.40	11.30	40.49
Administrative support	3,180	18.30	25.88	83.05	19,445	17.20	28.42	87.70
Service/ maintenance	853	20.86	28.37	38.33	6,833	23.88	26.38	39.07
Professional	8,189	19.51	22.00	61.08	56,808	15.82	21.74	59.77
Paraprofessional	4,761	27.64	24.88	63.05	22,622	28.87	24.63	73.01
Protective services	7,624	29.64	17.02	40.70	39,041	27.99	18.90	34.98
Skilled craft	457	7.65	18.59	2.84	7,403	7.67	21.63	2.97
Technical	1,356	12.24	22.05	45.79	11,580	12.72	19.87	43.13
Totals	27,237	22.78	21.50	55.48	168,668	20.09	21.99	53.99

Source: Texas Commission on Human Rights, 2002

conservative agendas within many suburbs and rural areas. Local school board elections, rarely attracting more than 10 percent of eligible voters, are often dominated by community groups, such as local organizations of the Christian Coalition. Consequently, board members may be mobilized citizens interested in controlling practices ranging from teaching methods to hiring of teachers.

State Board of Education   Heading Texas's system of public education is the **State Board of Education (SBOE***)*. Representing districts with approximately equal population (about 1.4 million), the 15 elected board members serve without salary for overlapping terms of four years. The governor appoints, with Senate confirmation, a sitting SBOE member as chair for a term of two years. Among the board's most significant powers are curriculum approval for each subject and grade; textbook selection and adoption for the public schools;[1] management of the Permanent School Fund; and certification of public school administrators, teachers, and counselors (a power shared jointly with the appointed State Board for Educator Certification).

Few Texans know the name of their SBOE member. Yet the board and its decisions are often the subject of media attention. Deep ideological differences divide the board's socially conservative members from its moderate and liberal members.[2] Openly hostile debates on subjects such as textbook adoption and public criticism surrounding possible conflict of interest in the selection of external portfolio managers and independent financial consultants have led some legislators to advocate reforming board procedures and others to threaten elimination of the SBOE.[3]

Texas Education Agency   With about 1,040 local school districts adminis-tering more than 6,300 public schools, many concerned citizens question whether additional layers of educational bureaucracy are needed. Already in place at the federal level is the U.S. Department of Education, with nearly 5,000 employees. In the Lone Star State, the **Texas Education Agency (TEA)**, headquartered in Austin, is staffed with less than 600 full-time employees. Created by the legislature in 1949, the TEA today is headed by the commissioner of education, who is appointed by the governor to a four-year term with Senate confirmation. The TEA accredits schools, oversees grade-promotion testing of elementary and secondary school students, grants waivers to schools seeking charter status and exemptions from cer-tain state regulations, administers about three-fourths of the Permanent School Fund, and supervises the Foundation School Program, which allo-cates state money to independent school districts (ISDs). Whenever a local school district fails to meet state standards, TEA officials are permitted by law to assume control of that district, after approval by the U.S. attorney general, until acceptable reforms are instituted.

Charter Schools   The State Board of Education has issued charters for about 200 schools that are not part of an ISD. The state provides some fund-ing ($4,500 per enrolled student in fiscal year 2005). Other money must be obtained from private sources. Drawing students from across school district lines, charter schools are exempt from some state regulations (including teacher-certification requirements), serve special groups (such as urban, low-income students), and practice various teaching strategies. Charter schools are under SBOE supervision.

Testing   Educators are sharply divided about how to assess student progress and determine graduation standards. After its inception in 1990, the Texas Academic Assessment of Skills (TAAS) drew cries of protest from many parents and educators. Social conservatives argued that this legislative-mandated testing program intruded excessively into local school operations, while African American and Latino critics charged that the tests were dis-criminatory. The TAAS was administered as an exit-level test to qualify stu-dents for high school graduation, and the Texas Education Agency rated districts and schools on their students' overall TAAS scores. In 2003, follow-ing more than a decade of use, the TAAS was replaced by the **Texas Assess-ment of Knowledge and Skills (TAKS)**. This new testing program for grades 3 through 11 was developed as a better measure of students' mas-tery of the Texas Essential Knowledge and Skills (TEKS), which is a core cur-riculum required by the legislature. Ordinarily, a student who fails to pass a test on three attempts must repeat the grade. For eleventh-graders, the TAKS is an exit-level test that covers language arts, mathematics, science, and social studies. Passing grades in all four areas are required for a diploma upon completion of the twelfth grade, but failing students are allowed to retake tests even after leaving school.[4]

Colleges and Universities

Texas has six public university systems and four independent state universities, along with its health science centers (including medical schools) that receive part of their funding from the state. The Texas Technical College System, whose colleges offer a wide variety of courses from meat-cutting to laser technology, are also state supported. In addition, the state's fifty community college districts rely on some funding from the state. With government funding, there is also state regulation.

Texas Higher Education Coordinating Board   The **Texas Higher Education Coordinating Board** provides some semblance of statewide direction for all public community colleges and universities. Membership on the board is at twelve but will reduce to nine in 2007. The nonsalaried members are appointed by the governor to six-year terms with Senate approval. Gubernatorial power also extends to designating two board members as chair and vice chair, with neither appointment requiring Senate confirmation. The coordinating board has approval authority for new academic programs, degrees, universities, university centers, community colleges, and technical colleges. Students who have problems transferring course credits from one Texas college or university to another may appeal to the board.

Boards of Regents   In Texas, a variety of public institutions of higher education function independently or within systems composed of two or more entities. Boards of regents for each of four independent state universities and for seven systems (six university systems and the Texas Technical College System) are appointed by the governor for six-year terms, with Senate approval.

Affirmative Action   Responding to pressure from interest groups representing racial and ethnic minorities and women, governments at all levels began to establish affirmative action programs as early as the 1960s. Universities and professional schools devised ways to consider race or ethnicity in admissions and scholarship decisions to assure the enrollment of more Latinos, African Americans, and Native Americans. Some white applicants, who were denied admission or scholarship benefits, challenged these affirmative action programs. In the case of *University of California* v. *Bakke* (1978), the U.S. Supreme Court ruled that race could be considered as one factor along with other criteria to achieve diversity in higher education enrollment; however, setting aside a specific number of slots for one race was not acceptable.[5]

Relying on the *Bakke* decision, the University of Texas Law School created separate admission pools based on race and ethnicity. In the case of *Hopwood* v. *Texas*,[6] the U.S. Fifth Circuit Court of Appeals held that the practice was unconstitutional. Subsequently the U.S. Supreme Court ruled in the Michigan case of *Grutter* v. *Bollinger* that race could constitute one factor in an admissions policy designed to achieve student body diversity.[7] In another Michigan case, *Gratz and Hamacher* v. *Bollinger,* the court condemned the practice of giving a portion of the points needed to guarantee admission to every single "unrepresented minority" seeking admittance.[8] In the years ahead, both the *Grutter* and *Gratz* rulings will provide guidance to legislators and university officials as they formulate admissions policies for Texas's institutions of higher education.

In response to the *Hopwood* ruling, pressure from Texas minority groups resulted in private and public initiatives to counter the impact of that court decision. In 1997, for example, Texas legislators mandated that 10 percent of every high school graduation class be admitted to tax-supported schools of their choosing, regardless of test admission scores.[9] This practice remains controversial, especially among applicants denied admission to the state's flagship institutions—the University of Texas at Austin and Texas A & M University in College Station.

Social Services

Social services include much more than governments handing out money to the poor. Politicians' most underserved constituencies include persons suffering from old-age infirmities, inadequate health care, malnutrition, physical disabilities, mental illness, and life-threatening diseases such as AIDS. But most needy persons are not organized to compete with special-interest groups and their high-powered lobbyists. Nevertheless, the Lone Star State has responded with social service agencies that provide assistance for millions of needy Texans.

The Health and Human Services Commission is an umbrella office that coordinates the policies of several social service agencies. Sweeping changes were launched in 2003 when the 78th Legislature passed H.B. 2292. The law consolidates functions of 12 social service agencies under the **executive commissioner of the Health and Human Services Commission**. This official is appointed by the governor for a two-year term and confirmed by the Senate. Health and human services not controlled directly by the executive commissioner are supervised by commissioners heading each of four agencies: Department of State Health Services, Department of Aging and Disability Services, Department of Assistive and Rehabilitative Services, and Department of Family and Protective Services. Commissioners heading departments are appointed by the executive commissioner with approval of the governor. (See Figure 8.1 for the commission's organization chart.) Administrative support services are centralized in the Health and Human Services Commission, which is responsible for developing policies and making rules for all agencies. In addition, the commission determines eligibility for food stamps, the Children's Health Insurance Program (CHIP), Medicaid, and long-term care services. Although consolidation of all agencies is expected to take from four to six years, significant steps were taken during 2003 and 2004.

Figure 8.1 The Consolidated Texas Health and Human Services System

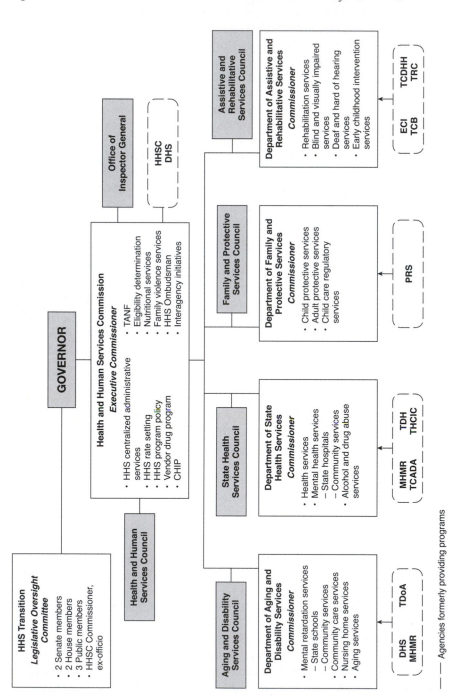

Source: Texas Health and Human Services Commission

Transformation plans that provoked widespread opposition involved replacing many local offices and caseworkers with call centers. Applicants for social services would be encouraged to use telephone and Internet communication to establish eligibility for social services. Call centers could be operated by private sector contractors rather than staffed by state employees.

Human Services

The executive commissioner has direct responsibility for the **Temporary Assistance for Needy Families (TANF)** program. It provides limited support for poor families with income below the poverty level, which was $18,850 for a family of four in mid-2004. At that time, a caretaker (usually a parent) with three children could receive TANF support amounting to $261 per month for a maximum of three years. Caretakers must sign a "personal responsibility agreement" forcing them either to work or to enroll in a job-training program. Children may continue to receive benefits if their caretaker seeks work but fails to find employment. Caretakers must be U.S. citizens or legal residents.

The federally funded food stamp program makes food available to elderly or disabled people, families, and single adults who qualify because of low income. About 80 percent of those who benefit from food stamps do not receive TANF support. Benefits vary, depending on income and the number of people in a household. In October 2004, for example, a qualified household composed of four people with a maximum combined monthly income of $2,043 could obtain groceries costing up to $499 each month. Paper stamps are no longer used for such purchases. Instead, a plastic "Lone Star Card," which resembles a credit or debit card, is used. For these and other benefits, log on to the State of Texas Assistance and Referral System at www.txstars.net.

Health, Mental Health, and Mental Retardation Services

Beginning in 1997, federal law replaced the national-state funding of **Medicaid** with block grants to the states. Part of President Lyndon B. Johnson's Great Society initiatives in the 1960s, Medicaid is designed to provide medical care for persons falling below the poverty line. Tangible resources not counted against the poverty-level limit are homesteads, personal possessions, and (in 2004) motor vehicles worth up to a total of $4,650. Not to be confused with Medicaid is **Medicare**, another Great Society initiative. A federal program providing medical assistance to qualifying applicants age 65 and older, Medicare is administered by the U.S. Department of Health and Human Services without use of state funds.

The Department of State Health Services performs a wide variety of functions, including public health planning and enforcement of state health laws. As with public assistance, state health policies are closely tied to several federal programs. One example is the Special Supplemental Nutrition Program for Women, Infants, and Children (WIC), which is a delivery system for food packages, nutritional counseling, and health care screening. Parts of the federal Medicaid program are administered by the Department of State Health Services.

Because diseases are a constant threat to human life and a drain on the economy, the Department of State Health Services is responsible for educating Texans about infectious diseases. Significant resources are invested in making the public aware of high-risk behavior that spreads sexually transmitted diseases. Acquired immunodeficiency syndrome (AIDS), the principal killer of men in their thirties, is unrivaled as a public health problem. Caused by the deadly human immunodeficiency virus (HIV) and commonly transmitted by sexual contact (both homosexual and heterosexual) and contaminated needles used by drug addicts, AIDS is an international epidemic. Texas trails only New York, California, and Florida in numbers of cases. During the 30 months between January 2001 and June 2004, the cumulative total of HIV/AIDS cases reported in Texas increased from about 57,000 to approximately 86,000. A related problem is the 100,000 cases of sexually transmitted diseases other than HIV/AIDS that are reported in Texas each year. Persons between 15 and 24 years of age account for about two-thirds of this total, but it is common knowledge that many cases are not reported by personal physicians.

Specialists treating persons overwhelmed by emotional problems often cite stressful, urban lifestyles as precipitating factors. Financial pressures, combined with family breakups, are causing record numbers of social problems that are not confined to any one socioeconomic group. For persons unable to afford private therapy, the Texas Department of State Health Services provides public mental health programs, but many people must wait years before receiving treatment in one of Texas's ten state hospitals. As a result, thousands of untreated, mentally ill Texans are detained in jails, incarcerated in the state's penitentiaries, or living on city streets. About 20,000 state employees are involved in providing mental health services throughout Texas.[10]

Supervised locally by county commissioner-appointed boards, thirty-five mental health community centers handle most cases of mental illness. Although these local mental health units receive some state funding, more than 50 percent of their operations are financed from county budgets.

State mental retardation programs are supervised by the Department of Aging and Disability Services. These programs are designed to help people within four categories of IQ scores: Mild (55-70), Moderate (40-54), Severe (25-39), and Profound (below 25). About 2.7 percent of all Texans are within these categories. Most of these people are within the mild range of mental retardation, but about 1 in every 1,000 Texans is severely or profoundly retarded. Campus-based mental retardation services are provided in eleven state schools, and other services are provided locally.

Employment

In 1995, the state legislature consolidated several job-training programs under the **Texas Workforce Commission (TWC)**. Matching unemployed workers with employers offering jobs is another important function of TWC. The agency is directed by three salaried commissioners who are appointed by the governor, with consent of the Senate, for overlapping six-year terms. The commission chair is paid $111,800 per year, and the salary for the other two commissioners is $109,200. One member represents employers, one is a representative of labor, and one represents the general public. The TWC collects an employee payroll tax that is paid by employers. This tax provides revenue used for weekly benefit payments to unemployed workers who are covered by the Texas Unemployment Compensation Act. The amount paid depends on wages earned in an earlier quarter (three months). In 2004, the maximum weekly compensation was $228 and the minimum was $52.

Texas's welfare reform program emphasizes local responsibility for employment training. Twenty-eight regional boards cover Texas's 254 counties, assisting welfare recipients and others in finding jobs. Each of the regional boards, composed of local business and labor representatives, is authorized to hire job training companies through a competitive bidding process.

Economic Policies

Have you ever complained about a high telephone bill, a big automobile insurance premium, or the cost of a license to practice a trade or profession for which you have been trained? Welcome to the Lone Star State's regulatory politics! For businesses seeking to boost profits or professional groups trying to strengthen their licensing requirements, obtaining changes in regulations can be costly but also rewarding. Less-organized consumers and workers often believe that they are left to pick up the tab for higher bills and fees, and, on occasion, inferior service.

Business Regulation

The **Railroad Commission of Texas (RRC)** and the state's Public Utility Commission (PUC) are among the most publicized agencies. This is because the former regulates the oil and gas industry, which has a declining but still important influence on the Texas economy, and the latter affects the telephone and electric power bills paid by millions of Texans.

Oil and Gas Texas does not have an energy department, much less a state-funded agency with a title that identifies it as a regulator of either the oil or the natural gas industries. Instead, the three popularly elected Railroad Commission (RRC) members function in several capacities, most of which have nothing to do with railroads. Today, the commission no longer "busts" railroad monopolies; rather, the RRC is primarily involved in granting per-

Texas Railroad Commissioners: Victor G. Carillo (Abilene); Michael L. Williams (Midland); and Charles R. Matthews (Garland) (Courtesy Texas Railroad Commission)

mits for drilling oil and gas wells, and performing other regulatory duties designated by the legislature. For example, appeals of municipally set gas rates for residential and business customers must be heard by the RRC. Other important functions of this agency include preventing waste of valuable petroleum resources, ensuring the safety of pipelines, and overseeing the plugging of depleted or abandoned oil and gas wells.

Public Utilities   State regulation of Texas's utility companies did not begin until 1975 with the creation of the **Public Utility Commission (PUC).** Its three members are appointed by the governor, with Senate approval, to overlapping six-year terms.

PUC's responsibility for overseeing telecommunications within Texas is limited by national policies. Federal law allows the Federal Communications Commission (FCC) to preempt state regulation of telephone companies. Ultimately, determining whose regulations apply is a matter for courts to decide.

Today, the operations of the Public Utility Commission exemplify what has been happening in recent years to regulatory policies nationwide. Business practices formerly controlled by rules made by government agencies are now governed more by market conditions. This industry-backed policy is termed **deregulation**. Its objective is to free businesses from governmental restraints and to depend largely on competition to protect the public interest.

Over the last decade, the Texas Legislature has caused PUC to shift from setting rates charged by telephone and electric power companies to a policy of deregulation that emphasizes competition. Allowing consumers to

Points to Ponder

In 2003, Texas had only 142 miles of toll roads, but motorists drove without charge on:
- 78,648 miles of city streets
- 142,477 miles of county roads
- 79,513 miles of state-maintained roads and highways that include:
  - ○ 40,990 miles of farm-to-market roads
  - ○ 16,183 miles of state highways
  - ○ 12,109 miles of U.S. highways
  - ○ 6,662 miles of frontage roads
  - ○ 3,233 miles of interstate highways
  - ○ 336 miles of park roads

Source: Texas Department of Transportation: *Annual Summary, 2003*, p. 35.

choose their telephone service supplier, for example, is expected to result in reasonable telephone bills and reliable service from companies that must compete for customers.

Insurance The **commissioner of insurance**, who heads the Texas Department of Insurance, regulates to some degree the more than $70 billion insurance industry in the Lone Star State. The Office of Public Insurance Counsel represents consumers in rate disputes.

At the beginning of 2003, Texans owning homes and automobiles were paying the highest insurance rates in the country. Rates for 95 percent of homeowners and 30 percent of automobile owners were unregulated and were rising rapidly. In response to a public outcry against high insurance rates, Governor Perry declared insurance reform to be an emergency matter requiring fast action by the 78th Legislature. Although the Senate and the House moved slowly, a law was enacted giving the commissioner of insurance authority to regulate all home insurers doing business in Texas.

On 1 December 2004, Texas began a largely deregulated "file-and-use" system for auto and homeowners insurance. Insurers are free to set their rates, but the commissioner of insurance is authorized to order reductions and refunds if rates are determined to be excessive. This system is expected to produce reasonable rates by promoting competition among insurance companies; but it remains to be seen whether the results will be significant competition, lower premiums, and more satisfied consumers.

Business Promotion

Some cynical observers contend that the business of Texas government is business. Others argue that boosting business strengthens the Texas economy and creates jobs that benefit the lives of all Texans. State agencies in at least three policy areas—transportation, tourism, and licensing—are administered to promote and protect economic interests.

Highways More than 79,500 miles of state highways were constructed and are maintained by the **Texas Department of Transportation (TXDOT)**. This agency is headed by a five-member commission appointed by the governor, with Senate concurrence, to six-year overlapping terms. Drawing no state salary, each commissioner must be a "public" member without financial ties to any company contracting with the state for highway-related business. Appointment of commissioners must reflect Texas's diverse population groups and regions. At least one commissioner must reside in a rural area.

Texans operate about 19 million registered vehicles, and most of them want more and better highways, but some Texans want better rail transportation, too. In 2003, the 78th Legislature enacted the Trans Texas Corridors plan pushed by Governor Perry. When completed, it will provide a 4,000-mile network of toll roads, utility lines, and rail lines. Meanwhile, vehicle traffic on existing highways grows more congested and dangerous. Part of the cost of Texas's overcrowded highways is an annual death toll of more than 3,500 drivers and passengers; half of these fatalities are alcohol related.

Tourism and Trade Responsibility for preserving Texas's natural habitats and for providing public recreational areas lies with the Texas Parks and Wildlife Department. The nine members of its governing commission are appointed on a statewide basis by the governor with senatorial approval. The governor also designates the chair of the commission. The commission sets fees for fishing and hunting licenses, and entrance fees for state parks. The department's game wardens enforce state laws and departmental regulations that apply to hunting, fishing, and boating activities.

Tourism is the third-largest industry in the Lone Star State. It involves promoting recreational travel and providing camping and hiking opportunities for Texas residents. In addition, tourism attracts big-spending visitors from other states and countries.

Increasingly, global economics creates linkages between state policy-makers and private interests. The Texas Department of Agriculture has a program for assisting Texas producers and manufacturers with export sales of agricultural commodities and goods. Finding international markets for other Texas products, attracting outside investment in Texas, expanding business in the state, and promoting tourism are functions of the Office of the Governor.

Certification of Trades and Professions More than 40 occupational groups are certified (licensed) to practice their respective skills by state boards and commissions. Reflecting Texas's shift to a service economy, half of the state's certifying agencies are health-care related. As a result of combined legislative and public pressure, each licensing board and commission now has at least one "public" member (not from the regulated occupation). All members are appointed to six-year terms by the governor, with approval by the Senate. Thus, from plumbers and electricians to physicians and nurses, occupational and professional standards are affected by the politics of gubernatorial appointments and senatorial confirmations or rejections.

Fiscal Policies

Most of the jobs that state agencies and elected officials have sought to bring to the state in recent years are **service-sector jobs**, including those in utilities, trade, finance, the professions, and government. Texas's tax system, however, remains land- and product-based.[11] It relies heavily on real estate taxes for local revenue and on sales taxes at the state level. Business activities of service-sector employers are often tax-free. Even as state government developed an increasing dependence on the sales tax as a major source of state revenue, it failed to tax the core businesses and assets of the service sector. Changes in Texas's economy, without corresponding changes in its tax system, have eroded the tax base so that the part of the economy generating the greatest amount of revenue pays the least amount in taxes.

Erosion of the tax base, coupled with an economic downturn, reduced federal funding, and an increased demand for government services in the early twenty-first century, placed the state in a precarious financial position. Yet Texans remained committed to pay-as-you-go government spending. The Lone Star State's **fiscal policy** (public policy that concerns taxes, government spending, public debt, and management of government money) did not deviate from its nineteenth-century origins. Today, the notion of a balanced budget, achieved by low tax rates and low-to-moderate levels of government spending, continues to dominate state fiscal policy. Consequently, state government, its employees, and its taxpayers face the daily challenge of meeting higher demands for services with fewer resources.

The state's elected officials appear to adopt the view expressed by economist Milton Friedman that "the preservation of freedom requires limiting narrowly the role of government and placing primary reliance on private property, free markets and voluntary arrangements." The 78th regular legislative session reflected this approach when the legislature responded to declining state revenues by reducing agency staffs, restricting government services, eliminating several agencies, and increasing fees for some licensed workers, while refusing to increase taxes.

Taxing Policy

Given traditional opposition to taxes, Texas residents have pressured their state government to maintain a low level of taxation. When additional revenues have been needed, Texans have indicated in poll after poll their preference for **regressive taxes** that favor the rich and fall most heavily on the poor ("the less you make, the more government takes"). Under such taxes, the burden decreases as personal income increases. Figure 8.2 illustrates the impact of regressive taxes on those earning different levels of income. The poorest 20 percent of Texans pay almost three and one-half times as much of their income for taxes as the wealthiest 20 percent.

Texas lawmakers have developed a tax structure that is among the most regressive in the nation. A general sales tax and selective sales taxes have

Figure 8.2 Impact of Regressive Taxes

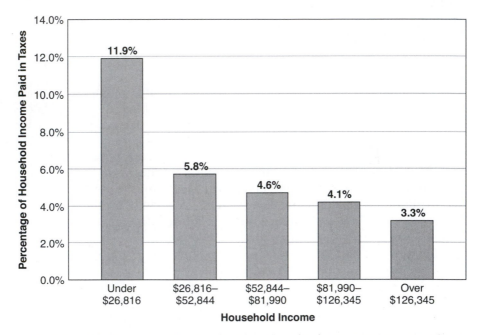

Source: Center for Public Policy Priorities, *The Texas Budget and Tax Primer: Where the State's Money Comes From and How It Is Spent* (Austin: Center for Public Policy Priorities, August 2002), p. 29. From *Texas Revenue Primer*, page 20 at **www.cppp.org/products/reports/revised2.pdf**. Reprinted by permission of Center for Public Policy Priorities.

been especially popular. **Progressive taxes** (taxes whose impact increases as income rises—"the more you make, the more government takes") have been unpopular. Texas officials and citizens so oppose state income taxes that the state constitution requires a popular referendum before an income tax can be levied.

To finance services, Texas government depends heavily on sales taxes, which rank among the highest in the nation. In addition, the Lone Star State has a dizzying array of other taxes. For example, Texas imposes taxes on bingo games, sulfur production, and oil and gas well servicing. Yet the sales tax remains the most important source of state revenue.

Budget Policy

Hostility to public debt is demonstrated in constitutional and statutory provisions designed to force the state to operate on a pay-as-you-go **balanced budget**. The Texas Constitution prohibits the state government from borrowing money "except to supply casual deficiencies of revenue, repel invasion, suppress insurrection, and to defend the state in war." The comptroller of public accounts must submit to the legislature in advance of each regular session a sworn statement of cash on hand and revenue anticipated for the succeeding two years. Appropriation bills enacted at that particular session, and any subsequent special session, are limited to not more than the amount

POINT   *COUNTERPOINT*

Should Texas Adopt a State Income Tax?

THE ISSUE

Even though Texas remains one of only seven states in the Union without an income tax, an increasing number of Texans suggest they might favor such a tax if property taxes or the sales tax were lowered. Democratic politicians are more likely to back an income tax, while Republicans are more likely to oppose it.

Arguments For a State Income Tax

1. *Tax Burden.* The Texas Constitution requires that any money received from a state income tax must be used to fund education. Two-thirds of collected revenue must reduce property taxes. In addition, state income tax payments are deductible from federal income taxes. Lower property taxes and federal tax deductions mean the average taxpayer will have a lower overall tax bill.
2. *Revenue Stream.* The state's tax base, relying heavily on a general sales tax on goods, is insufficient to meet the state's revenue needs.
3. *Economic Development.* One of the best ways to attract new businesses to the state is a qualified work force. Inadequate funding of schools has a negative impact on work force training and education. A high sales tax (the sixth-highest in the nation) inhibits business development and growth.
4. *Fairness.* Texas's tax system is too regressive (the fifth-most-regressive in the nation). An income tax would spread the tax burden more equitably.

> "Revenue from an income tax grows naturally (without rate increases) with the growth in the state's economy. . . . An income tax is also directly linked to an individual's ability to pay taxes. . . . In spite of all Texans have been told, an income tax is simply the best choice to meet our goals."

> —*The Best Choice for Paying for Public Education*
> (Austin: Center for Public Policy Priorities, January 2004)

Arguments Against a State Income Tax

1. *Tax Burden.* More state revenue will lead to greater spending by government. As a result, tax rates will increase. The tax burden actually increases faster in states with income taxes than in those states that do not rely on them.
2. *Revenue Stream.* The income tax fails to provide a dependable source of revenue. In 2002, during the most recent economic downturn, anticipated sales tax collections were 3.2 percent below projections, while income tax collections were 12.8 percent below projections
3. *Economic Development.* States with income taxes all have higher tax burdens and less personal income growth. These taxes also discourage savings.
4. *Fairness.* Income taxes are imposed across the board, but a sales tax is only paid by those who purchase goods.

(Continued on next page)

POINT COUNTERPOINT

"After all the tests are run and the results analyzed, the conclusion is clear, income taxes are nowhere near as efficient and effective as other forms of taxation, especially sales taxes. . . . They harm income growth, discourage savings and investments, and fuel unproductive increases in the size of government. . . . Lone Star State lawmakers should say loud and clear to those who advocate them: Don't mess with Texas."

—Richard Vedder, *Taxing Texans: A Six-Part Series Examining Taxes in the Lone Star State, Part I: The Worst Tax for Texas? Comparing Income, Property, Sales & Corporate Taxes* (Austin: Texas Public Policy Foundation, 28 February 2002).

certified unless a four-fifths majority in both houses votes to ignore the comptroller's predictions or the legislature provides new revenue sources.

Despite these constitutional provisions, casual deficits (unplanned shortages) occur periodically. These deficits usually arise in the **General Revenue Fund** (the fund available to the legislature for general appropriations). Although only one of nearly 400 funds in the state treasury, it is the critical fund in that maze of accounts. Like a thermometer, the General Revenue Fund measures the state's fiscal health. If the fund shows a surplus, fiscal health is good; if there is a deficit, fiscal health is poor. Less than one-half of the state's expenditures come from the General Revenue Fund. The remainder comes from other funds and is restricted to specific uses.

Spending Policy

Historically, Texans have shown little enthusiasm for state spending. Consequently, public expenditures have remained low relative to those of other state governments. Texas has consistently ranked forty-ninth or fiftieth in state spending per capita. Further, the state's voters have indicated their willingness to spend for highways, roads, and other public improvements; but they have demonstrated much less support for welfare programs, recreational facilities, and similar social services.

Revenue Sources

Funding for government services primarily comes from those who pay taxes. In addition, the state derives revenue from fees for licenses, sales of assets, investment income, gambling, and borrowing. When revenue to the state declines, elected officials have only two choices: increase taxes or other

Comptroller of Public Accounts Carole Keeton Strayhorn (Photo by Jack Grieder)

sources of revenue or decrease services. Although the 78th legislature meeting in 2003 increased some fees, it primarily chose to decrease services.

The Politics of Taxation

Imposed by governmental authority, a **tax** is a compulsory contribution for a public purpose rather than for the personal benefit of an individual. According to generally accepted standards, each tax levied and the total tax structure should be just and equitable. Of course, there are widely varying notions of what kinds of taxes and what types of structures meet these standards.

Sales Taxes　By far the most important single source of tax revenue in Texas is sales taxation. (See Figure 8.3 for the sources of state revenue.) Altogether, sales taxes account for 55 percent of all state tax revenue. The burden that sales taxes impose on individual taxpayers varies with their particular patterns of spending and their income level, because they are regressive taxes.

For more than 40 years, the state has levied and collected two kinds of sales taxes: a general sales tax and several selective sales taxes. First imposed in 1961, the limited sales, excise, and use tax (commonly referred to as the **general sales tax**) has become the foundation of the Texas tax system. The current statewide rate of 6.25 percent is one of the nation's highest (ranking as the sixth-highest rate among the 45 states that impose a sales tax as of January 2004).

Figure 8.3 Sources of State Revenue, 2004–2005

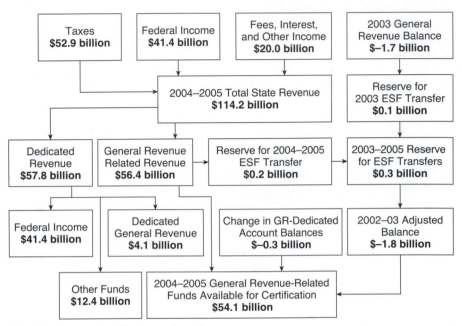

Note: Totals may not sum because of rounding.

Source: Office of the State Comptroller of Public Accounts, *Biennial Revenue Estimate 2004–2005.*

The base of the tax is the sale price of "all tangible personal property" and "the storage, use, or other consumption of tangible personal property purchased, leased, or rented." Among exempted items are the following: receipts from water, telephone, and telegraph services; sales of goods otherwise taxed (for example, automobiles and motor fuels); food and food products (but not restaurant meals); medical supplies sold by prescription; nonprescription drugs; animals and supplies used in agricultural production; and sales by university and college clubs and organizations (so long as the group has no more than one fundraising activity per month).

Two important items that are exempt from taxation are goods sold via the Internet and most professional and business services. As the volume of untaxed cybersales increases, Texas's sales tax revenue will decrease approximately 10 percent. Because the general sales tax primarily applies to tangible personal property, many services are untaxed. A sales tax is charged for dry cleaning, football tickets, and parking; however, accountants, lawyers, architects, and consultants provide their services tax-free. Proposals that would require these groups to charge and collect a sales tax have been strongly resisted. Because professional service providers and business represent some of the most powerful and well-organized interests in the Lone Star State, it is unlikely services provided by these groups will be subject to a sales tax. (See the chapter on "The Politics of Interest Groups.")

Since 1931, when the legislature first imposed a sales tax on cigarettes, many items have been singled out for **selective sales taxes**. For convenience of analysis, these items may be grouped into three categories: highway user taxes, sin taxes, and miscellaneous sales taxes. Road user taxes include taxes on fuels for motor vehicles that use public roads and registration fees for the privilege of operating those vehicles. The principal **sin taxes** are those on cigarettes and other tobacco products, alcoholic beverages, and mixed drinks. Sin taxes are among the easiest to increase in the state and, in 2004, became the centerpiece of Governor Rick Perry's proposal to fund the state's public schools. The governor sought to increase taxes on cigarettes and admission fees paid to "gentlemen's clubs." Perry, however, vigorously opposed increasing taxes on businesses. Additional items subject to selective sales taxes include hotel and motel room rentals (also called a "bed tax") and retail sales of boats and boat motors.

Business Taxes   As is the case with sales taxes, Texas imposes both general and selective business taxes. A general business tax is assessed against a wide range of business operations. Selective business taxes are those levied on businesses engaged in specific or selected types of commercial activities.

Corporations and other commercial enterprises operating in this state pay three general business taxes:

- Sales taxes, because businesses are consumers
- Franchise taxes, because many businesses operate in corporate form
- Unemployment compensation payroll taxes, because most businesses are also employers

The **corporate franchise tax**, which has been levied on business for almost 100 years, is imposed on corporations for the privilege of doing business in Texas. The tax is levied on the corporation's cash assets or annual income, whichever is greater. This tax produces about $2 billion in state revenue each fiscal year. Exempted from the franchise tax are banks, insurance companies, nonprofit corporations (such as churches and schools), and certain transport companies (mainly railroads and oil pipelines).

In addition, partnerships do not pay franchise taxes. In recent years, several major corporations, such as Dell Computer Corporation, have reorganized to avoid paying this tax. They have incorporated in Delaware and formed partnerships in Texas. The state loses almost $150 million per year as corporations take advantage of this tax loophole. Many professional groups, such as physicians and lawyers, organize as limited liability partnerships to protect their personal assets from creditor claims while also avoiding paying state taxes on their firms' earnings.

All states have unemployment insurance systems supported by **payroll taxes**. The payroll tax is levied against a portion of the wages and salaries paid to individuals to insure employees against unemployment. These amounts are paid into the Unemployment Trust Fund, which is distributed to workers who lose their jobs.

The most significant of the state's selective business taxes are levied on the following:

- Oil and gas production
- Insurance company gross premiums
- Public utilities gross receipts

These selective business taxes account for about 9 percent of the state's tax revenue.

One of the more important selective business taxes is the severance tax. Texas has depended far more than other states on **severance taxes**, which are levied on a natural resource, such as oil or natural gas, when it is removed from the earth. Texas severance taxes are based on the quantity of minerals produced or on the value of the resource when removed. The Texas crude oil production tax and the gas-gathering tax were designed with two objectives in mind: to raise substantial revenue and to help regulate the amount of natural resources mined or otherwise recovered. Each of these taxes is highly volatile, reflecting dramatic increases and decreases as the price and demand for natural resources fluctuates.

Death Tax   Texas collects a **death tax** equal to the amount that would be paid to the federal government in inheritance tax if the state did not levy such a tax. Therefore, if a federal tax is due on an estate, the amount of state inheritance tax is determined by an Internal Revenue Service computation called the federal credit for state death taxes. The state tax equals the amount by which the federal inheritance tax is reduced through payment of a state tax. Exemption from federal taxation has been set at $1,500,000 for 2004. By 2009, only estates in excess of $3.5 million will be taxed; in 2010, the estate tax will be repealed for one year. Therefore, the federal inheritance tax, and Texas's death tax, will be eliminated in 2010. Unless the law changes, death taxes will be restored in 2011 and exemptions will be limited to $1,000,000.

Tax Burden   The U.S. Census Bureau places Texas well below the national average for the tax burden imposed on its residents. In 2003, when state taxes alone were considered, the Lone Star State's average was $1,316 per capita, ranking it 50th among the 50 states. This amount was almost $600 less per person than the national average. A candidate's "no new taxes" pledge remains an important consideration for many Texas voters and will likely result in state officials' continuing to choose fewer services over higher taxes to balance the state budget.

Tax Collection   As Texas's chief tax collector, the comptroller of public accounts collects more than 90 percent of state taxes, including those on motor fuel sales, oil and gas production, cigarette and tobacco sales, and franchises. The Department of Transportation collects motor vehicle registration and certificate-of-title fees through county tax collectors' offices; the State Board of Insurance collects insurance taxes and fees; and the Department of Public Safety collects driver's license, motor vehicle inspection, and other such fees. The Texas Alcoholic Beverage Commission collects state taxes on beer, wine, and other alcoholic beverages. Although taxes represent the largest source of state revenue, there are other funding means.

Revenue from Gambling

Texas receives revenue from three types of gambling operations: horse racing and dog racing, a state-managed lottery, and bingo games. In addition, the Kickapoo nation, a Native American tribe near Eagle Pass, operates a casino. Because Texas has highly restrictive gambling laws, the tribe's gambling operations only allow players to compete against each other in games of chance. They cannot compete against the house as one would do in a Las Vegas casino. The state's other two tribes (the Alabama-Coushatta in East Texas and the Tigua near El Paso) are prohibited from operating casinos because of state law and the wording of one of their treaties with the United States.[12] Gambling proponents argue that legalizing more games of chance, such as video poker and casinos, would increase state revenue. Those candidates who share their view receive generous campaign contributions from these special interests. For example, in 2004, Governor Rick Perry's 2006 reelection campaign was given more than $230,000 in a single day by racetrack owners who supported placing video poker terminals at their facilities. Approximately two months prior to this successful fundraising event, Perry indicated that his office was investigating the possibility of amending state law to allow the establishment of video poker in the state. Although the proposal was submitted to the legislature in a special session in April 2004, it failed to pass.

Racing   Pari-mutuel wagers on horse races and dog races are taxed. This levy has never been a significant source of revenue for the state. In most years (including 2003), the Racing Commission collects less than its operating expenses.

Lottery   Texas operates one of 39 state-run lotteries. Chances for winning are 1 in 48 million. Under current rules, players have a better opportunity to win small prizes, but increased odds against winning the jackpot. In 2003, the 78th Legislature authorized participation in a multistate lottery. State officials selected Mega-Millions. Chances for winning are 1 in 135 million, but in July 2004, the winning ticket was worth $290 million.

The Texas Lottery Commission administers the state's lottery. Among its functions are determining the amounts of prizes, overseeing the printing of tickets, advertising ticket sales, and awarding prizes. This three-member commission must include one individual with experience in the bingo industry.

All profits from the lottery are dedicated to public education spending, rather than to the General Revenue Fund. This fact cannot be disclosed in lottery advertisements; however, the Texas Lottery Commission does publicize the information on its web site. In 2003, less than $1 billion went to the Texas Foundation School Fund. That amount constitutes a small portion of the state's annual budgeted expenditure of more than $17 billion on public education. Unclaimed prizes from the Texas Lottery revert to the state 180 days after a drawing. These funds are transferred to hospitals across the state to reimburse them for unfunded indigent medical care.

Bingo　Bingo games to benefit charities (for example, churches, veterans' organizations, and service clubs) are allowed by state law. There is a tax of 5 percent on bingo prizes, but the state's revenue from bingo taxes remains low. The Texas Lottery Commission oversees bingo operations in the state.

Nontax Revenues

Less than 50 percent of all Texas state revenue comes from the taxes analyzed above; therefore, nontax revenues are important sources of funds. More than half of these revenues (some 33 percent of the total funds in the 2004–2005 biennium) is derived from federal grants, but state business operations (such as interagency sales of goods) and borrowing also are significant sources of revenue.

Federal Grants-in-Aid　Gifts of money, goods, or services from one government to another are defined as **grants-in-aid**. In the 1960s and 1970s, federal grants-in-aid contributed more revenue to Texas than any single tax levied by the state. In 1982, when the state sales tax first exceeded federal funding, the principal losers were education, welfare, and health programs. As federal funding declined, Texas and most other states responded by reducing expenditures rather than raising taxes or redirecting spending. Over 95 percent of federal funds are directed to three programs: health and human services, business and economic development (especially highway construction), and education. For the 2004–2005 biennium, federal funds, including grants, were expected to account for more than $40 billion in revenue.

State participation in federal grant programs is voluntary. States choosing to participate must:

- Contribute a portion of program costs (varying from as little as 10 percent to as much as 90 percent)
- Meet performance specifications established by federal mandate

Funds are usually allocated to states on the basis of a formula. Factors commonly used in deriving a formula include lump sums (made up of identical amounts to all states receiving funds) and uniform sums (based on a number of items that vary from state to state: population, area, highway mileage, need and fiscal ability, cost of service, administrative discretion, and special state needs).

Land Revenues   Texas state government receives a substantial amount of nontax revenue from public land sales, rentals, and royalties. Sales of land, sand, shell, and gravel, combined with rentals on grazing lands and prospecting permits, account for approximately 3 percent of this revenue. The remaining 97 percent is received primarily from oil and natural gas leases and from royalties derived from mineral production on state-owned land. The General Land Office manages more than 20 million acres for the state and has responsibility for selling, leasing, and renting the surface and minerals of the property.

The Tobacco Suit Windfall   Early in 1998, the American tobacco industry settled a lawsuit that had been filed by the state of Texas. Over a period of 25 years, cigarette makers will pay the Lone Star State $18 billion in damages for public health costs incurred by the state as a result of tobacco-related illnesses statewide. These funds support a variety of health care programs, including the Children's Health Insurance Program, Medicaid, tobacco education projects, and endowments for health-related institutions of higher education. Payments averaged more than $500 million per year through 2003.

Business groups and others have suggested selling bonds backed by future payments from the tobacco settlement funds to private investors. This practice is called **securitization**. The major advantage of these bond sales is the immediate cash payment to the state. A serious disadvantage is that the bond prices would be heavily discounted because the private investors risk that settlement payments will not be made. This discount decreases the total cash the state will receive. Pressure to sell the funds will likely rise whenever the economy weakens.

Miscellaneous Sources   Fees, permits, and income from investments are major miscellaneous nontax sources of revenue. Fee sources include those for motor vehicle inspections, college tuition, other student services, state hospital care, and certificates-of-title for motor vehicles. The most significant sources of revenue from permits are those for trucks and automobiles; the sale of liquor, wine, and beer; and cigarette tax stamps. Income from fees and permits currently approximates $4 billion per year. These sources of state funding were increased in 2003 to improve state revenue.

At any given moment, Texas actually has on hand several billion dollars invested in securities or on deposit in interest-bearing accounts. Trust funds constitute the bulk of the money invested by the state (for example, the Texas Teacher Retirement Fund, the State Employee Retirement Fund, the Permanent School Fund, and the Permanent University Fund). Investment returns closely track fluctuations in the stock market. The Texas state comptroller is responsible for overseeing the investment of most of the state's surplus funds. Restrictive money-management laws limit investments to interest-bearing negotiable order withdrawal (NOW) accounts, treasury bills (promissory notes in denominations of $1,000 to $1 million) from the U.S. Treasury, and repurchase agreements (arrangements that allow the state to buy back assets such as state bonds) from banks.

Broader investment authority is given to the University of Texas Investment Management Co. (UTIMCO) to invest the Permanent University Fund and other endowments for the University of Texas System. This nonprofit corporation is the first such investment company affiliated with a public university in the nation. UTIMCO is allowed to invest in venture capital partnerships, which provide funding to new companies. Interest and investment income provide approximately 3 percent of the General Revenue Fund.

The Public Debt

When expenditures exceed income, governments finance shortfalls through public borrowing. Such deficit financing is essential to meet short- and long-term crises and to pay for major projects involving large amounts of money. Most state constitutions, however, severely limit the authority of state governments to incur indebtedness.

For more than 50 years, Texans have sought, through constitutional provisions and public pressure, to force the state to operate on a pay-as-you-go basis. Despite those efforts, the state is allowed to borrow money by issuing general obligation bonds (borrowed amounts that are repaid from the General Revenue Fund) and revenue bonds (borrowed amounts that are repaid from a specific revenue source, such as college student loan bonds that are repaid by students who received the funds). Commercial paper and promissory notes are also used to cover the state's cash flow shortages. General obligation bonds and commercial paper borrowings must have voter approval; other forms of borrowing do not require voter approval. **Bonded debt** that must be repaid from the General Revenue Fund has increased by almost 500 percent since 1988. Thus, many Texas voters approve both a balanced budget and bond amendments that authorize the state to increase its debt by borrowing money.

Bond Review   Specific projects to be financed with bond money require legislative approval. Bond issues also have to be approved by the Texas Bond Review Board. This board is composed of the governor, lieutenant governor, speaker of the House, and comptroller of public accounts. It approves all borrowings with a term in excess of five years or in an amount in excess of $250,000.

Economic Stabilization Fund   The state's Economic Stabilization Fund (popularly called the **"rainy day" fund**) operates like an individual's savings account. It is intended to be used when the state faces an economic crisis, primarily to prevent or eliminate temporary cash deficiencies in the General Revenue Fund. The "rainy day" fund is financed with any excess money remaining in the General Revenue Fund at the end of a biennium and with natural gas taxes that exceed 1987 collections. This fund has been used to provide temporary support for public education and the criminal justice system, as well as finance Texas's Enterprise Fund that is designed to attract new businesses to the state.

Budgeting and Fiscal Management

The state's fiscal management process begins with a budget and ends with an audit.[13] Other phases of the process include tax collection, investment of public funds, purchasing, and accounting. Each activity is important if the state is to derive maximum benefit from the billions of dollars it handles each year.

Budgeting Procedure

A plan of financial operation is usually referred to as a **budget**. In modern state government, budgets serve a variety of functions, each important in its own right. A budget is a plan for spending that shows a government's financial condition at the close of one fiscal, or budget, year and the anticipated condition at the end of the next year. It also makes spending recommendations for the coming fiscal year. In Texas, the fiscal year begins on September 1 and ends on August 31 of the following year. When referring to a budget year, the ending year is the one used, preceded by the initials FY for "fiscal year." For example, FY2005 began on 1 September 2004 and ended on 31 August 2005.

Texas is one of only seven states that has biennial legislative sessions and budgets for two-year periods—that is, on a biennium basis. Many political observers argue that today's economy fluctuates too rapidly for this system to be efficient. Voters, however, have consistently rejected proposed constitutional amendments requiring state appropriations on an annual basis.

Legislative Budget Board   By statute, the **Legislative Budget Board (LBB)** is a 10-member joint body of the Texas House of Representatives and the Texas Senate. Its membership includes the lieutenant governor, who serves as chair, and the speaker of the House of Representatives, who is vice chair. Assisted by its director and staff, the LBB prepares a biennial (two fiscal years) current-services-based budget. This type of budget projects the cost of meeting anticipated service needs of Texans over the next biennium. The comptroller of public accounts furnishes the board with an estimate of revenue that will be available over the same time period to meet projected expenses. The comptroller's revenue projections establish spending limits.

The board's staff also helps draft general appropriation bills for introduction at each regular session of the legislature. Furthermore, if requested by a legislative committee chair, staff personnel prepare fiscal notes that assess the economic impact of a bill or resolution. The LBB also assists agencies in developing performance evaluation measures and audits.

Governor's Office of Budget, Planning and Policy   Headed by an executive budget officer who works under the supervision of the governor, the Governor's Office of Budget, Planning and Policy (GOBPP) is required by statute to prepare and present a biennial budget to the legislature. Traditionally, the governor's plan has been policy based. It has presented objectives to be attained and a plan for achieving them. As a result of this dual arrangement, two budgets, one legislative in origin and the other executive, should be prepared every two years. In the closing decades of the twentieth century, governors often did not submit separate budgets. Governor Rick Perry, however, submitted budgets in 2001 and 2003, although his 2003 budget proposal allocated $0 for every spending category and made no attempt to set spending priorities or recommend reductions.

Budget Preparation   Compilation of each budget begins with the preparation of forms and instructions by the Legislative Budget Board and the Governor's Office of Budget, Planning and Policy. (See Figure 8.4 for a diagram of the budgeting process.) These materials are sent to each spending agency early in every even-numbered year. For some six months thereafter, representatives of the budgeting agencies work closely with operating agency personnel to prepare proposed departmental requests. By early fall, departmental estimates are submitted to the two budgeting agencies. These agencies then carefully analyze all requests and hold hearings with representatives of spending departments to clarify details and supply any additional information needed. At the close of the hearings, usually in mid-December, budget agencies traditionally compile their estimates of expenditures into two separately proposed budgets.

Each state agency requesting appropriated funds must submit a five-year strategic operating plan to the Governor's Office of Budget, Planning and Policy and to the Legislative Budget Board. Agency plans are then combined by GOBPP and LBB into a long-term strategic plan composed of three phases:

1. Statewide goals (for example, increasing access to higher education for students with disabilities) and proposed measures of specific government performance
2. Strategic priorities (for example, a commitment to achieve the goal in the immediate future) and external and internal factors that might affect the agency's ability to meet the goal
3. Strategic policies (for example, installation of elevators in all buildings and other facilities where higher education services are provided)

An agency's request must be organized according to the strategies the agency intends to use in implementing the next two years of its strategic plan. Each strategy, in turn, must be listed in order of priority and tied to a single statewide functional goal.

Thus, during each regular session, legislators normally face two sets of recommendations for all state expenditures for the succeeding biennium. Since the inception of the **dual budgeting system**, however, the legislature has shown a marked preference for the recommendations of its own budget-making agency, the Legislative Budget Board, over those of the Office of Budget, Planning and Policy and the governor.

Figure 8.4 Texas Biennial Budget Cycle

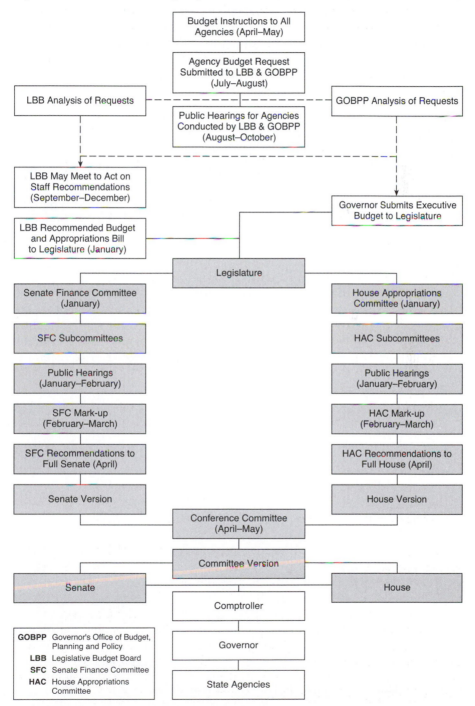

Source: Senate Research Center, *A Guide to the Budget Process in Texas* (Austin: Texas Senate, January 2003), p. 5.

By custom, the legislative chambers rotate responsibility for introducing the state budget between the chair of the Senate Finance Committee and the chair of the House Appropriations Committee. In subsequent months, the legislature debates issues surrounding the budget before approving it and sending it to the governor. The comptroller certifies the budget prior to signature. In 2003, Comptroller Strayhorn initially refused to do so, claiming the budget was not balanced. Ultimately, she certified the budget but cut her own agency's spending by $212 million to balance the budget. Whether this action was voluntary on her part remains questionable. In the next special session, important powers exercised by the Comptroller's Office were transferred to other agencies by the legislature.

The governor has the power to veto any spending provision in the budget through the line-item veto (rejecting only a particular expenditure in the budget). Through the exercise of the line-item veto in the 2004–2005 budget, Governor Perry eliminated six state agencies. Once approved, the budget is ready for implementation in the next fiscal year.

Budget Expenditures

Analysts of a government's fiscal policy look at public expenditures in two ways. One method is according to function—that is, the services being purchased (for example, education, highways, welfare, health, and protection of persons and property). Figure 8.5 illustrates Texas's proposed functional expenditures for fiscal years 2004–2005. The other method is according to

Figure 8.5 Texas Legislative Budget Board's Biennial Budget Recommendations for Fiscal Years 2004–2005

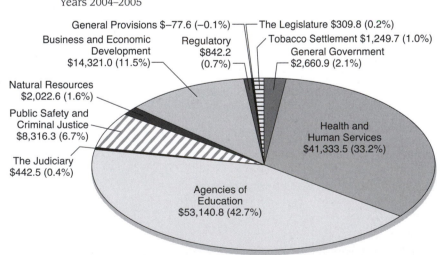

General Provisions $–77.6 (–0.1%) — The Legislature $309.8 (0.2%)
Business and Economic Development $14,321.0 (11.5%)
Regulatory $842.2 (0.7%)
Tobacco Settlement $1,249.7 (1.0%)
General Government $2,660.9 (2.1%)
Natural Resources $2,022.6 (1.6%)
Public Safety and Criminal Justice $8,316.3 (6.7%)
The Judiciary $442.5 (0.4%)
Health and Human Services $41,333.5 (33.2%)
Agencies of Education $53,140.8 (42.7%)

Total = $124,561.6 billion. The adopted budget was approximately $117 billion.
Note: Excludes interagency contracts. Totals may not add up because of rounding.

Source: Legislative Budget Board, *Summary of Legislative Budget Estimates for the 2004–2005 Biennium*, January 2003, p. 1.

the object of the expenditure, or objective expenditures (goods and services purchased to render the functional services, such as wages and salaries of public employees, medical assistance to needy individuals, and supplies and materials).

For more than four decades, functional expenditures have centered on three principal functions: public education, human services, and highway construction and maintenance. Similarly, three items have led all objective expenditures for most of that period: salaries and wages, medical and other assistance to needy individuals, and aid to public schools.

Budget Execution

In most state governments, the Governor's Office or an executive agency responsible to the governor supervises **budget execution** (the process by which a central authority in government oversees implementation of a spending plan approved by the legislative body). The governor of Texas and the Legislative Budget Board have limited power to prevent an agency from spending part of its appropriations, to transfer some money from one agency to another, or to change the purpose for which an appropriation was made. Any proposed modification by the governor must be made public, after which the Legislative Budget Board may ratify it, reject it, or recommend changes. If the board recommends changes in the governor's proposals, the chief executive may accept or reject the board's suggestions.

Purchasing

Agencies of state government must make purchases through or under the supervision of the Texas Building and Procurement Commission (formerly the General Services Commission). Depending on the cost of an item, agency personnel may be required to obtain competitive bids. This commission places greater emphasis on serving state agencies for which it purchases goods than on controlling what they purchase. The commission has seven members. Three are appointed by the governor, two are nominated by the speaker of the House but appointed by the governor, and two are appointed by the lieutenant governor. The commission also provides building and property management services for state facilities, including the Texas State Cemetery. The Council on Competitive Government is required to determine exactly what kinds of services currently provided by the state might be supplied at less cost by private industry or other state agencies.

Accounting

The comptroller of public accounts oversees the management of the state's money. This elected official is held responsible by Texas law for maintaining a double-entry system with such ledgers and accounts as are deemed necessary. Other statutes narrow the comptroller's discretion by creating numerous special funds or accounts that essentially designate revenues to be used for financing identified activities. Because this money is usually earmarked for special purposes, it is not subject to appropriation by the legislature.

Major accounting tasks of the Comptroller's Office include preparing warrants (checks) used to pay state obligations, acknowledging receipts from various state revenue sources, and recording information concerning receipts and expenditures in ledgers and other account books. Contrary to usual business practice, state accounts are set up on a cash rather than an accrual basis. In cash accounting, expenditures are entered when the money is actually paid rather than when the obligation is incurred. In times of fiscal crisis the practice of creating obligations in one fiscal year and paying them in the next allows a budget to appear balanced. Unfortunately, it complicates the task of fiscal planning by failing to reflect an accurate picture of current finances at any given moment. The comptroller issues annual and quarterly reports that include general statements of revenues and expenditures.

Auditing

State accounts are audited (examined) under direct supervision of the state auditor, who is appointed to a two-year term by the Legislative Audit Committee with approval by two-thirds of the Senate. The auditor may be removed by the committee at any time without the privilege of a hearing. With the assistance of more than 200 staff members, the auditor checks financial records and transactions on a random basis after expenditures have been made. Auditing therefore involves reviewing the records and accounts of disbursing officers and custodians of all state funds. Another important duty of the auditor is to examine the activities of each state agency to evaluate the quality of its services, determine whether duplication of effort exists, and recommend changes.

Future Demands

Elected officials have worked to keep taxing levels low. As a result, Texas has also kept its per capita spending levels among the lowest in the nation. Some observers believe that this limited funding is merely deferring significant problems in the areas of education and social services. Additionally, environmental concerns and homeland security demands strain the state's human and fiscal resources. A growing population; additional social service needs; an aging infrastructure; changing views of the role of government; and federal mandates regarding air standards, water quality, and national security are among the problems facing Texans, their government, and its agencies in the twenty-first century.

Points to Ponder

- Texas's largest school district (Houston Independent School District) enrolled 211,499 students in 2003–2004, and its smallest (Divide Independent School District in Kerr County) enrolled only 10 students in that same year.[a]
- In 2002-2003, Texas ranked 30th in the nation in average teacher salaries ($39,972 per year).[b]
- Texas ranked 48th in the nation on average SAT scores in 2002.[c]

Sources: [a]Texas Education Agency. [b]American Federation of Teachers. [c]The College Board.

Public Education

The state, together with local school districts, is responsible for providing a basic education for all school-age children Public education is the state's most expensive public service, accounting for almost 30 percent of the state's expenditures (approximately $17 billion per year) in the 2004–2005 biennium. The state's share of public school funding covers less than 40 percent of the actual cost. The balance is paid with local taxes and federal grants.

Sources of State Funding In promoting public education, Texas state government has usually confined its activity to establishing minimum standards and providing basic levels of financial support. The cost of three elements—salaries, transportation, and operating expenses—is shared by local districts and state government. Local funding of school systems is based primarily on the market value of taxable property within the school district, because local schools raise their share primarily through property taxes. Average daily attendance of pupils in the district, types of students (for example, elementary, secondary, or disabled), and local economic conditions are used to determine the state's share.

Funds to finance the state's Foundation School Program are allocated to each school system from the Foundation School Fund. This fund receives its money from the Available School Fund (revenue received from a variety of state taxes and income from the Permanent School Fund), the School Taxing Ability Protection Fund (money appropriated by the legislature to offset revenue reduction incurred by rural school districts), proceeds from the Texas Lottery, and the General Revenue Fund.

Funding Equalization A continuing controversy surrounding public school finance in Texas has been court-mandated funding equalization. The legislatively enacted wealth equalization plan, labeled the "**Robin Hood plan**" by its critics, requires wealthier districts (those with a tax base equal to $305,000 or more per student in 2003–2004) to transfer money to poorer school districts. The 78th Legislature abolished this method of equalization, but did not replace it either in the 2003 regular session or in a special session in 2004. The "Robin Hood plan" was also challenged in court and held to be unconstitutional. The state appealed the decision to the Texas Supreme Court.[14]

Public Higher Education

The state's public higher education system, just as its public schools, suffers from the dual pressures of increasing enrollment and declining state support. The Texas Higher Education Coordinating Board's Closing the Gaps initiative requires all public institutions to participate actively in increasing the number of Texas college students by 500,000 by the year 2015.[15] The 78th Legislature, meeting in 2003, reduced funding for community colleges almost 5 percent. Although university funding increased approximately 0.5 per cent, universities lost all state funding from the Texas Excellence Fund for research projects.

Community College Funding   State financing of public community or junior colleges is based on a "contact hour of instruction" rate for vocational-technical and academic courses. This rate is determined by calculating the hours of contact between an instructor and students. These two-year institutions use local property tax revenues, tuition, fees, gifts, and state and federal grants to finance their operations. In 2003, state funding per contact hour was reduced to the same level as it had been in 1995. During that same time period, costs increased. This gap in funding has been financed by students and local taxpayers.

University Funding   The 35 state universities and the Texas State Technical College System obtain basic financing from money appropriated biennially by the legislature from the General Revenue Fund. They also obtain money from fees other than tuition, such as student service and computer use fees (which are deposited in the General Revenue Fund), auxiliary services income (for example, rent for campus housing and food service fees), grants, gifts, and special building funds. The University of Texas and the Texas A&M University systems share revenue from the Permanent University Fund (PUF) investments, with the University of Texas System receiving two-thirds of the money and the Texas A&M University System receiving one-third.

Tuition Deregulation   In late 2002, the University of Texas System sought to eliminate legislative caps on tuition and fees. According to university officials, current funding limitations threatened the University of Texas at Austin's ability to remain a premier research institution. Despite fears that escalating tuition and fees would limit access to higher education for Texas's lower income students, the proposal became law in 2003.

Public community colleges and universities quickly moved to raise tuition. The state's community colleges raised tuition and fees on average almost 16 percent from 2002–2003 to 2003–2004. In that same period, university tuition and fees increased across the state, rising more than 20 percent at the University of Texas at Austin and Texas A & M University (College Station). The Texas Senate responded by appointing a study committee to review the impact of these increases, and the legislature ordered the Legislative Budget Board to conduct audits at the University of Texas at Austin and Texas A & M University.

Texas Tomorrow Funds   The Texas Guaranteed Tuition Plan and Tomorrow's College Investment Plan comprise the Texas Tomorrow Funds. The Tuition Plan provides a way for parents to save for their children's education and to lock in the cost of tuition and fees at the state's public colleges and universities. The program is backed by the full faith and credit of the state of Texas. As tuition and fees began to rise during late 2003, the state closed the funds to new participants. College living costs can be covered by investment in Tomorrow's College Investment Plan.

State Grants   Higher-education funding increases have been most significant in the area of student financial aid. Rather than give money directly to colleges, legislators across the country have preferred to provide funding to students and to allow students to select the institution at which the funds will be spent. The **TEXAS Grants Program** (Toward Excellence, Access and Success) provides grant funding to eligible students to pay all tuition and fees at any public college or university in the state. To qualify, a student must be a Texas resident, enroll in college within 16 months of high school graduation, show financial need, and have no convictions for a crime involving a controlled substance. The student must maintain a 2.5 grade point average in college to continue to qualify. Reduced funding, increased tuition, and higher than anticipated demand by returning students exhausted available funds for many entering college students in 2003–2004. The Teach for Texas program provides loan repayment assistance for eligible teachers. Information about both of these programs is available from the Texas Higher Education Coordinating Board.

Public Assistance

One of the characteristics of an economic downturn is rising unemployment and underemployment (in the latter, individuals work fewer hours than desired, are paid lower wages, or are overqualified for their jobs). As job losses and underemployment increase, so does the need for government services. Job loss in the early twenty-first century, as a result of an economic downturn in the United States and offshoring (in which jobs are outsourced to employees in foreign countries) increased the demand for social services from the state.[16] Rising health care costs and lower state revenue limited the amount of support the state could provide. Government limits on spending for welfare and restrictions on the amount of time individuals can qualify for Temporary Assistance to Needy Families (TANF) benefits present significant challenges to Texans and their government in the years ahead.

Texas has little or no control over many of these policy matters. The federal-state partnership that exists in the TANF and Medicaid programs places limits on state responses. Federal law also continues to shift greater monetary responsibility for public assistance services to the states through devolution. Texas's economy reacts to national and international economic conditions. Market conditions control the cost of health care services and other benefits. Yet poor children and adults rely on government to meet the basic human needs of food, health care, and shelter. A review of Texas's fiscal policies provides insight into how the state might address these issues in the future.

For the past three biennia, the cost of Medicaid and **Children's Health Insurance Program** (CHIP) exceeded budget allocations. Even though the 78th Legislature limited enrollment in both programs, with almost 150,000 previously eligible children losing coverage under CHIP through the end of fiscal year 2004, additional funding was required to complete fiscal year 2005. Much of the burden of the cost of care for these uninsured residents has shifted to local governments. Analysts project a continuing increase in indigent health care costs in the years to come. The ability of local entities to meet the social service needs of the state's low-income residents is one of the challenges of the twenty-first century.

Environmental Issues

A growing population requires the creation of more jobs in the Lone Star State. However, among Texas's many public policy concerns, none draws sharper lines of disagreement than how to maintain and nurture all forms of life while advancing business development that will provide jobs for Texas workers. Fewer arguments exist over why more action is needed for combating pollution. Texas industries produce more toxic contaminants (chemical waste) than do those of any other state. This grim reality is part of an increasingly complex problem that confronts local, state, and national policymakers. Federal policies give impetus to state environmental initiatives. Examples include rulings by the U.S. Environmental Protection Agency (EPA) and congressional directives in the Clean Air and Clean Water Acts.

Texas business people, who often complain about governmental red tape, usually support state policies designed to forestall federal regulations. Tracking corporate Texas's every step, however, is a growing army of public "watchdogs" (like the Sierra Club) who do much to inform the public concerning environmental problems.

Air and Water

The **Texas Commission on Environmental Quality (TCEQ)**, commonly called "T-sec," coordinates the Lone Star State's environmental policies. Six full-time, salaried commission members, an executive director, and about 3,000 employees oversee regulation of the environment in Texas.

State policymakers are continually involved in a balancing act as they respond to federal directives, local business pressures, and demands of individuals and environmental groups seeking stronger regulation of polluters. Texas's air pollution problems are not confined to the millions of motor vehicles on its roadways daily. Petrochemical and cement plants, refineries, smelters, steel mills, and a large variety of factories dot cityscapes statewide. Combined, these and other pollution emitters put the health of millions of Texans at risk.[17] Even the sparsely populated Big Bend National Park in West Texas has polluted air. For that reason, it is now designated as one of the 10 most endangered national parks in the United States.

Water contamination is another major area of TCEQ's responsibilities. Working with local prosecutors, the commission hears cases involving individuals and corporations alleged to have dumped toxic waste and other contaminants into the state's waterways. As with actions of other regulating bodies, TCEQ's decisions can be appealed to state courts.

Water will remain an important resource in a state that is primarily arid. The six-member Texas Water Development Board (TWDB) and its staff develop strategies for water conservation. In addition, they are responsible for collecting water-related data and for administering grants and loans from funds that have been established to support water supply, wastewater, and flood control projects.

Hazardous Waste

"Not in our backyard" is the rallying cry of incensed Texans faced with having their communities selected as storage and disposal sites for toxic materials. This waste can range in danger from high-level radioactive material that is potentially toxic for thousands of years to less harmful low-level radioactive waste to nonradioactive hazardous waste. Several West Texas counties (noted for sparse populations, undeveloped land, and little political clout) have been targeted by state and federal officials looking for places in which to dispose of industrial and residential waste. Increased accumulation of waste produced nationally will only intensify the demand for dumpsites in the years to come.

Generated largely by Texas's petrochemical industry, nonradioactive hazardous waste stored in landfills presents another environmental dilemma. Housing and commercial land developers covet landfill sites for their building projects. Pressured to relax regulations for cleaning up dumpsites in land-scarce cities, TCEQ has angered environmentalists with its tendency to approve less restrictive guidelines for dealing with this problem. As the state's population increases in the years ahead, even greater demands will be placed on the quality of its air, water, and land. Texans will continue to balance economic interests and environmental safety in making these decisions.

Homeland Security

Following the terrorist hijackings of four commercial passenger planes on 11 September 2001, federal, state, and local officials throughout the United States began giving more attention to preparations for preventing or coping with terrorist actions. In Texas, the Division of Emergency Management in the Governor's Office provides emergency response resources and information concerning disaster preparedness. Within the Texas Department of Public Safety, a counterterrorism intelligence unit handles reports of suspicious or criminal activities in which terrorists may be involved. The threat of bioterrorism has caused the Texas Department of State Health Services to compile information on that subject, and the Texas Department of Agriculture has done the same for diseases that terrorists could spread among the state's livestock.[18]

Most of the impetus for homeland security derives from the federal government. Yet, much of the cost is borne by the states. These unfunded mandates must be performed and financed by the state. As the United States continues to operate in an environment of heightened threat, increasing demands on the state budget for prevention and protection should be anticipated.[19] There is, however, no guarantee that Texans will be safer than they were in 2001. Safety is something that is not appreciated unless an attack is experienced or plans for an attack are uncovered.

Looking Ahead

In the years ahead, the state's governmental agencies will be forced to respond to the competing stresses of increasing demand and decreasing revenue. Doing more with less will be critical. In addition, taxpayers want better (at least from a business perspective) results for their money. This view is reflected in *Limited Government, Unlimited Opportunity* (2003), a study issued by Republican comptroller Carole Keeton Strayhorn. It concluded that Texas faced a "spending crisis, not a budget crisis" and that the basic challenge facing the Lone Star State's policymakers is to make government "smaller, smarter, and faster." Whether this government model will overcome the many challenges facing the state in the twenty-first century remains to be seen.

Another expensive governmental responsibility is the state's justice system. The next chapter, "Laws, Courts, and Justice," describes Texas's justice system, its cost, and its relationship to the state bureaucracy, particularly those public employees in the criminal justice system.

☆ **Chapter Summary** ☆

- The development, approval, and implementation of budgets by government agencies are important parts of the Texas political scene.

- State employees are Texas's largest work group.

- The state's 200-plus agencies provide a variety of services to Texans including public and higher education, social services, and business regulation and promotion.

- Texas has one of the most regressive state tax systems in the United States, because the Lone Star State relies so heavily on the sales tax and does not have a state income tax. Inability to tax Internet purchases and failure to tax most services cost the state significant revenue.

- Texas operates with a pay-as-you-go budget.

- Each biennium, the Legislative Budget Board and the Governor's Office of Budget, Planning, and Policy are required to prepare proposed budgets. Tax collection, investment of the state's surplus funds, and overseeing management of the state's money are responsibilities of the comptroller of public accounts. The state auditor is responsible for examining all state accounts to ensure honesty and efficiency in agency spending of the state's money.

- State revenue is used to provide services to Texas's residents. Most state money is used for public education (including higher education) and public assistance.

- Unfunded mandates and devolution are federal policies that increase spending at the state level.

Key Terms

sunset process	Medicare
State Board of Education (SBOE)	Texas Workforce Commission
Texas Education Agency (TEA)	(TWC)
Texas Assessment of Knowledge and Skills (TAKS)	Railroad Commission of Texas (RRC)
Texas Higher Education Coordinating Board	Public Utility Commission (PUC)
executive commissioner of the Health and Human Services Commission	deregulation
	commissioner of insurance
	Texas Department of Transportation (TXDOT)
Temporary Assistance for Needy Families (TANF)	service-sector jobs
	fiscal policy
Medicaid	regressive taxes

progressive taxes
balanced budget
General Revenue Fund
tax
general sales tax
selective sales taxes
sin tax
corporate franchise tax
payroll tax
severance tax
death tax
grant-in-aid
securitization

bonded debt
"rainy day" fund
budget
Legislative Budget Board (LBB)
    dual budgeting system
budget execution
Robin Hood plan
TEXAS Grants Program
Children's Health Insurance
    Program (CHIP)
Texas Commission on
    Environmental Quality (TCEQ)

 Discussion Questions

1. What services should Texas's government provide to the state's residents?
2. What are the advantages and disadvantages of a pay-as-you-go balanced budget requirement?
3. What are some benefits and some disadvantages of the "Robin Hood" plan for public schools?
4. Who should pay more for higher education—the state's taxpayers or students?
5. Has Texas dealt effectively with terrorist threats? Why or why not? Who should pay for this protection, the federal government or the state government?

Internet Resources

Center for Public Policy Priorities: **www.cppp.org**
Legislative Budget Board: **www.lbb.state.tx.us**
Office of the Texas Comptroller of Public Accounts:
    www.window.state.tx.us
Railroad Commission of Texas: **www.rrc.state.tx.us**
State Board of Education: **www.tea.state.tx.us/sboe**
Sunset Advisory Commission: **www.sunset.state.tx.us**
Texas Education Agency: **www.tea.state.tx.us**
Texas Health and Human Services Commission: **www.hhs.state.tx.us**
Texas Higher Education Coordinating Board: **www.thecb.state.tx.us**
Texas Public Policy Foundation: **www.tppf.org**
Texas Lottery Commission: **www.txlottery.org**

Notes

1. For textbook adoption details, see Dana Jepson, *Fact or Fiction: The SBOE's Role in Textbook Adoption,* Focus Report No. 77-17 (Austin: House Research Organization, Texas House of Representatives, 22 February 2002); and Diane Ravitch, *The Language Police: How Pressure Groups Restrict What Students Learn* (New York: Alfred A. Knopf, 2003).

2. See Dianne Patrick, "The Texas State Board of Education," in *Education in Texas: Policies, Practices, and Perspectives,* 9th ed., edited by Charles W. Funkhouser (Upper Saddle River, N.J.: Merrill, 1999), pp. 37–40.

3. Chase Untermeyer, "Partial Powers over Education Serve No One Well," *Dallas Morning News,* 15 December 2002.

4. Greg Mt. Joy, "Taking the TAKS," *Fiscal Notes* (October 2002): 1, 6–7.

5. *University of California Regents* v. *Bakke,* 438 U.S. 265 (1978).

6. *Hopwood* v. *Texas,* 78 F.3d 932 (1996).

7. *Grutter* v. *Bollinger,* 156 L Ed. 2d 304 (2003).

8. *Gratz and Hamacher* v. *Bollinger,* 156 L Ed. 2d 257 (2003).

9. See Michael May, "The Cream of Every Crop," *Texas Observer,* 6 July 2001, pp. 5–7; and Skip Hollandsworth, "Imperfect 10," *Texas Monthly,* April 2001, pp. 52, 54, 56.

10. Concerning problems at one state mental health institution, see Lucius Lomax, "Working the Plantation," *Texas Observer,* 11 June 1999, pp. 29–31. A different view is presented by Clint Shields, "New Directions," *Fiscal Notes* (June 2002): 1, 10–11. For a history of the Austin State Hospital, see Sarah C. Sitton, *Life at the Texas State Lunatic Asylum, 1837–1997* (College Station: Texas A&M University Press, 1999).

11. Billy Hamilton, "An Epic 100 Years Changes Texas," *Fiscal Notes* (December 1999): 1–5

12. For an interesting discussion of casino gambling and Texas's Native American tribes, see Kellie Dworaczyk, *Native American Gambling Operations: Are They Legal?* Focus Report 77-16 (Austin: House Research Organization, Texas House of Representatives, 12 February 2002).

13. For excellent discussions of the Texas budgeting process, see Senate Research Center, *A Guide to the Budget Process in Texas: Budget 101* (Austin: Texas Senate, January 2003); House Research Organization, *Writing the State Budget,* State Finance Report No. 78-1 (Austin: Texas House of Representatives, February 2003); and *The Texas Budget and Tax Primer: Where the State's Money Comes From and How It Is Spent* (Austin: Center for Public Policy Priorities, August 2002).

14. Sharon Hope Weintraub, *School Days and Legal Maze: Constitutional Challenges to Public School Finance in Texas* (Austin: Senate Research Center, September 2003).

15. Don W. Brown, John Opperman, and Steve Murdock, *Closing the Gaps by Moving Every Texan Forward: Demographics, Education, and the Future of Texas* (Austin: Texas Higher Education Coordinating Board,

28 November 2001), at **www.thecb.state.tx.us/ClosingTheGaps/ CTGMovingEveryTexanFwd.pdf**.

16. For a discussion of the impact of offshoring on a South Texas family, see Katherine Boo, "Letter from South Texas: The Churn," *The New Yorker*, 29 March 2004, pp. 62–73.

17. For more on air pollution in Texas, see Paul Burka, "Clearing the Air," *Texas Monthly,* December 2000, pp. 9–10, 12; Louis Dubose, "Lost in the Ozone," *Texas Observer,* 20 October 2000, pp. 12–15; Hope E. Wells, *Clean Air: Texas' Response to Federal Mandates,* Focus Report No. 76-24 (Austin: House Research Organization, Texas House of Representatives, 5 October 2000); and Travis Phillips, *Paying for Clean Air: New Funding Options,* Focus Report No. 78-7 (Austin: House Research Organization, Texas House of Representatives, 18 February 2003).

18. See Kelli Donges, "Bioterrorism: How Texas Plans to Respond," *Interim News* No. 77-2 (Austin: House Research Organization, Texas House of Representatives, 16 November 2001); and Dana Jepson, *Farm and Ranch in Biosecurity: Is Texas Prepared?* Focus Report No. 77-14 (Austin: House Research Organization, Texas House of Representatives, 22 February 2002).

19. Iris J. Lay, *Federal Policies Contribute to the Severity of the State Fiscal Crisis* (Washington, D.C.: Center on Budget and Policy Priorities, 3 December 2003), at **www.cbpp.org/10-17-03sfp.htm**. For a critical view of efforts to defend the United States against the terrorist threat, see Stephen Flynn, *America the Vulnerable: How Our Government Is Failing to Protect Us from Terrorism* (New York: HarperCollins, 2004).

SELECTED READING

★
——

*Memo Costs a State Employee Her Job**

W. Gardner Selby

Carol Jones was employed as director of governmental relations for the Texas Workforce Commission when journalist W. Gardner Selby, a reporter for the San Antonio Express-News, inquired about a memo that she wrote several months earlier. His story provides an insight into agency politics. Although not mentioned, the fundamental issue is whether public dollars should be used to lobby for legislation.

An employee has resigned from the Texas Workforce Commission [TWC] under fire for a memo she drafted last spring [2003] suggesting the agency should make use of "sugar daddy" lawmakers to succeed in the 2005 regular session. Referring to Rep. Mike Villarreal, D-San Antonio, and Democratic Sens. Eliot Shapleigh of El Paso and Judith Zaffirini of Laredo, who often file similar proposals, the 21-page memo states: "We should use the Villarreal, Shapleigh, Zaffirini strategy and get our 'sugar daddy' legislators to file several bills on the same topic so that we can at least get a few through." Describing those who lobby to keep favorite agencies from budget cuts, the memo states: "Everyone wants to protect his or her 'sugar daddy.'"

Carol Jones, the TWC director of governmental relations since December [2003], resigned Tuesday [27 January 2004]. She declined to be interviewed but released a statement saying the memo "represented simply my thoughts written on my own time on my home computer. . . . I never intended to imply any disrespect to the Legislature, but used what I considered to be a friendly colloquialism, which is the way I generally talk."

The commission, whose chairwoman is Diane Rath of San Antonio, oversees employee-training programs, unemployment compensation and child care subsidies for people trying to get off welfare and work full time. Larry Temple, its executive director, said he asked for Jones' resignation after requesting and reading the draft when a reporter called to inquire on it. "I read it one time, and that was enough," Temple said, calling it "too divisive, too partisan, a lot over the top."

Villarreal, Shapleigh and Zaffirini each said the "sugar daddy" reference seemed to compliment their commitment to changing laws to help children, and Villarreal credited Temple with "acting decisively." But he also said the draft memo showed the kind of attitude toward legislators "that will result in a divisive legislative process that places partisanship over the merits of good policy."

The agency provided a hand-marked copy of the memo, which addresses legislative and media relations, informal staffing and raising the agency's profile. Among its recommendations, it urges close contact with the conservative Texas Public Policy Foundation and Citizens for a Sound Economy "because they both have [Gov. Rick Perry's] ear." "Most Democrats will vote for bigger spending legislation," it states. "However, even for Republicans 'for the children' resonates whether the legislation has validity or not." A lobbyist who read the draft was impressed, saying "This is exactly like something you'd say, but never put down in writing."

Temple said he found no copy in his files, but might have received it when it was written last April [2003] when he was a deputy director. "I could very well have been given a copy of this" last year, Temple said. "I'm sent a lot of stuff. Some of it I read. . . . I don't remember. I really don't."

After Jones resigned, Temple began circulating the draft to state leaders with a note "to whom it may concern" stating it "does not represent the views of this agency nor my personal views." He said a similar packet also was being offered to interested legislators.

————————

When invited to respond to the article by W. Gardner Selby, Carol Jones submitted the following statement for publication in *Practicing Texas Politics: A Brief Survey:*

> The information in the San Antonio Express-News article does not provide a complete picture. Additionally, some information in the article is inaccurate. I will clarify the record below.
>
> 1. I resigned from the agency voluntarily because I didn't want public scrutiny harming my superiors or the agency. I was not fired. Never was I told nor was it intimated that I would be dismissed if I did not resign.
> 2. The memo in question had been reviewed by the individual who claimed to have fired me as well as the chair of the Texas Workforce Commission (TWC) and other top level officials. Larry Temple in fact referenced the recommendations in the memo in two separate planning meetings, and the restructuring of the department was partially based on the memo.
> 3. The same memo was cited as a reason for my promotion.
> 4. My superiors failed to publicly acknowledge their review or input and even went so far as to deny having seen the document.
> 5. Legislative priorities are set by commissioners of an agency, and governmental relations departments are charged with carrying them out. The memo I wrote was a draft plan for the TWC government affairs office to implement the policies established by the commissioners.

★

LAWS, COURTS, AND JUSTICE

*L*ady Justice is the symbol of American justice. With her sword demonstrating authority, her scales signifying fairness, and her blindfold symbolizing impartiality, she represents the ideal justice system. Most Texans share these same values. At times, however, significant gaps develop between the ideal and the reality. Lady Justice's dismay at the sloppy manner in which the Department of Public Safety's Crime Lab handles crime evidence in the opening cartoon highlights only one of many problems facing Texas's justice system in the first decade of the twenty-first century.

Incompetent representation of indigent defendants, inadequate access to attorneys and courts for poor people, excessive malpractice insurance premiums for doctors, wrongful incarceration of innocent people, allegations of racial profiling, a politicized judiciary, and a judicial system that is much less ethnically diverse than the population it serves are also characteristics of the Texas justice system. Technology now confirms what many feared—some innocent people are punished for crimes they did not commit. These faults erode confidence. Yet a democratic society depends on a justice system that is respected by and responsive to its citizens. Legal theorists such as Professor David Kairys suggest that the very survival of a justice system in a representative democracy depends on citizens' belief in the legitimacy of its authority. Concern about the growing mistrust of state justice systems by people of color, in particular, caused the American Bar Association's Commission on the 21st Century Judiciary to declare that the "systems are in great jeopardy."[1] In this chapter both the civil and criminal justice systems of Texas are examined. As you read, consider whether the criticisms and fears expressed above are reasonable.

An Introduction to Texas's Justice System

Texans have given substantial power to their justice system. The Texas Constitution and state statutes grant government the authority, in the appropriate circumstances, to take a person's life, liberty, or property. Significant connections between politics and justice in the Lone Star State result from state constitutional requirements that judicial officials (except municipal court judges) be popularly selected in partisan elections. Many Texas judges, however, obtain their offices initially when they are appointed to fill a vacancy caused by a judge's death or retirement before the end of a term of office. Such appointments, as well as elections, are usually influenced by political party affiliation. Although judges are involved in the policymaking process, they attract less public attention than do state legislative and executive officials; yet their decisions affect Texans every day. It is therefore important that the state's residents understand the role of the judicial branch.[2]

State Law in Texas

With more than 3,000 justices and judges, and almost that many courts, Texas has one of the largest judicial systems in the country. Counting the traffic violations that are dealt with by lower courts, millions of cases are handled each year. Texas courts deal with cases involving **civil law** (for example, disputes concerning business contracts, divorces and other family issues, and personal injury claims). They also hear cases involving **criminal law** (proceedings against persons charged with committing a **misdemeanor**, such as using false identification to purchase liquor and punishable by a fine and jail sentence, or a **felony,** such as armed robbery punishable by a prison sentence and a fine). A court's authority to hear a particular case is its **jurisdiction**. The law creating a particular court fixes the court's jurisdiction; it may be civil, criminal, or both. In addition, some courts have **original jurisdiction** only, meaning they are limited to trying cases being heard for the first time. Other courts are restricted to hearing appeals from lower courts and thus have only **appellate jurisdiction**. Still other courts exercise both original and appellate jurisdiction.

Sources of Law

Regardless of their jurisdiction, Texas courts are responsible for interpreting and applying state law. These laws include statutes enacted by the legislature, the provisions of the Texas Constitution, and judge-made common law that is based on custom and tradition dating back to the days of medieval England. The Texas Constitution is frequently amended by Texas legislators and voters (as discussed in the chapter "Federalism and the Texas Constitution"). Many new statutes are added after each biennial legislative session. For example, in 2003, more than 1,300 new laws became effective as the result of the work of the 78th Legislature. A court may apply a statute, constitutional provision, and common law all in the same case. Procedures that are followed in filing a case, conducting a trial, and appealing a judgment depend on whether the case is civil or criminal.

Points to Ponder

Laws passed by the 78th Texas Legislature:
- Prohibit driving Segway Human Transporters and similar devices on sidewalks and bike paths
- Bar Texas from recognizing same-sex marriages performed in other states
- Require drivers to change lanes or slow to 20 miles per hour below the posted speed limit when approaching an emergency vehicle that is flashing its lights

---

Newly enacted laws passed in each legislative session are compiled by the Office of the Secretary of State and published under the title *General and Special Laws of the State of Texas*. For easier reference, these laws are arranged by subject matter. Many of these statutes may be found in *Vernon's*

Revised Civil Statutes of the State of Texas, available from the West Group and on the Internet.

Code Revision

In 1963, the legislature charged the Texas Legislative Council with the responsibility of reorganizing Texas laws related to specific topics (such as education or taxes) into a systematic and comprehensive arrangement of legal codes. More than 40 years later, the Council continues to work on this project. Completed codes are found in *Vernon's Texas Codes Annotated*. In addition to piecemeal changes resulting from routine legislation, on occasion the legislature undertakes extensive revision of an entire legal code.

Courts, Judges, and Lawyers

Article V of the Texas Constitution is titled "Judicial Department." This article provides that all state judicial power "shall be vested in one Supreme Court, in one Court of Criminal Appeals, in Courts of Appeals, in District Courts, in County Courts, in Commissioners Courts [which have no judicial authority, as discussed in the chapter "Local Governments"], in Courts of Justice of the Peace and in such other courts as may be provided by law." In exercising its constitutional power to create other courts, the Texas Legislature has created municipal courts, county courts-at-law, and probate courts. These courts are referred to as statutory courts.[3]

The Texas Legislature continues to add specialized courts to meet specific needs of the state's residents. Among these specialized courts are "cluster courts," traveling courts that adjudicate only Children's Protective Services' cases. Major metropolitan areas are now required to have drug courts that are focused on treatment options rather than incarceration for substance abusers.

Texas's judicial system is complex. (See the structure of the current judicial system presented in Figure 9.1.) A court may have both exclusive and concurrent jurisdiction. A court that has **exclusive jurisdiction** is the only court with the authority to decide a particular type of case. **Concurrent jurisdiction** means that more than one court has authority to try a specific dispute. In that instance, a plaintiff selects the court in which to file the case. The same court may have original and appellate jurisdiction. Further distinctions are made regarding whether a court resolves criminal matters, civil cases, or both. Qualifications for judges also vary among the different courts, as shown in Table 9.1.

Local Trial Courts

The courts with which Texans are most familiar are municipal courts and justice of the peace courts. Together, these local trial courts handle, among other types of cases, charges involving Class C misdemeanors, the least

Figure 9.1   Court Structure of Texas

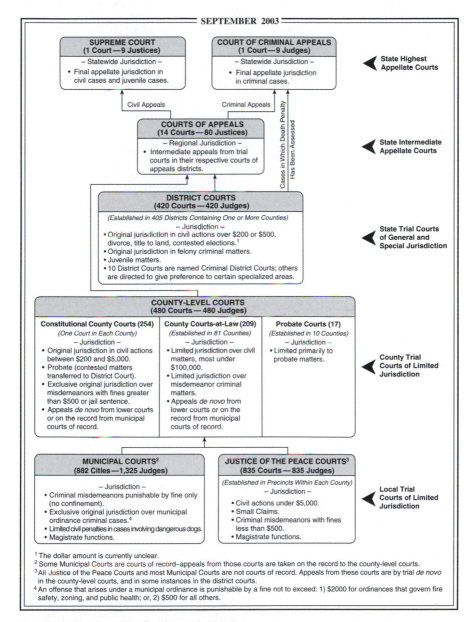

================ **SEPTEMBER 2003** ================

SUPREME COURT
(1 Court—9 Justices)
– Statewide Jurisdiction –
• Final appellate jurisdiction in civil cases and juvenile cases.

COURT OF CRIMINAL APPEALS
(1 Court—9 Judges)
– Statewide Jurisdiction –
• Final appellate jurisdiction in criminal cases.

◄ **State Highest Appellate Courts**

Civil Appeals   Criminal Appeals

Cases in Which Death Penalty Has Been Assessed

COURTS OF APPEALS
(14 Courts—80 Justices)
– Regional Jurisdiction –
• Intermediate appeals from trial courts in their respective courts of appeals districts.

◄ **State Intermediate Appellate Courts**

DISTRICT COURTS
(420 Courts—420 Judges)
(Established in 405 Districts Containing One or More Counties)
– Jurisdiction –
• Original jurisdiction in civil actions over $200 or $500, divorce, title to land, contested elections.[1]
• Original jurisdiction in felony criminal matters.
• Juvenile matters.
• 10 District Courts are named Criminal District Courts; others are directed to give preference to certain specialized areas.

◄ **State Trial Courts of General and Special Jurisdiction**

COUNTY-LEVEL COURTS
(480 Courts — 480 Judges)

Constitutional County Courts (254)
(One Court in Each County)
– Jurisdiction –
• Original jurisdiction in civil actions between $200 and $5,000.
• Probate (contested matters transferred to District Court).
• Exclusive original jurisdiction over misdemeanors with fines greater than $500 or jail sentence.
• Appeals *de novo* from lower courts or on the record from municipal courts of record.

County Courts-at-Law (209)
(Established in 81 Counties)
– Jurisdiction –
• Limited jurisdiction over civil matters, most under $100,000.
• Limited jurisdiction over misdemeanor criminal matters.
• Appeals *de novo* from lower courts or on the record from municipal courts of record.

Probate Courts (17)
(Established in 10 Counties)
– Jurisdiction –
• Limited primarily to probate matters.

◄ **County Trial Courts of Limited Jurisdiction**

MUNICIPAL COURTS[2]
(882 Cities—1,325 Judges)
– Jurisdiction –
• Criminal misdemeanors punishable by fine only (no confinement).
• Exclusive original jurisdiction over municipal ordinance criminal cases.[4]
• Limited civil penalties in cases involving dangerous dogs.
• Magistrate functions.

JUSTICE OF THE PEACE COURTS[3]
(835 Courts — 835 Judges)
(Established in Precincts Within Each County)
– Jurisdiction –
• Civil actions under $5,000.
• Small Claims.
• Criminal misdemeanors with fines less than $500.
• Magistrate functions.

◄ **Local Trial Courts of Limited Jurisdiction**

[1] The dollar amount is currently unclear.
[2] Some Municipal Courts are courts of record–appeals from those courts are taken on the record to the county-level courts.
[3] All Justice of the Peace Courts and most Municipal Courts are not courts of record. Appeals from these courts are by trial *de novo* in the county-level courts, and in some instances in the district courts.
[4] An offense that arises under a municipal ordinance is punishable by a fine not to exceed: 1) $2000 for ordinances that govern fire safety, zoning, and public health; or, 2) $500 for all others.

Source: Reprinted courtesy of the Office of Court Administration

Table 9.1 Texas Judges and Justices

Court	Judicial Qualifications	Term of Office	Annual Salary[a]	Method of Selection	Unexpired Terms Filled by
Local Courts					
Municipal Courts	Varies; set by each city	Varies; set by each city	Paid by the city; highly variable	Appointment or election, as determined by city charter	Method determined by city charter
Justice of the peace Courts	None	4 years	Paid by the county; highly variable	Partisan precinctwide elections	Commissioners court
County Courts					
Constitutional County Courts	Must be "well informed" in Texas law; law degree not required	4 years	Paid by the county; highly variable	Partisan countywide elections	Commissioners court
Statutory county courts (courts-at-law and probate courts)	At least 25; licensed attorney with at least 4 years experience; 2 years county residence	4 years	Paid by the county; highly variable	Partisan countywide elections	Commissioners court
State Courts					
District courts	At least 25; licensed attorney with 4 years experience; 2 years district residence	4 years	$101,700; county salary supplements; must be $1,000 less than court of appeals justices' salaries	Partisan districtwide elections	Governor and advice and consent of Senate
Courts of appeals	At least 35; licensed attorney with at least 10 years experience	6 years	$107,350 (justices); $107,850 (chief justices); county salary supplements; must be $1,000 less than Supreme Court justices' salaries	Partisan districtwide elections	Governor and advice and consent of Senate
Court of Criminal Appeals	At least 35; licensed attorney with at least 10 years experience	6 years	$113,000 (judges); $115,000 (presiding Judge)	Partisan statewide elections	Governor and advice and consent of Senate
Supreme Court	At least 35; licensed attorney with at least 10 years experience	6 years	$113,000 (justices); $115,000 (presiding justice)	Partisan statewide elections	Governor and advice and consent of Senate

Source: Office of Court Administration
[a]Through fiscal year 2005

serious category of criminal offenses. Both municipal judges and justices of the peace serve as magistrates of the state. In this capacity, they issue warrants for arrest of suspects and conduct hearings to determine whether a person charged with a criminal act will be jailed pending further court action or released on bail.

Municipal Courts   Judicial bodies in more than 880 incorporated cities, towns, and villages in Texas are known as municipal courts. The mayor of a general-law city serves as municipal judge, unless the city council provides for election or appointment of someone else to perform this function. Usually, municipal court judges of home-rule cities are named by city councils for two-year terms. Although they are not required to be licensed attorneys (unless presiding over a municipal court of record), more than one-fourth of Texas's 1,300 municipal judges have this professional qualification. The city council determines the number of judges and sets judicial salaries.

Municipal courts have limited civil jurisdiction in cases involving owners of dangerous dogs. They have no appellate jurisdiction. Their original and exclusive criminal jurisdiction extends to all violations of city ordinances, and they have criminal jurisdiction concurrent with justice of the peace courts over Class C misdemeanors committed within city limits. Municipal court judges are authorized to impose maximum fines of $2,000 in cases involving violations of some municipal ordinances (for example, regulations governing fire safety and public health). The maximum fine for violations of other city ordinances and state criminal laws is $500. If an individual is dissatisfied with the result of a municipal court ruling, the case can be appealed to the county court or a county court-at-law. Appeals are filed only in about 1 percent of municipal court cases.

If a city has a municipal **court of record** (a court with a court reporter to record the testimony and proceedings), a transcript of the municipal trial is made, and the appeal at the county level is based on that record of the case. Otherwise, cases that are appealed are given a trial de novo (a completely new trial). All incorporated cities are authorized to maintain municipal courts of record. Because of the expense involved, few Texas municipalities have such courts.

Justice of the Peace Courts   A justice of the peace, often called the JP, is elected for a term of four years by voters residing in a precinct with boundaries created by the county commissioners court. The number of precincts per county (one to eight) is mandated according to population by the Texas Constitution. The number of JPs (one or two) per precinct is also directed in part by that same document. Texas has approximately 835 justices of the peace, most of whom serve on a part-time basis. Annual salaries are set by county commissioners courts and range from a token $1 to almost $95,000.

Neither previous legal training nor experience is required for the position. Approximately 5 percent of Texas's JPs (usually in large cities) are lawyers and may engage in private legal practice while serving as a justice of the peace. Within a year after election, a justice of the peace who is not a lawyer is required by law to complete a 40-hour course in the performance of the duties of that office. Thereafter, the JP is supposed to receive 20 hours of instruction annually. Because failure to complete the training is a violation of a JP's duties under the law, arguably a noncomplying JP could be removed from office for official misconduct. However, such removal is highly unlikely.

Judicial duties of justices of the peace in urban areas constitute a full-time job, whereas in many rural precincts very few cases are tried. In addition to presiding over the justice court, a justice of the peace serves as an ex officio notary public and, like other Texas judges and justices, may perform marriages. A JP also functions as a coroner, who determines the cause of death when the county commissioners court has not named a county medical examiner. Justice of the peace courts have both criminal and civil jurisdiction. In all cases, their jurisdiction is original. In criminal matters, these local courts try Class C misdemeanors, but any conviction may be appealed to the county court or a county court-at-law for a new trial.

A justice of the peace depends on the precinct constable to handle any courtroom disruption. A constable, who is a peace officer with full law enforcement authority, is elected for a four-year term in each JP precinct. Most constables, however, leave law enforcement and crime detection to local police and the county sheriff's department. The principal function of constables is to serve writs (for example, a subpoena requiring appearance in court) and other processes issued by trial courts. In a precinct with a large population, one or more deputy constables usually assist the constable.

Exclusive civil jurisdiction of JP courts is limited to cases in which the amount in controversy is $200 or less, not including interest. Concurrent civil jurisdiction is shared with county courts and district courts if the amount in controversy exceeds $200 but is not more than $5,000. Appeals from a JP court of cases involving $20 or more are taken to the county level, where cases are tried de novo.

Small-Claims Courts Did the cleaners damage your sweater and then refuse to replace it? Did you work last week and now your boss is withholding your wages? **Small-claims court** is where you should seek justice. Presided over by the justice of the peace, a small-claims court can hear almost any civil dispute in which the damages claimed are for $5,000 or less, except for divorces, slander, or suits affecting title to land. Plaintiffs must pay a fee of up to $65 to bring a case against one individual. Additional amounts may be due if there is more than one defendant in the case. Because these proceedings are informal, parties to the suits often represent themselves. When the amount in controversy exceeds $20, the losing party may appeal to a county-level court.[4]

County Trial Courts

Every Texas county has a county court as prescribed by the state constitution, and some have one or more additional county-level courts. All are courts of record, and each is presided over by a single judge, who is elected on a countywide basis for a term of four years. The county commissioners court fills a vacancy on a county-level court. Annual salaries are set by the commissioners court of each county and vary from a few thousand dollars in sparsely populated rural counties to more than $120,000 in heavily populated urban counties.

Constitutional County Courts   Under the Texas Constitution, each of the states' 254 counties has a county judge who is supposed to be "well informed in the law of the State." County judges performing judicial functions—along with judges of county courts-at-law, district courts, and appellate courts—must take Supreme Court–approved courses in court administration, procedure, and evidence. Only one-fourth of Texas's constitutional county court judges are licensed attorneys.

Most of the 254 constitutional county courts have original and appellate jurisdiction as well as probate, civil, and criminal jurisdiction. In some instances, however, the legislature has created county courts-at-law to exercise such jurisdiction. **Probate** matters include establishing the validity of wills, guardianship proceedings, and mental competency determinations. Original civil jurisdiction of a constitutional county court is limited to cases involving between $200 and $5,000. Original criminal jurisdiction includes all Class A and Class B misdemeanors.

Appellate criminal jurisdiction extends to cases originating in JP courts and municipal courts. A constitutional county court's appellate jurisdiction is final with regard to criminal cases involving fines of $100 or less. For cases in which greater fines are imposed, the plaintiff may appeal to a court of appeals. Civil cases are heard on appeal from JP courts and the county court's decision is final with regard to those cases in which the amount in controversy does not exceed $100.

County Courts-at-Law   In counties with large populations, the burden of presiding over the county commissioner's court and handling many administrative responsibilities has left the judges of constitutional county courts with little or no time to try civil, criminal, and probate cases. Thus, the legislature has authorized more than 200 statutory courts that are most commonly called county courts-at-law. Statutory court judges, who must be licensed attorneys with at least four years of experience, relieve constitutional county court judges of some or all courtroom duties in more than 80 counties. With few exceptions, the criminal jurisdiction of county courts-at-law is limited to misdemeanors. Civil jurisdiction of most county courts-at-law is limited to controversies involving amounts of $200 to $100,000.

Probate Courts   Some constitutional county courts share probate jurisdiction with county courts-at-law. In the ten most populous metropolitan areas in Texas, the legislature has established one or more county-level probate courts to hear probate cases only. These courts are responsible for guardianship and competency proceedings, as well as admitting wills to probate.

State Trial Courts

Texas's principal trial courts are composed of 420 district-level courts of general and special jurisdiction (as of 2004). Each has one judge, who is elected to serve for a term of four years. Through fiscal year 2005, the minimum state salary for a district judge was set at $101,700 per year. Counties within a district may pay limited salary supplements. Although such salaries seem ample when compared with those paid for most jobs, in fact they are well below amounts earned by many attorneys. As a result, a large number of district judges now return to the more lucrative private practice of law after serving as a judge for only a few years.

Most state trial courts are designated simply as district courts, but a few are called criminal district courts. Each district-level court has jurisdiction over one or more counties. Heavily populated counties may have several district courts with countywide jurisdiction.

Qualifications for judges of district-level courts include U.S. citizenship, residence in the district for two years immediately before election or appointment, and a license to practice law in Texas. As a guarantee of practical legal experience, a district-level judge must have been a practicing lawyer, a judge of a court of record, or both for at least four years prior to election. As in the case of Texas judges in other state courts, a vacant judgeship (resulting from death, resignation, retirement, removal, or the creation of a new court) is filled by gubernatorial appointment with the advice and consent of the Senate. More than half of the judges in district-level courts initially reach the bench as a result of appointment.

District Courts　Most district court judges are authorized to try both criminal and civil cases, although a statute creating a court may specify that the court give preference to one or the other. All criminal jurisdiction is original. Except for cases transferred from constitutional county courts, misdemeanor jurisdiction is limited to offenses involving misconduct by government officials while acting in an official capacity. Felony jurisdiction extends to all types of felonies. Appeal following a capital felony conviction is taken directly to the Court of Criminal Appeals. Other criminal convictions are appealed to an intermediate appellate court.

District courts have exclusive original jurisdiction over civil cases involving divorce, land titles, contested elections, slander, and defamation of character. They have original civil jurisdiction in controversies involving $200 or more (however, one court of appeals held the amount to be $500). Thus, concurrent jurisdiction with lower courts begins at this level; above the maximum "dollar-amount" jurisdiction of those courts, district courts exercise exclusive civil jurisdiction. Appeals of civil cases go to courts of appeals.

Drug Courts　All counties with populations of 550,000 or greater are required to establish drug courts. These courts focus on rehabilitation and court monitoring of nonviolent drug offenders rather than imprisonment. Although advocates argue that treatment of low-level substance abusers is more successful than incarceration, a lack of state funding for court operations and concerns that rehabilitation gives the appearance of being "soft on crime" may limit the success of this program.

Appellate Courts

The Lone Star State's appellate courts consist of 14 courts of appeals, the Court of Criminal Appeals, and the Supreme Court of Texas. Each of these courts has three or more judges or justices, and all members are popularly elected for terms of six years. Terms are staggered so that one-third of the members are elected or reelected every two years. This arrangement helps to ensure that at any given time—barring death, resignation, or removal from office—each appellate court will have two or more judges with prior experience on that court.

Justices of courts of appeals, judges of the Court of Criminal Appeals, and justices of the Supreme Court of Texas must be at least 35 years of age and have had 10 years of experience as a practicing lawyer or 10 years of combined experience as a practicing lawyer and judge of a court of record. Decisions are reached by majority vote of the assigned judges after they examine the written record of the case; review briefs (written arguments) prepared by the parties' attorneys; and hear oral arguments by the attorneys. The Supreme Court of Texas and the Court of Criminal Appeals are authorized to answer questions about Texas law asked by federal appellate courts (for example, the U.S. Supreme Court).

Courts of Appeals The legislature has divided Texas into 14 state court of appeals districts and has established a court of appeals in every district. Each of these intermediate appellate courts is composed of a chief justice and from 2 to 12 justices. There are a total of 80 justices on the courts of appeals across the Lone Star State.

A court of appeals justice receives a state salary that is 95 percent of the salary of a Supreme Court justice. Through fiscal year 2005, the state salary for members of courts of appeals was $107,350. County governments in a district may provide limited salary supplements.

Courts of appeals hear appeals of civil and criminal cases (but not those involving capital punishment) from district courts and county courts. Final jurisdiction includes cases involving divorce, slander, boundary disputes, and elections held for purposes other than choosing government officials (for example, bond elections). Courts must hear appeals in panels of at least three justices. A majority vote of a panel of justices is required for a decision.

Court of Criminal Appeals Texas and Oklahoma are the only states in the Union that have bifurcated (divided) court systems for dealing with criminal and civil appeals. In Texas, the highest tribunal with criminal jurisdiction is the Court of Criminal Appeals. This nine-judge court hears criminal appeals exclusively. Noncapital criminal cases are appealed from the 14 courts of appeals. Capital punishment cases are appealed directly to the

☆ **How Do We Compare . . .**
in Salaries of Highest Court Justices and Judges?

Annual Salaries of Highest Court Justices and Judges (in annual dollars as of 2003, rounded to the nearest $1,000)

Most Populous U.S. States	Chief Justice/ Judge	Associate Justice/ Judge	U.S. States Bordering Texas	Chief Justice/ Judge	Associate Justice/ Judge
California	$186,00	$170,000	Arkansas	$134,000	$123,000
Florida	$154,000	$154,000	Louisiana	$118,000	$113,000
New York	$156,000	$151,000	New Mexico	$ 98,000	$ 96,000
Texas	**$115,000**	**$113,000**	Oklahoma	$110,000	$107,000

Source: *Survey of Judicial Salaries: Setting Judge Salaries* 28, no. 1 (April 2003); **www.ncsconline.org**.

Court of Criminal Appeals from district courts. Texans continue to resist the creation of a unified judicial system, which would have a single appellate court of last resort for both criminal felony and complex civil cases.[5]

Members of the Court of Criminal Appeals, including one whom voters elect as presiding judge, are chosen in partisan elections on a statewide basis for six-year terms. Annual salaries of judges of the Court of Criminal Appeals were set at $113,000 through fiscal year 2005. The presiding judge receives $2,000 more because of additional administrative responsibilities. A comparison of salaries indicates that judges and justices of Texas's highest appellate courts are compensated at lower levels than their counterparts in other large states.

In 2000, Presiding Judge Sharon Keller became the first woman elected to this position on the Court of Criminal Appeals. As of mid-2004, four of the remaining eight judges were women. There are currently (2004) no Hispanics or African Americans on the Court of Criminal Appeals. All members of the court are Republicans.

Supreme Court   Officially titled the Supreme Court of Texas, the state's highest court with civil jurisdiction has nine members elected statewide on a partisan basis: one chief justice and eight justices. Annual salaries for the justices and the chief justice are the same as those for the judges and the presiding judge of the Court of Criminal Appeals.

No Democrats have served on the Texas Supreme Court since Justice Raul Gonzalez resigned in 1998. For the first time in its history, as of September 2004, two African Americans were serving on the court. Chief Justice Wallace Jefferson, the first African American to join this body, was appointed by Governor Rick Perry in 2001. Perry elevated him to the position of chief justice in 2004. Justice Dale Wainwright became the first African American ever to win election to the court in 2002. Although three Hispanics have served on the Texas Supreme Court throughout its history, there were none on the court as of mid-October 2004. At that same time, two members of the nine-member court were female.

U.S. Supreme Court Justice Sandra Day O'Connor (right) swears in (from left) Texas Supreme Court Justices Michael H. Schneider, Thomas R. Phillips, and Wallace B. Jefferson in January 2003. Phillips resigned in 2004 and Jefferson replaced him as chief justice. (Harry Cabluck/AP Wide World Photos)

Without criminal jurisdiction, this high court is supreme only in cases involving civil law. Because it has very limited original jurisdiction (for example, issuing writs and hearing cases involving denial of a place on an election ballot), nearly all of the court's work involves appeals of cases that it determines must be heard based on statutory provisions. Much of the Supreme Court's work involves handling applications for a writ of error, which can be requested by a party who argues that a court of appeals made a mistake on a question of law. If as many as four justices favor issuing a writ, the case is scheduled for argument in open court. Approximately 10 percent of cases appealed to the Texas Supreme Court are accepted.

In addition to hearing motions and applications and deciding cases, the Supreme Court performs other important functions. It is responsible for formulating the rules of civil procedure, which set out the manner in which civil cases are to be handled by the state's trial courts and the appellate courts. The Supreme Court also has the authority to transfer cases for the purpose of equalizing workloads (cases pending on the dockets) of courts of appeals. The chief justice can temporarily assign district judges outside their administrative judicial regions and assign retired appellate justices (with their consent) to temporary duty on courts of appeals. Early in each regular session of the Texas Legislature, the chief justice is required by law to deliver a "State of the Judiciary" message, either orally or in written form, to the legislature.

Disciplining and Removing Judges and Justices

Each year, a few of Texas's judges and justices commit acts that warrant discipline or removal. Traditionally, the most common method of dealing with erring judges was to vote them out of office at the end of a term. Situations involving the most serious judicial misconduct were handled through trial by jury for judges at all levels and by legislative address or impeachment for state court judges. Although all of these methods are still available, the State Commission on Judicial Conduct now plays the most important role in disciplining the state's judiciary. This 11-member commission is composed of 5 judges, each from a different-level court; 2 attorneys; and 4 nonattorney private citizens.

The commission considers cases in which a judge is accused of failure to follow rules adopted by the Texas Supreme Court, incompetence, inappropriate conduct, or violation of the Texas Code of Judicial Conduct. The goal of the Code of Judicial Conduct is to set ethical standards for judges that reinforce the public's confidence in the judicial system.

The State Commission on Judicial Conduct has several options for the manner in which it deals with judges who come before it, ranging from private reprimands to recommending removal of the judge (although actual removal can only be decided by a seven-judge tribunal appointed by the Texas Supreme Court). In addition, the commission oversees Amicus Curiae, an employee assistance program that locates service providers for judges suffering from substance abuse or mental or emotional disorders. In fiscal year 2003, the commission resolved in excess of 1,000 complaints. Disciplinary sanctions were issued in approximately 60 cases. Summaries of these sanctions are available on the commission's web site.

Lawyers

Both the Texas Supreme Court and the State Bar of Texas play a role in regulating legal practice in the state. The Supreme Court is involved with issues relating to the training and licensing of lawyers. Although accreditation of law schools is largely a responsibility of the American Bar Association, the Supreme Court appoints the eight-member Board of Law Examiners. That board supervises administration of the bar exam for individuals seeking to become licensed attorneys, and it certifies the names of successful applicants to the court. The State Bar of Texas oversees the state's lawyers.

State Bar of Texas To practice, a licensed attorney must be a member of the State Bar of Texas and pay dues for its support. Although the state bar is well known for its high-pressure lobbying activities, the organization promotes high standards of ethical conduct for Texas lawyers and conducts an extensive program of continuing legal education. As an administrative agency of the state, it is authorized to discipline, suspend, and disbar attorneys. One of the primary purposes of the state bar is to maintain public confidence in the integrity of lawyers in the Lone Star State.

There are now (2004) about 70,000 attorneys in Texas, making 1 attorney available for every 339 residents. Although nearly 50 percent of Texans are Hispanics and African Americans, they represent only 11 percent of licensed attorneys. Almost 30 percent of the state's attorneys are female.

Legal Services for the Poor   Under the Bill of Rights in the Texas Constitution and the Sixth Amendment to the U.S. Constitution, individuals accused of a crime are entitled to be represented by an attorney. Courts must appoint attorneys for criminal defendants who establish that they are indigent (too poor to hire a lawyer). These attorneys are paid by the county. No assistance is available for cases brought by prisoners that challenge the constitutionality of their incarceration (habeas corpus proceedings), unless the defendant has been sentenced to death. Approximately twenty death row inmates in the Lone Star State, however, have benefited from the American Bar Association's Death Row Penalty Representation Project, which recruits large civil law firms to handle appeals for those sentenced to capital punishment.[6]

If these same individuals were trying to get legal help for a civil matter, little or no free assistance would be available. Individuals who have suffered bodily injury may be able to hire an attorney on a **contingency fee** basis in which the lawyer is paid from any money recovered in a lawsuit. Representation in legal matters such as divorce, child custody, or contract disputes, however, require the client to make direct payment to the attorney at the time services are performed. Even though there is an abundance of lawyers, 60 percent of Texans believe they cannot afford to hire one. Texas ranks last among the 10 largest states in per capita spending for legal aid in civil matters.

Self-Help Legal Software   One response to rising legal costs has been the publication of self-help books and software on a number of legal topics. It is possible to purchase interactive software, such as Quicken Family Lawyer, and legal self-help books, such as those published by Nolo Press, that will allow a person to write a will, obtain a divorce, or create a corporation. Legal documents that would cost hundreds, and sometimes thousands, of dollars if prepared by an attorney can be prepared at little or no cost by using self-help products.

Juries

A jury system enables citizens to participate directly in the administration of justice. Texas has two types of juries: grand juries and trial juries. The state's Bill of Rights guarantees that individuals may be charged with a felony only by grand jury indictment. It also guarantees that anyone charged with either a felony or a misdemeanor has the right to trial by jury. If requested by either party, jury trials are required in civil cases.

Grand Jury

A **grand jury** is composed of twelve citizens who may be chosen at random or selected by a judge from a list of fifteen to twenty county residents recommended by a judge-appointed grand jury commission. Members of a grand jury must have the qualifications of trial jurors and are paid like trial jurors (see the following "Trial Jury" section). As required of a trial juror, a grand jury member must not be under indictment for a felony or charged with a misdemeanor theft at the time of selection. The district judge appoints one juror to serve as foreman of the jury panel. A grand jury's life extends over the length of a district court's term, which varies from three to six months, although a district judge may extend a grand jury's term. During this period, grand juries have authority to inquire into all criminal actions but devote most of their time to felony matters.

The work of a grand jury is conducted in secrecy. Jurors and witnesses are sworn to keep secret all they hear in grand jury sessions. If, after investigation and deliberation (often lasting only a few minutes), at least nine grand jurors decide there is sufficient evidence to warrant a trial, an indictment is prepared with the aid of the prosecuting attorney. The indictment is a written statement accusing some person or persons of a particular crime (for example, burglary of a home). An indictment is referred to as a true bill; failure to indict constitutes a no bill. Some grand jury investigations are quite lengthy. In 2003 and 2004, for example, a series of Travis County (Austin) grand juries investigated use of corporate funds for campaign contributions to Republican candidates by the Texas Association of Business (TAB) and the Texans for a Republican Majority Political Action Committee (TRMPAC). This investigation resulted in several indictments in September 2004.

For misdemeanor prosecutions, grand jury indictments are authorized but not required. On the basis of a complaint, the district or county attorney may prepare an information, a document that formally charges the accused with a misdemeanor offense. The role of the grand jury is the same as for a felony—to decide on the sufficiency of any evidence.

Trial Jury

Although relatively few Texans ever serve on a grand jury, almost everyone can expect to be summoned from time to time for duty on a trial jury (**petit jury**). Official qualifications for jurors are not high, and many thousands of jury trials are held in the Lone Star State every year. To ensure that jurors are properly informed concerning their work, they are provided with brief printed instructions (in English and Spanish) that describe their duties and explain basic legal terms and trial procedures. In urban counties, these instructions are often shown as a video in English and other languages common to segments of the county's population, such as Spanish or Vietnamese.

Qualifications of Jurors   To be considered qualified, a Texas juror must be:

- A citizen of the United States and of the state of Texas
- 18 years of age or older
- Of sound mind
- Able to read and write (with no restriction on language), unless literate jurors are unavailable
- Neither convicted of a felony nor under indictment or other legal accusation of theft or of any felony

Qualified persons have a legal responsibility to serve when called, unless exempted or excused. Exempted from jury duty are individuals who:

- Are age 70 or older
- Have legal custody of a child or children under age 10
- Are enrolled in and attending a university, college, or secondary school
- Are the primary caregivers for invalids
- Are employed by the legislative branch of state government
- Have served as petit jurors within the preceding three years (only in counties with populations of more than 250,000)

Nevertheless, judges retain the prerogative to excuse others from jury duty in special circumstances. A person who is legally exempt from jury duty may avoid reporting to the court as summoned by filing a signed statement with the court clerk at any time before the scheduled date of appearance. In urban counties, prospective jurors can complete necessary forms on the Internet to claim an exemption.

Selection of Jurors   A **venire** (jury panel) is chosen by random selection from a list provided by the secretary of state. The list includes the county's registered voters, licensed drivers, and persons with identification cards issued by the Department of Public Safety. A trial jury is composed of six or twelve individuals: six in a justice of the peace court, municipal court, or county court; twelve in a district court. A jury panel generally includes more than the minimum number of jurors.

Attorneys are allowed to question jurors through a procedure called **voir dire** (which means "to speak the truth") to identify any potential jurors who cannot be fair and impartial. An attorney may challenge for cause any venire member suspected of bias. If the judge agrees, the prospective juror is excused from serving. Many individuals try to avoid jury duty by failing to appear (punishable as contempt for ignoring the court's order) or answering voir dire questions in a way that makes them appear biased.

An attorney challenges prospective jurors either by peremptory challenge (up to fifteen per side, depending on the type of case, without having to give a reason for excluding the venire members) or by challenge for cause (an unlimited number). Jurors may not be excluded on the basis of race or ethnicity. For a district court, a trial jury is made up of the first twelve venire members who are neither excused by the district judge nor challenged peremptorily by a party in the case. For lower courts, the first six venire members accepted form a jury.

When jurors are empanelled, a district judge may direct the selection of four alternates, and a county judge may require the selection of two alternates. If for some reason a juror cannot finish a trial for either a civil or a criminal case, an alternate juror may be seated as a replacement. Even if no alternate has been selected and a juror cannot complete service, the Texas Court of Criminal Appeals has ruled that in criminal cases once a jury has been empanelled, it must proceed to trial and judgment with only 11 members.

Compensation of Jurors   Daily pay for venire members and jurors varies from county to county. Each county can authorize payment at an amount not to exceed $50 per day, but most counties set payment for venire members at only $6 per day (the lowest in the nation) and pay for jurors at a mere $10 for each day of jury service. Employers are prohibited by law from discharging permanent employees because they have been summoned for jury duty or selected as jurors.

Judicial Procedures

Many Texas residents, as well as people from outside the state, appear in court as litigants or witnesses. As a litigant, for example, a person becomes a party to a civil case arising from an automobile accident or from a divorce or child custody matter. A person would become a party in a criminal case when accused of a crime such as theft. Witnesses may be summoned to testify in any type of case brought before the trial courts of Texas, but a court pays each witness only $10 per day for court attendance. In still another capacity, a citizen (even someone without legal training) may be elected to the office of county judge or justice of the peace. For these reasons, Texans should understand what happens in the courtrooms of their state.

Civil Justice System

As used in Texas, the term civil law generally refers to matters not covered by criminal law. The following are important subjects of civil law: **torts** (for example, unintended injury to another person or that person's automobile resulting from a traffic accident); contracts (for example, agreements to deliver property of a specified quality at a certain price); and domestic relations or family law (such as marriage, divorce, and custody of children by parents). Civil law disputes usually involve individuals or corporations. In criminal cases, an individual is prosecuted by the state. Nevertheless, a single incident may result in prosecution on a felony or misdemeanor charge and a civil suit for personal damages.

Limiting recovery amounts by injured parties, who claim they were damaged by some type of tort, is one of the most important changes in civil law in recent years. In a 2003 constitutional amendment election, Texas voters expressed their support for further limiting recoveries in medical malpractice suits when they chose to let the legislature cap punitive damages against doctors and other health care providers. A major justification for limiting recoveries in tort cases is that individuals and businesses must pay high liability insurance premiums for protection against the risk of lawsuit judgments. Three months after passage of the constitutional amendment capping recoveries, two of the five major insurance carriers in Texas requested rate increases. Only one announced that it intended to lower its premiums.

Civil Trial Procedure

Rules of civil procedure for all courts with civil jurisdiction are made by the Supreme Court of Texas. These rules, however, cannot conflict with any general law of the state. Rules of civil procedure are enacted unless they are rejected by the legislature.

Pretrial Actions   Civil cases normally begin when the **plaintiff** (injured party) files a petition, a written document containing the plaintiff's complaints against the **defendant** and the remedy that is sought—usually money damages. This petition is filed with the clerk of the court in which the lawsuit is contemplated, and the clerk issues a citation. The citation is delivered to the defendant, directing that person to answer the charges. If the defendant wants to contest the suit, he or she must file a written answer to the plaintiff's charges. The answer explains why the plaintiff is not entitled to the remedy sought and asks that the plaintiff be required to prove every charge made in the petition.

Before the judge sets a trial date (which may be many months or even years after the petition is filed), all interested parties should have had an opportunity to file their petitions, answers, or other pleas with the court. These written instruments constitute the pleadings in the case and form the basis of the trial. Either party has the option to have a jury determine the facts. If a jury is not demanded, the trial judge determines all facts and applies the law. When a jury determines the facts after receiving instructions from the judge, the judge's only duty is to apply the law to the jury's version of the facts.

Trial and Appeal of a Civil Case   As a trial begins, lawyers for each party make brief opening statements. The plaintiff's case is presented first. The defendant has the opportunity to contest the relevance or admissibility of all evidence introduced by the plaintiff and may cross-examine the plaintiff's witnesses. After the plaintiff's case has been presented, it is the defendant's turn to offer evidence and the testimony of witnesses. The plaintiff may challenge this evidence and testimony. The judge is the final authority as to what evidence and testimony may be introduced by all parties, although objections to the judge's rulings can be used as grounds for appeal.

After all parties have finished their presentations, the judge writes a charge to the jury, submits it to the parties for their approval, makes any necessary changes they suggest, and reads the charge to the jury. In the charge, the judge instructs the jury on the rules governing their deliberations and defines various terms. After the charge is read, attorneys make their appeals to the jury, at which point the jury retires to elect one of its members as the foreman and to deliberate.

The jury is given a series of questions to answer that will establish the facts of the case. These questions are called **special issues**. The judgment will be based on the jury's answers to these special issues. The jury will not be asked directly whether the plaintiff or the defendant should win. To decide a case, at least 10 jurors must agree on answers to all of the special issues in a district court, and 5 must agree in a county court or JP court. If the required number of jurors cannot reach agreement, the foreman reports a hung jury. If the judge agrees, the jury is discharged; otherwise jurors continue to deliberate. Either party may then request a new trial, which will be scheduled; unless the case is dismissed.

A jury's decision is known as a **verdict**. On the basis of a verdict, the judge prepares a written opinion, known as the **judgment** or decree of the court. Either party may then file a motion for a new trial based on the reason or reasons the party believes the trial was not fair. If the judge agrees, a new trial will be ordered; if not, the case may be appealed to a higher court. In each appeal, a complete written record of the trial is sent to the appellate court. The usual route of appeals is from a county or district court to a court of appeals and then, in some instances, to the Supreme Court of Texas.

Criminal Justice System

The State of Texas has identified more than 1,900 crimes that are classified as felonies. Less serious offenses are classified as misdemeanors. Features of the Texas Penal Code include **graded penalties** for noncapital offenses and harsher penalties for repeat offenders. Also provided is a two-step procedure for establishing whether a crime punishable by death (a **capital felony**) has been committed and, if so, whether a death sentence should be ordered.

Graded Penalties   There are first-, second-, and third-degree felonies, for which imprisonment and fines may be imposed in cases involving the most serious noncapital crimes. Some lesser offenses (especially those involving alcohol and drug abuse) are defined as state jail felonies (so-called fourth-degree felonies) and are punishable by fines and confinement in jails operated by the state. There are also three classes of misdemeanors (A, B, and C), for which county jail sentences and/or fines are levied. (See Table 9.2 for categories of noncapital offenses and ranges of penalties.) People who engage in organized criminal activity, repeat offenders, and those who commit hate crimes are punished as though they had committed the next higher degree of felony. This practice is called enhanced punishment.

Capital Punishment   Under the Texas Penal Code, a person commits murder if there is evidence of intent to kill or cause serious bodily harm to the victim. The presence of any of eight additional circumstances makes the crime a capital felony, for which the death penalty may be applied. In some instances the status of the victim changes the crime into a capital felony, such as:

- Being under the age of six
- Being a peace officer or firefighter
- Being a prison employee

Table 9.2 Selected Texas Noncapital Offenses, Penalties for First Offenders, and Courts Having Original Jurisdiction

Selected Offenses	Offense Category	Punishment	Court
Murder Theft of property valued at $200,000 or more	First-degree felony	Confinement for 5–99 years/life Maximum fine of $10,000	District court
Theft of property valued at $100,000 or more but less than $200,000 Aggravated assault, including a spouse	Second-degree felony	Confinement for 2–20 years Maximum fine of $10,000	District court
Theft of property valued at $20,000 or more but less than $100,000 Unlawfully taking a weapon to school	Third-degree felony	Confinement for 2–10 years Maximum fine of $10,000	District court
Theft of property valued at $15,000 or more but less than $20,000 Illegal recruitment of an athlete if the value of any benefits are more than $1,500 but less than $20,000	State jail felony	Confinement for 180 days–2 years Maximum fine of $10,000	District court
Theft of property valued at $500 or more but less than $1,500 Manufacture, sale, or possession of a counterfeit disabled parking placard	Class A misdemeanor	Confinement for 1 year Maximum fine of $4,000	Constitutional county court and county court-at-law
Theft of property valued at $20 or more but less than $500 Possession of four ounces or less of marijuana Sending sexually oriented unsolicited electronic mail	Class B misdemeanor	Confinement for 180 days Maximum fine of $2,000	Constitutional county court and county court-at-law
Theft of property valued at less than $20 Advertising, preparing, or selling term papers and reports used by others Using false identification to attempt to purchase an alcoholic beverage	Class C misdemeanor	No confinement Maximum fine of $500	Justice of the peace court and municipal court (if offense committed within city limits)

In other situations, additional circumstances related to the crime or the murderer change the status of the offense, such as:

- Occurring while another felony (for example, robbery or a terrorist threat) is being committed
- Receiving payment or the promise of payment for committing the murder
- Occurring during a prison escape
- Murdering more than one individual (including an unborn child)
- Murdering another inmate while in prison if the murderer was originally convicted of murder or certain other crimes

After a jury has found a defendant guilty of a capital offense, it must answer two questions:

1. Is there a probability that the defendant will commit criminal acts of violence that would constitute a continuing threat to society?
2. Is there mitigating evidence in the defendant's background, such as child abuse or mental retardation, that warrants a sentence of life imprisonment rather than death?

The jury must unanimously answer yes to the first question and no to the second question to impose the death penalty. In determining punishment, jurors may also consider impact evidence concerning suffering (physical, emotional, and financial) experienced by relatives of the murdered person. In the event the jury cannot reach a unanimous decision to assess the death penalty, the convicted felon receives life imprisonment. Anyone receiving a life sentence for a capital felony must be imprisoned for a minimum of 40 calendar years, without credit for good conduct, before becoming eligible for release on parole. An affirmative vote of two-thirds of the seven-member Board of Pardons and Paroles is required for granting such release.

If the death penalty is assessed, the prisoner has an automatic right of appeal directly to the Texas Court of Criminal Appeals, the highest state court to hear criminal matters. In this proceeding, the Court of Criminal Appeals reviews the trial record to determine whether any errors occurred. Fewer than 15 percent of convictions are overturned on appeal. Overturning a conviction does not mean that charges are dismissed. Rather, a new trial is usually scheduled, and the defendant is retried. In a separate proceeding, a convicted capital felon may also file a writ of habeas corpus to challenge the constitutionality of a conviction.

Prisoners who receive the death penalty cost the county and state taxpayers about $2.3 million on average for trial and appeal. Imprisonment for forty years in a single cell, on the other hand, would cost about one-third of this amount. Despite the economic cost, the death penalty continues to be assessed.

For nearly a century, death by hanging was the means of capital punishment in Texas. Then, between 1924 and 1964, a total of 361 persons were put to death in "Old Sparky," the state's electric chair, now on display in a

POINT *COUNTERPOINT*

Should Texas Eliminate the Death Penalty?

THE ISSUE

The federal government and 38 states, including Texas, impose the death penalty for specified crimes. Throughout the nation in 2004 there were approximately 3,500 men and women on death rows awaiting execution. In mid-2004, Texas had more than 450 inmates on death row (8 of whom were women). The Lone Star State leads the nation in the number of convicted felons executed since 1982 (approximately 320 through mid-2004) and is second only to California in the number on death row.

Concern about geographic and racial bias in the imposition of the death penalty has caused elected officials and organizations to take action. Governors in Illinois and Maryland have stopped executions in those states. Groups as diverse as the American Bar Association, the largest national organization of attorneys, and the American Civil Liberties Union, a group that challenges laws they believe violate the U.S. Constitution's Bill of Rights, support a moratorium on death penalty executions. This form of punishment remains highly controversial.[7]

Arguments For the Death Penalty

1. *Crime.* Those who commit heinous crimes deserve the death sentence.
2. *Use.* According to former Oklahoma Governor Frank Keating, only one-twelfth of 1 percent of those who commit murder have been executed.
3. *Innocence.* Convicted capital felons are protected by many procedural rights and appeals to assure innocent people are not put to death.
4. *Sentence.* Convicted capital felons are imprisoned for many years before they are put to death. Some inmates spend twenty years or more on death row awaiting execution.

> "Once [the] standard [proof beyond a reasonable doubt] is established in my own mind—and this is not easy, because you're dealing with another human being—if that standard is applied, I with no hesitation can deny clemency, because I believe if we love and elevate human life—that means innocent human life—for those who would intentionally, with malice, with violence, take another human being's life, that person has forfeited the right to live."
>
> —Governor Frank Keating (Oklahoma)

Arguments Against the Death Penalty

1. *Crime.* If society condemns murder, should government be in the business of executing its citizens?
2. *Use.* Although the death penalty may be used sparingly, it is also used more often if the victim is white, than if the victim is any other race. There are geographic disparities in the way it is applied, with some areas in the same state more likely to sentence a murderer to death than others.

Continued on next page

3. *Innocence*. Innocent people have received the death penalty. In the 30-year period from 1973 to 2003, according to a report by the American Civil Liberties Union, 112 death row inmates were found innocent and released from prison. Further, those sentenced to death row, especially the indigent, often did not have high-quality legal representation.
4. *Sentence*. Life without parole is a possible sentencing option for those convicted of homicide. It is costly to conduct capital trials. If life without parole were available, counties could save money in conducting murder trials.

> "Most people support the death penalty out of a deep desire for justice, believing that it is fairly applied with adequate opportunity for the protections afforded by due process of the law. In reality, the punishment is not reserved for the worst of the worst. Most often those with the worst lawyers and the worst luck get the death penalty. Class and race often stack the deck against defendants and victims."
>
> —Diann Rust-Tierney, Director of the ACLU Capital Punishment Project in *Dead-End: A No-Nonsense Resource on Capital Punishment* 1, Issue 1 (2003): 2.

museum in Huntsville. Subsequently, because of federal court rulings, no executions occurred in Texas until December 1982, when the first condemned murderer to receive an intravenous lethal injection was put to death.

Criminal Trial Procedure

Rules of criminal procedure are made by the legislature. The Texas Code of Criminal Procedure is written to comply with U.S. Supreme Court rulings regarding confessions, arrests, searches, and seizures. Additional rules of procedure have been adopted to promote fairness and efficiency in handling criminal cases.

Pretrial Actions Probably millions of illegal acts are committed daily in Texas. For example, many people drive faster than official speed limits allow or drive while under the influence of alcohol. After an arrest is made, but before questioning, a suspect must be informed of the right to remain silent, of the possibility that any statement may be used as evidence by the state, and of the right to consult with counsel (a lawyer). When a prosecuting attorney files charges, a suspect must be taken before a judicial officer (usually a justice of the peace) who names the offense or offenses charged and provides information concerning the suspect's legal rights. A person who is charged with a noncapital offense may be released on personal recognizance (promising to report for trial at a later date), released on bail by posting personal money or money provided for a charge by a bail bond service, or denied bail and jailed.

People who cannot afford to hire a lawyer must be provided with the services of an attorney in any felony or misdemeanor case in which conviction may result in a prison or jail sentence. Research from Harris County indicates that those with appointed attorneys are twice as likely to serve time in jail or prison as defendants who hire attorneys. The Texas Fair Defense Act establishes minimum attorney qualifications and standards for the appointment of counsel for indigent defendants charged with capital crimes. As of late 2003, of the thirty-three counties in which the death penalty is assessed most frequently, only two complied with the law. The "snowman-attorney" in the cartoon on page 344 represents what some believe is the quality of indigent legal representation in the Lone Star State.[8]

Under Texas law, the right to trial by jury is guaranteed in all criminal cases. Except in a capital felony case in which the district attorney is seeking the death penalty, however, defendants may waive jury trial (if the prosecuting attorney agrees) regardless of the plea—guilty, not guilty, or nolo contendere (no contest). To expedite procedures, prosecuting and defense attorneys may engage in plea bargaining, in which the accused pleads guilty in return for a promise that the prosecutor will seek a lighter sentence or will recommend community supervision. Usually, a judge will accept a plea bargain. If the defendant waives a trial by jury and is found guilty by a judge, that judge also determines the form and amount of punishment.

Trial of a Criminal Case   After the trial jury has been selected, the prosecuting attorney reads an indictment or an information. The jury is thus informed of the basic allegations of the state's case. The defendant then enters a plea.

As plaintiff, the state begins by calling its witnesses and introducing any evidence supporting the information or the indictment. The defense may challenge the truth or relevance of evidence presented and is allowed to cross-examine all witnesses. Next, the defense may present its case, calling witnesses and submitting evidence that, in turn, is subject to attack by the prosecution. After all evidence and testimony have been presented, the judge charges the jury, explaining the law applicable to the case. Both prosecuting and defense attorneys are then given an opportunity to address final arguments to the jury before it retires to reach a verdict.

Verdict, Sentence, and Appeal   A unanimous decision is required for the jury to reach a verdict of guilty or not guilty. If jurors are hopelessly split and the result is a hung jury, the judge declares a mistrial and discharges the jurors. If requested by the prosecuting attorney, the judge orders a new trial with another jury.

When a jury brings a verdict before a court, the judge may choose to disregard it and order a new trial on grounds that the jury has failed to arrive at

SARGENT © *Austin American-Statesman*. Reprinted with permission of Universal Press Syndicate.

a verdict that achieves substantial justice. In a jury trial, the jury may fix the sentence if the convicted person so requests; otherwise, the judge determines the sentence. A separate hearing on the penalty is held, at which time the person's prior criminal and/or juvenile record, general reputation, and other relevant factors may be introduced, such as facts concerning the convicted person's background and lifestyle as determined by a presentence investigation.

A convicted defendant has the right to appeal on grounds that an error in trial procedure occurred. All appeals (except for capital punishment cases) are heard first by the court of appeals in the district in which the trial was held, and ultimately by the Texas Court of Criminal Appeals.

Correction and Rehabilitation

Confinement in a prison or jail is designed to punish lawbreakers, deter others from committing similar crimes, and isolate offenders from society, thus protecting the lives and property of citizens who might otherwise become victims of criminals. Ideally, while serving a sentence behind bars, a lawbreaker will be rehabilitated and, after release, will obey all laws, find employment, and make positive contributions to society. In practice, approximately 25 percent of convicted criminals violate the conditions of

How Do We Compare . . . in Prison Population?

Prisoners Under the Jurisdiction of State Correctional Authorities (as of June 2002)

Most Populous U.S. States	Number of Prisoners	U.S. States Bordering Texas	Number of Prisoners
California	160,329	Arkansas	12,999
Florida	75,204	Louisiana	35,736
New York	67,065	New Mexico	5,772
Texas	151,782[a]	Oklahoma	23,385

[a]Includes inmates ready for transfer but still in local jails

Source: Paige M. Harrison and Allen J. Beck, Ph.D., *Bureau of Justice Statistics Bulletin: Prisoners in 2002* (Washington, D.C.: U.S. Department of Justice, July 2003, rev. 27 August 2003), **www.ojp.usdoj.gov**.

their release or commit other crimes after being released, for which they are re-sentenced to prison.

The number of Texans who are either imprisoned or supervised by local and state criminal justice authorities is larger than in any other state. In 2002 (the most recent year for which information is available), more than 735,000 Texans were either incarcerated, on parole, or under community supervision (formerly known as probation). In response to high crime rates in the early 1990s, the Texas Legislature lengthened prison sentences. Over the past ten years, the state's incarceration rate has grown by almost 140 percent, compared with an average national increase of approximately 50 percent.

The Texas Department of Criminal Justice

The principal criminal justice agencies of the state are organized within the Texas Department of Criminal Justice (TDCJ). This department is headed by the nonsalaried Texas Board of Criminal Justice, composed of nine members appointed by the governor (with advice and consent of the Texas Senate) for overlapping six-year terms, including one member selected as chair by the governor. The board employs a full-time executive director, who hires directors of the department's divisions. Each division director is responsible for hiring division personnel. About 42,000 Texans were employed by TDCJ in 2002 (the most recent year for which official figures are available). These employees are responsible for a prison population that fluctuates between 140,000 and 150,000 inmates.

The Correctional Institutions Division supervises the operation and management of state prisons, state jails, and other specialized facilities. Older prison units are located largely in East Texas, but recent construction programs have established several new prison units throughout Texas. State jail facilities, located across the state, are designed for nonviolent offenders. Private contractors operate seven prisons and five state jails. Figure 9.2 shows the location of prison and state jail facilities in Texas.

Figure 9.2   Facilities of the Texas Department of Criminal Justice, August 2002

Source: Texas Department of Criminal Justice

   Two agencies are responsible for convicted criminals who serve all or a part of their sentences in the community. The Community Justice Assistance Division establishes minimum standards for county programs involving community supervision and community corrections facilities (such as a boot camp or a restitution center). The Parole Division manages Texas's statewide parole and mandatory supervision system for convicted felons. The seven-member Board of Pardons and Paroles recommends acts of clemency (such as pardons) to the governor and grants or revokes paroles.

State Institutions of Corrections for Adults

Adult offenders who are sentenced to confinement on misdemeanor convictions are housed in a county jail or another type of community corrections facility. After being sentenced to confinement following a felony conviction,

An inmate student receives assistance from his teacher in a Windham Independent School District classroom. (Photo from Windham School: A National Leader in Correctional Education, Schools in the Texas Department of Criminal Justice. Photo courtesy Windham School District, Huntsville, TX)

an adult is supposed to be incarcerated in a state prison unit or state jail within forty-five days. When Texas prisons become overcrowded, they are unable to accept convicted felons in a timely manner. This has sometimes resulted in overcrowding in county jails.

The Prison   Correcting or modifying the behavior of convicted felons is a goal of TDCJ's Correctional Institutions Division. Training and instructional programs are used to rehabilitate inmates and equip them with a means for self-support after release. Discipline and education are the primary means of combating **recidivism** (criminal behavior resulting in reimprisonment after release). Every prisoner must be given a job but may elect not to work. The work these prisoners perform saves the state money and, in some instances, generates revenue for the state. Prisoners repair engines, perform all types of agricultural labor, and even make the wooden gavels used by the presiding officers of the Texas House of Representatives and Senate. Over half of Texas prisoners are enrolled in vocational and academic classes offered through the prison system's Windham Independent School District. College-level courses are also available. Approximately 70 percent of the prisoners have less than a high school education, one-third are functionally illiterate, and approximately 7 percent are classified as mentally retarded, having scored less than 70 on an IQ test. (Only 3 percent of the general population tests as being mentally retarded.) According to estimates by TDCJ officials, between 85 and 90 percent of prisoners committed crimes while under the influence of narcotics, were drug users, or were convicted of drug-trafficking crimes.

Prison Problems   During the 1980s, much controversy and litigation surrounded the Texas prison system. U.S. district court judge William Wayne Justice's ruling in *Ruiz* v. *Estelle* (1980) established the framework for a complete reorganization and expansion of the Texas penal system. For more than two decades, all or part of Texas's prison system remained under Judge Justice's supervision. State authorities regained full control in 2002.

At the beginning of the twenty-first century, Texas prisons face new challenges. An aging prison population adds to the cost of incarceration because of extra health care expenses. In a post-11 September, 2001, world, the state's correctional officers are engaged in the war on terrorism. Prison officials monitor inmate behavior and correspondence (especially letters written in Arabic, Farsi, and other Middle Eastern languages) in an effort to identify any attempts to recruit prisoners for terrorist groups or activities. Several gangs exist within the prison system. Many gang members and violent inmates are held in administrative segregation cells. Here, they have little or no contact with anyone other than corrections officers and primarily live in isolation. There is increased concern about how these individuals will integrate into society after their release. Despite segregation of these offenders, prison security remains an issue for both inmates and correctional officers. The federal Safe Prisons Program requires that prisoners who have become victims must be placed in protective custody within the prison system to avoid further abuse. There have been several successful escapes and frequent physical attacks on guards and other prison personnel. Low pay and difficult working conditions result in a high turnover rate of approximately 20 percent annually for correctional officers.

State Felony Jails   The Texas Penal Code provides for a system of state jails to house people convicted of state jail felonies. State jails are rehabilitation-oriented. Allowing judges to sentence offenders to "up-front" time (a period of incarceration preceding community supervision), the law also provides for substance abuse treatment and other support programs. Funding for treatment programs was substantially reduced in 2003.

Local Government Jails

Unlike the state felony jails, which are funded through appropriations made by the Texas Legislature, county and city jails are financed largely by county and municipal governments, respectively. Like penal institutions of the TDCJ, however, local government jails are used to control lawbreakers by placing them behind bars. These facilities too must deal with complaints of overcrowding and unsafe conditions.

County Jails   All but seventeen Texas counties maintain a jail. Eighteen counties have contracted with commercial firms to provide "privatized" jails, but most counties maintain public jails operated under the direction of the county sheriff. These penal institutions were originally established to detain persons awaiting trial (if not released on bail) and to hold individuals serving sentences for misdemeanor offenses. Jail facilities vary in quality and usually do not offer rehabilitation programs.

The Texas Commission on Jail Standards is responsible for establishing minimum standards for county jails, requiring an annual jail report from each county sheriff, reviewing jail reports, and arranging for inspection of jails. The commission determines appropriate population and staffing levels, and issues remedial orders to enforce its standards. In the case of an ongoing failure to comply with commission rules, a jail may be closed, or the commission, represented by the attorney general, may take court action against the county.

Municipal Jails   There are more than 300 municipal jails in the state. Some are used primarily as drunk tanks in which to detain people for a few hours after they have been arrested for public intoxication. In large cities these facilities often house hundreds of inmates who have been arrested for a variety of offenses ranging from Class C misdemeanors to capital murder. Those charged with more serious crimes are usually held temporarily until they can be transferred to a more secure county jail. The quality of municipal jail facilities varies greatly. A city jail is not subject to regulation by the Texas Commission on Jail Standards, unless it is managed by a private vendor or houses out-of-state prisoners.

Private Prisons

Both state and local governments have dealt with their prison crises by contracting with private companies to construct and operate prisons and prerelease programs. Texas now has more privately operated facilities than any other state. Those private prison units that house convicted Texas felons are under the supervision of the Correctional Institutions Division of the TDCJ. The Texas Commission on Jail Standards supervises privatized county and municipal units. Operators of private facilities must reimburse the state if state assistance is required to deal with an emergency, such as catching an escaped inmate or quelling a riot.

Supervision of Released Offenders

Although Texas prisons and jails are usually successful in isolating lawbreakers, these institutions have left much to be desired in the area of rehabilitation. Confinement is expensive for taxpayers and often produces embittered criminals rather than rehabilitated, law-abiding citizens. Thus, criminal justice reform measures in recent years have emphasized supervision of released offenders and effective rehabilitation.

Community Supervision   In cases involving adult first-time offenders convicted of misdemeanors and lesser felonies, jail and prison sentences are commonly commuted to community supervision, formerly termed adult probation. These convicted persons are not confined if they fulfill certain court-imposed conditions.

Parole Prisoners who have been incarcerated for some portion of their sentence may be eligible for parole. Felons who commit serious, violent crimes, such as rape or murder, must serve from 30 to 40 years of "flat time" (without the possibility of having prison time reduced for good behavior). Other offenders may apply for parole after serving one-fourth of a sentence or 15 years, whichever is the lesser (minus good-time credit, time off for good behavior). Prisoners who file two or more frivolous lawsuits against the state in a year, as determined by a court, can lose up to six months of good-time credit, thus lengthening the period until they are eligible for parole.

Application for parole is made to the Board of Pardons and Paroles. This board is composed of seven full-time salaried members appointed for six-year terms by the governor with advice and consent of the Senate. The Board's presiding officer employs and supervises eleven commissioners. A three-member panel comprised of parole board members and commissioners reviews applications and recommends granting or denying parole for felons who are imprisoned or in jail.

Granting and revoking parole are the major methods for controlling population in the state prison system. As parole approval rates decline, the prison population increases. When approval rates increase, the prison population is more likely to stabilize. A comparison of costs of imprisonment and other alternatives computed in 2002, the most recent year in which such calculations were made, is shown in Table 9.3.

Rehabilitation As prison sentences in Texas lengthened, emphasis shifted to providing rehabilitation programs for prisoners within two years of exiting the system. One such effort is Prison Fellowship Ministries' InnerChange

Table 9.3 Inmate Cost per Diem in Texas Criminal Justice Programs (FY2002)

Criminal Justice Program	Inmate Cost per Diem
Incarceration (TDCJ systemwide)	$44.01
Incarceration (death row—male)	$60.32
Incarceration (death row—female)	$131.82
Incarceration (state jail)	$37.35
Substance abuse felony punishment program	$52.25
Parole supervision (regular)	$3.07
Halfway house (state cost only)	$30.61
Intermediate sanction facilities (for parole violators)	$32.42
Community supervision	$2.13
Substance abuse treatment facilities (state cost only)	$67.56

Source: Texas Criminal Justice Policy Council. (Note: More current information is not available because the Council was eliminated in 2003 when Governor Rick Perry vetoed its funding.)

Freedom Initiative program. Prisoners voluntarily enroll in this intensive, Christian-oriented prerelease project. Provided free to the prison system, the program is an example of **charitable choice**, a movement that encourages collaboration between governmental agencies and religious groups to solve social problems. Whether such programs violate the establishment of religion clause of the First Amendment has not been determined.

Reentry Issues Completing a prison sentence does not end punishment for many felons. Although the state restores the right to vote to convicted felons once they have completed their sentences, there are many barriers to successful reentry to society. A felony conviction is grounds for divorce. Sex offenders must register and have this information made public for the rest of their lives. Those convicted of drug-related offenses cannot receive food stamp assistance. Ex-prisoners can be denied public housing and jobs.[9] As tens of thousands of released inmates return to society each year, researchers and public officials express increasing concern about these barriers to reentry and their impact on recidivism rates.

Juvenile Justice

Texas's juvenile justice system clearly distinguishes between youthful pranks and violent, predatory behavior. Generally, young Texans who are at least 10 years of age but under 17 are treated as "delinquent children" when they commit acts that would be classified as felonies or misdemeanors if committed by adults. Children are designated as "status offenders" if they commit noncriminal acts such as running away from home, failing to attend school, or violating a curfew established by a city or county.

State and Local Agencies

Under Texas law, each county is required to have a juvenile probation board that designates one or more juvenile judges, appoints a chief juvenile probation officer, and makes policies that are carried out by a juvenile probation department. Overseeing these county departments is the Texas Juvenile Probation Commission (TJPC). Its nine members are appointed by the governor with the consent of the Senate. The TJPC allocates state funds to county juvenile boards, trains and certifies juvenile probation officers, and sets standards for local detention and probation facilities. Supervising the rehabilitation and training of delinquent youths is the responsibility of the Texas Youth Commission (TYC). The seven members of the TYC are appointed by the governor with Senate approval.

Procedures and Institutions

Although juvenile offenders are arrested by the same law enforcement officers who deal with adult criminals, they are detained in separate facilities.

Counseling and probation are the most widely used procedures for dealing with juvenile offenders. An increasing number of delinquent youths, however, are placed on probation in local boot camps and residential treatment centers or committed to facilities operated by the TYC. An arresting officer has the discretion to release a child or refer the case to a local juvenile probation department. Other referrals come from public schools, victims, and parents. More than 150,000 Texas youths enter the state's juvenile justice system each year.

Court Procedures   Trials in juvenile courts are termed adjudication hearings. Juvenile courts are civil rather than criminal courts; therefore, any appeal of a court's ruling will be made to the appropriate court of appeals. Ultimately a few cases are appealed to the Texas Supreme Court.

A Juvenile Determinate Sentencing Law covers about twenty serious offenses. This sentencing provision allows transfer to an adult prison when the juvenile reaches 18 for as long as 40 years for juveniles who commit offenses such as capital murder and aggravated sexual assault. In addition, some juveniles who commit violent offenses are ordered to stand trial as adults and their cases are transferred to a district court. Any incarceration is in the state's adult prison system.

Texas Youth Commission Facilities   Juveniles who violate terms of probation or are found delinquent for a serious criminal offense may be confined to TYC training schools and boot camps located across the state. Over the past five years, there have been increasing claims of abuse in these facilities. During the same time period, the percentage of mentally ill youth sent to TYC increased to almost 50 percent of the total population. The commission also operates halfway houses for juveniles who need minimum supervision. It contracts with privately operated, community-based residential programs that provide vocational training, drug treatment, General Equivalency Diploma (GED) preparation, and other services.

Problems and Reforms: Implications for Public Policy

Throughout the late twentieth century, Texas's criminal justice system experienced a series of crises resulting from an increase in violent crimes and stiffer sentences for criminals. The state's civil justice system dealt with similar pressures from litigants using courts to resolve their disputes. The legislature responded (often slowly) with authorizations for more courts and judges and alternative means to resolve lawsuits. The Texas Legislature, however, refused to change judicial selection procedures. While these nineteenth- and twentieth-century problems have not yet been fully addressed, the legislature must also deal with the twenty-first century issues of technology and changing demographics.

Coping with Crowded Dockets

Few people will dispute the adage "Justice delayed is justice denied." Yet one of the most common problems facing Texas's courts is that of court dockets swelling with cases awaiting trial. One solution to the problem of over-loaded dockets is to provide more judges. Thus, from session to session, the legislature has established a growing number of courts. Cases may be trans-ferred from an overworked court to another court with a lighter docket (that is, a short list of pending cases).

With ever-greater frequency, litigants are encouraged to use one of the alternative dispute resolution procedures and avoid courtroom trials. To reduce court workloads, speed the handling of civil disputes, and cut legal costs, each county is authorized to set up a system for **alternative dispute resolution (ADR)**. Two frequently used ADR procedures are mediation (in which an impartial mediator facilitates communication between the parties in a conference designed to allow them to resolve their dispute) and arbitra-tion (in which impartial arbiters hear both sides and make an award that is binding or nonbinding, depending on the parties' previous agreement).

Collaborative divorce is another method for resolving disputes outside the courtroom. In 2001, Texas became the first state to pass laws that codi-fied this practice. The couple and their attorneys resolve all disputes in a nonadversarial manner. The procedure saves money and time for the par-ties and frees up the state's courtrooms for the resolution of more con-tentious disputes.

Judicial Selection

Almost two decades ago, Chief Justice John Hill resigned from the Supreme Court of Texas to fight for reform of the state's judicial selection system. In 2004, Chief Justice Tom Phillips also criticized Texas's "high-dollar, partisan system" of selecting judges when he resigned from the same court.[10] Many Texans agree with the Chief Justices' principal criticisms of the state's judi-ciary: that judges are elected as candidates of political parties and the expensive election campaigns of judicial candidates are financed largely with contributions from lawyers who practice in their courts and special-interest groups representing business and industry.

Critics of partisan election of judges tend to favor a merit selection model such as those used in Missouri and most other states. The **Missouri Plan** features a nominating commission that recommends a panel of names to the governor whenever a judicial vacancy is to be filled. The appointee then serves for a year or so before the voters decide, on the basis of his or her record of judicial performance, whether to give the new judge a full term or allow the nominating commission and the governor to make another appointment on a similar trial basis. Others, such as former chief justice Phillips, favor an **appointment-retention system** for all courts of record, in which the governor appoints a judge and the voters determine whether to retain the appointee.

Efforts to change the way judges are selected in Texas have consistently failed in the legislature. Texas remains one of only four states in which all judges (except municipal court judges) are chosen in partisan elections and then reelected through the same procedure. The other three states are Alabama, Louisiana, and West Virginia.

Texas's only meaningful reform has been in the area of campaign contributions. Fundraising limits have been set for judicial candidates. The amount any individual or law firm can now donate to a judge's election campaign is restricted.

Technology

From Internet divorces to video cameras at stoplights, technology now touches every aspect of the civil and criminal justice systems. Evidence that was the subject of science fiction only a few years ago is now commonplace in Texas courtrooms. Another subject that has gained significant attention in recent years is DNA evidence.

In Texas, postconviction analysis may be available for some inmates who were tried and convicted prior to the development of DNA testing. It is required for cases in which DNA-test results could make a difference in establishing innocence. The use of biological evidence in criminal cases became increasingly important after the invention of DNA testing in the early 1980s by geneticist Alec Jeffreys.[11] Results of DNA tests are often more reliable than eyewitness testimony and circumstantial evidence. As of March 2004, the Innocence Project at New York's Cardozo Law School reported that more than 140 inmates were released across the nation after DNA analysis proved their innocence. Thirteen of those individuals were from Texas. (For the story of the attempted exoneration of one such individual, see this chapter's Selected Reading, "DNA Testing: Foolproof?") In 2003, complaints surfaced about the quality of DNA testing conducted by the Houston Police Department's crime lab. Several inmates were released after retesting verified that their DNA did not match crime scene DNA. When DNA evidence is available, juries appear more willing to convict defendants. Because of this high level of juror confidence, state law now requires all public crime labs to be accredited and DNA evidence to be held for retesting.

The state of Texas compensates individuals who were wrongfully incarcerated. Someone found innocent after being imprisoned is entitled to $25,000 for each year he or she was wrongly incarcerated up to a total of $500,000. Continued technological advances will allow even more sophisticated and accurate testing and the likely release of a greater number of innocent prisoners.

Racial and Ethnic Diversity

Changes in the state's demography have begun to affect its justice system. The underrepresentation of African Americans and Hispanics in elected and appointed leadership positions is matched by their overrepresentation in the criminal justice system. If many Texans believe the laws are unfair or unfairly applied, then the justice system is jeopardized. In this environment, if the race or ethnicity of those enforcing the law is consistently different from those against whom the law is enforced, the system has even less credibility. These concerns were expressed by the American Bar Association when that organization ratified the report, *Justice in Jeopardy*, quoted at the beginning of this chapter.

The Texas Criminal Justice Reform Coalition, the American Civil Liberties Union of Texas, NAACP of Texas, and Texas LULAC reached a similar conclusion when they commissioned research on traffic stops and searches.[12] The study found racial profiling present in approximately 85 percent of Texas law enforcement agencies in which officers reported stopping and searching African Americans and Hispanics at significantly higher rates than Anglos. Interestingly, in many urban jurisdictions, the search of Anglos was more likely to reveal incriminating evidence than any other group.

Racial overtones were present in a case arising in the Panhandle town of Tulia. Thirty-eight individuals, mostly African American, served sentences on drug charges based on the testimony of an undercover investigator who was later indicted for perjury. All but three of the defendants were pardoned by Governor Rick Perry after the Texas Legislature passed a law ordering their release from prison and the Texas Board of Pardons and Paroles unanimously recommended the pardons. Instances of racial and ethnic bias are the subject of growing concern as Texas has evolved into a state in which African Americans and Latinos represent a near majority population, and Texas moves toward becoming a majority Latino state.

Looking Ahead

The Texas legal system is indeed confusing. From deciding which court should hear a case, because of overlapping court jurisdiction, to identifying its presiding elected officials—the judges and justices of the courts—the system appears to be shrouded in mystery and anonymity. Often understood only by those who use the system on a daily basis—Texas lawyers—the decisions of criminal and civil court judges affect every Texan. It is therefore critical that citizens understand this complex system that governs their lives. Whether the justice system is viewed as fair and responsive to the state's residents or biased and closed to them depends in part on their knowledge of it. This understanding plus changing demographics, rising costs, and greater reliance on science and technology will not only influence the Lone Star State's justice system but also the way politics is practiced in Texas in the twenty-first century.

☆ **Chapter Summary** ☆

- Public confidence in the judicial system is critical to its effectiveness.
- State law in Texas includes both civil law and criminal law. Texas courts and judges apply and interpret statutes and the common law.
- Both constitutional and statutory laws have been used to create the state's court system. Courts may have original or appellate jurisdiction, or both. There are local, county, trial, and appellate courts. Judges and lawyers are subject to regulation and discipline.
- There are two types of juries: grand juries (which determine whether there is adequate cause to bring a defendant to trial in a criminal case) and petit juries (which determine the facts in criminal and civil cases).
- The civil justice system includes contract cases, tort cases, family law matters, and juvenile justice cases. Significant reforms have occurred in recent years in tort law, as the Texas Legislature has limited the amount of punitive damages in these cases.
- Criminal law regulates many types of behavior. Less severe crimes are classified as Class A, B, or C misdemeanors and result in fines or detention in a county jail. More severe crimes include state jail felonies; first-, second-, and third-degree felonies; and capital felonies.
- More than 735,000 Texans were under the supervision of a state judicial or correctional officer in 2002.
- The juvenile justice system is administered through the Texas Family Code. Youths between the ages of 10 and 17 are subject to its provisions. In recent years, more juveniles have been placed in detention facilities operated by the Texas Youth Commission.
- Issues that remain problematic for the Texas justice system are crowded court dockets and the popular, partisan election of judges. Technological and scientific advances have had a significant impact on all aspects of the law in the Lone Star State. Possible racial and ethnic bias is an issue in many areas of the justice system.

Key Terms

civil law	exclusive jurisdiction
criminal law	concurrent jurisdiction
misdemeanor	court of record
felony	small-claims court
jurisdiction	probate
original jurisdiction	contingency fee
appellate jurisdiction	grand jury

petit jury	graded penalties
venire	capital felony
voir dire	recidivism
tort	charitable choice
plaintiff	alternative dispute resolution
defendant	(ADR)
special issues	Missouri Plan
verdict	appointment-retention system
judgment	

 Discussion Questions

1. Is Texas's justice system fair?
2. What are the advantages and disadvantages of Texas's court system?
3. What can be done to make the legal system accessible to more Texans?
4. What are the advantages and disadvantages of the death penalty?
5. What are possible reforms to the method of selecting judges in Texas?

Internet Resources

Death Penalty Institute: **www.deathpenaltyinfo.org**
Justice Policy Institute: **www.justicepolicy.org**
State Bar of Texas: **www.texasbar.com**
State Commission on Judicial Conduct: **www.scjc.state.tx.us**
Texas Law Help: **www.texaslawhelp.org**
Texans for Public Justice: **www.tpj.org**
Texas Department of Criminal Justice: **www.tdcj.state.tx.us**
Texas Department of Public Safety: **www.txdps.state.tx.us**
Texas Judiciary Online: **www.courts.state.tx.us**
Texas Youth Commission: **www.tyc.state.tx.us**

Notes

1. American Bar Association, Commission on the 21st Century Judiciary, *Justice in Jeopardy: Report of the American Bar Association Commission on the 21st Century Judiciary* (2003), <www.manningproductions.com/ABA263/finalreport.pdf>, p. i.
2. Of special interest to young college and university students is lawyer L. Jean Wallace's *What Every 18-Year-Old Needs to Know About Texas Law,* rev. ed. (Austin: University of Texas Press, 1997). Three other easy-to-understand books that explain Texas law are Richard Alderman, *Know Your Rights: Answers to Texans' Everyday Legal Questions*, 6th ed. (Houston: Gulf Publishing, 2000); Charles Turner and Ralph Walton, *Texas Law*

in Layman's Language, 6th ed. (Houston: Lone Star Books, 2002); and David M. Horton and Ryan Kellus Turner, *Lone Star Justice* (Austin: Eakin Press, 1999).

3. Annual statistics and other information on the Texas judicial system are available from the Texas Judicial Council and the Office of Court Administration at <www.courts.state.tx.us>.

4. The State Bar of Texas has a how-to manual for prosecuting a claim in small-claims court (*How to Sue in Small Claims Court*), available on its web site at <www.texasbar.com>.

5. For an excellent discussion of the development and adoption of the constitutional amendment granting courts of civil appeals criminal appellate jurisdiction, see former chief justice Joe R. Greenhill, "The Constitutional Amendment Giving Criminal Jurisdiction to the Texas Courts of Civil Appeals and Recognizing the Inherent Power of the Texas Supreme Court," *Texas Tech Law Review* 33, no. 2 (2002): 377–404.

6. James Kimberly, "Large Civil Firms Offer Life to Inmates on Death Row." *Houston Chronicle,* 2 September 2003.

7. Governor Frank Keating, "'The Death Penalty: What's All the Debate About?' A Call for Reckoning: Religion & the Death Penalty," *Pew Charitable Trust* (2002) at <pewforum.org/deathpenalty>; Governor Marc Racicot, "'The Death Penalty in the 21st Century,' A Call for Reckoning: Religion & the Death Penalty," *Pew Charitable Trust* (2000) at <pewforum.org/deathpenalty>; American Civil Liberties Union, "Death Penalty," <www.aclu.org/DeathPenalty>; and John Blume, Theodore Eisenberg, and Martin T. Wells, "Explaining Death Row's Population and Racial Composition," *Journal of Empirical Legal Studies* 1, no. 1 (March 2004): 165–207.

8. Equal Justice Center and Texas Defense Center, *Texas Death Penalty Practices: Quality of Regional Standards and County Plans Governing Indigent Defense in Capital Cases,* 2nd ed., November 2003, <www.equaljusticecenter.org>, p. i.

9. Ronald Fraser, "In Texas, Felons Do the Time—and Then Some," *Houston Chronicle,* 5 January 2004.

10. Chief Justice Thomas R. Phillips spoke about problems he identified arising from our current process of selecting state judges in his 2003 State of the Judiciary address delivered to a joint session of the 78th Texas Legislature and printed in the *House Journal,* 4 March 2003, 461–467. Phillips raised similar issues when he announced his resignation from the Texas Supreme Court. See Clay Robison, "Texas' Chief Justice Resigning," *Houston Chronicle*, 30 April 2004.

11. Howard Safir and Peter Reinharz, "DNA Testing: The Next Big Crime-Busting Breakthrough," *City Journal* 10, no. 1 (Winter 2000): 49–57; <www.city-journal.org/html/issue10_1.html>.

12. Steward Research Group, "Racial Profiling: Texas Traffic Stops and Searches" (Austin: Texas Criminal Justice Reform Coalition, February 2004) at <www.protex.org/criminaljustice>.

SELECTED READING

★

DNA Testing: Foolproof?*

Vicki Mabrey

> *Josiah Sutton's rape conviction rested on two significant pieces of evidence: victim testimony and DNA. When a DNA retest established that the original test results were inaccurate, Sutton was released from prison after serving more than four and one–half years for a crime he did not commit. On May 14, 2004, Governor Rick Perry issued Sutton a full pardon "by reason of innocence." The inadequacies of the Houston Police Department Crime Lab were the subject of a hearing before the Senate Committee on Criminal Justice in October 2004.*

In 1998, on an October night, a woman was abducted at gunpoint by two men from the parking lot of her apartment complex in Houston. She was driven in her car to an isolated spot and raped by both men.

Five days later, she passed a group of men on the street, and identified two of them to police as her attackers. Josiah Sutton, 16, and a friend were arrested.

"I never knew and I kept getting questions, 'What am I here for? What am I here for,'" says Sutton.

In jail, Sutton and his friend found out they were accused of kidnapping and rape. They said they were innocent, and Sutton's mother, Carole Batie, thought it was a case of mistaken identity that would be quickly cleared up.

"When I first got the police report, the description of the suspects did not fit Josiah's description at all," says Batie, Josiah's mother.

Police were looking for a 5-foot-7-inch man who weighed 135 pounds.

"Josiah's never been thin since birth, so at the time, I had proof and identification, his ID, that stated he was 6 feet tall, and 200 pounds," says Batie. "So, I said, 'OK, they should look at that and let him go.'"

But police thought they had their man and the evidence to prove it—semen taken from the crime scene that they could compare with Josiah Sutton's DNA.

"I knew that the DNA would be able to clear me," says Sutton, who voluntarily submitted a DNA sample. "I knew that DNA was something people had a lot of faith in, that I was told, you know, gave the truth."

Sutton's blood sample was taken to the Houston police department's crime lab, where analysts compared it to semen samples taken from the victim and from the backseat of her car where the rape occurred.

---

*Reprinted by permission of CBS News from <www.cbsnews.com/stories/2003/05/27/60II/printable555723.shtml>.

For two months, Sutton waited in jail. He says he was confident that the test would free him. They cleared his friend, but his lawyer had different news for him.

"He said, 'I just got your tests back. They came up with a positive ID on you, as far as the testing.' And I told him I said, 'No, that's impossible.' My exact words were 'There's no way on God's green earth.' And he said, 'Well, I'm sorry, man, but that's what they came up with.'"

The lab's report was definitive. It said that DNA consistent with Sutton "was detected on the vaginal swab taken from the victim and on semen 'Sample Number 1' found on the backseat of the car." It also said Sutton was a one-in-694,000 match.

It was a slam dunk for the prosecution. The jury took less than two hours to find Sutton guilty. He was sentenced to 25 years.

"I still don't believe it to this day," says Sutton. "It couldn't be right."

Like a lot of prisoners, Sutton continued to proclaim his innocence and he set out to prove it. He studied DNA in the prison library, and three years after his arrest, he handwrote a motion requesting a DNA retest. But he wasn't getting anywhere until something unexpected happened.

Two reporters at KHOU-TV in Houston received a tip from defense attorneys that there were problems in the police department's crime lab.

Anna Werner and David Raziq decided to investigate. They dug up transcripts and lab reports from several cases and sent them to a group of experts, including University of California criminology professor William Thompson, who has reviewed DNA evidence from labs all over the country.

How did the Houston police crime lab stack up?

"It's the worst I've seen," says Thompson. "This doesn't meet the standard of a good junior high school science project."

"I found consistent distortions of the statistical certainty of the DNA evidence. I found instances that looked like fudging of results, to fit the prosecution's theory of the case. And I found a lab that consistently failed to use appropriate scientific procedures."

KHOU broadcast their story about the crime lab last year [2003], and Carol Batie, whose son had been in prison for four years by then, was lucky she caught the 10 o'clock news.

"I immediately jumped up and I started thanking God," says Batie, Josiah's mother. "I said, 'Here is our key, this is our answer.'"

Batie convinced KHOU to investigate her son's case. And Werner and Raziq sent his file to Thompson, who says the mistakes in the lab's original report practically jumped off the page.

"After reviewing the cases for a couple of hours, I became convinced that Mr. Sutton was very likely to be innocent," says Thompson. "This appears to be a pretty clear example of misrepresentation." He then examined the crime lab's original DNA test strips from 1998 and saw that the analyst had reached conclusions that were just plain wrong.

Remember the lab report that said Sutton's DNA could be found in "Sample 1" on the backseat of the car where the rape took place?

"This sample here is the sample from the backseat, which according to the lab report matched Sutton, or which included his profile. Josiah Sutton's sample here, he has two markers on this system that are labeled 1 and 2," says Thompson. "The sample from the backseat has two markers that are labeled 2 and 3. It does not appear to have the 1 marker, which Sutton has. And that would indicate that the sample in the backseat could not have come from Mr. Sutton."

And with only a little more work, Thompson concluded that Sutton's DNA wasn't found in any of the samples.

"You have to think something's wrong, when a college professor can look at lab records for a couple of hours, and figure out that somebody who's been sent to prison for 25 years is likely to be innocent," adds Thompson.

His findings convinced police to have the DNA from Sutton's case retested at an independent lab. That test was conclusive: Sutton's DNA was not found in the sample. That convinced a judge who ordered him released on bail. Today, he is waiting to see if he will be pardoned.

60 Minutes II wanted to ask Houston police chief C. O. Bradford how his crime lab could have made such a terrible mistake. Bradford wouldn't talk; neither would the head of the crime lab. All cited an ongoing investigation.

As a result, *60 Minutes II* asked forensic scientist Elizabeth Johnson, who monitored Sutton's retest for the defense, to explain how this could have happened.

"[Most people] think it's absolute and black and white and infallible," says Johnson. "But it is not. The testing has to be performed correctly in the first place and interpreted correctly in the second place."

Johnson, who used to be director of a different lab in Houston, showed *60 Minutes II* how evidence can be tampered with or contaminated. She doesn't think that happened in Sutton's case.

Her theory is that it had more to do with a problem that's found in many cities when crime labs are located in police departments and analysts can feel pressured to be "cops in lab coats"—trying to make the science match the police department's case.

"Too much of the time the police or the detectives come in and they submit evidence and they stand around and visit for a while and start telling chemists their version of what happened in the crime," says Johnson. "That's a dangerous situation."

Thompson's theory is similar, and it's just as tough on the Houston police department's crime lab.

"I think that the Houston Police Lab has personnel that are not particularly competent, who are working under situations where they have incentives to distort their findings in favor of the police and prosecution," says Thompson. "So I think that we have a situation where they may be making up for their incompetence with bias."

Amid all the accusations about the crime lab, the Houston Police Department ordered an independent audit of the lab's technical operations. That investigation resulted in a scathing 50-page report that chronicled a litany of problems—everything from inadequately trained staff, to possible contamination of evidence, to unnecessarily using up all the evidence from a crime—making any future retesting impossible. The lab was shut down immediately.

Another investigation is now under way to determine if there was any intentional fraud committed by laboratory personnel.

But the story doesn't end there. Hundreds of other convictions in Houston are now being called into question. Harris County district attorney Chuck Rosenthal and assistant DA Marie Munier must review 10 years' worth of cases their office has prosecuted using evidence from the lab.

"It seemed like someone from the Houston police department would have had enough inquisitiveness to have looked at that," says Rosenthal.

But why would the district attorney's office accept everything on blind faith— especially when the defense is bringing in expert witnesses to counter what they are saying?

"We're not equipped with enough scientific knowledge to question a lab like that," says Munier. "So we basically go on good faith. Unless there's something that slaps us in the face, which is what this has all done to say, 'Hey, look, there is a problem here.'"

So far, Munier says they've reviewed hundreds of cases, and nearly 200 have been pulled for retesting—including the cases of 17 men awaiting execution on the busiest death row in the country.

How likely is it that some of these other defendants are not guilty, just as Josiah Sutton was innocent?

It's too soon to say, believes Munier. "There's probably more, but we don't know which ones they are yet."

Of the nearly 200 cases being retested, 15 have been completed. So far, in addition to Josiah Sutton, one other test has uncovered inconsistencies and is still being reviewed.

Glossary

African American   A racial classification indicating African ancestry.

alien   A person who is neither a national nor a citizen of the country where he or she is living.

alternative dispute resolution (ADR)   Use of mediation, conciliation, or arbitration to resolve disputes among individuals without resorting to a regular court trial.

Anglo   A term commonly used in Texas to identify non-Latino white people.

appellate jurisdiction   The power of a court to review cases after they have been tried elsewhere.

appointive power   The authority to name a person to a government office. Most gubernatorial appointments require Senate approval by two-thirds of the members present.

appointment-retention system   A merit plan for judicial selection, whereby a court vacancy is filled by gubernatorial appointment for a trial period before retention for a term is determined by a "yes" or "no" popular vote in an uncontested election.

Asian American   A term used to identify people of Asian ancestry (e.g., Chinese, Japanese, Korean).

at-large election   Members of a policymaking body, such as some city councils, are elected on a citywide basis rather than from single-member districts.

at-large majority district   A district that elects two or more representatives.

attorney general   The constitutional official who is elected to head the Office of the Attorney General, which represents the state government in lawsuits and provides legal advice to state officials.

balanced budget   A budget condition whereby total revenues and expenditures are equal, so there is no deficit.

Basin and Range Province   An arid region in West Texas that includes the Davis Mountains, Big Bend National Park, and El Paso.

bicameral   Term describing a legislature with two houses or chambers (e.g., Texas's House of Representatives and Senate).

bill   A proposed law or statute.

Bill of Rights   Composed of 30 sections in Article l of the Texas Constitution, it guarantees protections for people and their property against arbitrary actions by state and local governments. Included among these rights are freedom of speech, press, religion, assembly, and petition. The Texas Bill of Rights is similar to the one found in the U.S. Constitution.

biotechnology   Involves development and production of medicines, vaccines, chemicals, and other products to benefit medical science, human health, and agricultural production.

block grant A congressional grant of money that allows the state considerable flexibility in spending for a program, such as providing welfare services.

bond A certificate of indebtedness issued by a borrower to a lender that constitutes a legal obligation to repay the principal of the loan plus accrued interest. In Texas, both state and local governments issue bonds under restrictions imposed by state law.

bonded debt Borrowings obtained through sale of revenue bonds and general obligation bonds.

budget A plan indicating how much revenue a government expects to collect during a period (usually one or two fiscal years) and how much spending is authorized for agencies and programs.

budgetary power The governor is supposed to submit a state budget to the legislature at the beginning of each regular session. When an appropriation bill is enacted by the legislature and certified by the comptroller of public accounts, the governor may veto the whole document or individual items.

budget execution The process whereby the governor and the Legislative Budget Board oversee (and in some instances modify) implementation of the spending plan authorized by the Texas Legislature.

business organization An economic interest group, such as a trade association (e.g., Texas Association of Builders) that lobbies for policies favoring Texas business.

Campaign Reform Act Enacted by the U.S. Congress and signed by President Bush in 2002, this law restricts donations of "soft money" and "hard money" for election campaigns, but it has been challenged in federal courts.

canvass To scrutinize the results of an election and then confirm and certify the vote tally for each candidate.

capital felony A crime punishable by death or life imprisonment.

caucus A once-used nominating process involving selection of candidates by an informal committee of party leaders; also, a group of legislators organized according to party, racial/ethnic, or ideological identity.

charitable choice A movement that encourages collaboration between governmental agencies and religious groups to solve social problems.

Children's Health Insurance Program (CHIP) A program that provides medical insurance for children of low-income families.

chubbing A practice whereby supporters of a bill engage in lengthy debate for the purpose of using time and thus prevent floor action on another bill that they oppose.

civil law The body of law concerning noncriminal matters, such as business contracts and personal injury.

closed primary A primary in which voters must declare their support for the party before they are permitted to participate in the selection of its candidates.

colonia A low-income settlement, typically located in South Texas and especially in counties bordering Mexico, that lacks running water, sewer lines, and other essentials.

combined statistical area A geographic entity consisting of two or more adjacent Core Based Statistical Areas.

commissioner of agriculture The elected official who heads Texas's Department of Agriculture, which promotes the sale of agricultural commodities and regulates pesticides, aquaculture, egg quality, weights and measures, and grain warehouses.

commissioner of insurance Appointed by the governor, the commissioner heads the Texas Department of Insurance, which is responsible for ensuring the industry's financial soundness and protecting policy holders.

commissioner of the General Land Office As head of Texas's General Land Office, this elected constitutional officer oversees the state's extensive land holdings and related mineral interests, especially oil and gas leasing for the benefit of the Permanent School Fund.

commissioners court A Texas county's policymaking body, with five members: the county judge, who presides, and four commissioners representing single-member precincts.

commission form A type of municipal government in which each elected commissioner is a member of the city's policymaking body, but also heads an administrative department (e.g., public safety with police and fire divisions).

commutation of sentence On the recommendation of the Board of Pardons and Paroles, the governor may commute (reduce) a sentence.

companion bill Filed in one house but identical or similar to a bill filed in the other chamber, a companion bill speeds passage because committee consideration may take place simultaneously in both houses.

comptroller of public accounts This elected constitutional officer is responsible for collecting taxes, keeping accounts, estimating revenue, and serving as treasurer for the state.

concurrent jurisdiction The authority of more than one court to try a case (e.g., a civil dispute involving more than $500 but less than $5,000 may be heard in either a justice of the peace court or a county court).

concurrent resolution A resolution adopted by House and Senate majorities and then approved by the governor (e.g., request for action by the U.S. Congress or authorization for someone to sue the state).

conditional pardon On recommendation of the Board of Pardons and Paroles, the governor may grant a conditional pardon. This act of clemency releases a convicted person from the consequences of his or her crime but does not restore all rights, as in the case of a full pardon.

conference committee A committee composed of representatives and senators who are appointed for the purpose of reaching agreement on a disputed bill and then recommending changes that will be acceptable to both chambers.

conservative Someone who advocates minimal intervention by government in social and economic matters and who gives a high priority to reducing taxes and curbing public spending.

constitutional amendment process Article XVII, Section 1, of the Texas Constitution stipulates that an amendment must be proposed by a two-thirds vote of members in each chamber of the legislature and approved by a simple majority of voters in a general or special election.

constitutional guarantee Included among the U.S. Constitution's guarantees to members of the Union are protection against invasion and domestic violence, territorial integrity, a republican form of government, representation by two senators and at least one representative in the U.S. Congress, and equitable participation in the constitutional amendment process.

constitutional history of Texas Since promulgation of the Constitution of Coahuila y Tejas within the Mexican federal system in 1827 and the Constitution of the Texas Republic in 1836, Texas has been governed under its state constitutions of 1845, 1861, 1866, 1869, and 1876.

constitutional revision Extensive or complete rewriting of a constitution.

Constitutional Revision Commission Composed of 37 members appointed by a six-member ex officio committee, the commission prepared a draft constitution that was submitted to the Texas Legislature in November 1973. When the legislature convened as a constitutional convention in 1974, this document served as the basis for further drafting and debate in an unsuccessful effort to produce a new state constitution.

constitutional revision convention A body of delegates who meet to make extensive changes in a constitution or to draft a new constitution.

contingency fee A lawyer's compensation paid from money recovered in a lawsuit.

corporate franchise tax This tax is levied on a Texas corporation's capital, surplus, and undivided profits or on annual income generated from business within the state if that amount is greater.

council-manager form A system of municipal government in which an elected city council hires a manager to coordinate budgetary matters and supervise administrative departments.

council of governments (COG) A regional planning body composed of governmental units (e.g., cities, counties, special districts); functions include review and comment on proposals by local governments for obtaining state and federal grants.

county Texas is divided into 254 counties that serve as an administrative arm of the state and provide important services at the local level, especially within rural areas.

county attorney An individual elected to represent the county in civil and criminal cases, unless a resident district attorney performs these functions.

county auditor A person appointed by the district judge or judges to check the financial books and records of other officials who handle county money.

county chair Elected on a countywide basis by party members in the primaries, this key party official heads the county executive committee.

county clerk An individual elected to perform clerical chores for the county court and commissioners court, keep public records, maintain vital statistics, and administer public elections, if the county does not have an administrator of elections.

county convention A party meeting of precinct delegates held on the second Saturday after the first primary and precinct conventions; it elects delegates and alternates to the state convention.

county executive committee Composed of a party's precinct chairs and the elected county chair, the county executive committee conducts primaries and makes arrangements for holding county conventions.

county judge An individual popularly elected to preside over the county commissioners court and, in many counties, to hear civil and criminal cases.

county sheriff An individual popularly elected as the county's chief law enforcement officer; the sheriff is also responsible for maintaining the county jail.

county surveyor A person who makes land surveys for the county, if requested, but some counties do not fill the office.

county tax appraisal district The district appraises all real estate and commercial property for taxation by units of local government within a county.

county tax assessor-collector This elected official no longer assesses the value of property for taxation but does collect taxes that include the state motor vehicle license fees and the county property tax.

county treasurer An elected official who receives and pays out county money as directed by the commissioners court.

court of record Has a court reporter to record testimony and proceedings.

criminal law The body of law concerning felony and misdemeanor offenses by individuals against other persons and property.

crossover voting A practice whereby a person participates in the primary of one party, then votes for one or more candidates of another party in the general election.

dealignment Citizens abandon allegiance to a political party and become independent voters.

death tax Texas collects an amount equal to that which would be paid to the U.S. government if the state did not levy this inheritance tax. The exemption level will rise from $1 million to $3.5 million between 2003 and 2009.

decentralized government Decentralization is achieved by dividing power between national and state governments and separating legislative, executive, and judicial branches at both levels.

defendant The person who is sued in a civil proceeding or prosecuted in a criminal proceeding.

delegated power Specific powers that are entrusted to the national government by Article 1, Section 8, of the U.S. Constitution (e.g., regulate interstate commerce, borrow money, and declare war).

deregulation The elimination of government restrictions to allow free-market competition to determine or limit the actions of individuals and corporations.

devolution Devolution exists when financial and administrative responsibilities of the federal government are shifted to state and local governments, especially in the area of social services.

direct primary A nominating system that allows voters to participate directly in the selection of candidates for public office.

district convention Held on the second Saturday after the first primary and precinct conventions in counties that have more than one state senatorial district. Participants elect delegates to the party's state convention.

district executive committee Composed of county chairs within a district that elects a state senator, representative, or district judge, this committee meets to fill a vacancy created by the death, resignation, or disqualification of a nominated candidate.

dual budgeting system The compilation of separate budgets by a legislative budget board and an executive budget office.

early voting Conducted at the county court house and selected polling places before the designated primary, special, or general election day.

economic development An area with dilapidated housing and poorly maintained streets indicates the need for economic development to create jobs and encourage commercial activities. Municipalities may create tax reinvestment zones as an incentive for businesses to participate in economic development by locating in blighted inner-city areas.

economic interest group Trade associations and labor unions are classified as economic interest groups, because they are organized to promote policies that will maximize profits and wages.

electioneering Campaigning actively on behalf of a candidate; the total efforts made to win an election.

election judge Appointed by the county commissioners court to administer an election in a voting precinct.

elections administrator Less than 12 percent of Texas counties employ a full-time elections administrator to supervise voter registration and voting.

exclusive jurisdiction Authority of only one court to hear a particular type of case.

executive commissioner of the Health and Human Services Commission Appointed by the governor with Senate approval, this executive commissioner appoints (with approval by the governor) commissioners to head the Commission's departments of Family and Protective Services, Aging and Disability Services, Assistive and Rehabilitative Services, and State Health Services.

executive order The governor issues executive orders to set policy within the executive branch and to create task forces, councils and other bodies.

federal grant-in-aid Money appropriated by the U.S. Congress to help states provide needed facilities and services.

felony jurisdiction A court's authority to hear criminal cases involving capital felonies and first-, second-, and third-class felonies.

filibustering A delaying tactic whereby a senator may speak, and thus hold the Senate floor, for as long as physical endurance permits.

fiscal management process Involves budgeting, collecting taxes and other revenue, investing public funds, purchasing, accounting, and auditing.

fiscal note The Legislative Budget Board's assessment of the economic impact of a bill or resolution.

fiscal policy Public policy that concerns taxing, government spending, public debt, and management of government money.

frontier experience Coping with danger, physical hardships, and economic challenges tested the endurance of nineteenth-century Texans and contributed to he development of individualism.

full faith and credit clause It means that most government actions of another state must be officially recognized by public officials in Texas.

full pardon On recommendation of the Board of Pardons and Paroles, the governor may grant a full pardon. This is an act of executive clemency that releases a convicted person from all consequences of a criminal act and restores rights enjoyed by others who have not been convicted of a crime.

general election Held in November of even-numbered years to elect county and state officials from among candidates nominated in primaries or (for small parties) in nominating conventions.

general law city Municipality with a charter prescribed by the legislature.

General Revenue Fund Less than half of state spending comes from the General Revenue Fund, which is available for general appropriations.

general sales tax At the rate of 6.25 percent of a sale, the general sales tax is the largest source of tax revenue for the state. It is applied largely to the sale price of tangible personal property and "the storage, use, or other consumption of tangible personal property purchased, leased, or rented." Food (but not restaurant meals) and prescription medicine are among items exempted from the general sales tax.

gerrymandering Drawing the boundaries of a district (e.g., state senatorial district) to include or exclude certain groups of voters and thus affect election outcomes.

ghost voting A prohibited practice whereby one representative presses the voting button of another House member who is absent.

government A public institution with authority to allocate values by formulating, adopting, and implementing public policies.

Governor's Office The Office of the Governor is the administrative organization through which the governor of Texas makes appointments, prepares a biennial budget recommendation, administers federal and state grants for crime prevention and law enforcement, and confers full and conditional pardons on recommendation of the Board of Pardons and Paroles.

graded penalty Depending on the nature of the crime, felonies are graded as 1st, 2nd, and 3rd degree; misdemeanors are graded as A, B, and C.

grandfather clause Exempted people from educational, property, or tax requirements for voting if they were qualified to vote before 1866 or 1867, or were descendants of such persons.

grand jury Composed of 12 persons with the qualifications of trial jurors, a grand jury serves from three to six months while it determines if there is sufficient evidence to indict persons accused of committing crimes.

grant-in-aid Money, goods, or services given by one government to another (e.g., federal grants-in-aid to states for financing public assistance programs).

Great Plains A large area in West Texas extending from Oklahoma to Mexico, the Great Plains is an extension of the Great High Plains of the United States.

group leadership Leaders of groups tend to have financial resources that permit them to contribute money and devote time to group affairs.

Gulf Coastal Plains Stretching from the Louisiana border to the Rio Grande, Texas's Gulf Coastal Plains area is an extension of the Gulf Coastal Plains of the United States.

hard money Campaign money contributed directly by individuals.

high technology Technology that applies to research, development, manufacturing, and marketing of computers and other electronic products.

home rule city Municipality with a locally drafted charter.

impeachment Process in which the Texas House of Representatives, by a simple majority vote, initiates action (brings charges) leading to possible removal of certain judicial and executive officials (e.g., the governor) by the Senate.

implied power A power inferred by the constitutional authority of the U.S. Congress "to make all laws which shall be necessary and proper for carrying into execution the foregoing [delegated] powers, and all other powers vested by this Constitution in the government of the United States, or in any department or officer thereof."

independent candidate A candidate who runs in a general election without party endorsement or selection.

independent school district (ISD) Created by the legislature, an independent school district raises tax revenue to support its public schools. Voters within the district elect a board that hires a superintendent, determines salary schedules, selects textbooks, and sets the property tax rate for the district.

initiative Although not used at the state level in Texas, this is a process whereby individuals or groups in some states may gather signatures required for submitting a proposed constitutional amendment or a proposed statute to a popular vote.

interest group An organization that seeks to influence government officials and their policies on behalf of members sharing common views and objectives (e.g., labor union or trade association).

interest group techniques These techniques are lobbying, personal communication, favors and gifts, grassroots activities, electioneering, campaign financing by PACs, and (in extreme instances) bribery and unethical practices.

Interior Lowlands This region covers the North Central Plains of Texas extending from the Metroplex westward to the Abilene area and northward to the Wichita Falls area.

item veto Action by the governor to delete a line item while permitting enactment of other parts of an appropriation bill.

"Jim Crow" Limited by "Jim Crow" laws, African Americans were segregated and denied access to public services for many decades after the Civil War.

joint resolution Must pass by a majority vote in each house when used to memorialize the U.S. Congress or to ratify an amendment to the U.S. Constitution. As a proposal for an amendment to the Texas Constitution, a joint resolution requires a two-thirds majority vote in each house.

judgment (or decree of the court) A judge's written opinion based on a verdict.

jungle primary Louisiana conducts a jungle primary in which candidates from all parties compete in a single election. A candidate who receives 50 percent or more of the vote is elected; otherwise, a runoff between the top two candidates must be held.

junior college or community college district Establishes one or more two-year colleges that offer both academic and vocational programs.

jurisdiction A court's authority to hear a particular case.

labor organization A union that supports public policies designed to increase wages, obtain adequate health insurance coverage, provide unemployment insurance, promote safe working conditions, and otherwise protect the interests of workers.

Latino This is an ethnic classification of Mexican Americans and others of Latin American origin. When applied to females, the term is *Latina*.

Legislative Budget Board (LBB) A 10-member body chaired by the lieutenant governor, this board and its staff prepare a biennial current-services budget. In addition, the LBB assists with the preparation of a general appropriation bill at the beginning of a regular legislative session; and, if requested, it prepares a fiscal note that projects the cost of implementation and an impact statement that assesses the economic impact of a proposed bill or resolution.

legislative power The governor's legislative power is exercised through messages delivered to the Texas Legislature, vetoes of bills and concurrent resolutions, and calls for special sessions of the legislature.

liberal One who favors government regulation to achieve a more equitable distribution of wealth.

lieutenant governor Popularly elected, serves as president of the Senate, and is first in the line of succession if the office of governor becomes vacant before the end of a term.

literacy test As a prerequisite for voter registration, this test was designed and administered in ways intended to prevent African Americans and Latinos from voting.

lobbying Communicating with legislators or other government officials on behalf of an interest group or a corporation for the purpose of influencing the decision-making process.

local government Units of local government authorized by the Texas Constitution are counties, municipalities, school districts, and other special districts. These "grassroots governments" provide a wide range of services that include rural roads, protection of persons and their property, city streets, and public education.

maquiladora An assembly plant that uses cheap labor and is located on the Mexican side of the U.S.-Mexican border.

martial law Temporary rule by military authorities when civil authorities are unable to handle a riot or other civil disorder.

matricula consular Issued to Mexican nationals by Mexico's consulates in Texas and other parts of the country, this photo ID card is accepted as a personal identification credential by many banks and some local government offices.

Medicaid Funded in part by federal block grants and in part by state appropriations, Medicaid provides medical care for persons falling below the poverty line.

Medicare This is a program funded entirely by the federal government. Administered by the U.S. Department of Health and Human Services, it provides medical assistance to qualified applicants age 65 and older.

message power The governor's State of the State address at the "commencement" of a legislative session and special messages delivered in person or in writing are examples of gubernatorial exercise of message power to communicate with legislators and the public.

metro government Consolidation of units of local government within an urban area under a single authority.

metropolitan division County or group of counties within a core based statistical area that contains a core with a population of at least 2.5 million.

metropolitanization Concentration of people in urban centers that become linked.

metropolitan statistical area (MSA) A freestanding urban area with a minimum total population of 50,000.

micropolitan statistical area An area that has at least one urban cluster with a population of at least 10,000, but less than 50,000.

misdemeanor Classified as A, B, or C, a misdemeanor may be punished by a fine and/or jail sentence.

Missouri Plan A judicial selection process that features nomination by a commission that recommends a panel of names to the governor, followed by appointment for a period of one year or so before voters determine whether the judge will be retained for a full term.

moralistic culture   This culture influences people to view political participation as their duty and to expect that government will be used to
advance the public good.

motor-voter law   Legislation requiring certain government offices (e.g.,
motor vehicle licensing agencies) to offer voter registration applications
to clients.

multimember district   A district in which all voters participate in the election of two or more representatives to a policymaking body, such as a city
council or a state legislature.

municipal bond   General obligation bonds (redeemed from city tax revenue) and revenue bonds (redeemed from revenue obtained from the
property or activity financed by the sale of the bonds) are authorized under
Texas law.

municipal government   A local government for an incorporated community established by law as a city.

nanotechnology   Using materials on an extremely small scale (one billionth) to produce microscopic machinery.

national supremacy clause   Article VI of the U.S. Constitution states: "This
Constitution, and the Laws of the United States which shall be made in
Pursuance thereof; and all Treaties made, or which shall be made, under
the Authority of the United States, shall be the supreme Law of the Land. . . ."

Native American   A descendant of the first Americans, who were called
indios by Spanish explorers and Indians by Anglo settlers who arrived later.

neoconservatism   A political ideology that reflects fiscal conservatism but
accepts a limited governmental role in solving social problems.

neoliberal   A political view that advocates less government regulation of
business but supports more governmental involvement in social matters.

noneducation special district   A special district other than a school district or a community college district, such as a fire prevention or crime
control district, which is a unit of local government that may cover part of
a county, a whole county, or areas in two or more counties.

nonpartisan blanket primary   A nominating process whereby voters indicate their preferences by using a single ballot on which are printed the
names and respective party labels of all persons seeking nomination.

nonpartisan election   An election in which candidates are not identified
on the ballot by party label.

North American Free Trade Agreement (NAFTA)   An agreement among
the United States, Mexico, and Canada that was designed to expand trade
among the three countries by reducing and then eliminating tariffs over a
15-year period.

off-year or midterm election   A general election held in the even-
numbered year following a presidential election.

open primary   A primary in which voters are not required to declare party
identification.

ordinance   A local law enacted by a city council or approved by popular
vote in a referendum election.

organizational pattern   Decentralization is the pattern of organization for some interest groups (e.g., the AFL-CIO, with many local and statewide unions), whereas others are centralized (e.g., the National Rifle Association, which is a national body without affiliated local or regional units).

original jurisdiction   The power of a court to hear a case first.

parliamentarian   An expert on rules of order who sits at the left of the presiding officer in the House or Senate and is ever ready to give advice on procedural questions.

parole   Release from prison before completion of a sentence; the release is conditioned by good behavior of the parolee.

patrón **system**   A type of boss rule that has dominated some areas of South Texas.

payroll tax   Levied against a portion of the wages and salaries of employees in order to provide funds for payment of unemployment insurance benefits to these people when they are out of work.

permanent party organization   In Texas, the precinct chairs, county and district executive committees, and the state executive committee form the permanent organization of a political party.

petit jury   A trial jury of 6 or 12 members.

physical region   An area identified by unique geographic features—for example, the Gulf Coastal Plains and the Great Plains.

place system   A system in which city council candidates file for numerically designated places and all voters in the city vote in each place contest.

plaintiff   The injured party who initiates a civil suit.

platform   A document that sets forth a political party's position on issues such as an income tax, school vouchers, or public utility regulation.

plural executive   The governor, lieutenant governor, secretary of state, and elected department heads as provided by the Texas Constitution.

political action committee (PAC)   An organizational device used by corporations, labor unions, and other organizations to raise money for campaign contributions.

political culture   Attitudes, habits, and general behavior patterns that develop over time and affect the political life of a state or region.

political influence of interest groups   This a highly variable factor that depends largely on the size of a group's membership, financial resources, quality of leadership, and degree of unity.

political party   An organization that is influenced by political ideology but whose primary interest is to gain control of government by winning elections.

politics   The process employed by individuals and political parties to nominate and elect public officials and to formulate public policy.

poll tax   A tax levied in Texas from 1902 until a similar Virginia tax was declared unconstitutional in 1962; failure to pay the annual tax (usually $1.75) made a citizen ineligible to vote in party primaries or in special and general elections.

population shift Within Texas this shift has featured demographic movements from rural to urban areas and from large cities to suburbs.

postadjournment veto Rejection by the governor of a pending bill or concurrent resolution during the 20 days following a legislative session.

power group An effective interest group that is strongly linked with legislators and bureaucrats for the purpose of influencing decision making and that has a continuing presence in Austin as a "repeat player" from session to session.

precinct chair The party official responsible for the interests and activities of a political party in a voting precinct; typical duties include supervising party volunteer workers, encouraging voter registration, and getting out the vote on election day.

precinct convention At the lowest level of political party organization, voters convene in March of even-numbered years to adopt resolutions and to name delegates to a county convention.

president of the Senate Title of the lieutenant governor in his or her role as presiding officer for the Texas Senate.

presidential preference primary A primary in which the voters indicate their preference for a person seeking nomination as the party's presidential candidate.

primary election A preliminary election conducted within a political party to select candidates who will run for public office in a subsequent general election.

privileges and immunities Article IV of the U.S. Constitution guarantees that "citizens of each state shall be entitled to the privileges and immunities of citizens of the several states." According to the U.S. Supreme Court, this means that citizens are guaranteed protection by government, enjoyment of life and liberty, the right to acquire and possess property, the right to leave and enter any state, and the right to use state courts.

probate Probate cases involving wills and guardianships fall under the jurisdiction of county courts and probate courts.

procedural committee These House committees (e.g., Calendars Committee and House Administration Committee) consider bills and resolutions relating primarily to internal legislative matters.

proclamation A governor's official public announcement (e.g., calling a special election or declaring a disaster area).

professional group An organization of physicians, lawyers, accountants, or other professional people that lobbies for policies beneficial to members.

progressive tax A tax that requires people in each successively higher income bracket to pay at progressively higher tax rates.

public interest group An organization claiming to represent a broad public interest (environmental, consumer, civil rights) rather than a narrow private interest.

public officer and employee group An organization of city managers, county judges, or other public employees or officials that lobbies for public policies that protect group interests.

public policy Government action designed to meet a public need or goal as determined by a legislative body or other authorized officials.

Public Utility Commission (PUC) A three-member body with regulatory power over utilities such as gas, electric, and telephone companies.

racial and ethnic groups Organizations like the National Association for the Advancement of Colored People and the League of United Latin American Citizens, which seek to influence government decisions affecting African Americans and Latinos, respectively.

racial gerrymandering Drawing districts designed to affect representation of a racial group (e.g., African Americans) in a legislative chamber, city council, commissioners court, or other representative body.

Railroad Commission of Texas A popularly elected, three-member commission that is primarily engaged in regulating the production of natural gas and petroleum.

"rainy day" fund A fund used for stabilizing state finance when there is insufficient revenue to cover public education, criminal justice, or other important programs.

realignment Occurs when members of one party shift their affiliation to another party.

recess appointment An appointment made by the governor when the Texas Legislature is not in session.

recidivism Criminal behavior that results in reincarceration after a person has been released from confinement for a prior offense.

redistricting Redrawing of boundaries following the federal decennial census to create districts with approximately equal population (e.g., legislative, congressional, and commissioners court districts in Texas).

referendum The referendum process, not used in Texas, allows voters to gather signatures needed to challenge at the polls (and potentially to overturn) a law enacted by their state legislature.

regressive tax A tax whereby the effective tax rate falls as the tax base (e.g., individual income, corporate profits) increases.

regular session A session of the Texas Legislature that begins on the second Tuesday in January of odd-numbered years and lasts for a maximum of 140 days.

religious-based group A group like the Christian Coalition or the Texas Faith Network that lobbies for policies promoting its religious interests.

removal power Authority to remove an official from office. In Texas, the governor's removal power is limited but extends to staff members, some agency heads, and, with the consent of the Senate, to other appointees.

reprieve An act of executive clemency that temporarily suspends the execution of a sentence.

reserved power   The Tenth Amendment of the U.S. Constitution declares that "the powers not delegated by the Constitution, nor prohibited by it to the States, are reserved to the States, respectively, or to the people." Although not spelled out in the U.S. Constitution, these reserved powers include police power, taxing power, proprietary power, and power of eminent domain.

right of association   The U.S. Supreme Court has ruled that this right is part of the right of assembly guaranteed by the First Amendment of the U.S. Constitution and that it protects the right of people to organize into groups for political purposes.

Robin Hood plan   A plan for equalizing financial support for school districts by transferring tax money from rich districts to poor districts.

run-off primary   A "second primary" that is held for the purpose of nominating candidates for offices for which absolute majority votes were not obtained in the first primary held a month earlier.

secretary of state   The state's chief elections officer who is appointed by the governor for a four-year term.

securitization   Sale of bonds backed by future payments of tobacco settlements.

select committee   Created independently by the speaker, a select committee works on emergency legislation early in a session before substantive committees are appointed.

selective sales taxes   These are quantity-based consumption taxes on motor fuel, alcoholic beverages, and tobacco products.

senatorial courtesy   Before making an appointment, the governor is expected to obtain approval from the state senator in whose district the prospective appointee resides; failure to obtain such approval will probably cause the appointee to be "busted" by the Senate.

separation of powers   The assignment of lawmaking, law-enforcing, and law-interpreting functions to separate branches of government.

service sector job   Employment providing services of enterprises such as hospitals, hotels, bowling alleys, and data processing companies.

severance tax   An excise tax levied on a natural resource (e.g., oil or natural gas) when it is severed (removed) from the earth.

simple resolution   A resolution that requires action by one legislative chamber only and is not acted on by the governor.

sin tax   A selective sales tax on items such as cigarettes, other forms of tobacco, and alcoholic beverages.

single-member district election   Only one representative is elected to represent a district as a member of a policymaking body (e.g., city council, county commissioners court, state House and Senate).

small-claims court   Presided over by a justice of the peace, a small claims court offers an informal and relatively inexpensive procedure for handling damage claims of $5,000 or less.

social interest group   Included among groups that are concerned primarily with social issues are organizations in the areas of civil rights, racial and ethnic matters, religion, and public interest protection.

soft money   Campaign money donated to national political parties rather than to candidates.

sound bite   A 15-second statement of a candidate's theme that is communicated by radio or television.

speaker of the House   The state representative who is elected by House members to serve as the presiding officer for that chamber.

special election   An election called by the governor to fill a vacancy (e.g., U.S. congressional or state legislative office) or vote on a proposed state constitutional amendment or local bond issue.

special interim committee   A Senate committee appointed by the lieutenant governor to study an important policy issue between regular sessions.

special issue   A question that a judge presents to a trial jury for the purpose of establishing facts in a case.

special session   A legislative session called by the governor and limited to not more than 30 days.

Spindletop Field   Located near Beaumont, this oil field sparked a boom in 1901 that made Texas a leading petroleum producer.

standing committee   A Senate committee appointed by the lieutenant governor for the purpose of considering proposed bills and resolutions prior to possible floor debate and voting by senators.

State Board of Education (SBOE)   A popularly elected 15-member body that heads Texas's K-12 education system.

state convention   Convenes every even-numbered year to make rules for a political party, adopt a party platform and resolutions, and select members of the state executive committee; in a presidential election year it elects delegates to the national convention and names members to serve on the national committee.

state executive committee   Composed of a chair, vice chair, and two members from each senatorial district, this body is part of a party's permanent organization.

straight-ticket voting   Voting for all the candidates of one party.

stratarchy   A political system wherein power is diffused among and within levels of party organization.

strong mayor-council form   A type of municipal government with a separately elected legislative body (council) and an executive head (mayor), who runs for office in a citywide election and has veto, appointment, and removal powers.

substantive committee   Appointed by the House speaker, a substantive committee considers bills and resolutions related to the subject identified by its name (e.g., House Agriculture Committee) and may recommend passage of proposed legislation to the appropriate calendar committee.

suburbanization   Growth of relatively small towns and cities, usually incorporated but outside the corporate limits of a central city.

suffrage   The right to vote.

sunset process   Over a cycle of 12 years, each state agency is studied, and then the legislature decides whether to abolish, merge, or retain it.

superdelegate An unpledged party official or elected official who serves as a delegate to a party's national convention.

tax A compulsory contribution exacted by a government for a public purpose.

tax abatement Elimination of taxes for a limited period of time.

tax increment financing (TIF) A method for attracting business activity to an inner-city area. After tax values are frozen, incremental property taxes on increased values are dedicated to paying for public improvements in the area.

tax reinvestment zone (TRZ) Municipal tax incentives are offered to encourage businesses to locate in and contribute to the development of a blighted urban area. Commercial and residential property taxes are frozen.

Temporary Assistance for Needy Families (TANF) Replaced Aid for Families with Dependent Children (AFDC) in an attempt to help poor people move from welfare to the workforce.

temporary party organizations Primaries and conventions that function briefly to nominate candidates, pass resolutions, adopt a party platform, and select delegates to party conventions at higher levels.

Tenth Amendment See reserved powers.

term limits Restriction on the number of terms that can be served in a public office.

Texas Assessment of Knowledge and Skills (TAKS) A standardized test covering a core curriculum.

Texas Commission on Environmental Quality (TCEQ) The state agency that coordinates Texas's environmental protection efforts.

Texas Constitution of 1876 Texas's lengthy, much-amended constitution that is a product of the post-Reconstruction era.

Texas Department of Transportation (TXDOT) Headed by a three-member commission, the department maintains more than 79,000 miles of roads and highways, and it promotes highway safety.

Texas Education Agency (TEA) Administers the state's public school system that includes more than 6,300 schools.

Texas Election Code The body of state law concerning parties, primaries, and elections.

Texas Equal Legal Rights Amendment Added to Article 1, Section 3 of the Texas Constitution, it guarantees that "Equality under the law shall not be denied or abridged because of sex, race, color, creed or national origin."

Texas Ethics Commission Enforces state standards for lobbyists and public officials, including registration of lobbyists and reporting of political campaign contributions.

Texas Grange Known as the Patrons of Husbandry, this farmers' organization was well represented in the constitutional convention that produced the Constitution of 1876.

TEXAS Grants Program "Toward Excellence, Access, and Success," the program provides funding for qualifying college and university students.

Texas Higher Education Coordinating Board   A 12-member body (9 members in 2007) that provides some direction for the state's community colleges and universities.

Texas Workforce Commission (TWC)   A state agency headed by three salaried commissioners who supervise implementation of job training and unemployment compensation programs.

third party   A party other than the Democratic Party or the Republican Party. Sometimes called a "minor party" because of limited membership and voter support.

tort   An unintended injury to another person or to a person's property.

underemployment   Working fewer hours than desired, receiving lower wages than deserved, or being overqualified for a job.

undocumented alien   A person who enters the United States in violation of federal immigration laws.

unicameral   The term that describes a one-house legislature (e.g., the Nebraska Legislature).

universal suffrage   Voting is open for virtually all persons who are 18 years of age or older.

urbanization   Migration of people from rural areas to cities.

venire   A panel of prospective jurors drawn by random selection.

verdict   A finding of guilty or not guilty by a jury.

veto power   Authority of the governor to reject a bill or concurrent resolution passed by the legislature.

voir dire   Courtroom procedure whereby attorneys question prospective jurors to identify any who cannot be fair and impartial.

voter registration   A qualified voter must register with the county voting registrar, who compiles lists of qualified voters residing in each voting precinct.

voting precinct   The basic geographic area for conducting primaries and elections; Texas is divided into more than 8,500 voting precincts.

weak mayor-council form   A type of municipal government with a separately elected mayor and council, but the mayor shares appointive and removal powers with the council, which can override the mayor's veto.

white primary   A nominating system designed to prevent African Americans and some Mexican Americans from participating in Democratic primaries from 1923 to 1944.

women's organization   A women's group, such as the League of Women Voters, that engages in lobbying and educational activities to promote greater political participation by women and others.

Index